Creating Television

Conversations with the People
Behind 50 Years of American TV

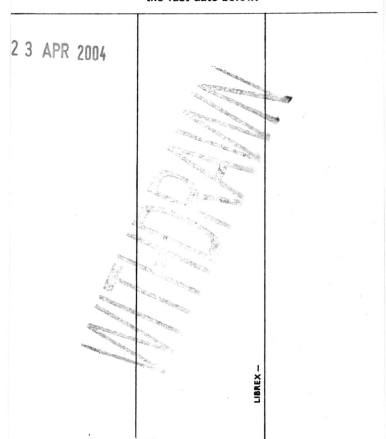

**Books are to be returned on or before
the last date below.**

2 3 APR 2004

LIBREX—

LEA's Communication Series
Jennings Bryant/Dolf Zillmann, General Editors

For a complete list of titles in LEA's Communication Series, please contact Lawrence Erlbaum Associates, Publishers, at *www.erlbaum.com.*

Creating Television

Conversations with the People Behind 50 Years of American TV

Robert Kubey

Rutgers University

LEA Lawrence Erlbaum Associates, Publishers
2004 Mahwah, New Jersey   London

Senior Acquisitions Editor: Linda Bathgate
Editorial Assistant: Karin Wittig Bates
Cover Design: Robert Kubey
Cover Layout: Marino Belich
Textbook Production Manager: Paul Smolenski
Full-Service & Composition: UG / GGS Information Services, Inc.
Text and Cover Printer: Hamilton Printing Company
Cover Photo Credits: Photo of Steve Allen, courtesy of Meadowlane Enterprises, Inc. &
steveallen.com; Jay Sandrich with Bill Cosby, courtesy of Jay Sandrich; the cast of *The Mary
Tyler Moore Show*, courtesy of Ed Asner; Bart Simpson, courtesy of Twentieth Century
Fox/Photofest; the cast of *Seinfeld*, Ron Howard with Henry Winkler, and Aida Turturro
with James Gandolfini all courtesy of Photofest.

This book was typeset in 11/13 pt. Minion.
The heads were typeset in ITC Symbol Bold and Minion Bold.

Lawrence Erlbaum Associates, Inc., Publishers
10 Industrial Avenue
Mahwah, New Jersey 07430
www.erlbaum.com

Library of Congress Cataloging-in-Publication Data

Creating television : conversations with the people behind 50 years of American TV /
    Robert Kubey.
        p. cm.
    Includes bibliographical references and index.
    ISBN 0-8058-1076-5 (alk. paper)—ISBN 0-8058-1077-3 (pbk. : alk. paper)
    1. Television broadcasting—United States. 2. Television producers and
directors—United States—Interviews. 3. Television actors and actresses—United States—
Interviews. 4. Television writers—United States—Interviews. I. Kubey, Robert William, 1952-

PN1992.3.U5C74 2004

                                                                    2003060386

Books published by Lawrence Erlbaum Associates are printed on acid-free paper, and their
bindings are chosen for strength and durability.

Printed in the United States of America

10 9 8 7 6 5 4 3 2 1

Contents

Preface

I began research for this book in 1987 as a fellow of the newly-founded Center for the Critical Analysis of Contemporary Culture at Rutgers University. My intent was to explore how television creators did their work and how creators' life histories, and their youthful experiences, influenced the work they did. I was curious to know how individual creativity survived in a collaborative, commercial medium like television.

In reviewing what is said in these interviews, it's notable that a fair number of interviewees talk about "going with their gut" or their "instinct." Chris Albrecht, the CEO of HBO, reports that a defining moment in his career occurred when veteran agent and producer Jack Rollins told him, "Listen to the gut of the performer. What's right for them, what they think is right for them, because nine out of ten times it will be right." Actor Henry Winkler made an unusual demand when first asked to play The Fonz, a demand that could have cost him the role. Asked how he had the nerve to do what he did, he says, "I went with my instinct. When I speak to young people, I say 'Your instinct is more powerful than you will ever know and when your instinct comes clear, do not second guess yourself, no matter what.'" Asked what makes his musical specials unique, Gary Smith says, "The show comes from here. I'm pointing to my stomach. I'm not pointing to my eye or my brain. If it doesn't work here, it doesn't work. This part, eyes and brain, are relatively easy. You can work at this, this is craft, this is technique. I am now pointing at eyes and brain. This can be learned. I don't think things in the gut can be learned. I think this is intuitive."

In the process of creating television, there are so many other people working on programs, and so many pressures—especially in a place like Hollywood—that it is easy to lose sight of what one is trying to create, and to let others redefine what you started out to do. One can quickly lose control, vision, and voice in a project.

One of the things that studying the interviews has taught me is how important it is to be clear in your mind (and your gut) what you want to accomplish. In any large endeavor, whether it's a television series or most anything else, you're going to work very hard and devote great effort. If you don't believe in the work, how will you possibly apply the necessary energies? If it somehow succeeds despite your ambivalence, you won't be happy or proud of the final product. If it is hardly seen or is never made, you might even be relieved. Any way you cut it, you'll be working at cross purposes with yourself.

But finding out what you want to do isn't always easy. For some, it may be the single hardest thing to do in life—finding one's path. I should say paths. The interviews also exemplify the different and circuitous routes people take in the development of a career, and a life.

Many of the interviews in the pages ahead are odysseys of becoming, of gradual self-actualization. Understanding how lives and careers unfold is among the valuable lessons that can be taken from the stories told in these interviews. The interviews also remind us that there are many forces in life that will interfere with and teach us *not* to listen to ourselves, our feelings, and our passion about something.

Another important lesson is that if the work matters, money isn't so crucially important. When wealth is discussed, creators who once didn't have much money and now have a great deal tell us that they've come to the conclusion that money isn't all it's cracked up to be. Neither fame nor money will buy happiness. Doing work that one likes and feels good about *can* bring happiness. Freud was well on the mark when he observed that work and love are the two elements of life critical to happiness. It's an idea worth repeating. After all, our culture is awash in messages that tell us hour after hour that the good life is one spent being acquisitive and self-indulgent.

Ultimately, these things go together: learning to go with what makes one happy, what feels artistically and creatively right, and the lesson that the greater rewards in life come from work (and love), not from material objects.

Having thought a lot about the life themes of the creators presented in this book, and the many others whom I've interviewed, I've had occasion to think of my own career path, and doing so helps me understand why I began this work and have stuck with it over the years. Some of the formative experiences in my early life occurred in community theater. In my childhood, theater taught many lessons about performance, about the teamwork and constant rehearsal involved in putting a show together, and also how the audience changed every night and how no two performances were ever the same. Later, as a teenager, I taught myself to make films. In my first year of college, I began to formally study psychology. My first paper applied psychoanalytic theory to understanding the filmgoing experience. I had no idea as a freshman that many years later my doctoral dissertation and first book, *Television and the Quality of Life*, would similarly explore how people experience television in the course of everyday life.

One of the findings from that research was how television viewing could inculcate and reinforce passivity in the viewer. Among the solutions proposed in the book, and in much of my subsequent work, is media education. In *Media Literacy in the Information Age*, my next book, each contributor focused on how media education was being developed in schools in their country as a way to foster more critical, active, and empowering use of the media (Kubey, 1997/2001). *Creating Television* is a third, related contribution insofar as rewarding use of media is brought about by understanding how media are created.

I've tried in the interviews, and in their editing, to bring each person alive on the page, so that you might get to know these creators of television as I have. I believe the book will be helpful to those interested in how television is created, and I hope it will contribute to more informed criticism and appreciation of the medium. (There might even be a reciprocal effect. As Walt Whitman wrote, "To have great poets there must be great audiences, too.") I also hope readers will see how people themselves are made, how people create themselves through their work. These individuals have brought television alive for me. I hope they do for you as well.

Acknowledgments

It was upon learning of the recent death of my college advisor, creativity psychologist Frank X. Barron, that I began to think of more than 30 years of personal connection to the psychology of creativity. Barron was already an eminent figure in the field when I first encountered him in the fall of 1970 at College V, the arts college, at the University of California at Santa Cruz. Barron wasn't the only psychologist interested in art and creativity at College V. Another was Pavel Machotka, with whom I worked, and from whom I also learned a great deal. One unforgettable psychology professor at Santa Cruz was Michael Kahn. It was in his class that I wrote "Psychoanalysis of the Filmgoer." In addition to providing a superb introduction to psychology and to Freud, Kahn had once been a television actor, especially in Westerns. I saw in Kahn that psychology and the performing arts could be related.

In 1976, as a doctoral student in the Committee on Human Development at the University of Chicago, I took a class in adolescent psychology with Mihaly Csikszentmihalyi in which I first learned about his newly emerging concept of flow (1975), became familiar with his studies in creativity, and that same year began to use the Experience Sampling Method to study audience experience and behavior. Mike chaired my dissertation work, and wrote *Television and the Quality of Life* with me. We have continued to publish together all these years later.

These were my key mentors in the psychology of creativity. For centuries, people have known that creative work is fostered by periods of apprenticeship spent with dedicated mentors. I have been fortunate to have had my share, and as we will see in the pages ahead, many television creators similarly identify critical mentors in their development.

This project began at Rutgers when I was a fellow of the Center for the Critical Analysis of Contemporary Culture. The Center was in its inaugural year yet still provided an intense interdisciplinary atmosphere thanks to the vision of founding director George Levine. The Center provided the initial financial support for this project. Additional funding came from Fordham University's McGannon Communication Research Center for the Study of Issues in Policy and Ethics, as well as from the Rutgers University Research Council.

I have learned a great deal from the writings of others. I am indebted to the pioneering work of Horace Newcomb and Robert Alley, Muriel Cantor, Todd Gitlin, Hortense Powdermaker, Leo Rosten, Robert Thompson and David Marc, and Joseph Turow, all academics who also have written about the creative people in the film and television industries. Thanks also to Jim Ettema and Chuck Whitney (1982) for their seminal edited volume, *Individuals in Mass Media Organizations.*

Most of all, I wish to thank the scores of very busy and charming individuals who generously permitted me the opportunity to talk with them about their work, their lives, and about creativity in television.

While in Hollywood, doing the interviews, I sometimes thought of myself as a cultural anthropologist as I made my way through the thicket of studios and offices across Los Angeles, Beverly Hills, and the San Fernando Valley. My stays in the area were made more comfortable by friendly natives who opened their local huts to me. Thank you to Don and Kay Bowen, Cynthia Cohen, and Marianne and Al Barbanell. At the end of an intense week of interviewing, I would happily leave their West Coast dwellings with a new stack of audiocassettes that I'd pack back with me on the plane east to Rutgers.

At Rutgers, Brent Ruben, Todd Hunt, and Dennis Mumby all served as early sounding boards. Among my graduate students, Barna Donovan was particularly helpful in reading and commenting upon many of the edited interviews. Computer guru Jon Oliver helped me solve innumerable computer glitches and has lent much appreciated moral support.

My faithful editor, Linda Bathgate at Lawrence Erlbaum Associates (LEA), has always been supportive, as has Larry Erlbaum, since the project's earliest inception. LEA's Paul Smolenski has been enormously helpful in all phases of the production process. Rebecca Homiski did a first rate job with the copyediting. I also wish to thank the very supportive and helpful production team of Donna Lee Lurker, Rose Gabbay and Jeff Barrie at University Graphics. Judy Ladendorf of Photo Permissions Group in Illinois and Buddy Weiss of Photofest in New York were helpful in locating photographs. Many thanks also to Jeff Cusson of HBO, to my friend Ray Solley and to Donna Bruton.

Over the years, many students and staff at the School of Communication, Information, and Library Studies at Rutgers helped me in many ways and with over 100 transcriptions. Thank you to Marsha Bergman, Angela DiMartini, Matthew Dvorin, Hiro Hirashiki, Julie Monagle, Paula Kantenwein, Elizabeth O'Shea, and Shirin Zarqa.

Thank you, finally, to my families. My parents were avid and very engaged audience members who conveyed to me, whether they meant to or not, an early appreciation of performance. I can still hear my father laughing at the antics of Phil Silvers as Sgt. Bilko. My mother got me started in theater and has always been supportive of my work. Thank you to my sons, Benjamin and Daniel, for understanding why I was out in the study "working on the book" instead of playing with them or watching something really cool on television. And greatest thanks to my wife Barbara who is always patient and supportive of my work and helped me figure out the right way to express more than a few ideas in the pages ahead.

—*Robert Kubey*
Highland Park, New Jersey

Creating Television

Conversations with the People Behind 50 Years of American TV

CHAPTER 1

Introduction

Bringing Television Creators to Life

The beginnings of television, depending on what you read, date back to Philip Nipkow's 1885 patent for the idea of a television scanner, Boris Rosing's 1906 electronic picture tube, Vladimir Zworykin's 1923 invention of the iconoscope, or Philo T. Farnsworth's 1927 patent on an "image dissector." But in America, television as a true, nationwide medium began when the networks first linked the country from coast to coast in 1951. In the half century since, the television industry has grown from a poor relation and spin-off of radio and vaudeville to the world's premier entertainment medium. People throughout the developed world spend more time watching television than doing any other activity but for sleep and work.

In the 1980s, American television truly went global. Programs like *Dallas* and *The Cosby Show* were regularly watched in more than 90 countries. In that decade, as American television's grip on the rest of the world was reaching new heights, a group of 50,000 fans nearly shut down the center of Athens when the cast of the American soap opera *The Bold and the Beautiful* visited the ancient capital.

Much of the world watches television, particularly American television, and is simultaneously fascinated by what goes on behind the scenes. There is a growing sophistication and curiosity among laypersons and scholars alike regarding how programs are created, how actors are cast in roles, how deals are made, and how ratings pressures affect programming decisions.

Long-standing theoretical work on the mass culture industries has informed this work, but purely theoretical treatments of the media industries often convey detached and unrealistic understandings of the roles of the people actually involved in the creation of popular culture products. The book you hold in your hands offers an opportunity to learn how leading professionals from the medium's first half century think about their experiences working in television. In so doing, the book offers real-world examples that both lend support to, and raise questions about, those theories long debated by scholars and researchers interested in the mass communication industries and the sociology and production of culture (see Chapter 2).

Over the past 17 years, I've interviewed 120 television professionals: writers, agents, actors, directors, producers, and studio and network executives. Chosen for presentation here are the 38 most interesting and revealing interviews (40 people in all, as there were two joint interviews). These are the conversations that have taught me the most about the industry and the people working in it.

Their careers span two, three, four, and in some cases, all five decades of television's first 50+ years. Of the 40, 13 worked in television in the 1950s, 20 in the 1960s, 26 in the 1970s, 31 in the 1980s, 29 in the 1990s, and 18 are active in the new century. Many were interviewed twice, years apart, to provide additional perspective on the decade just passed. Their breadth of experience lets them tell us how television was created and produced earlier in their careers and how much—and sometimes how little—the industry has changed over the years.

I typically began the conversations by asking the individuals about their youth and their start in television, often asking if they could pinpoint the earliest time they were doing something similar to what they now did professionally. I had many reasons for starting this way. One was to explore whether "life themes" could be identified—themes that might help illuminate the early sources of their talent or chosen area of work and expertise. If the hallmark of artistry is the expression of a creator's feeling, vision, and thought, and if we wish to explore whether certain individuals are indeed television artists, then we need to understand what elements of their personality, sensibility, and experience find expression in their work and where these elements come from. A background in lifespan developmental psychology influenced my use of this approach, as did others' work in the field of life themes and autobiographical memory (Bruner, 1994; Conway, Rubin, Spinnler, & Wagenaar, 1992; Csikszentmihalyi & Beattie, 1979).

As will be seen, many creators were able to recount such life themes as well as significant and formative childhood activities and events ("crystallizing experiences")—the very kinds of experiences that have been described by researchers studying creativity in other fields and that often are thought to help set the life course for a talented young person (Feldman, 1999; Walters & Gardner, 1986).

As a 3-year-old, Agnes Nixon often played alone and kept herself occupied for hours at a time making up stories using cut-out paper dolls from the Sunday funny papers, filing them away each week alphabetically in the phone book. As an adult, she became the medium's premier creator of soap operas, known for her character-driven stories. T. S. Cook was his Boy Scout troop's most accomplished campfire storyteller. Now he tells his suspenseful tales around the "cool fire" of television, before unseen troops numbering in the millions. Frank Dawson's rise out of poverty began when he won a photography contest in sixth grade. He would take this heightened visual sense with him as he rose to become one of television's highest ranking African American executives.

In tracing each practitioner's history and background, this book also documents the numerous ways that new talent enters and rises in the industry, as well as many of the impediments to entry and success. When young, some creators struggled with learning disorders, family dysfunction, and disapproving parents. As adults, many hit blind alleys in work or education before they found their way. Others had every advantage and were able to use a friend or relative's connections in the business.

In many instances, working closely with a key mentor made a critical difference in their creative careers. Apprenticeship is an especially old and well established tradition in the arts. Psychologists who study creativity have found it common in the development of creativity in most every field of endeavor (Gardner, 1983/1993; Getzels & Csikszentmihalyi, 1976; Piirto, 1992).

In observing such phenomena through these interviews, I have tried to bring individual television creators and their careers to life. The influential Frankfurt School theorists who developed their ideas about mass communication, art, and ideology at the University of Frankfurt in the 1930s believed that the creators of mass or popular culture were greedy hacks, producing escapist, kitsch material that softened up the masses for the goals of consumerism and the state.

There is doubtless some truth in this view, but Frankfurt School theorizing does not capture the actual experiences or lives of individual creators. *Creating Television* allows us to get to know 40 television professionals and gain an understanding of how their life histories, idiosyncrasies, and personal values are—or are not—reflected in their work. Some interviews document how commercial and institutional pressures can suppress and limit individual creativity, leading to a bland and predictable television product. For others, the constant deadline pressure is a valuable catalyst to creativity. We also see how individual creativity survives and is expressed within the system.

The case for television "auteurs"—writer-producers who put a unique, individual, and autobiographical stamp on television programs—was first made by Horace Newcomb and Robert Alley, through their interviews with 11 American TV producers in *The Producer's Medium* (1983). Their work influenced David Marc and Robert Thompson's 1992 comprehensive study of television producers, *Prime Time, Prime Movers*. Like Newcomb and Alley, Marc and Thompson were interested in how the biographies of the "authors of American television" were "manifest in their creations"; how television programs were, if nothing else, "human expressions born of human experiences" (p. 10). In Marc and Thompson's view, Newcomb and Alley established the importance of understanding creators' life histories:

> They demonstrated that despite the gigantic constituent corporate bureaucracies of this most massive of mass media—networks, advertising agencies, production companies, ratings organizations, federal regulatory authorities—the

autobiographical visions of individuals did manage to break through onto the television screen, just as the personal vision of artists had managed to reach expression in the older, preelectronic arts. (1992, p. 8)

This book also helps us understand how television creators' biographies are intimately linked to their work. A number of television auteurs, each with an identifiable personal style, are interviewed about their creations: Larry David (*Seinfeld*), Matt Groening (*The Simpsons*), Susan Harris (*Soap, Benson,* and *The Golden Girls*), and Edward Zwick and Marshall Herskovitz (*thirtysomething*).

But creating television is not confined to auteurs. To understand the creation of television more fully, we also need to know about the work, ideas, and background of other kinds of television creators and those who work closely with them. Thus, *Creating Television* also focuses on non-auteur producers, as well as writers, directors, actors, agents, and executives.

What do we make of the experiences and work of Dave Bell in documentaries, Jean Rouverol in soap operas, or Marty Pasetta in a variety of television formats? What do agents and executives do and what makes them tick? What can we learn from the actors who often bring a large part of themselves to the roles they play? And are there other kinds of creators who could be considered auteurs? What about Gary Smith, who brings a personal, designer's eye to the look and feel of musical specials and events programming?

The interviews explore the highly collaborative nature of television production while speaking to the problems inherent in collaboration. The complex bureaucratic maze of production can make it difficult for the individual creator to define, let alone enact, personal aims, ethics, or values. A television writer, in addition to trying to satisfy his or her own standards, must often juggle the demands of a fickle audience, an agent, other writers, producers, actors, studio executives, and a network with layers of executives and their deputies supervising development, quality control, promotion, finances, and standards and practices. Within this complex array of competing interests, how does the writer or producer maintain her own standards or place an individual stamp on his work? What conflicts are experienced with studio and network executives and how do the executives themselves experience the process? Because the interviews offer multiple perspectives, it is hoped that readers of *Creating Television* will develop a more nuanced understanding of how American television entertainment is made and how human needs, creativity, and commercial and organizational procedures and pressures interact.

Through some interviews, the reader will see how the production of television programming revolves around the goal of attracting and holding audience attention, and how the commercial pressures for audiences shape the content and form of what people see on television each day. Some in *Creating Television* tell us how television programming is developed methodically from initial concept to finished product and how particular elements are conceived from a program's earliest inception to maximize promotion and ratings potential. We also see how serendipitous creating television can sometimes be: how Zwick and Herskovitz suddenly got an idea the night before a pitch meeting at the network that became the television series *thirtysomething*. Or how network executive Bruce Sallan heard a classic rock song on the radio one morning driving to work and decided in an instant to make a TV movie by the same title.

The conversations also touch on relatively recent organizational and technological developments—from corporate mergers and takeovers and increased vertical integration to the growth of cable, the rise of the VCR, and the FCC's new financial-syndication ("fin-syn") rules—that have rocked and roiled the industry and resulted in a new business climate. What do these developments bode for the viewing public, culture at large, and for those considering a career in the industry?

The conversations also reveal what these television practitioners think about the impact of their work on audiences and what they believe are the responsibilities that come with working in so public a medium. Unbeknownst to many, television creators are among the medium's harshest critics. In these pages, they readily vent their frustrations with the industry and its products, painting a complex portrait of the conflict between art and commerce.

But in the end, this is a book of interviews and conversations that I want readers to experience on their own. I largely have limited my commentary and analysis to these introductory chapters and the introductions to each section and interview. My aim, from the beginning, has been to let the creators speak for themselves. I think you will find them bright and humorous, occasionally brash and opinionated, as well as engaging and very human.

I hope the book is helpful to those interested in how television is created, and that it contributes to more informed criticism and appreciation of the medium. I also hope readers will see how people themselves are made—how people create themselves through their work. These individuals have brought television alive for me. I hope they do for you as well.

HOW THE INTERVIEWS ARE ORGANIZED

The interviews are organized by profession. Almost everyone interviewed has worn at least two hats in his or her career; many have worn three or more. Therefore, it was often difficult to decide where to place each person.

The first section, "The Pioneers," lays important historical groundwork and introduces a variety of creators—writers, producers, performers, executives, and a technician—who began their careers in the 1950s or earlier. Some readers will gravitate to the names they know best, but "The Pioneers" is a good place to start.

Because the writer-producer is the key creative force in television, the second section is devoted to six writer-producers who have been associated with breakthrough television series. Then come three shorter sections focusing on writers, independent producers, and directors. Actors are in their own section—with the exception of Steve Allen and Sid Caesar, who are with the other pioneers. The chapter on agents includes a publicist. I put only three of the eight executives in a section called "A Different Kind of Executive"; the remainder can be found among the pioneers, producers, and agents.

CONDUCTING AND EDITING THE INTERVIEWS

In the course of working on this book, I interviewed 120 television professionals and worked with as many transcripts. Presented here are the 38 conversations that taught me the most about the industry and the people working in it.

I began the project speaking with middle-level producers, executives, and writers, as well as people at the top of the industry. From the outset, I knew I wanted to present each individual in his or her own words. As the work went on I concluded that the people toward the top of the industry, who had already achieved considerable success, were those who presented themselves most candidly. As these are also the people who have the most power to create television programs, I began to concentrate more on leading creators. Casting directors, editors, and publicists were also interviewed but I chose not to include them because, while their perspective on television production is quite interesting and important, I ultimately concluded that their interviews didn't contribute as much as the interviews selected for this book.

Initial Introductions, Referrals, and Arranging the Interviews

I introduced myself to most prospective interviewees via a cover letter on university letterhead in which I explained that I was a professor doing a book of interviews with individuals in the industry. In some instances, having been referred while visiting Los Angeles, the first contact was sometimes made by phone.

The project started with two people I knew in the industry and a list of others whom I wanted to interview. At the conclusion of many interviews, I would ask the person if he or she could suggest another good source, making a point of asking that I not be referred only to friends. I wanted to avoid talking with people who tended to think alike or shared the same political views or tastes.

I should add that I rarely had any direct contact or communication with each individual before the interview. I was almost always working through assistants or, in the case of actors, with publicists, who arranged the interviews.

Typically, I visited Los Angeles for a week of interviews, with each interview lasting 90 minutes to two hours. Over a third of the individuals were interviewed again 10 to 15 years after the first meeting. In these follow-up interviews, I asked how their work had developed and how they believed the industry had changed in the intervening years. The introduction to each interview notes which people were interviewed twice, and when and how far apart the conversations took place.

Editing the Interviews

The interviews were edited to allow the creator's personality, voice, and ideas to be heard as clearly as possible. In some cases, nearly half of what the individuals and I originally said was edited out. In most cases, much less was deleted.

Many of the deletions were my questions; I tried to pare them back to the minimum necessary for the interview to flow. Very few people talked about their childhoods and early careers without a good deal of prompting. I usually had to ask quite a few questions to draw the stories out.

Long discussions about an issue, perhaps of interest to only a very small number of readers, were not included; nor was material I thought too detailed, uninteresting, or obvious. The artistry—if there is any—in this book is in the interviews and in the editing. Many abridgements were made before I felt each interview read well enough for inclusion.

I sometimes reordered parts of interviews. If a person and I returned to a topic late in an interview and it made more sense to bring the two comments on the same topic together, I did so. If an interviewee stumbled in his or her speech or hemmed and hawed, I often cleaned up the resulting material.

On occasion, people asked to go off the record, so I would turn off the tape recorder. On two or three occasions, someone who had said something quite critical and specific about someone else in the industry would contact me later, realizing that the comment could prove hurtful if published. As each person had agreed to be interviewed and was helping me understand them and their industry, I respected their request to delete that material or the name of the individual. It was not my aim for the work to disturb careers or stir up problems.

RECENT DEVELOPMENTS AND HEIGHTENED COMPETITION IN THE INDUSTRY

In talking with creators over the last decade and a half and following up with many in the last few years, the interviews also gauge changes in the industry. For quite a few, it has become much more competitive, even more like a business than it once seemed, and much less enjoyable to work in. Among the reasons given are the media mergers and vertical integration that have come with deregulation, the "fin-syn" rule, and the fact that there are even larger pots of money to be won or lost than before (see the interviews with Alexander, Manson, Rich, Sallan, and Solley, among others). On the other hand, there *are* more markets and channels to which one can sell one's wares. (The FCC's financial syndication ruling now permits networks to own their television shows and not just disseminate them.)

The effects of deregulation are very much on the minds of TV creators. In 2002, the 150-member Caucus for Television Producers, Writers, and Directors formally called on the FCC to conduct a study of the effects of media mergers. In a letter to FCC chairman Michael K. Powell, the Caucus asked the FCC to consider how deregulation and growing concentration of ownership is decreasing program diversity. "The consequences of this new factor in our industry are—and this is no exaggeration—potentially catastrophic" wrote the Caucus (Associated Press, June 7, 2002). (David Levy and Leonard Stern have played important roles in the Caucus and discuss the organization in their interviews.)

Just three weeks earlier, Leslie Moonves, the president of CBS television, gave a speech to advertisers about the network's ratings prospects for the coming fall season. Remarking on the industry's return to normal following the events of September 11, he told the room of assembled advertisers, "Here we are eight months later, trying to stab each other in the back again" (James, May 18, 2002).

Individual Creativity in a Collaborative Medium

How do television creators do their work? When working under commercial pressures, and within complex systems of production and with scores of other people, how do they remain creative? Can their individual voices and visions be heard and seen? What impact can an individual's work have on the form or content of television? Does their work change television, and does television change society?

In the interviews that follow we learn what creators have to say about their experiences creating television, along with assessments of the industry, their personal impact, and the limits on and opportunities for creativity.

Ultimately, these are questions about television and social change and about the nature and value of art and creativity and their relationship to commerce. As will be seen, asking and answering such questions often involve value judgments about people, social class, art, and society.

Television does change, of course, but often many forces align to keep it the same. The industry relies on continuing series and familiar genres, and routinely feeds off successful shows in its breeding of spin-offs, sequels, and other imitations. In his thick-description study of the industry, *Inside Prime Time*, Todd Gitlin introduced the concepts of "recombinant culture" and the "hybrid pitch." In the hybrid pitch a writer-producer tries to sell a new television series to network executives by telling them, in one breath, that the prospective show is brand new—that no one has ever seen anything like it before—and in the next breath, that it is a blend of two familiar hit shows from the past.

NBC's enormous late-1970s failure, *Battlestar Gallactica*, is just one example of this phenomenon. It was pitched as an absolutely new, breakthrough show that would ably merge the *Star Trek* and *Bonanza* franchises. The program would put "*Bonanza* in outer space," with Lorne Greene holding the reins of the spaceship. Gitlin observed that what network executives were being sold, while new for the pitch session and marketing purposes, was ultimately a less than brilliant mixing of two tried (tired?) and true genres. I often learned of such pitches in the course of my travels in Hollywood.

Much of television *is*, in essence, novelty packaged in a safe context. TV delivers something very familiar, but just new enough that you haven't seen it before; something that may *seem* novel, but is not really new—at least not so new so as to scare off a potential audience or the advertisers.

In 1978, the Corporation for Public Broadcasting conducted a study of why imported British offerings such as *Masterpiece Theater* weren't watched more frequently by American audiences. Viewers in focus groups told the researchers that they didn't like not knowing the characters from week to week; that it required too much mental effort to watch a new program with so many unfamiliar characters and actors. They preferred continuing series, with familiar characters, sets, and storylines.[1]

The TV series became the key building block of commercial television early in the industry's history. A network's schedule, especially in prime time, is built around the episodic series because it reliably brings audiences back week after week, *and* because it permits the programs to be produced—or ground out on an assembly line, depending on your perspective—quickly and economically. There are scores, if not hundreds, of people involved in the production of a television series who help get a new program made each week, and their work has to be organized and systematized.

How do individual creators operate in such a system? If art requires an artist, can television be an art form if it is created by so many different people? Dwight MacDonald, reflecting the views of the Frankfurt School, had little doubt that the "Lords of Kitsch," as he called them, were technicians rather than creative artists:

> Mass Culture is imposed from above. It is fabricated by technicians hired by businessmen; its audience are passive consumers, their participation is limited to the choice between buying and not buying. The Lords of *kitsch*, in short, exploit the cultural needs of the masses in order to make a profit and/or to maintain their class rule. (1957, p. 60)

In summarizing this critique in *Popular Culture and High Culture*, Herbert Gans distilled three closely related, factual sounding statements on the process by which mass culture is created:

> That mass culture is an industry organized by profit; that in order for this industry to be profitable, it must create a homogeneous and standardized product that appeals to a mass audience; and that this requires a process in which the industry transforms the creator into a worker on a mass production assembly line, requiring him or her to give up the individual expression of his own skills and values. (1974, p. 20)

---

[1] The importance of the series, and "the familiar," to the success of television is explored further in the introductions to Chapters 3, 4, and 8.

There can be little question but that the first two assessments are on target. Just see the interviews with Lee Rich, David Levy, and Jean Rouverol among others. Television creators do unquestionably hone and accommodate their talent, skills, and vision to the commercial realities and constraints of the industry. But there are also creative ideas and storytelling innovations that creators bring to the small screen and that bring change to television content and form. Gans writes: "Popular culture creators fight as intensely for their own ideas as high culture creators, and thinking of the former as opportunistic hacks out to give an audience what it wants is an unfair and inaccurate surrender to a facile stereotype (p. 27)."

AUDIENCE SIZE AND THE HIGH VS. POPULAR CULTURE DEBATE

In understanding television and our attitudes toward popular culture, audience size should rarely be far from mind. I have long wished that a greater number of television creators—and ultimately the networks and cable channels they serve—could be satisfied with just one-third less audience. HBO understands the problem. It has revolutionized what is possible in American television by eliminating commercials and offering repeat showings of its programs, thereby reducing the necessary size of the audience at any given time. By producing just 13 episodes in each season of *Six Feet Under, The Sopranos*, or *Curb Your Enthusiasm*, HBO gives its creators the necessary breathing room.

It boggles the mind that programs offered by the traditional networks can be cancelled if they fall short of attracting an audience of 15 million viewers. (Not long ago, programs viewed by audiences of 20 to 25 million would sometimes be deemed ratings failures.) Consider for a moment, a Broadway play—a hit—that packs in a full house of 1,500 theatergoers each performance for six nights and one matinee every week. The audience of 15 million is 10,000 times larger than the one of 1,500. Put another way, the play would require over 27 years of nonstop, daily sell-outs to equal a single evening's television audience of 15 million.

But a television series doesn't have to draw millions of viewers just *one* night; it has to attract these huge audiences for each of its 22 annual episodes (30 to 40 episodes in the 1950s and 1960s). To appeal to such massive audiences, widely understood themes and tropes must be employed; as a result, mass audience television programs often steer down the middle in terms of taste, intelligence, and sensibility. Hence the repetitive, standardized quality of much television and the frequent criticism of the medium as a vast wasteland of bubble gum for the eyes. Because of its commercialism and its huge audiences, because of the sameness, the stereotyping, the exploitive tricks and plot twists, the action rising before each ad, there has long been a good deal of criticism of television and its creators, and by extension, its worthiness for analysis or study as art.

Though similar concerns and criticisms of mass culture arose well before the advent of television, especially by the Frankfurt School theorists in the 1930s, there was a resurgence in concern about mass culture among American intellectuals just a few years after television became widely popular. One such view is expressed here by Leo Lowenthal:

> The decline of the individual in the mechanized working processes of modern civilization brings about the emergence of mass culture, which replaces folk or "high" art. A product of popular culture has none of the features of genuine art, but in all its media popular culture proves to have its own genuine characteristics: standardization, stereotypy, conservatism, mendacity, manipulated consumer goods. (1957, p. 55)

In the same period, Edward Shils (1959) offered a similar but more revealing commentary on mass culture:

> I think we are not confronting the real problem: why we don't like mass culture. This seems to be the issue. We don't like it. It is repulsive to us. Is it partly because we don't like the working classes and the middle classes? . . . But the real fact is that from an aesthetic and moral standpoint, the objects of mass culture are repulsive to us. This ought to be admitted. To do so would help us select an aesthetic viewpoint, a system of moral judgments which would be applicable to the products of mass culture; but I think it would also relieve our minds from the necessity of making up fictions about the empirical consequences of mass culture. (pp. 198–99)

To be sure, the elitism associated with high culture and the high culture critique of popular culture are each inescapably tied to issues of class, how we think about commercialism and its aims, and what we believe constitutes art. And, of course, commercialism and class are inescapably tied to audience size and television's sheer popularity. The popular arts are just that: popular and art. But that doesn't make the status issues disappear. They were clearly apparent in the 1950s and they remain today in numerous conflicts over what should be taught in the English curriculum at the university, in clashes over cultural studies and, as we will see, in some assessments of the auteur approach.

In some quarters, there still exists the belief that only high culture is guided by true aesthetic standards (Bloom, 1988; Epstein, 2002), and by extension, that the creators and audiences of high culture merit superior cultural status owning to their artistry, taste and knowledge; what Pierre Bourdieu (1984) critiqued as "cultural capital." Indeed, according to Gans, popular culture is anathema to the high culture enthusiast because there is a fear that the high culture audience will eventually be wooed away and won over by kitsch, user-oriented culture. The fear isn't ungrounded. As we have seen, television *is* user oriented, audiences *do* like and seek out familiar programs that in the eyes of some are simply hackneyed and escapist. At the same time, for 30 years now, the fact that audiences actively seek out and enjoy popular culture has been seen by cultural studies advocates as an important phenomenon to understand from the point of view of the audience (or the interpretive community of readers, listeners, or viewers) and a critical feature of popular culture to champion (Hall, 1973, 1980).

But there are also false dichotomies and erroneous assumptions at play in the high culture critique of popular culture, all of which have been with us since before the beginning of television.[2] First, high culture also has its sponsors and markets to which artists respond. Leonardo da Vinci rarely stayed in one city for very long, constantly moving in response to changing market conditions. Mozart and Michelangelo similarly followed the predilections of *their* sponsors. Much of Dickens' and Twain's work was first published episodically in commercial publications. Second, the pantheon is never static. Just a century ago it would have been an outrage to see Dickens or Twain listed in the same English literature reading list with Shakespeare and Chaucer.

Popular culture is sometimes given short shrift because it is in the realm of leisure but also because the material under scrutiny is commercial, contemporary, and seemingly ephemeral. By contrast, the study of how the ancient Greeks and Romans spent their leisure time and entertained themselves, and what was written in their plays and how they were performed, has long been seen as having significant intellectual import.[3] Yet all that was created in the ancient world, or in the Renaissance for that matter, was once every bit as contemporary as were Twain or Dickens in their time, or the latest episode of *The Simpsons* in ours. This isn't to say that commerciality or contemporaneity put all art on a par. It is only to say that popular culture ought not be dismissed merely because it is commercial or contemporary, or because of class bias. After all, the patina of age is slowly and surely accreting on popular culture products; this factor alone is gradually making their study more acceptable to educational traditionalists. This is also why I believe that we can expect media education to become commonplace in schools by the middle of the twenty-first century, if not well before (Kubey, 1991). By the year 2050, film will have just celebrated its 150th birthday and television will be 100 years old.

But popular culture needs to be taken seriously even if the high culture stance *was* somehow thoroughly grounded in a widely agreed upon and perfectly enunciated aesthetic standard, such that one could authoritatively say that popular culture absolutely lacked a legitimate aesthetic. Social scientists and humanists would still be interested in television and popular culture,

---

[2] Speaking of false dichotomies, it's not as if television *never* presents dance, classical music, opera, or theater. For a comprehensive, historical review, see Brian G. Rose's 1986 handbook and reference guide to *Television and the Performing Arts.*

[3] Of course, many famous Roman leisure pursuits were especially debauched. The theater also suffered. Cicero was writing bitter criticism of the excesses and "ghastly horrors" of the theater as early as 50 B.C. By the 5th century, the church abolished the Roman theater as an art form because it was seen as so debased by commercial exploitation as to have lost any relevance to the good of society (Kubey & Csikszentmihalyi, 1990, p. 15).

and how they are created, if only for the reason that the audiences *are* so large, and because these widely experienced cultural products express and document the shifting psychological and sociological states—the hopes, dreams, concerns and nightmares—of the people and the societies in which they are produced (Arnheim, 1957; Cawelti, 1976; Munsterberg, 1916; Powdermaker, 1950; Wolfenstein & Leites, 1950).

As David Desser (2000) put it, television and filmic stories are "popular precisely because they answer, within structured fantasy, social, historical, psychological, or cultural issues within the culture that produces and consumes them" (p. 103). Or as Horace Newcomb and Paul Hirsch (1983) have written:

> Television is both a part of this cultural pluralism and currently its central component in American life. In its role as central cultural medium it presents us with its own multiplicity of meanings rather than with a monolithic presentation of a dominant point of view. Because it is, to a great extent, culturally written, television presents us with our most prevalent concerns, our deepest dilemmas. Our most traditional views, those which are repressive and reactionary, as well as those which are subversive and emancipatory, are upheld, examined, maintained, and transformed.

THE CHALLENGE OF CREATING QUALITY TELEVISION

Some critics of popular culture may fail to appreciate what is involved in its production. To understand how challenging it can be to make a single popular entertainment, consider Moss Hart's classic memoir, *Act One* (1959), about the mounting of his first successful Broadway play, *Once in a Lifetime*. Even with the expert help of George S. Kaufman, the most successful Broadway comedy playwright of the day, Hart worked intensely for years on this light, 90-minute comedy before it finally opened on Broadway and where it still might have failed. By comparison, some television creators hit their targets successfully each week for 22 weeks.

It's easy to laugh at the low quality of many a television program and scoff at the "hacks" who turn them out, but to create a program *well* on a regular basis is more difficult, I think, than many know. Once one learns the pitfalls and pressures, the many ways that a program can be interfered with, or a writer blocked, it is sometimes impressive that anything of quality gets made, especially at the pace required.

Reading the foregoing, more than one reader might conclude that I have been influenced by my subjects' point of view. I no doubt have been. But this is among the reasons I have presented the individuals in interview form, to let readers make their own assessments.

I liked the great majority of the people I interviewed and found them bright and engaging. My experience, incidentally, seems to be the norm. Todd Gitlin observed that the television creators he interviewed possessed "real intelligence," and found himself "liking almost all of them" (1983, p. 14). The same goes for Muriel Cantor and her assessment of the television producers she interviewed in the late 1960s (1971).

Some of the harshest contemporary criticism of television and its creators, or of latter-day Frankfurt School critics for that matter, is often on target in the abstract and sometimes in actual practice, but such views need to be held up to a more complex reality of how individuals actually function in the industry, how they are both frustrated and gratified in the process of creating their programs. There *is* much poorly crafted television product churned out every season. Indeed, one of the questions explored in the pages ahead is why television *isn't* better, what the obstacles and impediments are to a better product. There are many such obstacles and through the interviews one sees patterns and themes develop: interference from the network, too many cooks spoiling the broth; overdependence on focus groups, ratings, and demographics; a short-sighted obsession with the bottom line. And we see a significant solution in the creative freedom extended by HBO.

The interviews also permit us to see how individual talent and vision survives in television. For some, early talents and propensities were nurtured in childhood; other times they are stymied or lost and then rediscovered. Horace Newcomb and Robert Alley were right: "the autobiographical visions of individuals . . . manage to break through onto the television screen" (1983).

ESTABLISHING AUTHORSHIP: THE AUTEUR APPROACH

How is artistry and authorship to be established in the collaborative media? Scholars and critics have wrestled with this question for some time, particularly in film. In the next few pages I wish to focus on how the auteur approach in film began and on some of the problems in its application, and then discuss how the auteur approach came to be applied to television.

Auteur theory first developed when critics and scholars began formally to study film through the lens of a given director's body of work (*oeuvre*). Andre Bazin, then the editor of the influential journal *Cahiers du cinema*, is often credited with laying groundwork for auteur theory by persuasively arguing—in Europe of all places—for the quality, and even the *superiority*, of the American film and its diverse and distinctive genres. By raising the status of the American film, especially in largely neglected genres like the western and crime drama, Bazin also raised the status of many American filmmakers whose work had been previously ignored. Building on Bazin, in the 1950s and 1960s, François Truffaut (1954), and then Andrew Sarris (1968), began to formally argue that the principal author, or auteur, of a film was the director and that it was the director who gave a film, or series of films, their distinctive artistic and cinematic quality.

The enterprise wasn't focused exclusively on film aesthetics. They also wanted—and succeeded—to raise the status of film, as well as film criticism, closer to the levels established in the fine arts. Indeed, Truffaut publicly called for a *politique des auteurs*, and would later tell Sarris that the auteur approach was "a polemical weapon for a given time and a given place" (Sarris, 1962/1979, p. 661).

Some dismiss the auteur approach for these motives. Aaron Sultanik, for example, criticizes what he characterizes as a deliberate effort "to give film history a group of superstar figures of similar stature to the 'artists' of the past . . . to upgrade the 'public' and 'private' identity of the medium, to underline the notion to both the general filmgoing public and academia that film is an art and not a business" (1986, p. 84).

But we ought not to devalue the approach with such reasoning. The important question is whether the auteur approach works or comes up short. Does it contribute to the analysis, evaluation, appreciation and understanding of film—or television? Or does it cause too narrow a focus on the director in film or the producer in television, to the exclusion of others' contributions? More to the point, does it keep us from attending to critical aesthetic features of film or television?

On the one hand, it seems inevitable that people would come to better understand and categorize work in any art form by looking for themes and styles that distinguish works from one another, and the body of each artist's work from others'. Such an approach would surely help us better understand and appreciate individual works. David Marc and Robert Thompson answer the critics of auteurism this way:

> What critic would dare review a book without mentioning the name of its author? The very heart and soul of the artistic act is the communication of a creator's emotion, perception, and thought to an audience. To deny the animating influence of the creator's personality in a film is to place it (and by implication, the entire medium) outside the realm of art. (1992, p. 6)

On the other hand, one can overapply the auteur approach. Should we consider all of Picasso's thousands of sketches, paintings, doodlings, and sculptures significant simply because they are Picasso's? If deemed an auteur, a film director's entire body of work does tend to rise in stature while sometimes very good, nonauteur films are diminished by comparison. What happens to the assessment of the films of a director who works well in different styles but never becomes known for a singular style or type of movie? By not being identified as auteurs, do such directors' artistic achievements pale unfairly in revisionist comparison?

How *do* we settle on the creator in a collaborative medium? In theater, which is said to be a writer's medium, we know and identify plays by their authors: Aristophanes, Shakespeare, Molière, Ibsen, Chekhov, O'Neill, Williams, Ionesco, Mamet, Wasserstein. The choice to focus on the playwright makes sense because plays are produced and performed many times under hundreds, and even thousands, of different directors. And most plays are performed as the playwright's dialogue was originally written. It's easy to see why theater is called a writer's medium, even though directors, actors, and set designers make enormous creative contributions to how a given production of a play is interpreted, performed, and experienced.

With film and television things are more complicated. First, each involves an even more complex, collaborative enterprise than does theater. Second, unlike theater, perhaps the most crucial part of the artistic process in film and television is involved in how performances and scenes are "staged" and composed for the camera, shot (i.e., recorded), and edited. And third, because it *is* recorded, the work can be viewed and studied again and again and the contributions of each of the numerous collaborators can be closely critiqued, evaluated and reevaluated over the years. In theater, but for occasional film or tape, the only stable product *is* the script.

Is Film a Director's Medium?

Because of the success of the auteur approach, and because it is a very useful way to think about film as art, we do focus on the director as the key film creator: Hitchcock, Fellini, Riefenstahl, Kirosawa, Bergman, Welles, Kazan, Spielberg, Ford, Allen. Still, we shouldn't blindly accept that film is a director's medium or, for that matter, that television is a producer's medium. More consideration is needed.

Understandably, screen and television writers don't much like the auteur approach. They have long lamented their second-class status (for example, see the interview with Jean Rouverol). *Should* Orson Welles be deemed the auteur of *Citizen Kane* when Herman Mankiewicz wrote most of the screenplay, albeit with Welles' assistance? What about Robert Towne's classic screenplay for *Chinatown*—who should be considered the author of the film: Towne or Roman Polanski, the director?

We also need to remember that there was a time when American film, like television, was itself a producer's medium, with films closely supervised by the studio moguls and production executives of the day: Louis B. Mayer, Jack Warner, Irving Thalberg, Darryl F. Zanuck, Samuel P. Goldwyn. Nearly two decades before the advent of the auteur approach in film, sociologist Leo Rosten (1941) wrote this about the prominence of the movie producer in his book *Hollywood: The Movie Colony:*

> In the final analysis, the sum total of a studio's personality, the aggregate pattern of its choices and its tastes, may be traced to its producers. For it is the producers who establish the preferences, the prejudices, and the predispositions of the organization and, therefore, of the movies which it turns out (pp. 242–3).

More recently, film historian Thomas Schatz (1988) employed archival materials from the studios to make a persuasive case that it was the studios and the producers, more than the directors, who were the significant forces in film in that period. His assessment of the emphasis on the director in the auteur approach, at least with regard to movies from the studio era, is unforgiving:

> Auteurism itself would not be worth bothering with if it hadn't been so influential, effectively stalling film history and criticism in a prolonged stage of adolescent romanticism. But the closer we look at Hollywood's relations of power and hierarchy of authority during the studio era, at its division of labor and assembly-line production process, the less sense it makes to assess filmmaking or film style in terms of the individual director—or *any* individual, for that matter. The key issues here are style and authority—creative expression and creative control. (p. 5)

Still, it *was* the producer who played the critical role at the studios. As Schatz tells us, Frank Capra wrote a letter to *The New York Times* in 1939 in which he complained that "about six producers today pass on about 90 percent of the scripts and edit 90 percent of the pictures."

In the studio era, a production executive *would* often select material, as well as the director, the writers, and the stars. He would see dailies, sometimes make critical decisions in editing, and approve the film's final cut. Some directors were accorded very little control or freedom under this system, but others, like Capra, received a great deal more.[4]

Gone with the Wind offers an extreme but instructive example of the difficulty in determining a film's authorship. Some credit David Selznick with being the critical force behind the movie: "He bullied, coaxed, wooed, and dragged the film into being as directors fell by the wayside" (Thomson, 2002, p. 11). Four directors worked on the movie, including Selznick. But is there a principal auteur of *Gone with the Wind*? Some might say that the book's author, Margaret Mitchell, should stand as the critical author, even of the film. Others would point to Sidney Howard, the primary screenwriter, who had previously adapted the novel into a Broadway play. Some might point to Victor Fleming, who got the final directorial credit and won an Oscar for best director. Probably the best answer is that there *was* no single auteur of *Gone with the Wind*—there were many.

The Auteur Approach in Television

Most people know television series by their stars, and sometimes by their producers: Serling, Bochco, Lear, Spelling, Quinn Martin, Edward Zwick and Marshall Herskovitz, Agnes Nixon, Susan Harris, Lee Rich, Garry Marshall, David E. Kelley, and Aaron Sorkin. We hardly ever talk about television in terms of the director, and when we know the writer in television, he or she is almost always the producer. In television, the producer is the key creative force (more on this in Chapter 4). The producer creates and runs

---

[4] Capra titled his 1971 autobiography *The Name Above the Title*. Doing so may be one of the reasons that Joseph McBride chose to title his 1992 biography of the director, *Frank Capra: The Catastrophe of Success.*

the show and it is the producer who, more than anyone else, with rare exception, is the creative mind and manager behind a series and its programs.

In television today, and certainly since the early 1960s, the producer remains in charge, conceiving of the program and often writing, or helping to write, the original treatment. Indeed, the television producer is more critically involved and often lends more personal vision to the final product than did the powerful movie producers of the studio era. Consequently, many of the interviews in the pages ahead were done with individuals who are, or who were at one time, producers. No single profession helps us understand better how television is created.

In the late 1960s, sociologist Muriel Cantor (1971) completed the first formal study of television creators, interviewing 59 leading dramatic television producers, missing only a few of the entire group then working on network programs in Hollywood. In the book that resulted, *The Hollywood TV Producer: His Work and His Audience*, Cantor documented the central role of the producer.[5] In the book's foreword, former television producer Frank La Tourette wrote that the television producer is "unlike the producer in the theater and motion pictures. From a creative and executive standpoint he is the most powerful force in television" (p. vii).

In the 1980s, Newcomb and Alley (1983) took an important new step, formally applying auteur theory to television in their book of interviews with 11 major producers, *The Producer's Medium*. Newcomb and Alley demonstrated that one could discern the hallmarks of auteurism in television. There were distinctive similarities in each producer's television series—in the content and issues and in the tone and style of the storytelling. The significance of *The Producer's Medium* in applying auteur theory to television, and the value of using interviews with creators as a means to do so, is recounted by David Marc and Robert J. Thompson (1992):

> Proclaiming television, in the title of the book, to be *The Producer's Medium*, Newcomb and Robert S. Alley offered readers a series of revealing interviews with, and critical essays about, some of American television's most important and prolific video artists. . . . *The Producer's Medium* had two particularly significant virtues. First, the interviews with the various producers firmly established the primacy of the producer as the auteur of the American commercial television series. . . . The Newcomb and Alley study was replete with anecdotes and observations from specific working producers. These personal oral histories had the effect of translating a theory into an undeniable assumption about how television production functioned. . . . Second, and more important for most people interested in understanding television, the critical sketches offered by Newcomb and Alley constituted a potent statement on the application of auteur theory to American television. (pp. 7–8)

Marc and Thompson applied and extended auteur theory to television, adding new perspective. In *Prime Time, Prime Movers* they covered the work of over 50 creators, 26 with their own chapters. Nearly all were television

---

[5] At the time there were no leading female producers working in television drama.

producers. However, Marc and Thompson wisely point out that there are other sorts of auteurs in television. They argued, for example, that comedians like Jackie Gleason, Milton Berle, Lucille Ball, Sid Caesar, and Red Skelton, each with their own show in television's first decade, ought to be considered the auteurs of those programs. Their point is reinforced by veteran comedy writers Bob Schiller and Bob Weiskopf in their interview in Chapter 3, just a few pages ahead.

There is also recognition that during the first decades of television production, at least in some instances, creative control could be seen as resting with the studios—just like Schatz's argument about film in the studio era. In a book edited by Robert J. Thompson and Gary Burns (1990), three essays advance the idea of "studio as auteur." Each essay focuses on a different studio: Warner Bros., Desilu, and Screen Gems. David Marc wrote the one on Screen Gems, Thomas Schatz the one on Desilu, and Christopher Anderson the one on Warner Bros.

Of course, the networks also play a critical role and mustn't be neglected. It is the networks, in some ways like the old movie studios, that tell television studios, production companies, and their producers about their precise programming needs: for example, that they need a new comedy on Tuesday nights that will attract an older female audience. This is what producer Susan Harris was told by NBC before she created *The Golden Girls*. The rationale and impetus for the series came from the network, based in its analysis of competing audience demographics. But the series' creation was given over to Harris. As will be seen, the networks sometimes exercise a great deal of control in the development of a new series (see the interviews with Frank Dawson, Lee Rich, and others). And just as different directors worked under more or less constraint within the old studio system in movies, so too, depending on the network and the producer, will a television network and a given producer work more or less closely in shaping a particular series.

So where does this leave us? Quite simply, there are auteur producers and nonauteur producers in television, just as there are auteur and nonauteur directors in film. There are producers of vision and of little vision. There are artists and there are hacks. And as some of the interviews in this book show, there are producers who might be considered auteurs who work outside the series format, and there are creators other than producers who lend their own personal vision and artistry to the programs they make.

One can err by working too exclusively with a strict, single-creator thesis when studying collaborative media. In doing so, we run the risk of neglecting the substantial contributions of other creators as well as other critical features of film and television aesthetics.

To my mind, the auteur approach is best seen as a vehicle, a way to better understand and appreciate art and creativity in film and television. Just as paradigms in the sciences and humanities bring about more or less commentary and illumination, living shorter or longer lives based in their practical utility, the auteur approach will be with us as long as it continues to help us see more than might otherwise meet the eye.

Interviews

CHAPTER 3

The Pioneers

Creating the First Decade

Here are 11 individuals whose television roots reach back to the medium's earliest years. Some started off in radio, before television became a national medium. For example, Grant Tinker, David Levy, and Lee Rich each started in advertising. Much early television, like radio, was produced and controlled directly by the sponsors and their advertising agencies.

Like radio, television needed to attract large audiences and get them to return regularly. And like radio, the new medium found its early successes having the same likable and familiar personalities appear predictably at specific times each week. Because many of television's earliest successful shows were built around great comedic talents—Gleason, Berle, Caesar, Skelton, Allen, Burns, Benny, and Ball—one could argue that television was, in its earliest days, an actor's (or a comedian's) medium and that *these* individuals were the first auteurs of television.

The interview with Bob Schiller and Bob Weiskopf, who wrote *I Love Lucy*, speaks to this phenomenon. In this interview you'll read the thoughts and opinions of the oldest television comedy writing team in history, one that worked on *The Jimmy Durante Show, December Bride, Make Room for Daddy, Our Miss Brooks, Pete and Gladys*, and later, *Maude*, and *All in the Family*.

Sid Caesar's *Your Show of Shows* and *Caesar's Hour* helped define early television comedy. Caesar's only rivals in those years were Jackie Gleason and Milton Berle. Gleason started in 1950 and Berle launched his first show in June of 1948. Caesar followed six months later in January of 1949 with the *Admiral Broadway Revue* and then *Your Show of Shows* in 1950. From Caesar one gets a sense of what it was like to perform live on television before the largest audiences in history. Caesar also tells us why he believes increased corporate and commercial influences have affected television negatively in the years since.

Leonard Stern's experience in the medium goes back to writing for Milton Berle, Phil Silvers, and Jackie Gleason. It was his idea to turn

The Honeymooners from a sketch into a full-length program. Stern is a wise comedy veteran and well worth your attention. After *The Honeymooners*, he became the head writer of *The Steve Allen Show* and later created *Get Smart*.

Steve Allen was the first host of *The Tonight Show*. As the program's first star, his most significant single contribution was pioneering the late night talk and variety program format with which we are all so familiar—right down to the tradition of starting the show by performing, then moving to a desk to interview guests. Allen was extraordinarily talented; he wrote thousands of musical compositions, scores of books, numerous essays, short stories, and poems and also acted in film. We discuss his legendary creative process.

Following Steve Allen is Fred deCordova who produced *The Tonight Show* for the second and third decades of Johnny Carson's 30-year reign. Before *Tonight*, deCordova produced *The Jack Benny Show* and *The George Burns and Gracie Allen Show*, and in film directed Ronald Reagan in *Bedtime for Bonzo*. In his long history in show business and through his *Tonight* position, deCordova, at one time or another, worked with most every American celebrity of the twentieth century.

Agnes Nixon is one of the two most successful and celebrated creators of soap operas in the history of the medium. She began her work in radio in 1948 with the original "Queen of Soaps," Irna Philips. She moved to television in 1951 and still keeps her hand in to this day. Among her early credits were *Search for Tomorrow*, *The Guiding Light*, and *As the World Turns*. She is best known for creating *One Life to Live* and *All My Children*. In the interview, we talk about the process of writing soap opera, how subtext is scripted, and the reasons for the genre's form, pace, and mechanics.

David Levy, one of those who started their TV careers while in the advertising business, eventually became vice president for programming at NBC. His interview is the most serious in this section. Levy fought, and lost, an early battle to limit violence and sexuality on television and was ultimately forced to leave his position at NBC after testifying before a Senate committee investigating the business. He continued to fight for higher standards until his death in January 2000. While at NBC he was involved in the development of *Dr. Kildare, Thriller, Hazel, Car 54, Where Are You?, Saturday Night at the Movies*, and *Alfred Hitchcock Presents*. Later, he produced *The Addams Family*.

Like Levy, Grant Tinker started out in advertising. One of his earliest jobs was helping to keep score for Allen Ludden on the original radio version of *The General Electric College Bowl*. Years later, Tinker would found MTM Enterprises with his wife Mary Tyler Moore, and produce her show along with *The Bob Newhart Show, Rhoda, The White Shadow, Lou Grant, Hill Street Blues*, and *St. Elsewhere*. Later, as chairman and CEO at NBC, he led the network through a number of its most successful years with shows such as *L.A. Law, Cheers, The Golden Girls, Night Court, Family Ties, Miami Vice*, and *The Cosby Show*.

Lee Rich also came to television through the advertising industry. He is best known for the hit series that came out of his production company,

Lorimar. Rich had eight television series on the air simultaneously one season, including *The Waltons, Eight Is Enough, Dallas, Falcon Crest,* and *Knots Landing.* Later he would become the CEO of MGM/UA. We spend only a bit of time on his early years, but he provides a good bridge between television's origins and the later years, as his programs were massively popular from the late 1960s to the 1980s.

Finally, we have Carroll Pratt, the man who put the laugh tracks on many of the comedy programs over the first 40 years of television, learning his trade from "the father of the laugh track," Charles Douglas. As we will learn, sound technicians not only "sweeten" comedy with laughs, but also heighten crowd reactions during award programs, rock concerts, and figure skating. And though Woody Allen and Sid Caesar have denigrated the laugh track, Pratt claims they both have used it.

Four of the 11 pioneers are still working in the industry, five full decades since they began. Four of them have passed away, all in 2000 or 2001: Steve Allen, Fred deCordova, David Levy, and Bob Weiskopf.

Sid Caesar

SID CAESAR

Sid Caesar, Milton Berle, and Jackie Gleason were the first big comedy stars of American television. Caesar was best known for his broad, physical comedy and pantomime, his highly expressive and plastic face, and his mastery of dialects and doubletalk. He has attributed his ability with dialects to helping out at his father's Yonkers luncheonette as a boy, listening to one table speak Russian, another Italian, another French or German.

Later he worked as a waiter and "tummler" at Avon Lodge in the Catskills. Tummler is a Yiddish word for a funmaker or clown, a "live wire." In the Borscht Belt of Catskills summer resorts, a tummler would serve as a social director or entertainer. (Other famous tummlers include Berle, Jerry Lewis, Danny Kaye, Joey Bishop, Buddy Hackett, Phil Silvers, Shelley Winters, Red Buttons, and Tony Curtis.)

When World War II came, Caesar worked as a saxophonist and clarinetist in the Coast Guard and began performing in service shows. He started in television in 1949 paired with the great comedienne Imogene Coca in the *Admiral Broadway Revue* which, as Caesar explains, was cancelled because it was too successful. Admiral didn't have the capital to meet the increasing demand for television sets that the show had stimulated *and* support the program. The program was also unusual because it ran on two networks at once, NBC and the old DuMont network.

Caesar stayed with NBC, hosting the classic *Your Show of Shows* from 1950 to 1954 and then *Caesar's Hour* from 1954 to 1957. Both were produced live. The writing team for *Your Show of Shows* is the most vaunted in the history of the medium: Mel Brooks, Neil Simon, Woody Allen, and Larry Gelbart. Along with Imogene Coca, Caesar performed now-classic sketch comedy opposite Carl Reiner and Howard Morris.

Caesar later struggled to control his use of alcohol and tranquilizers, recalling those years in his 1982 autobiography, *Where Have I Been?* Memorable films include *It's a Mad, Mad, Mad, Mad World* and *Grease,* and a number of Mel Brooks movies including *Silent Movie* and *The History of the World, Part 1.* In 2001 Caesar won the Career Achievement Award from the Television Critics Association.

In this interview, Caesar maligns the increasing corporate and commercial influences on television and their negative effect on the resulting product. He also discusses what it was like to perform live before 50 million viewers in the earliest days of the medium.

How has television changed over the years?

> When I was involved there weren't too many network people between a performer and the audience. Nowadays there are as many people as they can shove in between you and the audience. If they could shove in some more, they would.

When people from one business get involved in another business you automatically have a problem. What if I walked up to you and said that you are now in charge of Carnegie Steel? We have a bridge that will weigh about 850,000 tons, maybe a million, now do you want to put the number 4 iron in or do you want to put the number 17 iron, or mix it with the ingots or how much tungsten do you want to put in it? Would you know what I was talking about?

No, I wouldn't.

It's the same thing in show business.

Didn't network executives want to break up Your Show of Shows *because they thought they could make more money by spreading the talent around and make more shows?*

They made a corporate decision. They said Imogene Coca was going to have her show, Max Liebman was going to have his show, and I was going to have my show. Lightning had struck us as a team and I said, "Why are you doing this? If it's not broke don't fix it." Unfortunately, they have the last word.

What they don't understand is that once you get a team, like Imogene and myself, it's magic. You don't just put two people together and they're funny. There has to be a chemistry between them. One and one doesn't always make two—not in this business. But they only look as far as the next quarter. And sometimes not even as far as next week. And sometimes they don't have the patience for that. So it's not a building mentality, it's a "Does it work *now*?" mentality.

What they do now is make packages and deals. They go to a talent agency and say "I got this name, that name, and this name." Well, this name and that name and this name might not necessarily work. They may be very talented people, but the chemistry that goes on between them isn't right. A lot of times they can't understand it because they are so blinded by numbers and by . . . what do you call it . . . ?

Demographics?

Demographics, yes! Boy, they get looped into that demographics. "If you have the four-year-olds you've got to have a giraffe in it. For the four-year-olds to the seven-year-olds, I think we should have a poodle dog. No, I don't think a poodle dog—I think we should have a dog from Mars."

If you were the head of one of the networks, what would you do to make things better?

If I got a group of talented people, I would give them their heads and let them do what they want to do. I hired them because I like what they do, right? Then let them do what they want to do. All I would do is censor them if they're going too far because they're going into people's homes. But let them do their work. Don't get in their way.

Can you comment on laugh tracks?

A laugh track is a phony thing right from the start. If everything gets a laugh, then nothing is funny. If everything is funny, then nothing is funny. If you fail in comedy, you can't fool the people.

In the very early days of television, it's my understanding that your show, Admiral Broadway Revue, *was actually cancelled because it had become popular.*

That is a fact. I couldn't understand why the show was going off when it was doing so well. Admiral was used to selling 500 to 600 television sets a week in those days and all of a sudden they were selling 5,000 to 6,000 sets a week. They couldn't keep up with orders. So they had to make a corporate decision: whether they were going to put the money into a capital investment or continue with the show. They couldn't afford both. So they went with capital investment. That's why they had to cancel the show.

In general, do commercial pressures in television end up producing a poorer product or a better product?

Most of the time I would say a poorer product is the result because their first consideration is money. I can understand that but if you want to make money, you have to understand *what* is making the money. You can't just say, "OK, let's make more money." If a program that's been very, very popular starts to go down a little bit, they should think about how they can help it, not how to destroy it.

Now a program is done many times and many people have looked at it, and everyone puts in their two cents. You don't get a pure thought. A pure thought is a very rare thing today. Instead you get a compilation of a lot of thoughts put together that is a lot of mish-mosh.

There are some people in Hollywood who are just concerned with making a buck and don't care what they turn out—and that's where the schlock pictures and the schlock television programs come from. We've seen enough car smash-ups and absolute sadism coming through the tube.

And there are people out here who have very high standards and who want to make something good. But the kids take it all for granted. The kids now buy these videos and they have horror parties. They watch these horror pictures, with people being dismembered. Cruelty is becoming fun. It's becoming like Rome. Let's get a couple of gladiators. Let's see some real blood.

Maybe we're in our decline.

You mean the rise and fall of the American Empire? That's what it is. When you start making cruelty an entertainment, this to me is insane.

Can you describe how you got your first TV show? You had lunch with Pat Weaver and it just sort of happened didn't it? It doesn't happen like that anymore.

Of course it doesn't. We had a meeting in a restaurant and Pat Weaver and I were looking at the menu and Pat said to Max Liebman and me, "Do you want an hour, a half hour, or an hour and a half?" He kept looking at the menu so I thought he was talking about what we'd order to eat. I joked that in an hour they could kill a deer or something for us to eat. In an hour and a half we could get an elephant and cook it. He said, "No, no, no. Do you want a half hour show, an hour show, an hour and a half?" It was as simple as that. I looked at Max and said, "Let's go for the hour and a half." When I walked out I said, "My God, an hour and a half. Whose going to write this?" But we took a chance and said hey, why not.

Can we talk about writing?

That's the most important thing. "If it's not on the page, it ain't on the stage." Writing is the most important thing. On *Your Show of Shows* we had people like Neil Simon and Mel Brooks.

And about performing live?

You had one chance, that's it. As you do it, it goes out over the air. I get writers who come up to me today and say, "How long did it take you to do the hour and a half show"? I say, "About 90 minutes." Then they ask, "After you finished, where'd you put the laughs in? How did you edit it?" I say, "You don't understand. As we did it, it went out over the air."

"Well, if something didn't get a laugh, what did you do?" I say, "If it didn't get a laugh, it didn't get a laugh. It died."

How did you feel going out live in front of 30 million people?

Fifty million people. I have nothing to compare it to. You went out, and the only reason we did it was because no one told us we couldn't. And we didn't do 20 shows a year, or 22 or 26. We did 39. Thirty-nine hour and a halves.

Because the show was live would you get comments the very next day from people on the street?

Not the very next day—that night. If you were good they told you so. If you were bad they told you. You didn't have to go out and get the paper to see what the critics said. The people told you.

A person on the street would tell you that you weren't good that night?

Absolutely.

Were they generally right?

Absolutely. You don't play down to an audience. You play up, because they're smarter than you think.

It sounds as if you were getting much better feedback 50 years ago before the Nielsens and People Meters than performers get today.

That's right. Because they told you right away whether you were good or bad. Also, when people know it's live and you make mistakes, or a prop doesn't work, or a sound effect doesn't happen they're with you, they know that you're doing it live, right then, right there. The audience becomes part of the show.

For a time, you were the biggest star on television. Did you enjoy the success and the money?

You don't realize what 39 shows is. Nine-and-a-half months of the year was devoted strictly to getting the show out every week. You don't just throw that over your shoulder.

Let me give you the rundown of how a show was done live: When you have a Saturday night show, you have Sunday off and you can do whatever you want with it. Then you'd come in Monday morning bright and early and you'd sit down and stare at a blank paper. Nothing is prepared in advance. You start to get ideas. But the show has to be written by Wednesday night because Thursday you have to put it on its feet. You have one day to put it on its feet and memorize it because we had no cue cards and no Teleprompter. On Friday you show it to the technicians, because they have to know what to prepare for, what to shoot, and what scenery to make and all the other stuff, and the music has to been arranged. Saturday was the show. When do you get time to enjoy your money?

Robert Weiskopf and Robert Schiller (r)

BOB SCHILLER AND BOB WEISKOPF

No writing team in the history of Hollywood, film or television, endured longer than Bob Schiller and Bob Weiskopf. After 37 years writing together, they were still chalking up screen credits in 1991. They've won Emmys, Peabodys, and a Golden Globe. In 1988, they won the Writers Guild's Paddy Chayefsky Laurel Award for their contribution to the literature of television.

Schiller and Weiskopf began writing separately in radio, before network television even existed. Weiskopf wrote for radio legends like Rudy Vallee, Eddie Cantor, Bob Hope, and Fred Allen starting in 1940. Schiller wrote on radio classics like *Duffy's Tavern*, *The Jimmy Durante Show*, and *December Bride*. Ed Wynn and Jack Benny also employed their talents.

Their longest series run together was *I Love Lucy*. Later they wrote for *Maude, All in the Family*, and *The Flip Wilson Show*. Other credits include early classics such as *Make Room for Daddy, Our Miss Brooks*, and *Pete and Gladys*. Their most memorable episodes include "Lucy and the Grape Stomping" and "The Attempted Rape of Edith Bunker."

We met in their offices at the old Sunset-Gower studios, which then housed the production company of Witt-Thomas-Harris. Thirty years earlier they had been on the same lot writing *I Love Lucy*. Both men were in their early 70s when I met them in the late 1980s, and as one can tell in the interview, they retained a very quick and comic rhythm to their banter. The two men were an important part of a half century of radio and television comedy. I felt honored being in their presence.

Robert Weiskopf died on Valentine's Day, 2001, at the age of 86.

Schiller: I was born in 1918 in San Francisco. My father was a man of the cloth: He sold coats and suits. My father and mother both dealt with things humorously. I grew up with humor.

We moved to Los Angeles when I was 11 and my cousin would send me the *California Pelican*, which was the University of California humor magazine. He got me interested in reading [Peter] Benchley and [James] Thurber and [S.J.] Perlman. Consequently, everything I wrote involved humor. I was writing humor in junior high school, high school, and at UCLA. I went in the army and wrote funny stuff for *Yank* and *Stars and Stripes*. Came back after five years and got a job on *Duffy's Tavern* in 1946.

Duffy's Tavern was a very well-known radio program. It was very similar to *Archie Bunker's Place*, which I worked on 30 years later. You'd do a monologue with Duffy and he did malapropisms like Archie's. So that was my introduction to professional writing.

What are some of your other credits?

Schiller: On radio I did *Ozzie and Harriet, The Jimmy Durante Show, The Mel Blanc Show*, and *December Bride*. I went to New York in 1950 and became the head writer of the Danny Thomas television segment of *Four Star Revue* once a month. I also did the *The Ed Wynn Show*. I eventually came back to Los Angeles and in 1953 I met Mr. Weiskopf.

Weiskopf: In grammar school we were asked to write an article for a neighborhood paper. I won a $5 prize. Comedy is all I've ever written. Writing is very hard and I've never wanted to write very much. I've always been involved in writing against my wishes. Saying funny things and thinking funny things—that came easier. At the University of Chicago there were about six close friends who were all very humorous. Four of us wound up in this business. The two who achieved a great deal of success kept after me. They really nudged me.

How come you didn't have the ambition they had?

Weiskopf: I like to use the word "drive." I've never had it, but apparently I've done allright without it. Finally, I quit my job in Chicago. I thought my folks were gonna kill me 'cause I was making $50 a week in 1939. I came out here in 1940 to work in radio. In three weeks I got a job.

Weren't most of the radio shows still in New York then?

Weiskopf: Not comedy. The comedians loved the weather out here. I was working for Jack Benny and Eddie Cantor. Eddie Cantor was my first job. Then I got a job with Rudy Vallee and John Barrymore's radio show.

The girl I met at the University of Chicago was as we say now, Asian. We were married in 1941, and the war came along and with that, the evacuation of the Japanese on the West Coast. I said "The hell with this, I don't want to bust up my marriage," so I quit my job and we moved back to Chicago so my wife wouldn't go to one of those camps.

How did the two of you meet and how did you start your career together?

Weiskopf: Everything folded in the east with television. I very reluctantly came back here but because of the Japanese experience we were concerned about our half-Japanese child. We heard that UCLA had an elementary school and figured that it would be a good environment for a Eurasian. Our friends knew someone who knew about the school and arranged an appointment. The person they knew was Bob's then wife. That's how we met. We went over there to find out about the school.

How quickly after that did you start writing together?

Weiskopf: I had a deal to do some Danny Thomas scripts and I did a couple of them by myself. It was kind of lonely working alone and I was looking for a partner. I remembered meeting Bob Schiller, that he was a writer, and that we liked each other. So I called his house and found out that he was in New York working for Red Buttons. When he came back he gave me a call. That's what happened.

To what do you attribute the success of your relationship? My guess is that you have spent more time with each other than with your wives by this time.

Schiller: Well, I've had a lot of wives.

Weiskopf: He's had a lot of wives.

Schiller: My first wife is no longer alive, my second wife is in Africa, and I've been married to this lady for 19 years.

Weiskopf: I've had only one wife for 46 years.

Schiller: To what do we attribute the longevity of our relationship? Never once, ever, in these 33 years have we ever agreed on anything.

Weiskopf: Yes we have.

Schiller mentioned that he came from a humorous home. From what did the humor in your house spring?

Schiller: Being Jewish I suppose.

Weiskopf: Oppressed people are funny. Like blacks are funny.

Schiller: The way you deal with anti-Semitism is to get them laughing instead of fighting. You're always looking over your shoulder. When you're accepted you can hardly accept the fact that you're accepted. You always feel that somebody's going to drop a shoe or something on your head. It's too good to be true.

You've been successful in this business for over 40 years and you still have that feeling?

Schiller: I always think that the Jews are on borrowed time. That they are always in jeopardy.

Do either of you have a theory about what makes things funny?

Schiller: Well, that's something that nobody's really been able to explain. There have been a lot of theories about what makes people laugh. "The unexpected."

Weiskopf: I'd agree with that. You think crooked.

Much humor is related to aggression.

Weiskopf: Yes. Hostility where other people get in trouble but not you. You don't fall on a banana peel and hurt your hip, but somebody else does and you laugh.

Schiller: It's indirect aggression. Freud said that all wit is hostile but that still doesn't explain what comedy is.

There is occasional humor that isn't hostile. Puns, for example.

Weiskopf: When we sit down to write a script and it isn't funny the problem in so many cases is that there is no conflict.

Once you have a show cast are you writing very much with the actors in mind?

Schiller: Oh, sure.

Weiskopf: It's better if you do. But we're writing a show right now and we don't know who's going to be cast.

Schiller: A thing for Nancy Walker called *Momma's Boy*. It's a bad title. We're gonna have to change it. It implies he's a wimp and we don't want him to be a wimp.

It's a new show, and we're doing a shake-down cruise right now and it's hard. You don't know how these people are going to react or even who they are. We know how she acts and we know how he acts because they did a pilot, but the subsidiary characters are all up for grabs.

Both of you have pitched things at the networks. Sometimes you get responses that I assume have made you feel that some executives don't understand comedy.

Weiskopf: Very few people agree on humor.

Schiller: Nobody agrees.

Weiskopf: NBC previewed a comedy special to the critics and it got horrendous reviews. But Brandon Tartikoff came on at the end and praised the new writing and the performers and this reviewer said, "His line praising the thing was the funniest line in the whole show."

I'm saying Brandon Tartikoff doesn't know his ass about humor. A lot of people don't. Tartikoff was one of the big wheels at NBC and he goddamnit should know better. Schiller's defense of him was, "Well nobody knows anything." My answer to that is that he's supposed to know. He's in the job and he's getting a lot of money and how can you be that wrong? And frequently that wrong. He signed up Cosby, but Cosby was turned down by the other networks first. He was just lucky I guess.

Don't you think that a network executive has to praise his company's shows even if he doesn't like them?

Schiller: My point is that nobody hits a home run every time, and you never know what's going to be funny. You never know what's going to catch on. If you had told me nine years ago that one of the longest running shows on television was going to be *Facts of Life*, I would have told you to have your head examined. I didn't think it would last two weeks. But the thing goes on and on and on. They found an audience and apparently they're doing something right. There are a lot of shows like that and there are a lot of shows that are good that are taken off the air.

Weiskopf: And a lot of shows in the drawer that never got on.

Schiller: A lot that we've written that never got on.

You're often working with young comedy writers who are in their 20s. Do they remind you of yourselves 50 years ago? Are they the same kinds of guys that you were?

Weiskopf: No. Everything is different.

Schiller: These kids grew up on television.

Weiskopf: I worked with funny comedians, very prominent comedians. Eddie Cantor and Fred Allen. These were funny people and we wrote jokes so they could say funny things.

Bob Schiller with Lucille Ball

Do you write comic dialogue straight onto the paper, or is it always a process of batting things around and then it goes on paper.

Schiller: The latter. Then you have to refine a line, because as the saying goes, "The shortest distance between laughs is a straight line." Most humor is very precise. It's spoken or said, rather than read. It has to sound proper to your ears. You get a syllable in there that is wrong and you lose a laugh, so you have to refine each line.

W. C. Fields used to carry a thesaurus around with him on the set, doing just what you're talking about, honing a line precisely. How has the industry changed? For better or worse, and why?

Schiller: The industry has changed for the worse, I think because it has grown, like everything else, almost like fungus. There are layers on layers of people separating you from the final product. When we wrote *Lucy* there was no one between us and the show. We wrote it in this building, by the way, and nobody interfered with you and there were no outside writers. Now there are layers of people telling us and our compatriots how to write.

When you go to the network you never know which urchin you're going to have to deal with. They're young people who have definite ideas about what comedy should be but they're nervous and shaking at their own end over what their network needs are.

Weiskopf: There is also a lot of politics in this business. The public doesn't know that the networks have prior commitments. For example, we know a writer who was the cocreator of one of the most popular shows on the air and he has signed his name to two on-the-air guarantees, which means 13 episodes of each. That's a lot of money. The reason he got 13 episodes was because he was a cocreator of a popular show. The networks have these commitments which they have to fulfill. This sometimes explains how a piece of crap gets on: "Well guys, we had a commitment with so and so." Steve Martin got a couple of shows on that I thought were just god-awful.

Schiller: Often times the network will cut their losses and buy out.

When these kinds of deals are struck, it may clog up the system for new material and new talent. But then the people in power tell me that there's a dearth of talent in Hollywood.

Schiller: There aren't a hell of a lot of funny performers, let's face it.

Weiskopf: One of the reasons we're here today is Nancy Walker. In the old days you'd say did you *see* Jack Benny, did you *see* Jackie Gleason.

Schiller: Did you *see* Red Skelton, did you *see* Eddie Cantor?

Weiskopf: But, today you don't say did you *see* Michael J. Fox, even though he's the big star. They'll say, did you see *Family Ties*, did you see *Facts of Life*?

You're arguing that there are fewer great comedians.

Weiskopf: Oh, absolutely.

Schiller: Yes.

Weiskopf: I think television comedy is at a very low level.

Are people growing up in less dire straits? Do you need poverty to be funny?

Schiller: The three funniest men in America today are black: Cosby, Pryor, and Murphy. They are funny men. Used to be almost all of them were Jewish. So comedy often follows adversity.

Weiskopf: Or anguish.

Schiller: There's also a difference between comedians and actors who can play comedy. Carroll O'Connor is a comic actor. He has no following except as Archie Bunker. Let's just take the difference between Ed Wynn, who was a buffoon, not really a person, and Cary Grant. Those are the two extremes.

Weiskopf: There are a few who kind of bridge the gap. The first I can recall is Danny Thomas, who was a comedian, but a very good comic actor. He was terrific and he did a terrific television series. Bill Cosby fits that picture.

My assumption is that financially, neither of you have had to work for some time.

Schiller: He doesn't, I do.

You've had three wives.

Schiller: He's had one wife, no orthodontia, and he lives in the valley.

That leaves Mr. Weiskopf. Why are you still working?

Weiskopf: Because my wife thinks I'll die if I don't work.
Schiller: She feels, as I do, that retirement is the first step to the grave. You have to feel productive, that you're contributing to something. I don't buy this whole American dream of working until you're 65 and then going fishing. I think that's a lot of crap.

You're both around 70. Is there ageism in the industry?

Schiller: A lot of our friends are out of work and they are just as good as we are. We've just been lucky. There are young people running the networks now and they want young ideas.
Weiskopf: Your experience doesn't mean a thing.
Schiller: It should. We've obviously had our share of credits and proved that we can still fill the bill.

I understand there's more rewriting these days than in the past and yet Lucy *and* The Honeymooners *were great comedies and rarely rewritten.*

Weiskopf: Norman Lear came to our first reading of the *Maude* show. He read the script and said, "It's pretty good if you work on it." And then I heard Lear asking the actors what *they* thought. I almost fell through the floor. Jesus Christ what are you asking the actors what they think for? This is a weekly show; we have to do it tomorrow. If you ask a bunch of people, especially actors, what they think of something, they can't say, "I think it's pretty good." They say, "Well I don't know about my motivation." This isn't a play. It's on in one day. I don't give a fuck what the actors think. That's their problem. If they don't like it they can leave.
   Do you know what gets on the air when you stay till 4:00 in the morning doing rewrites? Convince me that the crap you think of at 4:00 in the morning when you're exhausted and you've gone through three, four, five and six versions is the best? I don't believe it for a minute, and that's become the habit.
Schiller: I'd take some of the blame away from Norman. He's not the only one who demands rewrites.
Weiskopf: We got a show that an outside writer wrote for *Maude* that Norman didn't like. He didn't want to do it. It was sitting up on the shelf and we all liked it, but Norman didn't want to do it. One week we got into a bind and we were desperate and it ended up being one of our

Leonard Stern

best shows. So Mr. Lear can be wrong. I don't want to denigrate Norman because he was very helpful. He is very gifted and a great organizer.

We did a show on rape on *All in the Family*. We were nominated for an Emmy. We had a meeting with two ladies who were from a rape institute who were helping us with the script. Norman was critical of the script. The two women came to me and said, "This is one of the best scripts on rape we've seen." I'm telling you that if those two women hadn't said that, we'd have been up all night, or two nights, or three nights. I'm not always correct in my way of operating. But, he's not always correct in his way either.

Have you produced as well as written?

Schiller: We produced the last three years of *Maude*. We had our own show called *All's Fair* with Dick Crenna and Bernadette Peters. That was an interesting show. That was what would happen if Jane Fonda made it with Bill Buckley. That was the premise of our show.

Is that the show in which you hired Ben Stein to consult?

Schiller: We needed some input on the right wing and he had done a favor for the studio, then Tandem, by running a thing in the *Wall Street Journal* saying, "Here's a great pilot that you'll never see called *Mary Hartman, Mary Hartman*." It created more emphasis to sell that series, so they owed him a favor at the time. So we hired him. I did the audience warm-up and used to introduce him as our in-house fascist. He thought that was hilarious.

When you were writing I Love Lucy *or* All in the Family *with a large group of writers were you still working as a team?*

Schiller: We worked as a team. Whoever writes the first draft gets the credit. Because if you get the credit you're getting the residuals.

LEONARD STERN

Leonard Stern is a true pioneer of television comedy writing. He was there at the beginning, writing jokes for Milton Berle, and then wrote for *The Jackie Gleason Show* in its first year. It was his idea to expand *The Honeymooners* from a sketch in the Gleason show to a full length program. From Gleason, Stern moved on to two other comedy classics: *The Phil Silvers Show* (a.k.a., "Bilko") and *The Steve Allen Show*.

During a lull in his career, he invented Mad Libs and launched the publishing firm of Price Stern and Sloan. Later, he created *Get Smart*, one of the notable comedy hits from the mid-1960s, and received one of his Emmys for an episode written with Buck Henry. Later, he helped create *He and She*, with Paula Prentiss and Dick Benjamin, as well as *McMillan and Wife*. Stern was on the ground floor with Norman Lear and Grant Tinker in founding the Caucus for Television Producers, Writers, and Directors in 1974.

We met twice, first for breakfast in Beverly Hills in the late 1980s with the most expensive pancakes I've ever had, and then again in the late 1990s in his office at Tallfellow Productions in Los Angeles. As the name of his production company suggests, Stern is a tall man with gray hair, and immediately likable—like a friendly uncle who'd never steer you wrong.

I grew up in New York. My dad was an auctioneer and a city marshall. My mother was a housewife. I wrote my first play in elementary school at age 12. In high school I wrote three shows and wrote the humor column in the newspaper and edited the yearbook.

I went to college at New York University and then I went into the army. My degrees came from North Carolina State. My major was journalism, my minor was psychology.

When I was at NYU, one of my classmates edited the humor magazine. He had contacts with publicists, and one of the publicists who worked for Milton Berle. My friend and I submitted jokes to Berle, and Milton was responsive to them. This was the late 1940s.

When we met Berle he looked at us and said, "You're older than you look. This joke is seventy years old." One of the jokes turned out to be a very, very old joke. He befriended us. Milton is an exception to the idea that comedians are uncomfortable with their writers. He reveled in the association, and at 17, was identifying me as one of his writers.

We started writing material for standup comedians. The best known of that group were the Ritz Brothers. We did many of their routines. This led to our writing for Phil Baker and Dinah Shore here in Los Angeles. Then Abbott and Costello gave us an opportunity to punch up a movie called *Africa Screams.* Then we did an original for them, *Abbott and Costello in the Foreign Legion* at Universal. From there, Universal put us on contract, and we did Ma and Pa Kettle movies. It was marvelous on-the-job training.

Eventually, the impact of television undermined the spirit of movies. Work was hard to find. My agent said there was an opening on the *Gleason Show.* Would I come East for four weeks?

So I was with the *Gleason Show* in his first year on CBS. On a plane flying East, I had the idea that "The Honeymooners" sketch could possibly be extended to a full program. I had seen the potential and they were already expanding the sketches. They were developing a life of their own.

The Honeymooners defies one of the rules of television. Subsequent to doing *The Honeymooners*, if you devised a program that revolved about a family having problems, the network would tell you it couldn't work.

The Honeymooners became the most exhilarating beginning one could hope to have in television. Early on we found the writing exhausting, so we split into teams of two each. Marvin Marks and Walter Stone wrote together and Sid Zelinka and I worked together. Andy A. J. Russell joined the organization as the fifth writer and the swing man, working with each of us on stories. In the third year, we added Herb Finn and Andy joined Sid and me as a team, and Herb went to work with Marvin and Walter. In the fourth year, we split into three teams, and that's the 39 episodes that everyone knows.

When you thought of expanding the sketch to a full show did you go to Gleason with the idea?

Yes. As soon as my plane landed in New York, I went to the Park Sheraton to say hello and pitch the idea. We had been friends. Actually we lived together for two weeks in Vegas, a memorable two weeks in our lives.

I eventually found him. He was not easy to find, even on his own show, because he would only surface for the day of the show. He would hide in different places.

It's said that he didn't rehearse much.

Absolutely true. He didn't have any options. We always finished the script the night before the show or the morning of the show.

How has the status of the comedy writer changed?

Today, it seems that a writer's talents are regarded as ephemeral. In the past, the writer was more highly respected and consequently, categorized as the enemy. If you are totally dependent on any particular talent, then you've got to feel uncomfortable in the presence of that skill. What you had in the early days was a recognition by the owners of the studios that they could control everyone, but they were totally dependent upon the writer. They couldn't get started without him. There's nepotism in Hollywood but I've never seen a relative ever appointed as a writer.

Many comedians could replace their director or their producer, but could not write for themselves. As a result, they increased the numbers on their writing staff, and writers became a nondescript group. The star could call them the boys, the fellas, the guys, the kids. "Hi, Gang." We went to an era where writers accepted that categorizing. It was ingrained that the writer had to be suppressed.

The pecking order in the studios is also very interesting. In the old days, in most dining rooms, with the exception of the star writers, in concentric circles, you had the heads of the studio and the officers of the studio, then the producers/directors, and on the periphery were the writers, who, if they turned their chairs around, could eat for much less, with the crew.

Returning to The Honeymooners. *It appears that there was little blocking. Gleason constantly paces back and forth. It must have been difficult for the cameramen.*

It was photographed like a football game. He was the ball and everybody stayed with him.

Did you consider Gleason to be a genius?

Yes. And he had a trust of his writers that was unusual. He might be at war with us from time to time, but remember that he didn't see what he was going to do until he was about to do it.

Trixie was a weak character. Could the show have actually been negatively affected if she had been stronger?

We should have written Trixie's character better. I believe she was a victim of the writer's ancient superstition that three is a funnier number than four.

Could they have found a better actress?

That was never considered. I don't think Jackie would have ever replaced anyone. He had a fierce loyalty. He had a tough experience with the first actress who had done Alice. She was blacklisted. He fought for her on the principle of her talent.

It's been written that Carney was incredibly insecure and in awe of Gleason.

Art is inherently shy and retiring. I have worked with him many times. He is a private person, the antithesis of the man you see on the screen. And Jackie is flamboyant. So, in a social situation, one dominated the other, but in work they were more equal.

What did you work on after The Honeymooners?

This was the Bilko show, on *The Phil Silvers Show*. I then had an opportunity to do *The Steve Allen Show* as the head writer and director.

I was given carte blanche by NBC to create whatever departments I wanted and to pursue my own point of view, along with Steve. Those became four exciting years because we found Don Knotts, Louis Nye, Tom Poston, Bill Dana, Pat Harrington and we also brought imaginative comics such as Tim Conway, Jim Nabors, Lenny Bruce, and Mike Nichols and Elaine May. And with writers such as Herb Sargent, Stan Burns, Buck Henry, Bill Persky, and Sam Denoff.

Those were nine great years. I was part of three of the highest rated shows in the history of television. Four with *The Honeymooners*, one with Bilko, and four with Steve Allen. There were many awards. Peabodys, Emmys, Golden Globes.

Then we came out here and I couldn't get any work. I moved my family out here and we were in a transitional period in television. The

Louis Nye, Leonard Stern, Don Knotts, Tom Poston (l-r) on The Steve Allen Show.

type of material we were doing was no longer being done because there weren't any comedy stars available. Actors were coming into prominence in comedy and the focus changed.

I literally had a Mad Hatter conversation once. It was like a tea party where I was interviewed to do a comedy, but they didn't want it to be funny. And I said, "Could you rephrase that?"

Who were you talking to?

It was an executive at a large studio. I said, "What I think you are saying to me is you don't want bad writing, you don't want the jokes to be apparent." And he said, "No, Leonard, we don't have anybody that is funny, I don't want to put them under any stress." And I asked, "It is comedy, without any humor?" And he said, "Yes." This led me to a line that I used later when I started to see some of these shows. I said they should be accompanied by a smile track.

What shows were you talking about?

The Donna Reed Show, My Three Sons, Father Knows Best, Ozzie and Harriet. Soft comedy. They had a different approach with a different type of performer who was not a Lucy or Gleason or Berle who was going to sustain the program with their own personal dynamics.

To maintain my sanity and create some income, I went in a completely different direction and wrote a children's game, created with Roger Price, called Mad Libs.

You created Mad Libs? My brother and I used to play it and now I play it with my sons. Sometimes we'd make up our own.

Right, of course, anybody that was wise knew that they could do that. We counted on everybody being lazy. My publishing company and I are in children's books and humor books. Mad Libs became the foundation of Price Stern and Sloan.

Then I sold a script called, *I'm Dickens, He's Spencer.* It was extremely well received, but it didn't last. The reviews were marvelous and as a result I became a partner in Talent Associates with Dan Melnick and David Susskind and we produced *Get Smart. Get Smart* became our flagship in comedy.

We did many shows over the years. One that was a personal favorite of mine, that didn't last more than a year, was *He and She*, with Paula Prentiss and Dick Benjamin. Ultimately we did *McMillan and Wife*.

That is really rather different for you.

Yes. I started to enter the mystery genre. I tried to find the equation, the common ground, and I realized that a joke and a mystery are not dissimilar. We mislead, misdirect, and surprise. A good joke structure is almost a mystery reduced to the simplest form.

Am I right in thinking that the structure of the deals back then was such that if Get Smart *had been produced a few years later that you would have made a great deal more money?*

Yes. That was prior to the separation of the networks from their distribution. So, yes, with *Get Smart*, if one had owned the negatives I don't think you can calculate the money because here it is twenty years later and it is still running sometimes two or three times a day in a city. According to distributors and salespeople, hundreds of millions of dollars.

Then I started to do films and did a movie with George Burns called *Just You and Me Kid*, which I directed and cowrote.

Anything else on your bio that I should get?

The unique aspect of this is that I think I have created 22 television shows, 19 of which went to series.

Don Adams, Leonard Stern, and Buck Henry (l-r) receiving the Emmy for Outstanding Writing Achievement in Comedy for Get Smart, *1967. Buck Henry received a best screenplay Oscar™ nomination the same year for* The Graduate.

Prior to the 1970s, the network was run essentially by two people in New York and two people in L.A., in terms of creative decisions. There would be four people who were empowered to say yes or no. There might be six, in total, in a department. You could meet in a restaurant and you would present an idea and he would say, "Okay, go ahead." Then he'd say, "I have to catch a plane so you go ahead and notify everybody out here that I bought this."

So why did the networks change?

They became the repository of other people's investments. You used to go to Screen Gems, or to Universal, or to Columbia and pitch your ideas, or you would go independently to a network. But most instances the supplier put the money up for the pilot and the networks did not get involved. Now the networks put money into pilots and the studios have become reluctant to do so because they were making many pilots and the networks were only selecting one in eight for presentation, so that they could hardly recoup from a show unless it was a hit.

There are over 100 vice presidents at NBC. With so many people, are they trying to protect themselves from risky decisions?

I think you've defined the abdication of the visceral response. Now they use tools and devices. No one is accountable. There are so many escape routes.

This abdication of responsibility is fascinating. The iconoclast or the gifted, controversial person is expendable. There are so many contributing causes. One is a reverence for mediocrity.

On that point, how much better could American television be?

Oh, I think it is better than it is thought to be because it is often easier to be negative. But if you asked is television as funny as it once was, I would say, "No." Is it as creative? I feel no. Does it tend to duplicate and replicate? Yes. Why? Because it is no longer controlled by individuals.

An individual would have an aesthetic sense?

Right, or a realization of their own values. Gleason would not do the kind of show Caesar would do. Lucy wouldn't do a Red Skelton sketch, yet they were both clowns. So everybody had their own stamp and sought people who could write for them. So each show had a uniqueness. Now a writer can go from one show to another.

In a way you are saying things today are more homogenized, synthesized, standardized, and created within narrow parameters.

Yes, there is a truth to this. When you go through the filtering system and the networks pass on everything, everything has to resemble everything else. The antidote is to invest in those talents that you believe in and leave them alone. Let them have creative control. Don't interfere. Comedy was the province of individuals. Notice how unique and

Leonard Stern and Don Adams (Agent 86, Maxwell Smart)

different they were. I have to believe there are men and women out there today who have a point of view.

Will talent win out in the long run?

Yes. Talent within the network will win out if you have gifted executives who are empathic to the creative process. I think once they start to feel that they have prestigious jobs and are admired by their peers and they don't have to go elsewhere to seek acknowledgment, I think you will find that people will stay in the jobs longer. Plus, the networks can now retrieve some financial involvement in the back end of projects. Now they can divide the spoils.

What do you think about the FCC and what they have done in terms of deregulation?

I think they have done a disservice in many areas to quality because it is a myth that with a competitive market the product will improve. Programming has become less diverse. These days we have a much more restricted marketplace.

You are involved with the Caucus for Television Producers, Writers, and Directors. How was it founded?

Originally it was an outgrowth of the hyphenate (the writer-producer) problem within the Writer's Guild. The hyphenate almost became disenfranchised in the guild. There was resentment about writers who were also producers and that they were discriminating against writers and that they were losing their identity within the guild.

It became a crucial issue. And then when the Writer's Guild went on strike, the hyphenate writers performed their duties as producers and were fined by the Writer's Guild. There was a court decision in favor of the writers who didn't go to work, but functioned only as producers.

This group of men and women felt that they had no representation. But being loyal to the Writer's Guild, they ultimately recognized that it was to their mutual benefit to remain in the Writers Guild. But screenwriters talking to directors and producers for the first time felt the need to meet again. So the Caucus was formed, and then it became sort of a conscience of the industry and we've been working together now for over 25 years.

Can you point to any successes?

If I were asked to describe the Caucus in a sentence, I would say, if you don't mind a lofty term, it is the conscience of the industry. We established liaison committees with each of the networks, so that when something that we feel is abusive happens on a show, the producer or individual involved will not have to do battle with the network. We collectively give them some protection and have reduced interference by the networks.

There are other examples, such as the alcohol and drug abuse program, that is a direct result of the Caucus. We avoid showing alcohol as the solution to a problem. And we don't present it in such a casual manner that everyone feels that they have to come home and have a drink. So we started to do effective programming within the industry.

Is most everyone who is well known and successful in production and writing in the Caucus or do you wish you could get more?

In its prime the Caucus represented 90 percent of prime time television. Today it is probably in the low 70s. Among the founding members were Norman Lear. Grant Tinker was our chairman for two years.

What would happen to the quality of TV if it were more heavily government funded?

I can't say, categorically, that it would improve appreciably. It would depend on the pool of talent. Maybe there are only just so many good people in any field of endeavor. I think you might have a wider choice of ideas presented to you if there were true freedom. Somebody is always in charge and I don't know why a bureaucrat would be any more qualified than a network executive.

The important thing is for writers to control their ideas and to express them in the manner in which they conceived them. If you are given a choice, creative freedom, or money, I would have a feeling that most people would choose creative freedom. Maybe I'm idealistic and naive.

Do you think the American television audience is conditioned to expect a lower quality product? Is there an underestimation of the audiences' intelligence?

I think a tremendous amount. Audiences are brighter than we perceive them. Whenever something is good it somehow finds a fiercely loyal audience, and it generates a letter-writing response. Having been the recipient of letters from the width and breadth of the country, one is surprised by the literary content. Audiences will find well-written programs—take *Seinfeld* and *Frasier* as two examples.

What makes a situation comedy work?

I think a distinctive personal point of view is very important. With Gleason, it was the magnificent characters in interplay and they certainly are timeless. With Berle, it was that ability to say in any given 60 seconds, 20 jokes with rapid-fire delivery. These were people who could entertain by themselves. They could hold the audience. Cosby surrounds himself with gifted people, the standards are upgraded tremendously, and we find that we're back to a funny man at work, or a funny woman.

What is it about a Gleason or a Cosby that resonates with the audience?

I think the audience has a strong identification with the personalities and with the situation. I think there's a universality about Cosby, and the idealization that all of us would like to have a father of comparable wisdom and gentility. So that's our fantasy father. Gleason reflected everybody doing battle against the system. His get-rich schemes and so on.

For the show to have been so successful one must assume that there are millions and millions of men and women thinking about getting rich quick.

I am confident that is true. I also feel that when he's flawed or fails, they are comforted, because vicariously, they have experienced the worst with him. Also, remember that he had a marvelous reward. He had this tremendously supportive wife.

Steve Allen

STEVE ALLEN

Steve Allen died in 2000 at the age of 78 and left behind a remarkable record of creative accomplishment. A proper biographical entry would run many pages.

Steve Allen was a renaissance man in the performing and literary arts. During his life he wrote over 50 books, scores of magazine essays, stories, and poetry, and composed more than 8,500 songs—some of them hits, although he couldn't read music. *The Guinness Book of World Records* lists him as the most prolific composer of modern times. Among his standards are "This Could Be the Start of Something Big" and "Impossible." Judy Garland, Mel Tormé, Sarah Vaughn, and Ella Fitzgerald have all performed his music.

His books range from *How to be Funny* to a serious treatment on migratory labor, *The Ground Is Our Table*. His last book was *Vulgarians at the Gates: Trash TV and Raunch Radio*, in which he savaged what he saw as lowered standards of talk and behavior in popular culture. He began a letter-writing campaign to improve broadcast media.

In 1953, in New York, he started *The Steve Allen Show*, which moved the next year to the NBC network as the original *Tonight Show*. He thus created and pioneered the late night talk and variety show format. Allen typically opened each show at the piano, where he would talk, bespectacled as always, often playing one of his original songs. He would then move to the desk

where he would ad-lib or interview a guest. He helped fill the 90 minutes with audience gags that long since became a staple of late night talk shows. Allen hosted *The Tonight Show* from 1954 to 1956 before handing it over to Jack Paar so that he could concentrate on his primetime comedy series, *The Steve Allen Show*. During his *Tonight Show* run he starred in the title role of *The Benny Goodman Story*, one of his nine movies.

After *Tonight*, Allen's most notable television credit was *Meeting of Minds* for PBS, which he created, wrote, and hosted from 1977 to 1981. Each week, four different figures from history appeared in the period dress of their times to discuss important issues and theories. Episode one presented Teddy Roosevelt, Cleopatra, Thomas Aquinas, and Thomas Paine. The program won a Peabody, an Emmy, and other awards.

As our time was limited and his autobiography is still in print, I focused my questions on his renowned creativity and his assessments of television and the audience.

You're one of the great polymaths of the 20th century. A renaissance man. When do you sleep?

My sleep requirements, I regret to report, are considerably in excess of the norm in that my natural cycle is in the 10-to-11-hours-per-night range. I have always envied those such as Chou En-lai and Thomas Edison who, it is said, required only a couple of hours sleep in each 24.

Have you ever had writer's block?

I fortunately never have had a dry period in creativity. I carry pocket-size tape recording equipment with me at all times and when an idea emerges I instantly trap it. Others on my staff do the transcribing and filing.

There is something remarkably—or strangely—natural about all the things I do professionally. I am a musical illiterate, but am nevertheless referred to in *The Guinness Book of World Records* as the most productive composer of modern times. As a child I had some difficulty in being instructed formally at the piano, but from the first the ability to compose manifested itself.

Are there others to your knowledge, who possess a similar range across so many endeavors?

I have no idea whether there are others with the same degree of versatility. Noel Coward was one such. So is Peter Ustinov.

How often do you believe talent rises to the top in television?

A separate book could be written on this question. As regards acting talent, the list of truly gifted actors and actresses is quite short. Consequently

Steve Allen authored over 50 books.

if a law was passed that only truly talented performers could be hired for films, few pictures would be made. As regards writing, I suppose the same is true. There is a small minority of gifted practitioners, but thousands who have the minimum requirements to be called professionals.

You originated The Tonight Show. *Why do you think it caught on?*

The original *Tonight Show* became successful, I suppose, primarily because it was carried at 11:30 at night, when viewers were relaxed, and half asleep. It would not have succeeded at all had it been aired at 8:00 in the evening opposite big-league entertainment.

Do you think there are key explanations for why some people become stars and others don't?

I'm not aware of any one answer that applies to all cases. Some performers capture our attention and long-term respect by the brilliance of their talent. But there's a much longer list of no-talents and mini-talents who have their admirers and fans. Your question implies that there is an important degree of rationality as regards the factor of success. I'm not aware of any evidence for this. Luck plays a big part. Some actresses succeed because they make themselves sexually available to directors, producers, or studio executives. Other people succeed because of their physical appearance.

The first to find laughs in The Tonight Show *audience.*

Is television today better or worse than it was in what many call the golden age of the 1950s?

In some ways television is much better today; in other ways it's worse. It's better as regards the production of television films, news, documentaries, the coverage of athletic events and other public spectacles.

Ever since *All in the Family*, it's also been better at producing situation comedies, as compared to the 1950s. It's worse, however, as regards big-time sketch comedy. There's been nothing of that sort on the networks in prime time for several years, and programs such as *Saturday Night Live* are a pale imitation of the best sketch comedy shows of the 1950s.

Does a certain narrowness of vision on the part of studio or network executives interfere with the creative process?

As regards impediments to creativity—it took me 18 years to get *Meeting of Minds* on the air.

Is there ageism in the industry, with regard to performers or writers?

Yes, certainly, there is such a thing as ageism in the television industry. Part of this grows out of the fact that many executives are in their 30s. Another factor of the equation is that Americans, generally speaking, have little sensitivity to talent but are almost morbidly fascinated by success.

Jayne Meadows as Cleopatra with Steve Allen on Meeting of Minds, *1967.*

Do you believe the attention span of the American public has grown shorter? Are we "over-entertained." Are we any more or less happy than we once were?

Yes, people today are "over-entertained." I see absolutely nothing that can be done about this, however. The attention span of the American TV-viewing public—as I see it—is now equivalent to that of a gnat.

The public is certainly no happier or content than it was, say, before 1950. They are often distracted and, as we have agreed, entertained, but that may provide chiefly moments of surcease from the general unease characteristic of the human predicament in the twentieth century and—of course—characteristic of human life in this vale of tears anyway.

Given your views, do you think we should teach about the media in schools?

I have felt for a long time that since young people will watch television—whether they should or not—TV and film ought to be used more commonly as part of the formal educative process.

Fred deCordova

FRED deCORDOVA

Johnny Carson held *The Tonight Show* throne for 30 years. When Carson would look to his right to address "Freddy," whom the audience rarely saw, he was talking to Fred deCordova, his *Tonight Show* producer and besides Carson himself, perhaps the person most responsible for Carson's long reign. Before deCordova came to the show, Carson had been firing producers one after the other. But deCordova lasted 20 years in what some called the second hottest seat in show business.

At the time of our interview in 1989, Mr. deCordova was 79 and had spent almost all of his years in show business, working with virtually every notable American entertainer of the twentieth century. Born in 1910, deCordova got started in show business as a stage manager, working for 10 years for the Shubert theater system in New York. He briefly directed on Broadway, and moved to Los Angeles where he spent five years at Warner Bros. and another five at Universal, ultimately directing nearly 40 films, most notably *Bedtime for Bonzo* starring Ronald Reagan. Then he moved to television, producing *The Jack Benny Show* and *The George Burns and Gracie Allen Show*, and directing *My Three Sons*.

We met in deCordova's office inside one of *The Tonight Show*'s portable, prefabricated buildings at the NBC Burbank Studios. Arranged on a wall behind deCordova were scores of colored 3 × 5 cards arranged to represent scheduled guests for the next three weeks of *The Tonight Show*.

Meeting deCordova, I was immediately struck by his poised and incredibly smooth manner, a man ideally suited to the task of working with the biggest stars in show business. We talked about his rise in show business, how he ran *The Tonight Show*, and the keys to its long success. On September 17, 2001, Fred deCordova died at the age of 90.

✯   ✯   ✯

My mother was a show girl and a not-too-successful actress and my father had been a close associate and a friend of George M. Cohan. So my entire approach to life started with show business anecdotes and show business personalities.

I went to Northwestern University, where I majored in sociology. It's not something that's been of great value in this business. German and geology were my minors. The last year I was scrambling for credits to get my degree. The actual move into show business came at Harvard, where I got my law degree. One of my classmates was Johnny Shubert, who was the only son of the Shuberts.

Another important "Johnny" in your life?

Oh, yes. The Shuberts owned practically all the legitimate theaters in the country. When we finished at Harvard he asked me what I was going to do and I said, "I don't know, what are you going to do?" He said,

"I'm going to work for my father J. J. Shubert. Would you like to come along and be with me?"

I learned a little bit about the Shubert protocol, found out that it was dull, and so I became an assistant stage manager at the Winter Garden Theater in New York. From 1933 to 1943, I progressed from assistant stage manager to stage manager to general stage manager for the Shuberts, and then to producer of their summer operettas, and then a rather unmonumental but acceptable success on Broadway as a director. That in turn lead to my coming to Warner Bros. in Hollywood as a director in 1943.

What kind of contract would you have signed at that point? You hadn't directed a film.

You signed a director's contract and the first year you were assigned to a very well-known director. In my case, it was Mike Curtiz who directed *Casablanca*, among other things. I had directed an awful lot of stars in New York, but had no idea where to put a camera or what lens to use, or the differences between fade out and dissolve. I was Curtiz's dialogue director, a position that doesn't exist anymore.

You worked with the actors rehearsing dialogue?

Yes. And I would practically climb up the director's behind and hear what he was saying to somebody, a cameraman or a sound man. After about seven months of that, Curtiz told Jack Warner, "I think he's ready." That lead to four-and-a-half years at Warner Bros. and five at Universal where I directed a total of 37 pictures, I think.

What would you say is your most notable film?

Bedtime for Bonzo.

But that's because of what happened to one of the stars.

It was a successful picture. Absurd, but the monkey was good.

You don't want to comment on the monkey's costar.

He was as he is now: a consummate-appearing person. He knew all his lines. He was helpful, he had a sense of humor. All the things that you see in the president today, the good things. I found him just another extremely pleasant, competent, and personable young man.

Like many people in Hollywood.

Yes, the assumption that everybody out here is strange and unusual and absurd is not true. An awful lot of people have had pretty good backgrounds before they got into show business.

Did you want to get out of the "B"s and direct "A" features?

I never believed I was going to knock Billy Wilder or Willy Wyler off their pedestals. At the end of my five years at Universal it seemed to me,

Director Fred deCordova with Barbara Lawrence
(l) and Diana Lynn, from Universal's Peggy, *1950.*

and I think to the motion picture industry, that it was time for me to move into something that would be more prestigious than the pictures I was making. I did that by signing with CBS and immediately producing the *Burns and Allen Show*. From that moment on, practically every thing I have done has been with major stars.

After *Burns and Allen*, I produced *December Bride* with Spring Byington and the pilot of *The Bob Cummings Show*. Then I went with Jack Benny and did a year of his weekly shows, and a number of his specials.

Is there a connection between you, Jack Benny, and Johnny Carson? After all, Carson's comedic persona is a conglomerate of Jonathan Winters, Stan Laurel, Jackie Gleason, and particularly Jack Benny reaction shots. Carson also had a deep affection for Benny did he not?

Yes. Years ago I did a special with Jack and Lucille Ball and a new young and personable comedian named Johnny Carson. We then used Johnny on several of the Benny specials. Then, while I was doing *My Three Sons*, Johnny and his then-wife Joanne (that's prior to Joanna; I never met Judy his first wife)—Joanne and Johnny asked if I would be interested in producing *The Tonight Show*. In September I will have completed 17 years with Johnny and he will have completed 25.

When I've watched you produce the show I've seen a different Fred deCordova. A bit gruff.

My humor is often the "get the fuck out of the way" kind of humor, but it has always been accepted as humorous in attitude rather than gruff. During shows and rehearsals, my primary thrust is to see that everything's done correctly and should I either notice something not being done correctly, which has happened, or I believe that I have a creative or constructive idea, I want to make sure I am heard. If it is gruff, I don't mind being told I'm gruff. Terse would be more like it.

What's your responsibility on The Tonight Show? *What do you do?*

Everything, everything. I make sure that for an hour each night we are able to provide to the public the best possible blend of comedy and music, and guests and guest hosts. That also involves supervision of all comedy material with the exception of the monologue, which is Johnny's baby.

What about comedic interactions between him and a guest—are you supervising that?

Johnny has in front of him a series of questions which hopefully will be bright and amusing and which will cause answers that we have already determined might be interesting.

How much of what Carson does with the guests is scripted? Don't the writers try to find jokes out of the guests' stories so he's prepared?

No, the writers have enough to do to come up with their comedy spots. Essentially what Johnny gets is a series of questions that we have determined should interest him and interest the audience. However, with somebody like Burt Reynolds, Johnny might talk to the writers and see if they can come up with something. But that's only with people whom he has enormous faith in.

The notes come to me and I read them in a comparatively short space of time. I have read them at three and deliver them to Johnny at 3:15 and the show is taped at 5:30.

You're being deluged with things from around the country. Do people do outlandish things to get on the show?

Not so much. It's a business and still primarily involved with agencies and press agents. Letters which say, "My aunt is enormously amusing to the neighbors," go to a coordinator who is involved exclusively in the discovery of civilians. Civilians are people who don't essentially make their money in show business, but who are fascinating people.

So the person who sends in a videocassette is not beset by an insane fantasy. It might get consideration.

Yes. Rarely does a videocassette come in that somebody doesn't see at least once. It is our desire, not just the public's desire, to keep finding new people and, as a great scholar said, it ain't easy.

What's the ratio of people who are interviewed by a talent coordinator and the people who actually get on the show?

Well think about your own private life, there are a lot of people who are talented in what they do, but not necessarily effective as conversationalists. You can be the best actor in the world and perform superbly what somebody else has written for you to do, but not be so good on a chat show. I would say that the face-to-face interviews would be about 4 to 1 and the telephone inquiries that begin before a face-to-face interview would be that much again.

So there would be a 16 to 1 ratio. What else do your talent coordinators do?

They discover people. They look at many, many more tapes than reach this desk. They see movies, plays, nightclub performances, comedians in action, sports figures, and conversationalists. Anything that could be of value to *The Tonight Show* is scrutinized in some fashion.

You have all these talent coordinators looking for new talent and yet there is a sense among some people that The Tonight Show *has become staid. I've also heard that Carson can be rather particular about who he wants to have as guests and tends to like to visit with the same people.*

No, he doesn't.

You don't agree with that?

I not only don't agree with it, I know it's not so.

You know that these rumors get circulated.

Yes. Whenever any new nighttime talk show host comes along, we hear the glowing reports of the competition contrasted with the "stodginess" of *The Tonight Show* and then the others disappear and we keep on. Johnny is the most aware person I can possibly imagine, sometimes frustratingly to me. He'll say, "My God, haven't we had that person on too often or too recently?" We make a conscious effort anytime we have a "regular" on the show, any person who appears at least once or twice a year, to combine that booking with somebody new who has never been on—so that we don't present the same picture of a show that we might have done six months ago. So I am under constant pressure, and it is one of the reasons the job is so challenging, to make a different mix night after night.

You might have a comedian who you know you want to have on and a singer you know you want to have on, and for some reason you decide not to have them both on the same night. How do you make such judgments?

You should know by experience what makes a show. I don't know how you learn that except by experience or possibly some native brilliance. Sometimes you wish you had three more guests to put on because everybody isn't wonderful and you wish you could have stayed with the opening guest.

People do move down the couch rather quickly sometimes. Is that your decision and can Carson override it?

Yes on both counts. That decision is based on my recognition of how interested he is in the guest as well as the ability to see whether the reaction of Johnny and the audience warrants staying another two or three minutes with that guest or going to a commercial a little early and bringing somebody else on. That's one of the great advantages of sitting where I do. I can have eye contact with him and I can have eye contact with the audience behind me, rather than working out of a booth.

Are you watching a monitor as well?

Yes. To see what may be apparent in a close-up what might not be as apparent at a distance. Also on the monitor is an electronic timer, so I see automatically how long they've been on and how much time that leaves the other guests.

When someone gets bumped from the show is that only because an earlier guest was better than you had anticipated?

Or that there is not enough time to do justice to that person. I would rather stretch with a guest who is out there than bring somebody new out and say, "We only have three minutes, but how is your new picture coming?," or whatever. It's also why we rarely close with a comedian whose routine has been timed in advance and runs six minutes, let's say, and we have 5 minutes and 30 seconds left.

Is it a problem to bump someone who has flown out from New York or Chicago? Do they always get another chance?

No, or he may say, "Go fuck yourself," he may not care, or he may not want to.

There is nothing contractually that guarantees an appearance? A young comedian might have told all his friends and family that he's going to be on and then get bumped and never appear. That could be rough.

Sure, but nobody said this is a darling business. You never say, "I don't give a shit," but those people have often been told: "It is possible that if Jonathan Winters is remarkably funny, that you may not have as much time as we'd like to give you or none at all. But you are of course paid whether you appear or not."

I think there is a sense among the public that the show is a juggernaut and that it runs itself, and that you and Peter Lassally could vaporize and the show would be just as successful. Or does art conceal art, that is, is the show successful in part, because you make it look so effortless?

I'm not going to tell you that I am unnecessary, but I will tell you that there is one person who is absolutely necessary to the success of the show and that person is Johnny. He has surrounded himself with people who presumably know what they are supposed to do and that includes Ed and Doc and me and Peter. Essentially it is a very professional organization and it has lots and lots of experience both with guests and comedy. It would be wrong of me to say that I am irreplaceable, but I am not sure how easy it would be for somebody to do both everything that has to be done on the show *and* to maintain as close a friendship with the star as I have over these years.

And that is a major portion of what has made me as successful— whatever that word means—as I have been. With very few exceptions, I have remained close friends on and off the stage and screen with the stars I have worked with. That permits me to be more critical and more helpful. Because the advice or comment is coming from a friend.

Carson feels he can confide in you?

He confides in me as much as he confides in anybody. He did not tell me he got married. He is a bad example because he is an extremely private person. He lets people know what he wants them to know and he let's very few people know even that. But I believe that the past stars whom I have been associated with learned that they could trust me. I think they know that I will be in on time in the morning and will devote the work day and part of the work night, even after show hours, to what I think is the good of the show.

I assume you are always fine-tuning things on The Tonight Show *but you never want to get away from some fundamental thing that has made this such a long-running show.*

Well that gives rise to the theory that the show doesn't change very much. Indeed it doesn't and we don't want it to. The fundamental thing we do used to be called vaudeville. That's what we do. That's why you rarely see anything extremely serious. It is essentially a show of humor.

Johnny is more than able to talk to [William F.] Buckley or [Henry] Kissinger or whoever it may be. But I think that when you bring those people on—not necessarily those two, but people who are serious in their endeavors, or their endeavors are in a serious field—there is a great deal of clicking off of sets around the country. That is not what they tune in to see, except on rare occasions. They are here to be amused. It's 11:30

at night, 10:30 in the midwest. They tune in at the end of the day to have a pleasant time before they go to sleep.

(An assistant enters with the morning mail. On top is a sheet filled with numbers.)

Are those the overnight ratings that just came in?

That's right.

What can you read into them? Do you have a sense of what causes your ratings to slip?

It slips. It never used to slip at all until Ted Koppel came on. All of us have enormous regard for him, but his ratings are liable to be higher during a period in which the public is seeing the inside of something in Washington or . . .

Jim and Tammy Bakker.

Yes, and rightly so because we're watching that too. Because it's interesting to us.

If morning after morning you've seen the ratings not slip much, I would think that you wouldn't always take a look.

I look just to see that they haven't.

What else do you use the ratings for?

To find out, for instance, that a station in Houston might regularly have a lower average than San Francisco or Dallas. I want to know what the overall problem in Houston is. Is our affiliate there always lower?

If the ratings were lower in Houston, would you ever decide to bring in a country-western singer and promote it more than usual in that area to bring up your viewership?

No, because if there's a good country-western singer, Barbara Mandrell, or Roy Clark, or the Oak Ridge Boys, we would book them anyway because they are good guests. It is quite possible that the promotion area at NBC would target extra air time promotions to make that city more aware that such a person was on.

What is it about Johnny Carson that appeals to the American public?

I don't know.

You really don't know?

No . . . well all sorts of things. He's a monument of good taste. He will not go for a cheap laugh. That's it in general. He has a proper, in quotes, "background." He's an avid reader. He will read everything from the plumbing digest to *Modern Dentistry.*

Is that really true?

Oh, it is really true. It's unbelievable.

He reads Modern Dentistry?

It inspired one of our sketches. He caught me one morning and said, "Did you see this month's edition of *Modern Dentistry?*" and I almost fell down. I said, "Come on John, what the fuck are you talking about?" And he said, "There's an article in there about hypnotism where the patient doesn't even know that he has been to the dentist and I think that would make a good comedy sketch."

Isn't part of his broad appeal based in being able to appeal to men and women?

Men respect him and women are attracted to him. Practically nobody who has been in the public eye as long as he has doesn't have that crossover. I'm not making the analogy to Gable, but men liked to see his pictures and women liked to see his pictures. They fantasized differently of course.

He's also somewhat unpredictable and that keeps people interested in him, like Jack Paar but in a different way.

Yes, the emotional content of Paar is not there with Johnny, but the paranoid part of Paar isn't there either. Johnny is what he is supposed to be, and is meticulous in being what he is supposed to be. He doesn't stretch to be something else.

Carson's appeal is heightened by the camera work on the show. You use three cameras and one is trained on Johnny. To always get the reaction shot?

And we have a director, Bobby Quinn, who is infallible. He's been with Johnny since the beginning. He was with Paar. It is hard to think of the last time you wanted to see a reaction of Johnny and the camera wasn't on him. It's not always on him, but mostly on him.

What's the future for you and The Tonight Show?

We've just signed for a year or two more and if I live and Johnny lives and the show stays on the air, it will be 19 years for me and 27 years for him. And by that time I will be much too old to do anything.

What year were you born?

1910.

That's amazing. You look great, you must have an incredibly good doctor.

No, I don't go to doctors. If you go to a doctor, he's liable to find out that something's wrong with you that you don't know and I don't want to hear it. I go if I break my leg. But I don't believe in checkups or anything like that. I smoke and drink and make every attempt to stay far away from exercise. So far it's worked.

Agnes Nixon

AGNES NIXON

Agnes Nixon is the most renowned and celebrated creator of television soap operas in the history of the medium. Amazingly, she began telling stories when she was 3. Nixon was an only child; to keep herself occupied she would cut out comic strip characters from the Sunday funny papers and tell stories with them. She's been telling character-driven stories ever since.

Nixon began in radio and was there at the beginning of television's creation. She apprenticed with the first "Queen of Soaps," Irna Phillips, in 1948, writing for the radio soap opera *Women in White*. With Phillips, in 1951, she cocreated and wrote for six years on *Search for Tomorrow* and then cocreated and wrote for three years on *As the World Turns*. She was also headwriter on *The Guiding Light* from 1959 to 1967 and helped rescue *Another World*. Nixon is best known for creating *One Life to Live* in 1967 and *All My Children* in 1970. Both are still running on ABC in the early afternoon, more than 30 years later.

In the interview we learn about the multiple stages involved in writing soap opera and how subtext is deliberately denoted in scripts and heightened via reaction shot cutaways. Her important innovations include bringing more ethnic and religious diversity to the characters in soap opera and addressing contemporary social issues. After our interview, in response to a question I had asked about whether she had ever had the wish to write more enduring, literary works, she wrote in a letter, "To me, being good—that is, talented—is not nearly so important as perhaps 'doing good.'" Ms. Nixon believes that in reaching 9 million viewers a day, soap opera permits her to do good.

In 1993, Agnes Nixon was inducted into the Academy of Television Arts and Sciences' Hall of Fame. In 1981, she received a special Emmy for her contribution to daytime television. She was the first woman and the first writer to receive this award.

A TV screenwriter told me that he was the best storyteller in his Cub Scout troop. The kids used to beg him to tell stories around the campfire at night. He said, "Now I just write stories for a bigger campfire." Does that ring a bell for you?

Well, I just write stories for bigger paper dolls. I used to play paper dolls, long before I could read, and I would tell stories with the dolls. I was maybe three when I started. I cut out the Sunday comic strip characters. This was in the early 1930s. I kept all the cutouts in an old telephone book arranged alphabetically. I kept them segregated in terms of the characters and the clothes they wore. I organized them and played like that for maybe five years. I favored the women. The men didn't have very interesting clothes, you know. I'd have daytime and evening dresses for the women. I'd spend hours and hours at it.

I was an only child and though I don't think I was lonely, I was alone a lot. My mother worked. My parents were separated when I was two months old. We lived with my grandmother and several unmarried aunts. I had no peer group and not many playmates.

So you created a little world for yourself?

Yes, I really did. I also did a lot of plays in school. I had an aunt who told us stories. My mother's family was Irish and they told stories. I was also interested in acting, was a veteran moviegoer, and was attracted by the glamor. I went to a conservative Catholic girls school in Nashville. My mother was a bookkeeper in an insurance company and my father lived in Chicago. My first two years of college were at Saint Mary's Notre Dame, a Catholic women's college in South Bend, Indiana, across from Notre Dame. I transferred to Northwestern in my junior year to study speech and drama.

Two people at Northwestern changed my life. One was Alvina Krauss. She died many years ago. The other was Professor Lucerette, who was in the public speaking department. He was a poet. I just adored that man. Alvina taught me acting and to know a character, not just when you see them on stage or on camera, but from the moment they're born. You had to know what their story was. Lucerette taught me to see beyond what the eye first picks up, to see everything with fresh wonder.

How is this important to your work as a writer?

An actor may do thousands of performances but must always give the impression that it's the first time.

So between those two professors, you learned that any character has an elaborate past that brings them to a point in time in which they behave spontaneously.

Yes, yes, that's right. And of course I write character-oriented shows.

Three days after I finished Northwestern I got an interview with Irna Phillips who was the queen of soap opera. I gave her a script I had written for a Northwestern play workshop and she hired me. She used the story I wrote for six months of soap episodes.

Were those radio days?

Yes, that was radio. Television was just coming in in 1949.

Did you contact her through one of your professors?

No. It was very strange. Do you really want me to tell you about it?

Is it interesting?

I think it's very interesting. My father sent me to college. He was a poor boy in Chicago's Southside, wanted to be a doctor, but didn't have the money for med school. After he and my mother separated, he went into his own business—no one else had done it—making burial garments.

He would hang around funeral parlors looking for business. He wanted me to go into business with him. He said I didn't have any talent.

He actually told you that?

We didn't have the very best relationship. He was a very sick man. Very successful and very sick. But I was determined to write.

One of his friends was a very eminent doctor, head of Cook County Hospital in Chicago. My father said, "This crazy kid of mine thinks she could be a writer. How can I get it out of her head?" The doctor said, "Well, I have this patient . . . ." Irna Phillips, it turns out, was a hypochondriac. So the doctor got me an appointment with Irna Phillips.

I went to see her scared to death. The alternative, working for my father, was so abhorrent. She read the script aloud with her secretary sitting there. She put it down and said, "Would you like to work for me?" I tell you, I could have flown down the elevator shaft. I was hired as an associate writer. A dialogist. It means you get an outline, and then write the dialogue. Television was moving in, and actors were moving to the coast. I really wanted to go east, and so I did. I wrote some shows and freelanced for two years during the golden age of television. I wrote for *The Hallmark Hall of Fame*, and *Philco Playhouse*.

Then I got married. We moved to Philadelphia, and I had four children in just a little under five years, so it was a little difficult. It was hard to get into New York for meetings. Then Irna called me and asked me to come back and work with her. I did, for a few months as associate writer on the *Guiding Light*, and then we created *As the World Turns*.

I stayed in Philadelphia. We did it all by mail. Then there was a Procter & Gamble show called *Another World*, which had only been on for a year and a half, and it was about to be cancelled. It was doing very poorly in the ratings. They asked me if I thought I could write it. It became a very, very successful show.

That gave me my track record. Before that I had a low profile. I was a housewife, and soap opera wasn't big news then. William Morris became interested in representing me. That's when I got more exposure.

ABC wanted me to create a show for them, a soap opera, *One Life to Live*. It was my show. I owned it and my husband and I packaged it. I was still a terrible businesswoman, so my husband watched over that end of it. Then ABC was interested in my doing another show, and a year and a half later we put on *All My Children*, which premiered January 4, 1970. It is still an extremely popular show. It is probably my biggest success of all. Finally, I created *Loving*. Twelve-thirty is *Loving*, 1:00 is *All My Children*, 2:00 is *One Life to Live*.

Is it true that daytime television supports the networks?

That's true, because nighttime shows do 22, at the most 26, originals a year. We do 260. Nighttime television gets bigger bucks but the networks lose money the first time around.

Agnes Nixon with the cast of All My Children. *Thirtieth anniversary party.*

It looks like you've never had a failure. Is that accurate?

No failures.

Earlier you referred to Irna Philips as the queen of soaps. Now this term is applied to you, and has been for some time. How do you feel about that?

I've always also tried to do public service by presenting contemporary issues and disseminating information to viewers, among them teenage prostitution, child abuse and wife abuse, alcohol, drugs, AIDS, and racial prejudice.

Has yours been a key influence in causing the soap opera to come of age?

I think so. That's what I hope, anyway. It started when I used to read the reviews of different books and plays, and the cliched denigration was, "It's a soap opera." It really angered me, and I thought, "Wait a minute, perhaps we can do more." Perhaps soap opera is an arena for something more and really, it is, because it is the form of entertainment nearest to real life.

How do you create and develop a soap opera?

Each episode has to be plotted. You first put it down in an outline form, act by act, scene by scene. The outline then goes through several associate writers. Each one does a whole script, so each outline has to be fairly detailed before it moves on.

Now we use computers. We write a long-term story projection which tells us what's going to happen for six to eight or ten months. That gets updated every now and then. And it goes to the network for approval.

Then there are the weekly outlines. The daily outlines are done in braces of five a week. They also go to the network, and then once they are OK'd they go out to associate writers. Outlines are done about six weeks prior to taping, and then by the time associate writers get them, and they're edited, it's probably three or two weeks before taping. We have a week on tape. The show that was on today was taped a week or more ago.

Actors receive the script how long before taping?

The night before.

That's amazing. What about the director?

The director gets it three weeks before.

If the actors get it the night before, it's blocked and rehearsed and performed all on the same day. There must be very good actors who simply cannot do soap opera because they can't deal with the pressure and the quick memorization.

Yes. And actors very seldom go to the Teleprompter. There is a Teleprompter operating, but it's sort of "losing face" for an actor to use it.

Have you had conflicts with the network over content?

The only one I had was way back when I was doing *Guiding Light*, when I first decided we should do something more serious. I had a friend who died of cancer of the uterus, which could have been cured had it been caught in time, and I decided I wanted to give a character on the show that. I went to P&G, and they said, "No way," and the network screamed as well.

They said, "We have public service time." Of course, public service time was ghetto time: late-at-night, Sunday morning—when people are asleep or at church. I kept dogging them. Then they insisted, "All right, do it, but you can't say 'cancer,' you can't say 'uterus' and you can't say 'hysterectomy.'" Then *I* screamed. It was virtually impossible.

I got letters from women afterwards, saying that if it hadn't been for the show they might have died. Women were ostriches then—they wouldn't go to a doctor. After their last baby was born they never went back. The doctor whom I consulted, my own ob-gyn, had three women who came to him, who hadn't been back there in many years, and he said, "Why are you back?" and they said, "I saw this story on television."

The letters got me really hooked on this kind of thing. I did a story about a young woman who's an alcoholic, on *Children*, and got a letter from a woman hooked on Percodan, had been taking 40 a day, and she said, "When the girl in the story got help from a rehab center, I knew I had to, too."

You mentioned earlier about "hooking the audience" on a story. How do you do that?

"Make them laugh, make them cry, make them wait." But you can't attenuate. You can't make them wait too long.

How do you know what's too long?

By instinct. The audiences have gotten so sophisticated and smart today that they are the first to say, "This is going on too long." While you make a story last longer you have to have things that happen.

Do you get letters to that effect? Do you dip into the mailbag to get a sense of how the audience is responding?

Yes. I want to read all of it. Now the networks have focus sessions in which they question audience members. I go to them, and also get transcripts of them. A soap opera must also be interesting, have believable characters, and interesting, believable situations, which resonate somehow with the audience. It's an ensemble effort. It isn't just what the writers do. The actors are so fabulous, and they have a charisma that comes across. The actors will find values I didn't know were there, and that sparks the writer's imagination—to go someplace else with that character that hadn't been thought of before.

You said in another interview that "Loving is what everyone wants. It's lack of loving that causes the most unhappiness."

Yes, I think that loneliness—not being loved, being unwanted, abandoned, and all the things which are part of that—is one of the prime movers of humanity. Love makes the world go 'round, and lack of love causes a lot of problems. I write characters so that stories come out of them, instead of the other way around.

Do you think loneliness on the part of the audience motivates viewing?

By and large, the audience is made up of the people who are alone at that hour, but *AMC* is one of the most taped shows in all of television. Working people watch it at night.

Are you ever concerned about people becoming overly dependent on television?

When I was raising my children they weren't allowed to watch television until Friday night. I think that parents should monitor their children's viewing until they are old enough to be selective.

So you would lay the responsibility of so-called "addiction" to TV, with the viewer, not with the producer of the show?

Absolutely. No one makes them turn it on.

But you do try to hold your audiences for as long as possible.

Yes, we all do. That's how we sell soap.

Do you think that the denigration of the soap opera form is related to sexism?

I know from my mail that we have an awful lot of males watching our shows, but I do agree that the soap opera woman is considered "brainless." I stopped letting it bother me a long time ago, and I think there's been less of that sort of criticism.

Can you comment on Dallas *and what have been called primetime soaps?*

Dallas is a soap opera, but it's a nighttime soap opera, and there is a difference because they put out only 26 episodes a year. Because they only do one hour a week they really have to move the story along. I would not like to do a nighttime soap opera because I could not develop my characters as I feel they must be developed.

Also, I never found out on *Dallas* why J. R. is such a bastard. On our soaps people know what "slings and arrows of outrageous fortune" have happened to the characters at some point in their lives. There's no time for nuance in a nighttime soap.

What does it mean to you to be a writer?

I think a writer writes from her experience, grief and frustration, happy times and sad times, dreams and fantasies, not to mention all the experiences of all her friends and what she has read. Look at the Brontë sisters—they never left their little parsonage.

Does it become easier once a character is cast and they take on a life of their own, to write stories for them?

Yes, then I have a face. It's harder, when I'm creating a show and don't have a face. I sort of conjure up a face, and then I look for an actor.

Have you had the experience of casting someone who looks exactly the way you had envisioned the character?

Yes, Susan Lucci (Erica).

Are there tricks you've learned to get the creative writing juices flowing?

One has to learn that you can't wait for the muse. You have to write. I get caught up in the writing totally. I have a one-track mind, and if I let other things enter in, then I'm dead.

My shows deal with subtext. Subtext is a word that's in almost every scene of every outline. Subtext is what she's really feeling and not saying. Sometimes I'll start out with the subtext, and it will be even more important than what she's saying, and we want to make sure that the viewer understands that though Erica is putting on a great front, she's really terrified inside, she's that little girl whose father left. Sometimes

David Levy in his Addams Family *office, 1964.*

we put in the script at the end "don't forget to play the subtext of Mark being afraid he has AIDS."

This affects the camera work. Sometimes the camera will not be on the person who's speaking. What the camera shows, the audience sees. The camera is saying to the viewer, "You're hearing what Mark is saying, but look at the effect it's having on Erica, who is saying nothing."

DAVID LEVY

No voice is more clear and adamant about the decline of standards and practices in television than David Levy's. Levy started with Young & Rubicam in 1946, developing daytime radio and then TV. He joined NBC in 1959 and spent two critical years battling to keep television the more sedate, family medium that he thought it should be.

Levy's recollections are of historical importance. We see through his experience precisely how standards about violence and sexuality began to change in network television just as the 1960s were getting under way. After testifying about sex and violence in television to Senator Dodd's committee investigating television, and refusing to take the blame for the very excesses he had fought, Levy was presented with an untenable situation at NBC and was forced to leave the network. (For a more detailed account of Levy's experience at NBC one should read his article "How Sex and Violence came to Network Television" [1992]. Also of interest is James Boyd's 1968 book on Dodd, *Above the Law*. He focuses on the television hearings and Levy's involvement on pages 188–193.)

At Young & Rubicam, Levy was responsible for the development of *Father Knows Best*, *Maverick*, *Our Miss Brooks*, *I Married Joan*, and *The Life of Riley*. As vice president for programming at NBC, Levy developed or brought to the network such shows as *Dr. Kildare*, *Thriller*, *Hazel*, *Car 54, Where Are You?*, *Saturday Night at the Movies*, and *Alfred Hitchcock Presents*. He helped put Johnny Carson on *The Tonight Show*.

Later, as an independent producer, he created *The Addams Family* and *Bat Masterson*. He later formed Wilshire Productions, Inc., and served as president and executive director of the Caucus for Television Producers, Writers, and Directors, an industry group that fought for stricter ratings of sex and violence while under Levy's leadership.

Levy authored three books, all which focus on corruption either in politics, television, or advertising: *Network Jungle*, *Executive Jungle*, and *Potomac Jungle*. We met twice; first in 1987 and again in 1997. After decades of fighting for better television, David Levy died in January of 2000 at the age of 87.

I always wanted to be a writer. I was writing plays when I was 15 and had plays produced when I was studying economics and business at the

University of Pennsylvania. When I graduated I worked selling on the first floor of Macy's. My parents didn't think that that was the right result for four years of education. This was in 1934, during the Depression, so I went back to graduate school to the Wharton School for a one-year course to get my master's.

Where did your interest in theater come from?

My girlfriend was in plays, so I tried out, too. My twin brother was writing poetry. We were omnivorous readers. We went to the library every week together.

After I finished graduate school I got a job in merchandising. During that period I was sending ideas in script form to advertising agencies. I was writing every kind of radio show. I had a flair for dialogue. I wrote for the audience participation shows and they'd be transcribed so the dialogue seemed very natural.

I began to write a daytime serial for Sears-Roebuck, broadcast on three radio stations, called *Sally at the Switchboard*. At the same time I was running a store in Syracuse. Eventually I left that and concentrated

Radio days, directing K. T. Stevens in a radio play from the ABC series Manhattan at Midnight, *1941 or 1942. NBC originally had two networks, red and blue (see the mike). The FCC split RCA and NBC into two networks and the Blue Network became ABC.*

Levy dictating in his office at Young and Rubicam, 1950. In television's early years, many programs were produced by advertising agencies.

on writing. I was invited with 40 other writers to try out for a radio show called *We the People.* I was one of three survivors.

Then I went in the navy for two years where I was put into writing training films. Then I was switched to the Treasury Department because of my radio background. I became chief of the Radio Section in the War Finance Division. I came back in 1946 and was put in charge of daytime TV–radio for the ad firm of Young & Rubicam. (In the early days of television, many programs were created and produced by advertising companies, not by the networks that distributed them.)

I was there for many years. I began as a writer, then became a producer. Everything was experimental. I was on the ground floor. I supervised everything that we did. I wrote commercials. We did animations. I was involved in every kind of production.

I grew with Y&R from being writer and producer, to supervisor, to vice president. Then I was made VP in charge of programming–development. I eventually got an invitation to join NBC and finally accepted after they met my terms. I told the president of Y&R, to whom I was very attached, that I was leaving. He was visibly distressed. I told him that the reason I was leaving the advertising agency business was because my instincts were in the creative side of programming. The agencies were then turning that over to the networks because of the changing economics of the industry.

I felt at that time that there were six major switches to the American mind: the three chief executive officers at the networks, and the three VPs in charge of programming. All other jobs in the networks were really unimportant. This was an opportunity to exercise within the network a sense of social responsibility. That's what motivated me to leave. I wanted to have a major voice in television.

You joined in 1959, but you were there for only two years.

I left in the fall of 1961. My decision to leave after such a short time was complex. The networks were all being investigated in 1960 to 1961 by Senator Thomas Dodd, chairman of the Senate Subcommittee on Juvenile Delinquency. TV was a factor, in his opinion, in causing sex and violence. The network was very pleased with my initial testimony, but I ran into problems with the president of the company, Robert E. Kintner, a very able executive, who was without question the architect of sex and violence on TV. He started it at ABC, under that very title, "Sex and Violence."

He simply ordered it on the network. He lectured me about it at program board meetings. But he would order it out of the minutes. I was only at NBC about four or five weeks when I got this lecture. It was absolutely astonishing what I was told. We were trained at Y&R not to even recommend suspense or mystery shows before 10:00 at night.

It was Mr. Kintner's opinion that these elements would attract an audience and it was what he had done at ABC. The reason was that ABC was the third network. They did not have the lineup of stations and they did not have distribution of CBS and NBC. So, in order to get more visibility, he decided he would make his programming a little more enticing by injecting sex and violence.

Sex and violence attracted younger audiences. He was interested in increasing ratings with programs such as *Hawaiian Eye, The Untouchables,* and *77 Sunset Strip.* Clint Walker on *Cheyenne* was photographed frequently with no shirt on. Kintner liked the idea of men showing their bodies.

He wasn't just titillating the males with females, but females with males. We had a show with Dick Powell where an actor was in a scene going to bed and he's wearing pj's. I remember Kintner telling me, "The next time he does that, he doesn't have to wear the pj tops." I told that to Dick Powell and he just roared with laughter. When you compare it to what's going on today, it was innocuous. Of course, a tremendous leak in a reservoir begins with a little hole in the dike. That's what happened.

In June 1961, just three weeks after I first testified, Kintner decided that I should be reassigned to the news division in India. This would keep me out of the country for months. I later learned that Walter Scott had made contact with my successor just a couple of days *after* my testimony, not before as he had first told me.

I was summoned to Walter Scott's office. He said, "We're going to make a change in the Programming Department. You've done a great job." I interrupted, because I knew immediately what was in the air and I said, "Look, Winston Churchill said it correctly, 'If you're going to commit murder, you have no obligation to be polite.'" He said, "Bob [Sarnoff] wants to see you." We walked into Kintner's office. He said, "You're very creative. We would like you to be an executive producer in the news department. Put your name on programs. You'll get air credit. Bill McAndrew wants you very much and you could go down to India for three or four months." Scott appealed to me to make a deal and there were these lengthy duels. Sarnoff stormed out at one time.

I said I did not want any other job, and if you ever change my job, the job that you offered me must be of an equal policymaking function. I will not just take another job. You're not going to do with me as you have done to some of my predecessors. I had the option of being the sole determinant of whether they violated the contract, and if they had and I didn't want the job, they had to pay me in full on my contract. So when they offered me the job in the news department, I said it was a breach of contract. I had a four-year contract. I said that is not a job of equal policymaking function. I don't have to accept it, and you are required to pay me in full, plus the RCA incentive plan.

I was called back to the committee and testified in executive session but Dodd never used what I had said in questioning later witnesses such as Kintner or in his own testimony before the Senate Ethics Committee.

Six years later Jack Anderson wrote in the *Philadelphia Bulletin*, "Despite this attempt to muzzle him, Levy testified freely and frankly behind closed doors. But Dodd never released the transcript, thus succeeding in muzzling Levy where NBC had failed. However, this column has now obtained a copy of the suppressed transcript. 'Relucant at first to name Kintner, Levy finally acknowledged under cross-examination that Kintner had championed sex and violence first at ABC, then NBC.'"

I would also hold the U.S. Senate Ethics Committee accountable. These men condoned, by their silence, this kind of behavior on TV.

How so?

Senator Dodd was charged with conduct unbecoming a senator. He was censured because he engaged in double bookkeeping. He would charge people for a speech *and* his transportation and then he would book it to the government. And he pocketed campaign funds to build a home.

He closed down the hearings on TV sex and violence and had allegedly been paid off. There were rumors that payments were made via a network through a talent agent. The committee never issued an official report and there's evidence in Boyd's book that NBC went out of its way to influence Dodd to clamp down on the hearings. The issue of selling out a hearing was never touched on by the Ethics Committee. They only went after the financial end of it.

You're saying that if people like Kintner, Dodd, and others had made the proper ethical decisions at a particular time that we would not have the medium that we have today?

One man can make a difference. John Bansoff is the man responsible for cigarette advertising being off TV and radio. One man can make a difference. You must never underestimate that.

What were the programs you developed at NBC?

Bonanza. I started the use of feature films on network TV with *Saturday Night at the Movies.* I put on *Hazel, Car 54, Dr. Kildare,* and *Thriller.*

And at Young & Rubicam?

Father Knows Best, and *Maverick, Our Miss Brooks, I Married Joan,* and *The Life of Riley.*

I put Johnny Carson on *The Tonight Show.* It was my decision. I said, "Johnny, you have the job. I have a lot of authority, but I just want to run it by the president and the chairman and then we'll make the deal." He actually began after I left the network. We couldn't enter a deal then because he was under contract. I said, "When you're free, come and see me." He probably doesn't want to remember how he was discovered.

What was it about Carson that attracted you?

I was in charge of daytime radio and TV so I was aware of Johnny Carson (Carson hosted a daytime game show, *Who Do You Trust?*). I knew a genuine wit when I heard one. He was not a jokemaster. He was a natural born wit and a straight shooter. So, when I recommended him, Kintner said "He'll take Jack Parr's place?" I said, "You bet. He's ten times the man Jack Parr is." Jack Parr is very bright and very able, but he is in no way in the league with Johnny Carson. I never heard from Johnny Carson from the day I first met him, but that's par for the course. Nobody shows any gratitude in Hollywood.

I gave David Wolper his very first network assignment. When he sees me or bumps in to me, he always remembers I gave him his first network deal. But you don't hear him making a statement in public. He'll make it to me, but not in public.

I started Sam Peckinpah with his first series. I was a major factor in Mark Goodson's career. I received gratitude from Mark Goodson, Sam Peckinpah, and Robert Redford in a small way.

In my effort to reduce sex and violence I had made a special trip to Hollywood and met with every producer, giving them instructions on what they were not to do on our shows. No injections of false elements of sex and violence.

I was the chief exponent. So much so that I read every script of every new show for eight weeks on NBC. I personally wrote to every producer on those eight shows and our supervisor at NBC, so they would know where the head of programming stood. The schedule was going to reflect my policies.

What was it that compelled you to be so against sex and violence in the media?

At Young & Rubicam we were very straightlaced. For example, they discouraged as a policy recommending game shows, giveaway shows, with a lot of money. Why? Because in John Young's judgment, that simply appealed to the avarice of people. Not a good idea to do that.

Are you saying your position was solely an outgrowth of 20 years at Young & Rubicam?

A lot of it was. But a lot of it was my heritage and my parents. I was raised very properly, let's put it that way. With a basic respect for the difference between right and wrong. I learned very early on that if you open up a dike to let one thing through, you don't know what else is going to come pouring out. And that's what happened in TV. That's why I wouldn't permit any profanity of any sort. No exceptions.

The producer of *Laramie* objected to my eliminating a murder scene. He wrote back to me that he intended to put that scene in because it had been passed by the Program Practice and Standards Department. I wrote back to him, "You do it at your own risk because the standards of the Programming Department are far higher than Standards and Practices." I said to my associates, "We're going to have a totally clean network. We're not going to have sex and violence."

I wrote every producer, from Alfred Hitchcock to Walt Disney. We will not have any profanity. We will never take the Lord's name in vain. There will be no exceptions. None, because if you do that, you start a hole in the dike. There will be no profanity, and no ugly words. I even ruled out the word "lousy." Elevation was a very important word to me.

What did you do after you left NBC?

I began to write a novel and began to create some shows. In 1962, I created a show called *Herbert*, that missed out only because it was preempted by *My Favorite Martian*. I had the same basic idea and wrote it as a short story.

Then I had thought that I could develop a good comedy show based on the cartoons of Charles Addams. I developed that into *The Addams Family*.

I created *The Phyllis Diller Show* [*The Pruitts of Southampton*] for ABC, and *Sarge*, an action adventure police show, starring George Kennedy. This was in the 1970s. I developed *Name That Tune* and *Face the Music*. I also created a cartoon version of *The Addams Family*, Then I did Don Rickles' first show, which was not very good. We lasted 26 weeks. I did a number of pilots for Paramount, for Jackie Gleason's company, and for Red Skelton's company. I produced movies of the week.

Most everybody out here gets typed. I have never been typed because I have probably created more widely different kinds of programs than anybody in the history of the business. I created a number of anthology shows, the show that discovered Grace Kelly called *Hollywood Screen Test* on ABC. But I have also created westerns, comedy shows, and game shows.

To what degree do you think that TV is responsible for problems of violence and sex in society? Or is TV just reflective?

I think it's both. I was watching a daytime serial the other day. I watched a young woman and young man kissing each other like they were about to swallow each other. That is teaching young people that this is the way to kiss. That would have been absolutely taboo in my time and as an executive I would have ruled it out. You now have scenes in the bedroom with promiscuity, infidelity, premarital sex. It all has a sense of approval and the actors become role models.

When I was a youngster the neighborhood was like a village. We didn't have radio. There were kids selling extras on the street corners. A murder was rare. Foreign news was buried on page three. You only got the local news. Nowadays, the world's become local. Now you have thousands of murders and thousands of sexual incidents.

Aside from content, what about the form?

The pace is faster. Today it's hyped up. It's hyped up on MTV, in all TV shows, but also in the theatre and motion pictures. The emphasis is on merchandising and licensing. It's happened in kid's programming. One hundred percent of the program is an advertisement for a toy.

What do you think the increased pace does to the attention span of the public?

It makes it difficult for the typical viewer to be patient. If they were to watch *Marty* today, or *Requiem for a Heavyweight*, or *Patterns*, they'd say, "Come on, get on with it." Look at the Coca-Cola or Pepsi-Cola commercials today—the cuts are just fractions of a second. Everyone is clamoring for a moment of attention. Maybe someday someone will get it by being very quiet.

Are you optimistic for the future?

Will Durant made a little speech out here one day. He said, "Speak out against anything that's pornographic, speak out against tastelessness." I took that to heart. So I am one who speaks out.

The commercial networks sell three elements every day without the advertisers paying a penny. A commercial shows the product in color and in use. Right? You can't sell cigarettes on television. But you can see a whole show where the hero's smoking cigarettes. You're not allowed to sell hard liquor on television, but characters are always seen drinking hard liquor. You've never seen a TV commercial selling guns or revolvers or rifles, but you see it every day of the week on TV and you see them in use. They're being sold.

You have a conflict of art and business, and television is essentially a business. Artists are always the ones who are frustrated and they fight to get quality. The trap is that this great invention has been taken over by commerce, and commerce dictates that each network pursue the objective of winning every half hour on the half hour and winning a specific segment of the public.

They are not obligated to service youngsters, and they're not obligated to service older people. They're incidental. The networks don't care if they watch or not. They want to get the 20 to 50 year range—the range has gotten a little older of late. It was 18 to 34 for a long time.

When I was at NBC I went to Young & Rubicam and sold them on the concept of buying Friday nights, our weakest night. I said, "I'd like to program a night where the advertisers buy without regard to ratings. That would not be a criteria. We will have only one criteria—excellence." We sold the idea to General Motors, Proctor & Gamble, and General Foods. I then went to the management of NBC and said, "I can sell out Friday night totally. We program the entire night, week after week without any regard to ratings." It was rejected.

I went to Richard Rodgers and Walt Disney and I said, "I'd like to put on an evening of entertainment. You furnish the entire evening." Both said they would do it. But I could never get it through the management.

William Paley at CBS made a proposal some years ago of doing a couple of hours a week without regard to ratings provided the other two networks did it, too. They wouldn't do it. I wrote to him as executive director of the Caucus for Producers, Writers, and Directors. I demanded that he take the lead. I said, "Have the guts to do it, the others will follow." He didn't do it.

If you could decide that American television would not be permitted to have any advertising at all, would you come down on that side, or would you say that there are good things to be said for advertising?

As a theory, commercials pass on information to the public. It might be very worthwhile not to interrupt the programs, but to have a clutch of commercials between programs. One wit said, "The problem with television is that it's commercials interrupted by programming." That's what it's become.

Many people in the industry say, "When you think about how much programming we're putting on, it's amazing that the quality is as high as it is." What do you say?

That's a cop out. Quality is a neverending objective. I think the system today is deplorable. The whole institution is organized so that the head of programming has many vice presidents under him, all of whom are designed to take the onus of making a bad judgment call away from him.

Producer David Wolper presenting the Distinguished Service Award of the Caucus of Producers, Writers, and Directors to David Levy (l). Levy helped found the Caucus. Caucus Chairman and producer, Charles Fries (r).

You think that's why the networks are top-heavy? When I last counted, there were 180 vice presidents at NBC.

Of course. There's a proliferation of network executives. The areas of responsibility are fragmented. There's no reason under the sun why the head of programming isn't reading the scripts and commenting on them. He doesn't have to read every single show. It's just escaping responsibility.

The other problem is that the executives are meddlesome and intrude on the creative process, which is one of the reasons why the Caucus was formed. It's primary objective—besides the exalted effort to elevate public taste through what the networks offer—was to eliminate so much of the creative interference, not only in program content, but in the approvals of all personnel that participate on the program. In my day, I didn't give approval of the composer, the film editor, the cinematographer. I didn't think that I was more expert than the producer I hired, because he had great credentials for being a producer.

Today, you have many people functioning as producers who are not producers, they are managers of talent, agents, and they become executive producers through the muscle of their contact with talent. But the fact is that the networks meddle too much in the creative process. They should rely on the producer. If he isn't doing the job, fire him. Drop the show.

Does every network have an approved list of producers and writers?

Of course. They'll all deny they have such a list. This is one of the curses of the business. You lose a lot of bright people who flounder and can't break through. As a result, you don't have the diverse elements there should be.

The networks do hire writers with no background. In fact, the writer who's a veteran may be hard to sell. One older writer I know had his agent tell him, "I can sell your students with no credits easier than I can sell you." There is a quiet discrimination against the old producer-writer.

Not so much the director, because the director means money saved on the screen. They hire directors who are in their 50s, 60s and even 70s. But you won't find many writers that old.

The emphasis is on execution in television. The idea comes second. People at the network think ideas are a dime a dozen. Well that's not quite true. It's the idea that generates whatever's on the screen.

We're talking now 10 years since our last interview. Have you ever regretted walking out at NBC?

Oh yes.

Could it have come out differently?

It might have come out differently had I acted differently with Kintner. Instead of getting up and saying thank you for your fairness, I had two options. I could've gone in to see Bob Sarnoff, who was his boss, with whom I was quite friendly. I never did. He summoned me a couple of weeks later. But I could've said to Kintner, "This is all nonsense, we have a season opening up in six weeks, I put it together. It's a great season. Don't do this right now. I'm telling you not to do it. I will not accept that decision. You'll have to find some other way to handle whatever is on your mind." It may not have had any impact on him, the fact that I might have said something different because he was gunning for me and I knew from day one that I had crossed him.

I get the impression that you feel more regret about the way you handled it now than you might have 10 years ago.

Well, yes. One of the saddest things is meeting a former executive who is lamenting some incident that took place 30 years ago. I've met people like that, and I say, "For God's sake, get over that—don't dwell on it." Then I find myself in the same position if I'm prodded as you're prodding me. I don't think of it every day. But this was a key turning point in my life. And if I had taken Kintner head on and said, "I won't let you do that Bob, wait till the season's launched" . . . but I didn't do that.

In the 30-odd years since the period at NBC, have you loosened up your own view very much?

Not really.

Well you would have had to loosen up a bit or you couldn't watch TV today without being appalled much of the time.

I am. We are in the midst of a cultural pollution that is just as dangerous as the environmental pollution.

And some people can't assess it because they don't know anything different.

Because they live in it. They're surrounded by it. They don't analyze it, they don't think about it.

Some of us are going to take Jack Valenti [president of the Motion Picture Association of America] on, if I'm still around to do it, because he is not a friend of parents of children. At a big panel event in Peoria about television ratings a few months back that was televised, Jack kept saying that to change the age-oriented system that he had put through, he'd have to hear from real parents. Well, they had real parents and real children at this meeting and they just tore to shreds his rating system and he was asked to comment. I've never seen him in the media where he didn't have anything to say.

He said he had no comment. He didn't know what to say. He sat with me in a debate over a year ago in the Los Angeles Convention Center, and I said to him, "Jack, it says here that you watch *NYPD Blue* with your youngest child and have no problems with that." He said this was correct. I said, "I have one question Jack: How old is your youngest child?" He looked like an arrow went straight through him, and he said "27." He told the truth, but he didn't speak with candor. He concealed the real truth.

Has television become more commercial over the years?

Just measure the amount of time now that's given to commercials and other clutter.

What was it in the early sixties, how many minutes per hour?

Three minutes per half hour.

So, six an hour. Now it's about 16. Considering that programs tend to run about 22 minutes, there are nearly 16 minutes left each hour for ads and promotion.

TV is less an art than it is a commerce.

What do you think the future holds?

The network business will never be the same or as good as it can be until the networks are severed from their parent companies and are independent companies again. Networks are not independent.

This is interesting, because your politics are conservative but on this front, you're talking antimonopolistic practice and you sound like a left-wing democrat.

I'm an independent.

I know you were trying to obtain what you felt was rightly yours with The Addams Family. *You sued the filmmakers on* The Addams Family *movie.*

I sued Paramount.

Can you tell us a little about that? How did the idea for the program come to you?

I was walking down the streets of New York with two of my former assistants. We passed a bookstore, and I said, "We just passed a great new comedy show." We walked back and they both looked in on all the covers and I pointed to the cover of the Addams Family characters. They weren't called the Addams Family. None of the characters had a name. It was Charles Addams' work.

They said "You can't make a comedy out of that, they're macabre, vicious, etc." I said, "You forget, I put *Father Knows Best* on the air. This is *Father Knows Best* in costume. I'm going to make this man and woman the most loving father and mother, husband and wife, that television ever saw. The children are going to be very well behaved. They're all going to be different. They'll be slightly askew. So that when the parents see the son posing in front of the mirror with a Boy Scout hat on, they're astounded."

At any rate, 64 episodes of *The Addams Family* were produced. I wrote on every one. I never permitted a producer, I was executive producer. When we went on the air, it was *The Addams Family*. Charles Addams had never named any of the characters until I compelled him to and we named some of them together.

He didn't name any of them in the comic strip?

No. Never a name. I named Cousin It.

Now those were still the days when you might not have owned as big a chunk of things as you might have years later.

I owned a substantial chunk.

So you still get residuals?

Not residuals. I'm a profit participant.

So your deal making was not so bad?

I was a good dealmaker. I made all the deals at Young & Rubicam while I was there for TV and I drove very hard deals in favor of our company.

The Addams Family ran two years on ABC. It should've run six or seven years. There was a reason for it: It was my first show out of the box since I'd left NBC. Bob Kintner was still president of NBC and he wanted to kill the show. He put the biggest things he could opposite it. They all failed. CBS put on *Hogan's Heroes*. That worked very well.

Did you have a hand in the movie?

No, I had nothing to do with the movie. I was excluded.

You sued because you felt they had infringed or used material that you had developed?

No, the reason I sued—I wasn't going to sue at all, but Mark Goodson said, "hey—how come you're not participating in the movie?" And I said, "Well, I don't know if I have any rights." We discovered that Paramount didn't have any contract but I couldn't find one either. Mark persuaded a top lawyer who took on the case. And I always said to him that I wasn't sure that I didn't sign a contract.

Grant Tinker

So you didn't have the standing that Goodson thought you might have.

No, because there was no signed contract.

It never went to court?

No, it was dismissed. It never went anywhere. It was black and white that I had given up my ownership of any ideas created in that show. I did that in order to get the show on the air in the first place.

GRANT TINKER

Perhaps not since Irving Thalberg reigned as head of production at MGM in the 1930s had Hollywood so admired one man as much as Grant Tinker when he was at his height at MTM in the 1970s and later at NBC in the 1980s. Not a bad word was to be heard about Tinker, and not just because for a number of years he was the most influential single person in television. Tinker's self-effacing manner is legendary. In this interview he deflects compliments but a rare egotism is exhibited, a character trait usually kept hidden.

Tinker started his career in radio with NBC in 1949 and held numerous positions at the network and in advertising. With his former wife, Mary Tyler Moore, he helped create *The Mary Tyler Moore Show*, and with its success Tinker formed MTM Enterprises, where some of the best and most popular television programs of the 1970s were created: *The Bob Newhart Show*, *Rhoda*, *The White Shadow*, *Lou Grant*, *Hill Street Blues*, and *St. Elsewhere*. As chairman and CEO of NBC, Tinker was associated with *L.A. Law*, *Cheers*, *The Golden Girls*, *Night Court*, *Family Ties*, *Miami Vice*, and *The Cosby Show*. Except for *M*A*S*H*, there are few popular and critically acclaimed television programs from that era in which Tinker did not participate.

During his six years at NBC, profits jumped 800 percent from $48 million in 1981 to more than $400 million in 1986. After turning NBC around from the number three to the number one network, Tinker returned to California to start his own production company, GTG (Grant Tinker/ Gannett). Tinker had an unprecedented on-air commitment with Lawrence Tisch and CBS that guaranteed CBS first shot at 10 or more GTG shows. GTG did launch one of the more expensive failures in television history, *USA Today*, and did not do terribly well after that.

Tinker wanted his own studio, so Gannett paid $24 million for the old Laird Studios in Culver City, where *Gone With the Wind* and *King Kong* were made. We met in Tinker's office at GTG, just a stone's throw from where the white Selznick International Productions sign was once seen swinging lightly in the breeze at the beginning of Selznick's movies.

And so we began. This was the late 1980s. We caught up again by phone 10 years later. Material from the two interviews are combined here.

☆ ☆ ☆

My biography is so prosaic. I can be real quick about it. I was born and brought up in Stamford, Connecticut. I was there till I was 17, went to Dartmouth until I turned 18 and was accepted into the service toward the end of World War II. I went into the air corps, spent two years, and got out at the end of '45 and went back to Dartmouth and by a little acceleration finished up by February of 1949.

I majored in English. I did my thesis on Richard Brinsley Sheridan. He wrote a couple of Restoration comedies that looked quite a bit like three-camera comedy today. I wasn't looking ahead to the *The Mary Tyler Moore Show* or anything, but there is a connection.

After college I went to New York to be in publishing. I knew zilch. I thought I'd sit around in a tweed jacket and read all day. That sounded like a great way to make a living to me.

Anyway, nobody cared. I was knocking on doors. Nobody wanted to talk to me. One day somebody told me that they were hiring over at NBC for an executive training program. It was an unstructured, unformed, unplanned trainee program and I spent the 10 months being sent to department after department. I delivered mail and did a lot of scut work. I began to understand how the thing worked.

I was just about to get married and I said, "I've got to have a real job." They gave me the lowest job in the operations end of the radio network. I learned how a network works. At the end of 1951 I left and went to Radio Free Europe for a year, intending to go to Istanbul where they were supposed to open a facility. Instead, I worked for a year on 57th Street. Istanbul was looking more and more remote all the time.

One day I ran into a guy who was in personal management, just a schleppper kind of guy that I'd known, and I went in with him for a couple of years. We managed people like Bob and Ray and Bill Stern. I recruited Allen Ludden, who was at WTIC radio in Hartford, to come down and start a thing called *College Bowl*.

Allen and I created that show—mostly Allen. We sat down and created the "toss-up" and "bonus" questions. We went to the engineering department at NBC and got them to design a buzzer with an interrupt so that when one guy pressed from Notre Dame, the guy from Minnesota couldn't buzz in.

We did it on radio. I was the producer and he was the star. I would stand in front of him and keep score on a blackboard. These were the declining days of radio and the budgets were very low. The game went very quickly sometimes, and I would get lost and fall behind in the score, and Allen would panic. I have some great memories of that.

We did a couple of other network radio shows together, and in 1953 we did a local early morning television show right in the *Good Morning America* studio on spit. We had a little weather girl. We had a monkey. The opening shot of the show was wonderful. We'd take the camera out on the street. Allen, who commuted from Dobbs Ferry, would come up the street, and we would show him arriving. He would walk right into the studio. The doors would open wide, and we were on. Like *The Today Show.*

One morning, Allen was late and the camera was looking for him and the music had started. There was a dog across the street, and the cameraman fixed on the dog who took a dump right on camera. Probably a first and last on TV.

Anyway, I did that for two years. I learned more in those two years than in any two years of my working life. And then somebody offered me a job in advertising at McCann-Ericson to be the director of program development.

I worked for McCann for three or four years and paused briefly at Warwick and Legler, which had the Revlon account. Revlon at that point had been very tarred by the quiz show scandals. They were looking to clean themselves up, so they hired a squeaky-clean guy like me, and did squeaky-clean things, like the *Andy Williams Summer Show.* I was handling that rather happily when Benton & Bowles asked me to join their television program department. That was like a network—with sponsors like Procter & Gamble, General Foods, and Johnson Wax. At any one time we'd be buying and supervising 12 or 15 shows.

In any way would you say that it was a better system then?

Yes, I think it was a better system. Because of the diversity of customers. Think back to the eclectic nature of those schedules. We've slowly closed up the openings for new major network shows. There was more diversity in the program schedules and that was a better way of doing it as opposed to everybody's show looking the same.

Was there counter-programming in those days?

Yes, because you did still work with the network. In fact, it was very hard to get your shows in the right places. It was done by clout and by guile and you got sort of good at it. There was a lot of good training in there, in those years.

When I was at McCann I made my first little mark by inventing something which just occurred to me one day, the "5:00 report." We were always into espionage. I had spies like Ed Vane at NBC, and I had a guy at ABC who got his information from Fred Pierce, who was in the research department, and I had a guy named Don Foley at CBS, and I would phone these people each afternoon because they were in areas that would hear about scheduling changes at the network. I would get the information about time periods and sponsors dropping in or out. They would say "Bristol Meyers is going to give up half of Thursday at 9:00, where *Rawhide* is."

I would hurriedly prepare a "5:00 report," which went immediately to all our agency account people. They were also looking for a decent time period for their clients. The whole thing might come down in

20 minutes. If you missed a slot, it was gone. At the most, the slot was maybe there overnight before a bright guy or quick fellow at an agency gobbled it up. A valuable time spot—half an hour or a full hour—was so coveted and hard to get that if we could pull it off for one of our clients, the agency was suddenly a hero.

I was spending more time in Los Angeles and my marriage was winding down—or over. I was practically living at the Bel Air Hotel.

It was a wonderful time of my business life. I was learning a lot because I was beginning to learn how the product was made. And then I was asked to come back to NBC and sent out to Los Angeles to be in charge of NBC's west coast programming. I was finally a guy on the scene. It was a terrific job and it got me known in the production community.

I was then promoted back to New York as head of programs, which I did for only a year. Then I just didn't want to stay in New York for reasons related to how the company was running above me. A guy named Bob Stone was the number two man at the network, a giant pain in the ass. He fed the natural caution of a very good guy named Don Durgin who was running the network, and I just felt NBC was sinking slowly, and so I decided to hell with it, and I returned to California with Universal in 1967.

Head of programs was a job I had always wanted. I thought I'd never want any other job, but when I spent all day in Don Durgin's office trying to get a "yes," and was getting too many "no's I just thought, "Who needs it?" Also, by that time, I preferred California as a place to live, and so I quit and I came back here.

I jumped right over the desk and suddenly became a seller. A week after I left I was back selling in my old office at NBC.

It seems often that the most savvy people in this industry—probably most industries—are people who've been on both sides of the desk, buying and selling.

I think that's right. It's certainly helpful. But it's a little disorienting for a while. It was traumatic for me to be back in my own office selling in exactly the same room I was used to buying in. Anyway, I did that for two years at Universal, then I went to Fox for a year. While I was at Fox, Mary did a special with Dick. Mary and I had been married eight years.

Dick Van Dyke?

Dick Van Dyke. It was a wonderful special that CBS loved, and it sort of reintroduced them to Mary who had been a star on Dick's series, and then she had gone and done some forgettable movies at Universal.

One was with Elvis Presley called Change of Habit. *She played a nun who falls in love with Elvis.*

Gee, you know your stuff. She also did one with Julie Andrews, *Thoroughly Modern Millie*. That was about the only halfway-decent one. The rest of them were pretty bad. Anyway, CBS looked at the special and said,

"Geez, we want her back on the network." They gave her a series commitment which in those days was an even rarer commodity than it is now.

She turned to me and said, "Well how do I do this?" I went to Jim Brooks and Allan Burns, two writers that I had worked with at Fox, and I asked them if they would like to become a team. They fashioned the show that everybody now remembers. And on the strength of that we started MTM. Eleven years later Thorton Bradshaw asked me to come back to NBC.

You mentioned having spies at the networks. Is there real espionage in this industry?

Maybe someone has done that, but I don't think so. I think that we're all too square to do that. There was a lot back in those days when I was at McCann.

Does it run through your mind on occasion, that you've been the equivalent of a modern-day Selznick or Zanuck, but in the TV business?

No, it doesn't. I think of myself as more of a . . . I don't know what I am. I'm sort of a bastard. I'm not a creative guy, in the way Jim Brooks and Allan Burns are, or an actor, like Mary. I'm none of those things. I love to schmooze and hang out with those people and I'm good at it. I'm good at expressing my appreciation, and have great respect for what they can do and for what I can't. At the same time, I'm really not a businessman, though I have some of that ability. I *am* a pretty organized guy.

You may have been the perfect hybrid to do what you were doing.

Well, towards the end of my time at NBC, I said to a good friend, "You know, I am really fucking good at this job, this job of running NBC." Don't put this down in terms of my having done a solo there. I was CEO of NBC at a time when a lot of us all did some very good work and restored a company that was at death's door. It was a team effort. But in truth, I was the right guy at the right time for that job.

Some people have said that the reason that you left NBC was because you did the job so well that you filled up their schedule with successful programs, had no more room, and that you then wanted to do it again at CBS.

The thing with CBS was not the same. GTG made a deal with CBS because they had great need. We were trying to do what we did years earlier with MTM and CBS with Mary and Bob, *Lou Grant* and *Rhoda*. We did the CBS deal because Tisch and Paley came and said, "How can you help us," and I said, "Well, in a way that will also be helpful to what I want to do."

Were you offered a similar job at CBS to the one you had at NBC?

I have said no comment to that before. Let's just say they had some problems that looked very much like the ones NBC had some time ago and it was only natural that someone like Larry Tisch, particularly being new to the business, would be walking around saying, "What should I do?" But, if I wanted to be in a job like that I would have stayed in the one I had.

NBC is 8,000 people and in a business with a lot of ritual and ceremony and preordained things to do every day, at least when you're chairman, and this new venture is a little hands-on thing that is a lot more fun, is twenty minutes from my house as opposed to seven hours. . . . It was just time, you know.

What key things happened at NBC to turn the network around?

You need building blocks. Even the explosion of *The Cosby Show* was only one night of the week. There were a lot of other things that had to happen; *The Golden Girls* and *Miami Vice* on other evenings around which nights could be built.

On a digression for a moment: the name Lou Grant, and your first name. Was it just a coincidence?

You would have to ask Jim Brooks or Allan Burns. Grant is a fairly common name, or it may have been their little joke. My contribution there was not the name of the character. It was to suggest that they read Ed Asner. That was one of my few creative contributions. Ed had never done anything like *Lou Grant* before. He played a lot of dummies. In fact, it was remembering him in a terrible Fox television movie in which he played a police chief. He kidded a little bit in that part and that made me think he could do comedy.

What, in your view, makes for a popular or good television series?

I could give you a very general answer. Good execution. Hitting the target you aim at, whatever that target is. It can be high or low, it can be *The A-Team*, or it can be *Hill Street Blues*. There's an appreciation on the part of the audience when you advertise what you plan to do and then you do it and hit the target dead center. But some people set their sights lower.

To what degree could television be a lot better than it is, or to what degree do you need the program mix of very different sorts of programs?

That's the department store school of programming as opposed to the boutique. In my life, the analogies would be the boutique of MTM where you only had to be so big and you could do just what interested you versus the department store of NBC where you couldn't. For one thing, there aren't enough creative people.

Could you ever have a boutique network?

No. That's too much of a good thing and the audience is too eclectic. You've got to appeal to all of their varied tastes and desires. If you give them nothing but headier stuff, they will all go across the street and look at something that's on a lower level. Incidentally, what bothers me about some violent programs—say *The A-Team*, to just pick on it for a minute—was not the lower target. It was the way in which they did the job. They didn't do it with creative sweat. They did it with stunts and automobile crashes, and bloodless violence which is another evil.

Still, how much better could American television be than it is?

Not much I guess, given the front and the back, the beginning and the end. The end being the audience and what it wants. And as for the front, which is the creative input, there just aren't enough good creative people that you can find. They may be out there, but we don't let them in.

A lot of old guys like myself, don't get spun-out enough to make room for the new blood to be spun-in. And, there are too many mediocre suppliers and creative people in the business who are not forced out, thereby opening the windows and doors and letting new blood in. Better blood.

When you come right down to it, there just aren't a whole lot of wonderfully talented, creative people, going over to the networks and saying, "Here's our stuff." There's a limited number that are carved up among the networks.

It's also true that there is a bureaucracy that isn't brilliant, if indeed it isn't venial. When I was at NBC in the 1960s, I didn't even have a program development guy. Now the halls are teeming with program development people, and by and large a lot of them are sort of a negative factor. Of course, they aren't sitting there *trying* to be stupid. In fact if you spend some time with those guys, and you probably have, there are a lot of bright, young people.

Compare television to Broadway or the movies. Think of the huge, relentless appetite of TV: seven nights, multiple networks, going all the time, and in comparison, a few plays, and a few movies every year. Television's batting average is a lot higher than the people who are mounting plays and producing movies.

On the question of a shortage of talented people, isn't the attraction of becoming a success in this industry so great that thousands of capable people are attracted out here every year to give it a try?

I think there are more people than we find, and this is a fault in our business. And I'm one who has never figured out how to right this wrong. We do not have enough ways, enough doors and windows, as I've said, for these aspiring people, not all of them so brand new, some of them 40 years old perhaps, to get out of the University of Iowa and into the creative mix out here.

On the other hand, Tony Bill said years ago that if you're smart enough to write a screenplay or TV show that's going to be a hit, then you ought to be smart enough to know how to get it on the right desk.

Well, it's easy for Tony Bill to say, but in truth, there are a lot of reasons that people can't do it. Still, the writer is the one guy who can sit in a room by himself, write something, and try to figure out how to get it read. You're right to think in terms of writers, because it all starts with that, and without them, nothing starts. But if you're a potentially good director it's a different story.

I'll also give you an indictment of the creative people. Friends of mine, Steven Bochco, Bruce Paltrow, Gary Goldberg. They're all coworkers and very good friends. When I was at NBC I asked a writer named Bill Froug, an old practitioner who'd been teaching at UCLA for a while, a sort of burnt-out writer, to come to work and just sit around and solicit and read material. He agreed and went to about 8 to 10 schools, all the obvious ones: UCLA, USC, NYU, Carnegie. He went where he thought there would be hotbeds of potential writing talent and the stuff began to come in and he began to get very excited. He would send it over but he came to me months later and said, "Forget this. They won't read it." He would call up Gary Goldberg and say, "I'm going to send you something. I'm so excited about this guy, for *Family Ties*," and Gary just could not get around to it. You see, it's our own fault.

Earlier you were talking about the networks being top heavy with executives in development. Why are there all those people?

Insecurity of people at the networks, I think, partly. Show business is such a crap shoot. Whether you're writing plays, producing movies, or making television shows, you're bound to anticipate failure as much as you want success and so you have all these layers that I think are counterproductive in many cases.

Brandon Tartikoff and I used to have discussions about this. He was from a different generation and he didn't agree with me that you didn't need all those people. One way of letting Brandon do his job was to let him have all his people and the result speaks for itself.

What sounding boards do you use? Do you make a point of paying close attention to the comments of friends, colleagues, the ratings, people you might meet on a plane?

I don't meet people on planes. I am the most antisocial bastard you'll ever meet on a plane. You won't meet me on a plane, because I burrow into something, desperate not to talk to the guy next to me, or the fat lady, or whoever it is.

I have only two rules. One, you associate with the really superior, creative people. It's a great rule to live by. Two, trust your own visceral reaction, your instincts. I guess mine are pretty good, if not great. God knows I've been wrong. But if I live by those two rules, then everything seems to work out OK.

Many people say television improved during your time at MTM and at NBC, and many people credited you with that.

If you mean I was a party to it, I might cop to that, but I certainly wasn't responsible for it. I happen to like a kind of television done by a certain level of creative person and I like to hang out with those people and I idolize them and recruit them when I'm in business.

How important do you think television is to our culture?

I think it's probably incredibly important in ways that those of us in the forest probably don't think about often enough or even understand, but I would probably not be at the top of the list of those who should try to articulate why it's important, or how it's important. It just seems important to me for two reasons: one, that anything we spend too much time with has got to have an effect, particularly on young minds. And second, the great sadness of it all, is that for every hour you spend watching television, it's an hour you haven't read a book, or done something that is a constructive activity. That's probably immeasurable.

I guess, among television's sins, the most obvious and the most mentioned are making a bad or mediocre product; the witless forgettable product that many of us sit through all the time. If television were only more daring and more diverse in its offerings. TV is just repetitiously giving you situation comedies and dramatic shows that all look rather alike.

Given this wonderful machine, it's a shame we don't use it better, and more meaningfully. On the other hand, given the relentless appetite that I talked about, I think it's remarkably good much of the time.

Would the overall quality of television be significantly better if somehow the networks could decide to reconsider the profits that they are shooting for and accept a prime time audience of 20 million as a success?

Damn right. You now have hit on something that is not going to get better. It's going to get worse. The fact that the networks all fell into bottom line–oriented hands exacerbates the problem. They say, "I want this news division to be a profit center, or damn close to it." I say to those people, "Get out of the business. If you want to maximize your profits, go and get another business—buy T-bills, whatever the hell will do it for you—and let's let the guys who don't just think of the bottom line own the networks." When I was at MTM and we owned the company, a private company, we did whatever the hell we wanted to. It's the devotion to those shareholders that is the problem, and that some executives see their duty as delivering the biggest bang for their buck. That bothers me.

How has the proliferation of television and cable networks changed the industry?

It's much harder to succeed than it used to be. You just don't get the big audiences that we got with only three networks, except in very rare cases. You have to settle for a lot less: the programmer, the network, and the advertisers. Either you're niche programming, or you're looking for a particular demographic.

Then there's content. Cable does things that network television would never have done, and hasn't yet done, in terms of matching cable. And it is also dragging over-the-air broadcast television along.

Lee Rich

You think standards have dropped?

It's obviously more permissive. I'm personally offended by some of the things I see and hear. I'm totally offended by Mr. Karmazin putting Howard Stern on at 11:30 on Saturday night as a *television* show. There used to be people called *broadcasters* and I don't think there are broadcasters any more. I think TV does have some sins to answer for, in the area of gratuitous sex, violence, and language.

LEE RICH

Lee Rich is something of a legend in television. He began his career at the Benton & Bowles advertising agency where he spent 14 years, leaving as senior vice president in charge of media and programming. In the 1950s and early 1960s, much television was created and produced by the advertising agencies themselves, and in those years Rich was associated with the production of *The Dick Van Dyke Show* and *The Andy Griffith Show*, among other programs.

Rich cofounded Lorimar in 1969, and at one point in the 1980s had eight television series on the air at once including *The Waltons, Eight Is Enough, Dallas, Falcon Crest,* and *Knots Landing.* Over Rich's 17 years at Lorimar, the company won 36 Emmy Awards. *Dallas* became the first television program to run in as many as 90 countries worldwide. At Lorimar, Rich was a master television producer, a man with a clear vision of what each series was designed to do and with the organizational and business ability to launch and oversee a whole stable of weekly productions.

In 1986 he became chairman and CEO of MGM/UA where he was responsible for both movies and television. While Rich was in charge, the studio produced *Rain Man, A Fish Called Wanda, Moonstruck, thirtysomething,* and *In the Heat of the Night.*

Lee Rich has received many honors including an Emmy, three Peabody Awards, four Humanitas Certificates, and two Christopher Medals. He has been twice named "Television Showman of the Year" by the Publicists Guild.

I first spoke to Rich when he was running MGM/UA, and then again 10 years later when he was back in independent production. Lee Rich is an especially enjoyable interview subject because he seems to hold nothing back. He's a man with strong opinions and a clear, unsentimental understanding that the function of American television is entertainment and the accumulation of advertising revenue.

My father was a banker but I didn't want to be in the banking business. I wanted to be as far away from it as I possibly could be. But business was the area my head was in. I wanted to be in the advertising business and studied marketing at Ohio University. I'm still doing marketing and advertising.

I got a job the summer after college in an ad agency for $90 a month. We would put together TV shows that we took to the network and got on the air. I didn't produce the shows but was deeply involved in their formulation and marketing. Eventually I came to California and started producing shows.

When you started Lorimar and you had The Waltons, Eight Is Enough, *and* Dallas, *some of them on simultaneously, how did you manage to supervise all those programs?*

You're only as good as the people you have.

How did Lorimar get started?

I started Lorimar with just my secretary. I started by doing movies of the week and miniseries. Then *The Waltons* came along. *The Waltons* gave us a great deal of momentum. We got other series then. We got *Eight Is Enough* on the air.

Is there a vision or is there a thread through, if not all of the series you've produced, at least some of them?

With *The Waltons*, I just thought it was time for a show of that kind. *Eight Is Enough* I always knew would work. It has all the things people can identify with.

I believe a television series, to be truly successful, has got to have people you can identify with or people you can dream about being. *Miami Vice* works because young people look at it and say, "Jesus, I'd like to be him. Look at the broads, look at the excitement." *Eight Is Enough* is everybody. *The Waltons* was so perfect. People said "That was exactly like my family," which was generally bullshit. What that person was saying in effect is "I *want* my family to be like that."

The Waltons was written from a book called *The Homecoming* by Earl Hamner. He and I were executive producers of *The Waltons*. I took that book and did a two-hour movie of the week called *The Homecoming*. That formed the pilot of what *The Waltons* was gonna be. In actuality it was Earl's life. Earl was John-Boy. That's who he was.

There's a lot of symmetry between The Waltons *and* Eight Is Enough. *Is there a Lee Rich stamp?*

No, I don't think there's a Lee Rich stamp. I did *Sybil*, I did *Helter Skelter*. It is my job to entertain the public. I'm not out to change their morals. I'm not out to change their views about politics or religion, or anything. I'm there to entertain them. And as long as they like what I give them, they'll view my product. If they don't, they won't.

I know some people have made fun of *Dallas* and *Knots Landing*. Grant Tinker made fun of them. But fine, make fun of them. The point is: the American public likes them. The medium is an entertainment medium in my opinion.

You talked about the appeal of The Waltons. *What's the appeal of* Dallas?

I think *Dallas* is everybody's dream. People are looking at it saying, "See they have problems too, regardless of how much money they have."

J. R. is rich, but he is not really happy.

That's right. It makes people say, "Well, shit. You know, having the money is not necessarily the answer. They're unhappy."

You have money. Is it true that money doesn't buy happiness?

Oh, there's no question about it. Money doesn't necessarily buy happiness. It may buy some comfort, but it may not buy happiness.

At its height, Dallas *was seen in over 90 countries around the world. Was there anywhere it didn't work?*

The only country it never worked in was Japan.

Do you think the appeal of Dallas *is similar in each country?*

I think in many countries it's probably curiosity about the way the American rich live. That could be a part of it. I think the same thing that makes the American public view is probably true for some of the other countries around the world.

Let's talk about the power of television.

The medium is universal. Go and see shacks and shanties, the poorest housing in the world, and you see those television antennas, no matter how poor it is. It's there. A house can have nothing but they have a television set. Television has become the prime entertainment of the world. My mother, God rest her soul, used to watch wrestling in the early days of television. She loved it.

I think television is the single most important form of entertainment in homes today. And it has been for years. People are more sophisticated today: they're pickier, they don't watch everything, they've become critical, they've become so sophisticated, so knowledgeable about the media, but it's still the single biggest form of entertainment.

I think the quality of television has gone up remarkably. I'm talking about the pure quality of the thing, the writing, the set decoration. You go back and look at the so-called golden age of television, which is total bullshit, and you will see the difference.

Look at comedies. Look at *Cheers.* I love *The Honeymooners.* I still sit and laugh at *The Honeymooners.* It was unbelievable. But I sit and laugh at *Cheers.* It may not be a roar, but it's a different kind of laughter because it's a different kind of show. They're beautifully written. The writing has improved, the acting has improved. I think it's all improved. I thing it's much better than it was.

Who determines the quality of American television?

The American public. Because of every time they watch, or turn it on, or turn it off. Nobody has to watch. You just turn it off if you don't like it. But who's to determine what's quality?

Grant Tinker has said that he felt the tragedy of American television was that so little stuck to your ribs.

Tinker sets himself up as a god of what television should be. And what is this bullshit about sticking to your ribs?

Many programs leave one with a rather empty feeling after watching.

You have an empty feeling after eating Chinese food, too. It's your perception of it. Maybe my perception is totally different. You or I are not the criteria for what is good or bad. What we feel is not necessarily what's right. The American public, in their numbers, will tell you what they like. I may not like a movie. I may think that *Predator* is a real piece of garbage. The American public, spent $47 million viewing it.

What do you say to the argument that while the public may be entertained by things such as Predator, *or things that are simply base, or that cater to the lowest common denominator or their instincts, the industry should be above that, the industry should try to entertain and to elevate.*

So, what's your argument, that they shouldn't have that on the air?

Let me just tell you something. The television medium is an advertising medium. That's basically what it is. And as long as a ratings systems exists, and as long as it is a very profitable thing, and as long as it will deliver profits, that's basically what we have to live with. That's what it is.

It's like every other medium. You get a titillating best seller, written by Sidney Sheldon, and a great biography of Eisenhower or Churchill and the Sheldon will sell copies and that's the way the world goes.

Look at *Harpers*, which is a fine magazine, and look at their circulation and look at *People* and see what their circulation is. It always happens that way. Sure, every once in a while we get one with tremendous quality and *also* tremendous popularity and that's great, that's ideal. But that doesn't happen very often.

What does a producer do?

A producer does exactly what it sounds like. Somebody has to put all the pieces together. Somebody else may come up with the idea and then turn it over to somebody who will do it and put it all together. A guy who is making sure it gets done, the pages are shot, and the whole thing is done on a day-to-day basis. Out of 10 shows we had at Lorimar, I had 8 of them on the air at once.

How thin were you spread?

I had people helping me. I had a routine. On series that were on the air longer than a year, I would read the first six scripts and look at dailies for about the first three shows. On shows that were new, I would watch them pretty much most of the time.

So for each series, is there a vision that you're trying to hold?

Always. If I started them off, I want them to stay on that path. In *Dallas*, for example, you have to keep the character of J. R. in very clear perspective. You can't let him wander off. He motivates the show. It's making sure that you're using all the characters and making sure that they all work together.

There's thousands of things that happen on a day-to-day basis. Casting, production problems, budget problems, dollar problems, actor problems, all kinds. Network problems.

Give me an example of a network problem.

Interference. The big problem with the network, is that somebody wants to become a hero. My answer to them when they start telling me things is, "When you get your name up on that picture, when your name is up there, I'll let you do it."

But what you find is if you listen to them, they will tell you, "Hey why don't we put that character in and make him purple." So you put the character in and you make him purple and when they're all sitting in the room watching the picture, somebody will say, "Who the hell made that character purple?" They don't stand up and say, "I did it." They don't say a word. So under those circumstances, I tell them to go fuck off. Really.

When you're trying to get a deal you gotta go through the whole ritual of the idea, the script, the pilot, and all of that. And you sit and you talk to these guys at this level, 'cause you can't go above levels. The guy says, "You know, I think it would be great if we shot this in Boston." People say, "OK, we'll shoot in Boston, that's a pretty good idea." You walk out of the room and say, "Hey it's going to cost $100,000 more to shoot in Boston." So you go down the aisle to the business affairs guy and you say, "Hey Harry, the jerk over here told me to shoot it in Boston. You owe me $100,000." Business affairs says "Screw, I'm not going to give you the money." Now you go back to the guy and the guy says, "Well, I want to shoot in Boston." And that's what goes on. They give him the job and they automatically think that they're gonna control everything.

They do that, in part, because they have to report to someone higher up. They need to be able to report that they've done something.

Of course! That's right, that's exactly right. My answer to them is very simple. Fellas, you get your name up on that show, you can do whatever the hell you want. Some of them are very bright and they have a very good idea.

You didn't have any formal training in drama, or any particular love for theater or drama, and yet you've become someone who has been responsible for an incredible amount of the entertainment that people see. Why are you good at it?

I have no idea. I like it. I suppose that has something to do with it. If I had gone to heaven and this had happened to me I couldn't be happier. I wouldn't want to do anything else. I enjoy what I do. I've been very fortunate and very lucky.

Why do you keep doing it?

Because it's the way I'm built. I love working.

You still love to see a program on the air that's yours?

Oh sure. It's very exciting.

I would think it was more exciting earlier on than it is now.

No, strangely enough I think it's the same.

Let's talk for a minute about all the takeovers. There are a lot of people who are worried about it.

I think it's going to make our lives a lot different, and more difficult. You're dealing with people who don't understand the business and are looking at it from a pure dollars and cents standpoint. But I think that they will recognize that programming makes it all happen. I think where the squeeze will come is in the business aspects of the television industry. Which in turn may have some effect on the quality.

Of course, if they chop down the number of people at the networks, fewer executives would waste your time.

Oh, I'll give you another one. If they stop making pilots, which prove nothing, they could save even more money.

You resist the notion of pilots?

Oh, I have always. I can make a pilot that can sell. But, it may never resemble the series that I put on the air. I'll put guest stars in it. I'll put fancy music in it. I'll do all kinds of things. I always maintained that pilots are made for the people in New York. Mr. Paley and all those other people who want to see pilots.

My view is if you want success on the air, why don't you do a bible of what the series is about? Why don't you write six scripts because the first six episodes are going to prove a great deal? And then do a 5- or 10-minute tape of the casting that you're suggesting. So you have a bible, you know where this series is going, and you have six scripts and you're able to read them and say, "Damn it, this series is good."

Everyone goes to New York. It's so ridiculous. It's totally degrading, it really is. It's like a group of people waiting for fish to be thrown at them. They take all these pilots to New York and people look at them. A whole room full of people look at them. They look at that pilot and they say, "Gee, that's a good pilot."

I did a pilot once with James Franciscus and Linda Evans for CBS, a brilliant pilot. I paraded Linda Evans around in a white bathing suit. I mean, two very attractive people. I forget who wrote it or produced it, but I sold it. I got an order for 13 weeks, and I realized after I sold it that I didn't know what the hell was going to happen after the fourth or fifth week. I truly didn't know. And needless to say, the show just went on its butt.

This business of going to New York and showing the pilots, and getting orders from the networks is not much different than a big show that a fashion designer puts on, and then receives orders for clothing.

Yeah, but in fashion you see it and you know the people can do it. He has shown you his entire line in dress manufacturing. Television doesn't need pilots. Do you know how much money they spend on pilots? Do you know what better things they could do? A half-hour pilot costs $1 million. Five scripts might cost you $100,000. A little tape and a bible will cost you another $50. For $200,000, you've got the whole thing. An hour pilot these days costs you almost $2 million.

Don't some executives have difficulty envisioning the scripts? They need to see the program produced as a pilot?

That's bullshit.

But some people can't read a script and envision how it would play.

Well then, they are not in this business.

But they are, that's one of the problems.

Well, I'm not talking about them. The point that I'm making is that if you're looking for greater quality on television, here's one of the ways to get it. You talk to any writer, any creator and he'll tell you that's what he wants to do.

So, what perpetuates it?

Because the people back in New York want to see pilots. I have been fighting this battle for years, and of course I will never win.

You've received three Emmys and three Peabodys and many other important awards.

I'm delighted. I truly am.

Anything else that we should get down about your views on television?

We have to understand that television is an entertainment medium and that as long as it involves profits, the bottom line, and ratings, it will continue to be a popularity medium.

As CEO at MGM/UA you produced Being There. *In* Being There, *Kosinski is saying some very critical things about the American public and television.*

What did Kosinski say?

He's concerned about what's happening to the minds of the American public by virtue of watching so much TV.

I happen to think the minds of the American public are more advanced today than prior to television.

Some people believe the attention span of the public is growing shorter. It's harder and harder to hold the attention of the viewing public.

It means we have to work harder to do it better. This is the only medium I know where the ratings are published in the newspapers, and everybody knows who's number one and who's number two. Same thing in the movie business. They all now know the grosses.

The general public is aware of what the top-grossing film is at any given time?

Without a question. Movies are the greatest word-of-mouth business in the world. The public is so aware about a picture that they know in advance whether it's going to work. Everybody knew *Ishtar* wasn't going to work. The smell wasn't there.

The public knows in advance whether a movie is good or bad?

Oh yeah. The audience can. We've made people so sophisticated in the television area, particularly, that they have become the world's greatest experts.

How important are tracking surveys and the Nielsen ratings? How much attention do you pay to them?

I pay a great deal of attention. That's what I live and die for. I've got to pay a great deal of attention.

If you see a drop in a particular demographic group, do you say well, we need to do something to bring back those audience members?

Yeah. But anybody who gets angry at Nielsen shouldn't be in this business. That's one of the rules. You may not like it and I've heard people criticize them. Then get out of the business, for Christ's sake. There are certain rules in the business—we all may not like them, but if we're going to be in the business, then let's live by the rules.

In addition to pilots, are there other rules that exist that you think are wrong?

I think that we have got to give opportunities for shows to live. I think one of the things that has happened, because of the ratings and profit wars, is that shows are cancelled too fast, before they give them the chance to breathe and to live a little.

We last met just about ten years ago. How did the industry change in the 1990s?

The industry has changed a great deal. I think that if nothing else dollars have changed the industry. The fact that the networks have lost such a tremendous amount of the share of their audience, the fact that within the past God knows how many years, you've got at least another 50 different channels of communication. I mean you can go to USA, HBO, Showtime, wherever. Sometimes it's good, sometimes it's bad.

I would think that a producer, a seller in this market, would like that there are so many more buyers.

That's true. However, a network transmitting programming can only pay dependent on the size of their audience. And since the audience is smaller, they can't pay for quality programming. So it's good, but it's bad. I think you have to make a lot of adjustments today. You've got to figure out ways of making programming at reduced costs. And audiences have more trouble finding a show now.

If you're going to meet a person, and you know him, you meet him at one place all the time. He's your friend and you say, "I'll meet you there, right Charlie?" Years ago, the audience knew the show. They knew *The Waltons* was on at 8:00 Thursday night. Today, they move the shows around willy-nilly, you don't know where the hell they are.

I would tell the networks to give programming a chance. Years back, on *The Waltons* we got an order for 13 episodes. Today, you get an order from a network for eight episodes, six episodes. A show was canceled the other day that appeared on television for two or three weeks. The three original networks have only 50 percent of the audience. I don't believe that they have done enough to keep their share of the audience.

Eventually their market share had to erode with all of the competition.

There's no question about it. It *all* will erode. I don't know who will be left. Maybe they'll all be left with 5 share points, or 10. Viewing habits have also changed. Computers take up a tremendous amount of time and have become a major part of our society.

Still, a lot of people will not be playing around with computers at home at night and after a day working at a computer, many people will still want to watch television.

But there will be a goodly portion that will be on the computer, and they will be young people. I really don't know. I only know one thing. I know that a bottle is empty unless you put something in it. Put milk in it, it becomes a milk bottle. You put liquor in it, it becomes a liquor bottle. I don't give a damn what the thing is, what's going on up there, in the computers, you need programming.

The entertainment business, both the movie business and the television business, are going to go through drastic changes. And they have gone through changes. I mean the movie business is ridiculous right now, truly ridiculous.

How so?

Well, look what they're spending. I mean it's ridiculous. They make a movie for $100 million and it lasts three weeks and it's gone. It's gone!

I had lunch with Lew Wasserman the other day, who still knows more about this industry than anybody, and he said a very interesting thing. He said, "We've been through crises like this in the movie industry and what will happen will be one of two things. Either one company will go out of business, just like United Artists went out of business, and that will bring everybody to a standstill. Or the exhibitors will put a stop to it." Because the way a movie works now, in the first couple of weeks, the first week anyway, the studio gets anywhere from 70 percent to 90 percent of the box office and the exhibitor gets 30 percent or less. The second week it gets to be pretty even, depending upon the movie. By the third week, when the exhibitor is anticipating getting his money, the movie is out, its gone, finished.

Since I talked to you last, the FCC ruled that the networks could own a percentage of their negatives where previously that had been prohibited. Now they can own all of a program.

It's the worst thing that's ever happened in the industry. It should have been regulated in some fashion because today the networks are putting more of their own shows on the air than anybody else. You could get to the point of it being a monopoly. If I take a show to a network today, the chances are very good that the network says, "I'll take half."

Or they each have their own production companies. NBC Productions, CBS Productions. They are fully staffed, they hire writers, they hire producers and they make their own shows. So what do they need me for, or anybody else? It's becoming very, very difficult.

It's been good for them. All you have to do is look at the financial records of the networks. The networks don't lose money. They have always made money.

The last time we talked you were at MGM/UA.

I was at MGM for three years, and when I arrived there we had 1.9 percent of the movie market. When I left three years later, we had 14.5 percent. We did *Rain Man, A Fish Called Wanda, Moonstruck,* and I also started a television department there and we did *thirtysomething* and *In the Heat of the Night.* Then I came here.

Now that you're an independent player again, can you contrast how different that is?

I'd rather be CEO than independent. But the movie business I wanted to get out of. It's just ridiculous. It used to be a better business than television. Now? Forget it.

It used to be that writers thought if they wanted more freedom they'd have it in film, but that's not even true anymore.

Without a question. And now, it's just a rotten business.

When you were CEO, did you wake up with any more or greater energy than you do now?

No, I'm always here early in the morning. I stay late, I work just as hard.

I always get a sense that you love what you do and you're intensely involved.

It's all I know. I'm doing what I'm supposed to do.

And you're as happy and as eager and as excited now?

I may not be as happy, but I'm as eager and I'm as excited as I've always been.

Carroll Pratt at the controls of his laugh machine.

CARROLL PRATT

Carroll Pratt is the president of Sound One, a small company with two assistants. When we met in the late 1980s, Pratt's company was placing over 80 percent of the laugh tracks and audience effects on network programming. He had won three Emmys for his work. Pratt began his career as a sound man at MGM and learned his craft from the "father of the laugh track," Charles Douglas.

I met Pratt at a postproduction house on Sunset Boulevard where he was laying down the laugh track to a short-lived NBC sitcom called *The Marbleheads.* It turns out that there's a lot more "sweetening" in television than I realized. Pratt also sweetens award shows where the audience isn't applauding loud enough, and rock concerts where the audience needs to sound insanely enthusiastic. He even sweetens figure skating. To match acoustics, he has audience reactions from Carnegie Hall, the London Palladium, and the Kennedy Center. There are specialized laughs and audience sounds broken down by gender and race, whistles for when "foxes" enter the room, and hoots and "whoo-ees" for the entrances of certain ethnic stars.

Though legendary comedians from Woody Allen to Sid Caesar have denounced the laugh track, Pratt reports that both have worked with him. As we talked, Pratt demonstrated the machine.

My father was a sound engineer in radio and later worked in film. I followed him and began working at MGM in 1939. The war soon broke out and I went into the air force as a pilot and was taken prisoner of war.

In 1950, CBS was having problems with shows where the audience had been rained out and the reactions had been too small. They were also doing a lot of audio work after an audience left because they didn't get enough reaction during the show. Charles Douglas, who was a technical director at CBS, saw the need and developed a very basic, crude laugh machine which consisted of a large wheel. Douglas was the father of the laugh machine.

The demand came fast and he started freelancing. He left CBS and made a new machine which was somewhat more sophisticated. It all burgeoned so fast because producers who were doing filmed shows without audiences immediately saw the advantage of having a laugh track.

They had just started working on *I Love Lucy.* Douglas was working long hours. He needed a second person and asked me to go with him. That was the beginning of the inuring of the American public with this beast of a laugh track.

Did you call the laugh track a "beast" because the audience has been conditioned to accept and expect it?

Exactly. It has made itself needed. Comedy started out in the infancy of television with audiences. But then there were all those sitcoms that came out of Screen Gems—*Dennis the Menace, I Dream of Jeannie,* and *The Patty Duke Show*—which were shot with a single camera. They were shot with the motion picture technique and had no audience. But the feeling was that if you could just get a stimulus, the people sitting alone at home would enjoy the show more with audience accompaniment. And that was proven to me by ASI, the people here in town who study audience reactions.

We took the worst *Dennis the Menace* and added a laugh track to it. Then they took their best show without a laugh track and ran it time and time again for several different audiences and the bad show got the best reaction.

That was carried even farther by Columbia, Screen Gems' parent. A producer, Mike Frankovich, did a movie called *Cat Ballou* and ran it thousands of times, like all producers do, in different theaters to watch reactions. Then he was flying to New York to a meeting and they had it playing on the airplane. He sat there with the headsets on and didn't enjoy the show. Something was lacking.

They thought that for drive-in movies, where there is no one around you, and for aircraft, it would be wise to provide a stimulus there, too. And it was proven that it worked. Then they got into distribution problems.

Back to Charles Douglas' second laugh machine. How did it work?

He used his own style of magnetic tape. It was basically mechanical and not electronic in its cueing and procedure, but the layout was the same. He started with smaller laughs and went up to big laughs. He was doing a lot of Bob Hope and Jack Benny programs where the big laughs were much bigger than those we have now.

The business continued to burgeon and my brother came with us because Charlie wanted to preserve secrecy. Charlie was very secretive about the whole operation. He had big locks on the machine. I stayed with him 21 years and my brother stayed with him about 17 years. Finally, it was time to leave.

My brother had already left—he was retiring to Tasmania—but he wanted to build a better laugh machine and we knew the head engineer at Glenn Glen Sound, who had these transports in mind as a way to do it. So my brother went with him and formed a corporation and as soon as I could get Charlie through the season without leaving him in the lurch, I went with the corporation. We developed into Sound One and I have been president ever since. I'm going to retire this year.

How does your machine work?

The machine consists of endless cassettes that loop around in a regular mounting, the same as a household audiocassette player. We run them at high speed for fidelity. One tape contains shorter laughs and chuckles. There are about 30 to 35 different chuckles before we get around to the start again. We mix them to avoid the feeling of repetition. Hopefully you'll never hear the same laugh in a show twice. In addition to operating the machine with buttons, I also have a foot pedal that puts little tails on the laughs so you don't hear an abrupt cut-off. Some laughs stop rather suddenly, so I use the foot pedal to put a little extension on them.

They also intensify from small to large. If I were doing something in Carnegie Hall, for example, I might have to go clear out to get the largest laughs and some with applause. We have thousands of different laughs depending on the house. I have Carnegie Hall, the London Palladium, and it goes on and on. Each one has different acoustics.

If you're sweetening a Kennedy Center production, might you ever put Carnegie Hall laughs and applause in Kennedy Center?

Absolutely. I do it if it matches. It's just getting the same acoustical match.

It appears that you have multiple drawers in the machine and a total possibility of 10 different tapes.

Yes, there are 10 transports. Of the 10, normally we have 8 of them provided with material. We have one that is applause and one where the applause comes in a segue form. The applause starts with a few people and goes up to a full house. Different tapes are being activated as I go along. So this is the first one [low applause], a few more [growing louder], a few more [louder still] and that's it.

I understand you also have tapes of black audiences. When you worked on The Jeffersons *would you bring different tapes to a session?*

Yeah. We have strictly black laughs and "oohs."

Does that mean there are racially mixed audiences, too?

Yeah. One of my guys does *The Cosby Show.* It's shipped out here every week from New York. There's a large black attendance but they don't sound black at all. I don't know whether it's a matter of sophistication or choice, but *The Jeffersons* and *Good Times* had a very black sound to them.

The audience would talk to the actors constantly but I don't hear that much anymore, even in black shows. Still, in a show we're doing now called *Bustin' Loose*, the producer would like to have more of an ethnic sound.

What other kinds of sounds can you make?

Well, naturally, we do "oohs" and "aahs," cheers and whistles, and at a rock concert there would be much carrying on and clapping.

I understand that nowadays, in 1987, your fee is $145 an hour. What happens when you have to fly to New York? Do you charge by the hour?

Oh yeah, I give an estimate. Part of it's man-hours. Most of it's just expenses to get there.

Is the machine patented?

Very loosely. It's made up of components. When we left Charlie Douglas, morally and ethically, more than patent-wise, we went a whole different route to get to the same end just so we wouldn't infringe.

It seems to be a fairly simple machine.

You're right. But we have a very well-known, highly reputed electronics firm in Boston designing a new state-of-the-art machine for us. We're into R & D. But technology is moving so fast we put a hold on it because of other developments. If we stay with what we've planned, the same computer memory and circuitry, I would say it would cost between $60,000 and $100,000 to build a prototype.

There are only two companies in Hollywood making laugh tracks, yours and Douglas'. How come no other company has come along?

There have been several different laugh machines made by the majors. Universal made one, MGM made one, and they have one at CBS, NBC, and ABC. Mostly it's dollars and cents. They'll hire a man to operate it but the bookkeeping end of the business comes along and says, "Wait a minute, this guy is sitting here doing nothing." We also have a huge library because we have collected from so many different sources. We pride ourselves on our technique of editing them and bringing them about. The biggest part is not the machine, it's the library and the technique of the guy. And, to train a man you've got to deficit-spend. We're going to train him for at least six months before we let him touch a show. It took me almost a year before Charlie let me do it.

I would think that it could be learned more quickly.

But there is no rehearsal time. Your reaction has to be correct immediately.

In other words, it would sound more wooden if I tried to do it, than when you do it?

Probably, unless you had time to rehearse it three or four times.

You can do it on command.

Exactly. That's where we're saving the producer money. There are always producers who start off wanting the indigenous laughs of a particular show. They'll say, "I want not only my stage, not only my show, but I want *this* particular show." He'll say to an editor, "Take those laughs, mount them up and roll them in." But to do a half-hour show like that from scratch would take somewhere in the vicinity of 16 hours, maybe 24 hours of work time to roll those all in. We can do a show in an hour and a half.

Sometimes there is a lot of visual editing and you'll have a crescendo of a laugh chopped off. We've got to tail off that laugh to make it sound natural. Or perhaps they shot all day and had to do the stunt work after the audience went home, so we've got to incorporate that into the same sound. In other words, there are often mechanical things that we're worrying about more than just sweetening.

A great many comics deny that their work is sweetened.

Sid Caesar says that the laugh machine is awful and he'll never use one. I have laughed at everything he's ever done. And Red Skelton. These are our greatest detractors—the ones that use us most. They're not going to say to the public, "I get my big laughs from a machine."

I'm sure you know the scene in Annie Hall *where Woody Allen is upbraiding his friend for sweetening a sitcom. Did you have any reaction to that?*

Well, I've worked with Woody Allen on a TV special he did in New York. I sat with him there for a long time. He sat and drew sketches of me and was paranoid about the machine and then when he began using it, he saw where it was saving him time and making things work.

Does sweetening go on in other countries?

England does it very badly, Mexico does it very badly. They have very rudimentary equipment.

Do you ever sweeten live programming?

Oh yeah. We just sit there and do the show. Like the Academy Awards. Telethons we have to sweeten. All the artists come for free and the producers feel the only thing they cannot let them do is fall on their ass. On telethons I have a charity rate. I give them a much better rate.

What do the Academy Awards need to be sweetened with?

We do applause, laughs, and cheers. Not as much with the Oscars. With some of the awards shows, unfortunately, a lot of the people leave after they get their award and by the end of the evening there is no one left. The audience flags after a while, enthusiasm flags, and the show will slow down.

For the Oscars, they also hire people to sit in the empty chairs because the camera is frequently showing the audience. Are any sports sweetened?

Not very often. Every year I do the skating championships. Usually they retape all the background music to the skater's performance so they take away all the audience reactions when they change the music.

When somebody is setting up a budget and has a line item for you, what do they call it?

Audio sweetening. They call us everything on credits.

If you get credits, does that mean you also receive awards?

Yeah, I got three Emmys. I got one Emmy for *M*A*S*H*. Another was a Motown show. Some of the shows I worked hardest on are not the ones I've got Emmys for. Like the last Streisand thing. I worked my butt off on that show.

Why does Barbra Streisand need sweetening?

There are so many different reasons. She is such a perfectionist that she won't let a note go by if there is anything wrong with it. She has perfect pitch and she will just sing that one note and it'll lay in like it was built for it. In doing that, they take away a lot of the live audience reactions. She knocked out all the ambience. So that was redone.

You took a call a minute ago and somebody was hiring you for a rock concert at Capitol Center in Washington. You asked him what kind of show it was and I heard you say, "lots of enthusiasm." He's telling you in advance to think about what tapes to bring to that session.

Right.

What's "enthusiasm," besides applause?

Screaming at a rock concert, just insanity.

How much comedy and variety do people watch on TV that isn't sweetened?

I would say not over 5 percent. We do game shows. All the game shows are sweetened. And we do TV show segments within feature pictures, too.

People often joke that some of the laugh tracks are so old that we are actually listening to dead people laugh. Is that true?

Sid Caesar said that. No, every slack season we take two months to edit shows that had the best audio from the year before. We'll take those shows and break them all down, which is very tedious, and make our standard basic tracks for the following season. So none of our stuff is more than a year old.

Was it ever accurate to say that a third of the audience was deceased.

Yes, early on, before our company was formed. There just wasn't that big a library.

If somebody asks you to save a show, can you save it?

Possibly—and I say this only after many years. Possibly a show with no laugh track would improve with a well-done laugh track. Something that was done with good taste. But you can't make a funny show funnier by laughing at it louder.

But you would never say you wouldn't sweeten a show because it's not funny. You're hired guns, like lawyers.

We're whores.

When a show's not funny the laugh track seems to cheapen the product. It really sounds "canned."

That's exactly right. I think the best laugh guys in the business are those who don't like the laugh track. We should all train ourselves downward. If we're just left alone, I think we come out with a fairly tasteful product. I'm not saying that out of ego, but just out of experience. I've been "laughing" for 31 years and I know that when I laugh at something that isn't funny, it's going to make people think less of my business.

One thing I feel strongly about is that if you go to a movie or watch a TV show where the musical composer has done his job, you never realize the music is playing. It's all lending itself to the effect that the art form should have. If a laugh track is well laid in, I feel that the best compliment is someone coming to me and saying that the show got through without a laugh track. And that happened to me on *My Three Sons* and it happened to me on *M*A*S*H*. I think that's the greatest compliment an operator can have.

CHAPTER 4

Writer-Producers

Creating Breakthrough Television

If you were to focus on the early days of dramatic television, and writers like Paddy Chayefsky and Rod Serling, you might conclude that television was a *writer's* medium. Before the *The Twilight Zone*, Rod Serling wrote classic television dramas such as *Requiem for a Heavyweight*, and Paddy Chayefsky wrote *Marty*. Each was quickly made into a movie.

Serling, like no television writer before or since, became extraordinarily well known introducing and providing an epilogue for each episode of *The Twilight Zone*, many of which he wrote. In producing *and* writing *The Twilight Zone*, Serling was among the industry's early "hyphenates": a writer-producer *and* unquestionably a television auteur.

The Twilight Zone was a breakthrough. Serling used the series—miscategorized as science fiction in the view of some—to tell searching, thought-provoking stories about the human condition: the compelling and serious stories he wanted to tell on television but could not have on a regular basis if he had stuck with the melancholy weight and style of *Requiem for a Heavyweight*. To this day, *The Twilight Zone* is in a class by itself.

SETTING THE SERIES TEMPLATE

In series television, the producer puts a system together, a production apparatus of writers, coproducers, directors, actors, editors, and technical crew members. The beauty of a series is that once developed, the sets, writers, and continuing characters are all in place and each week's program can be produced in time for its air date. The producer, along with senior writers and others, develops the series' plan for the season, and then oversees the creation and production of episodes, each at a different stage of development. Producers sometimes have more than one series on the air at a time—Lee Rich once had eight.

With 22 episodes to produce each season—and in the old days, as many as 30 or 40—a template is a necessity, and it is the producer who creates and sets the template: the style, tone, subject, theme and characters. If the producer is a hyphenate, he or she will create the template by writing a treatment: a detailed overview of the series, its concept, the setting, the kinds of stories that can be told, and descriptions of the main, continuing characters and how they interact. Then, if commissioned, the writer-producer will write the pilot. If the pilot is produced and aired and fares well with the network, the producer may receive a commitment to produce a number of episodes, sometimes 5 or 6, preferably 13; rarely more than that since the mid-1990s or so. Once the series is picked up and the template set, the producers and writers can focus on each episode, and new premises and situations for stories.

There *is* a monetary incentive. For decades now, the carrot dangling in the eyes of series creators is to reach the industry gold standard of four or more years of "negatives" (88 episodes) and the opportunity to sell the series' syndication rights for hundreds of millions of dollars—the better part of a billion dollars each in the case of *Seinfeld* and *The Cosby Show*. (Syndication sales explain why a comedy punch-up writer—or script doctor—like Bob Ellison, who appears in Chapter 5, is so well compensated.)

Keeping the writing level up is the biggest challenge in television and many a series has lost its way when it lost its writer-producer. The quality of *Seinfeld*'s final two years fell off once Larry David, who had created the series with Jerry Seinfeld, left the program. Susan Harris admits that she has become something of a "creative deserter." After her experience with *Soap*, writing so many episodes by herself, on subsequent series she would write only the treatment and pilot, leaving much of the weekly writing to others.

WRITING WITH A PERSONAL STYLE

Larry David and Susan Harris, along with Matt Groening, Allan Burns, and Edward Zwick and Marshall Herskovitz, are all writer-producers. Discernable in their work is a personal style, a recognizable auteur's point of view in the subject of the stories and how they are told. Each has a more or less distinctive voice in television: Larry David in *Seinfeld* and *Curb Your Enthusiasm*; Susan Harris in *Soap, Benson,* and *The Golden Girls*; Matt Groening in *The Simpsons* and *Futurama*; Allan Burns—along with James Brooks—in *The Mary Tyler Moore Show* and *Rhoda*; and Ed Zwick and Marshall Herskovitz in *thirtysomething, My So-Called Life, Relativity,* and *Once and Again*.

In the interviews we see how the creators' personalities and autobiographical experiences are expressed in their work. Indeed, there is a detectable personal angst expressed by many of the creators in these interviews—especially by those who write comedy—an angst that is inseparable from the style and satirical edge of their programs. Often, their voices can be heard most explicitly through the dialogue they write for the characters they create.

Each of these creators has been associated with the creation of a breakthrough program. *The Simpsons* broke new ground in delivering scathing social satire by way of animated characters, while simultaneously reviving the primetime animated cartoon. *Seinfeld* was the first TV comedy to be about "nothing," studiously following the producers' mantra that there be "no hugging" and that "no one ever learns anything." Though immensely likable, each character took turns being more selfish and self-absorbed than the next; the objects of their varied obsessions broke new ground, making great comedic art out of the personal minutiae of everyday life. In *thirtysomething*, Zwick and Herskovitz explored new television terrain by basing their stories in their characters' psychological responses to events rather than on the events themselves.

Both *Seinfeld* and *thirtysomething* mark high points in the gradual trend in television toward characters with more complex inner lives. We also see it in *The Simpsons*' thought bubbles, and in Susan Harris' and Allan Burns' work as well.[1]

Allan Burns also came out of a background in cartooning and, like Groening, worked in close collaboration with James Brooks. Responding to the incipient women's movement, in 1970 Brooks and Burns built *The Mary Tyler Moore Show*—and later *Rhoda*—around a new kind of female sitcom character, a single working woman who was both independent and positively portrayed. Susan Harris similarly extended the development of the socially relevant comedy in merging the soap opera and situation comedy genres in *Soap*, where she confronted societal taboos and raised controversy with biting satire. She continued to do so, although in more muted fashion, in *Benson* and *The Golden Girls*.

THE WRITING PROCESS

Writing is the means by which these creators began to make their voices heard in television. Once writer-producer status is obtained, a considerable amount of control follows. When I started work on this project, I assumed that writers who wanted more artistic freedom would often gravitate to film, but Susan Harris and others, changed my thinking. As she points out, "A writer of films has very, very little control. No control compared to a writer in television." The old vaudeville line is as apt now as it was then: "If it ain't

---

[1]This trend toward a more realistic and recognizable interiority to characters in the theatrical arts has been going on for some time, with perhaps the most significant modern turns coming in the first half of the twentieth century and the development of the Method in theater, its passage to film, and the related influences of Stanislavsky and Freud (Kubey, 1992).

Susan Harris

on the page, it ain't on the stage." Television *is* a producer's medium, but nothing happens without writing.

Writing may well be a gift, but it also requires hard work and discipline. Allan Burns makes sure he writes every day. By spending many hours at it, some writers sense that they become a channel for the material they create. Burns says, "Like there's something that's floating around out there and somehow it comes out through you. It sounds a little pretentious to say that, because it's a little like saying, 'Well, I have this God-given gift or something.' I just feel that you hook into something that you don't quite understand."

Neither Harris nor Burns believe that they have funny personalities. Spending time with each, I would have to agree. But each has an idiosyncratic, skewed view of the world. Writing is their medium, and when they take pen to paper what they write turns out to be funny. Harris reports that she would try to write drama but it would come out as comedy instead. She couldn't help it.

Having the gift and exercising it is critical, but sustaining stories and making them work is particularly difficult. Writers have to work especially hard to master story structure. Larry David explains that the *Seinfeld* trademark of weaving disparate parts of the storyline together for a satisfying and coherent sort of haiku began almost accidentally. However, once discovered, it became a challenge to make that keep happening and have it appear seamless without telegraphing the audience where the story was going.

Learning story structure and television writing can take time, experience, and often, a good mentor. Matt Groening, who only had experience telling the shortest of stories in his syndicated comic strip *Life in Hell*, tells us how he had to learn the discipline of longer storytelling from James L. Brooks, his cocreator on *The Simpsons*. For Susan Harris, Garry Marshall was a key mentor, as was Norman Lear.

All of these writer-producers have worked with a key partner or mentor. Writing for television often involves collaboration. Zwick and Herskovitz have worked with each other for 20 years now. Pioneers Schiller and Weiskopf wrote together for nearly 40. And Larry David's fondest memory from his *Seinfeld* years is of the hours spent alone in a room with cocreator Jerry Seinfeld, making one another laugh.

SUSAN HARRIS

Susan Harris is the most successful female writer-producer in the history of American television and is credited with helping change the image of television's female characters. When she began writing for *Maude* there were no women on the writing staff of a program whose title character was a female.

Harris is the creator of *Soap, Benson,* and *The Golden Girls.* I interviewed her at the home she shares with husband and colleague, Paul Witt. I gained entry to the ultramodern house by identifying myself through a TV camera mounted in a large brick wall. Once approved for entry, a large gate opened electronically with a futuristic hum.

Harris greeted me at the front door, dressed in black, and gave me a tour of the house. In the master bathroom, an Emmy serves as a jewelry hanger. The interview took place in her darkened library. Harris wore dark glasses throughout.

This interview is especially instructive. We learn about the challenges of writing for television and film, how Harris approaches her craft, and how rare she believes it is to find good writers or lead actors in Hollywood. We also learn how a writer might go about breaking into the industry and her views on the quality of television and about working with network executives.

Of particular interest are the challenges she faced writing *Soap*, and the surprising psychological impact of becoming wealthy. *The Golden Girls* was up for its first syndication sale when we spoke, and they expected to garner somewhere between $100 and $300 million in the sale. However, we learn that money isn't all that it's cracked up to be, a cautionary tale echoed in the interviews with Lee Rich, Larry David, and Matt Groening.

We began with my asking how she began to write for television.

I was a housewife. I had a baby, and my husband and I split up and I needed a way to earn a living. One night I was watching television and I said, "That's garbage, anybody can do that."

So I sat down, wrote a teleplay, and sold it for an existing series called *Then Came Bronson*. I wrote it with a friend. She knew the creator, who got it to the producer. They read it, loved it, and they happened to need a script and we sold it to them.

Is that the easiest way for someone to break into writing for television—to try freelancing a script for an existing show with characters already developed?

Oh, definitely. Because even if they're not going to use it for their show—and a lot of times they're not because odds are they've done a similar story line or it's not going to work—it's still a wonderful thing for your portfolio. If it's a good script, you'll get a job on some other show because of it.

Many outsiders think that it's easy to write for television.

That's what a lot of people think about writers, period. I've gone to the dentist and had the dental hygienist say to me, "I would be a writer if I had the time." There was a cartoon in the *New Yorker* of two guys talking at a cocktail party and the one said to the other, "Oh a writer. I'd be a writer if I had the time." So that's all it takes. I'd be a brain surgeon if I had the time. People have a misconception about writing.

Where did you go to college and what did you study?

I went to Cornell for a while and then I went to NYU. I studied English. It was an academic dead end.

But you had an affection for reading and writing. There are a lot of books here in your library.

Yes, something you don't see much of in California. It's something I've noticed over the years. You go into people's houses and they don't have books. It doesn't seem to be the case for New Yorkers.

What did you do after Bronson?

Love, American Style. Garry Marshall took me under his wing and he really taught me the craft. I did a lot of *Love, American Style*s and I did *The Odd Couple, Barefoot in the Park, The Partridge Family.* Then I met Norman Lear and I did a few shows of *All in the Family.* He asked me to be on staff and I turned it down. I never wanted a staff position.

What would that have meant?

It would have meant regular hours. What was so lovely about writing for me was that it left me available to my son, who was a baby. I could do it all at home, and whatever hours I wanted. So I was never interested in a staff position.

Then I did some *Maude*s, a few pilots, and then did *Fay* with Paul Witt and Tony Thomas. Since then, I have only worked with Paul and Tony and have done a show called *Loves Me, Loves Me Not* which I think only went for six episodes, and there was *Soap, Benson,* and *I'm a Big Girl Now.*

What was your level of involvement and screen credits for each of the Witt-Thomas shows?

I created *Soap.* I wrote all the episodes. I was executive producer. I created *Benson,* and wrote a couple of episodes. *I'm a Big Girl.* I created it. I don't even remember if I wrote any of them. And then I created *Golden Girls.*

There were a couple of disasters. There was *Hail to the Chief.*

Is Soap *or* The Golden Girls *your biggest hit?*

Golden Girls is by far the biggest hit. It finished fifth this year. We've never had a show with those kind of numbers. *Soap* was usually around 20th. *Golden Girls* will probably go up for sale next year. But you need four years of a show, four years of negatives, to have a really decent sale.

Because Golden Girls *is such a hit, you stand to increase your income by some magnitude. How significant is that for you?*

Let me put it this way. I still *think* poor. I have to ask my business manager once a month if I can still fly first class. That's really a euphemism for, "Am I still OK?" I'm asking, "If I never work again, is there money there?" I still think that there's been some sort of mistake. I never had money my entire life really. I still don't grasp the concept that there is that money there. But on the other hand, it doesn't really change anything. Once you get a house and the car that you want, it doesn't change your life.

It doesn't make you happy?

God, no. It doesn't do anything really except alleviate the worry of money.

Can you speak to the myth of money equaling happiness?

It does give you a certain amount of freedom to pick and choose and do what you want, or not do anything at all. Beyond that it does nothing for the inner person at all. That's not what it's about. And that's a very big surprise because you think that when you get there, it's going to be different and it was a little depressing, actually.

For a certain amount of time, life for me was attaining certain goals. When I started writing, it was being able to get assignments. Once I got assignments, it was being able to have my own show. Once I had my own show, it was about having that show be a hit. So there were always goals to attain. When I attained them all and saw that it made no difference, that was the point at which I got a little depressed. What now?

Now the point is really to find out what makes me happy. And having money allows you to do that. You have more time to find out.

Are you thinking about doing something entirely different?

Right now I am writing a screenplay, which makes me much happier than writing television. But what happens *after* I write it is most likely not going to make me very happy. Because a writer of films has very, very little control. No control compared to a writer in television. So I'm not so sure I'm going to like what happens after it's written. If I don't like it enough, I probably won't want to write any more movies. I don't know. I've thought about going to school again. I've thought of writing prose, which terrifies me.

What makes a television program work with an audience?

I can only deal with comedy because that's my area. The audience has to like to watch the people they watch every week and the characters have to be believable. You have to like the people you see, you have to care about them, and you have to be entertained. I think one of the reasons that *Golden Girls* is successful is how much the audience loves those four women.

How did the concept come to you?

Through NBC. They said something about doing a show about old people. The demographics of the country were changing.

Actually for many years, older people have had a lot of disposable income and the TV networks were very slow in catching up to that fact. Why are the networks often so slow?

Well, they're a business. They're corporations and they have to answer to stockholders. Businesses are conservative outfits. They're not going to take big chances. They're in a business to make money above everything else.

Nobody wants to put their neck out and take a chance. They make safe decisions and want to make an exact copy of *The Golden Girls* so if it doesn't work, nobody can find fault.

One network tried to copy The Cosby Show *with a show featuring Flip Wilson.* Animal House *was a big hit in theatrical release, so there were two TV shows that fall about fraternities. But these copycat shows rarely do well. Is safety a sufficient excuse for bad decision making?*

You generally don't have a lot of creative people at the network. You do at times. When we brought *Soap* to ABC there was a creative bunch of people there: Tom Werner, Marcy Carsey, and Freddie Silverman. They were willing to take chances. You had the same thing at NBC. Brandon Tartikoff, who's terrific and will take chances, and will stick with you. After Marcy, Tom, and Fred left ABC, it was a bunch of very uninspired people.

Are the people at the networks who make decisions about scripts well read?

Not at all. They are busy watching television. I don't think they have time to read. When they read, they mainly read scripts.

Does being well read help you in your writing?

No. At times it will make it tougher. I wrote something the other day that had all these literary references in it. I referred to Henry James and to Henry Miller, and Paul Witt, who I work with said, "This is hysterically funny but nobody is going to get it. It's a 2 percent joke." Every once in a while I'll argue and get to keep my 2 percent joke.

You've pitched ideas for new situation comedies to the networks, and you've been turned down on occasion. What are you told when you're turned down? Does it make sense?

No, it hasn't always made sense. There was a time Paul, Tony, and I went to ABC. We had a prior commitment and what we wanted to do was a family comedy. This was before *Cosby*. ABC said, "No, that's soft, it's not gonna work. How many people are going to be interested in that? We'd rather have you do something crazier." That's when we came up with *Hail to the Chief*. Well, a family comedy would have been just perfect.

Americans were ready for a family comedy, but instead we came out with this lunacy called *Hail to the Chief* that no one could relate to. Once we saw it on its feet we saw that no one would want to watch it because there were absolutely no characters that were real, that you could identify with. It was cancelled and it should have been cancelled because it simply didn't work. That was a case of a network turning something down, encouraging you to do something else, losing your objectivity and

The production company of Witt, Thomas, and Harris. Susan Harris with partners Paul Witt and Tony Thomas (r). [Trivia note: Tony Thomas is the son of Danny Thomas, the brother of Marlo Thomas, and the brother-in-law of Phil Donahue.]

going ahead and doing it. It was something that we had never done before and it turned into a disaster.

Have the networks put much restraint on your work?

We go in and say this is what we want to do and, generally, they say go ahead and do it. So there are very, very few restraints. There are no restraints on us really. But television is a compromise and I know what the restrictions are. It's never something that I have to think about. I'm not going to sit down and write offensive stuff. So I really don't have a lot of battles with standards and practices. They bent the rules completely for *Soap* and let us do just about anything we wanted.

Could the quality of American television be significantly better? How good or bad is it?

I think it's pretty bad and I think television could certainly stand to improve. But like I said, it's very difficult. It's a business and people are not particularly courageous. Advertisers are not a particularly courageous bunch of people. Those are the people you're dealing with and nobody takes a lot of chances. If nobody's taking chances you're going to see a level of mediocrity. Television doesn't reflect life. It's certainly major steps behind films.

What have you written that didn't get high ratings but that you were proud of?

Fay had very low numbers and we thought it was a damn good show and should have worked. But it was a grown-up show. It was ahead of its time. It was the first show about a divorced woman who was having a life and who actually slept with somebody. They didn't give it much of a

Susan Harris, standing, fifth from left on the set of Soap

chance and they yanked it after eight or ten episodes. But it was also in a suicide slot. It was opposite some blockbuster.

It's a rough business. I don't expect to do any more television. I'm tired of it. I'm very tired of television.

How draining is it?

When you have to do it every week, like I did on *Soap*, when you're responsible for getting a show on the table every week, it's incredibly draining and you burn out. The hours were endless. The first year and a half, I wrote them all. I had nobody with me.

Give me a picture of what your life was like during that time.

I would be at work by 9:30 in the morning and an early night was getting home at 7:30, 8:00, and I would have to work right through on weekends. I never stopped writing. I couldn't afford to get the flu, because there had to be a script on the table every Monday and there was no one else to do it.

My son was nine and it was a very difficult time. Towards the end of *Soap*'s run it was not so late. I really had it down to a science. But it wasn't a time I look back on. . . . It was a very, very unhappy time for me. It was a terribly unhappy time. I vowed after that time to never, ever do it again. And I haven't.

Paul Witt calls me a creative deserter. I will create a show, and that's it. I'm gone. Everybody knows that up front, that I will never do what I did on *Soap* ever again. Because I had no life.

Does your work ever make you extraordinarily happy?

Not extraordinarily happy, but the happiest I am is when I'm writing something that really pleases me and that I take pride in. That did happen with *Soap* when I finally got somebody on staff that could write and some of the burden was lifted. The hours weren't as crazy as they had been and I could actually enjoy what I was doing. It happened with the pilot of *The Golden Girls*. I really loved writing it.

Is it difficult to have to write around commercial breaks, or can it help give a structure to the script?

Well, you know that vaguely around page 17 that there should be an "act out."

An "act out"?

Yeah, end of Act One should roughly be around the end of page 17. I have written shows where that act break is later. The act break for the spin-off I've written for *Golden Girls* was on page 32 in the early drafts. I knew that was completely wrong and that I had to have the commercial way before that. But eventually it worked out.

Can it wreck the writing to have to conform to commercial breaks?

No, not at all. I don't see why it would have anything to do with that. Look at England, where they don't have to worry about those things. They can run programs 43 minutes in length. They just stop when they stop. It doesn't matter. By and large, most of British television is terrible. It amazed me when I was over there.

Are there hindrances to a better TV product that we haven't talked about?

What makes for a poorer product is the fact that you have to turn a product out every week and there is a paucity of really good writers and really good directors. Given the time factor it's almost impossible to do terrific work. That has nothing to do with the fact that it is a commercial business. Even if you had the luxury of time, you don't have the writers. We have had enormous problems, just as does everyone else, staffing our shows. They just aren't out there.

But there are so many aspiring writers.

They are terrible. There are mostly terrible writers out there. We get scripts sent to us all the time which we read hoping to find the next Jim Brooks or Allan Burns. The next talent. Stu Silver, who wrote the last few years of *Soap* with me, sent us a play that he wrote for Off-Broadway, and you could just see in those pages a raw talent, an original mind. We grabbed him and we were right. It's very rare.

Talk about what you mean by an original writing mind in television. Some people think it's just simple dialogue.

That's why your dentist would say, "If I had the time I would write." You *can* learn the craft. That's teachable and that's learnable. But you can't learn to be special and there are not a lot of very special writers out there. There are not a lot of very special directors. For example, nobody can touch Jay Sandrich in television. Jay directed *Soap, Mary Tyler Moore,* and *Cosby.* You can't touch him.

And you have the same problem with actors. We were trying to cast a comedy show last month and found it almost impossible to cast because this year they produced 60 comedy pilots and there was nobody left. There was nobody. We couldn't find terrifically funny leading men or leading women.

So there are a lot of factors that go into the mediocrity of television.

If what you say is true about the special nature of the writer, this assumes that you are such a person. What makes you that way?

I don't know, I don't know. It just happens. This is not going to be a satisfying answer. I just sit down and I write and it happens.

It is not something I have thought about. I've never considered myself funny. I still don't really consider myself funny. It was a surprise to me that I wrote comedy. When I sat down to write I thought I would write drama, except that everything was coming out funny. I would sit down after writing *Bronson,* which was kind of a mix, and I decided I would write a medical show. But I couldn't make it serious.

You don't strike me as a funny person.

I'm not a funny person. I'm only funny on paper. I'm around the funniest people in the world and they're funny. Carl Reiner is funny. Mel Brooks is funny.

What's happening in the writing that makes it funny?

It's a kind of twisted way of looking at the world. Especially at the aspects of life that aren't too thrilling. The disasters. Looking at getting old, and looking at death.

I'm just now touching on the things that concern me most in my writing. The themes that you see running through what I write aren't all that different from Herb Gardner's preoccupations when he writes, or Woody Allen's when he writes. The urgency of time and death. It's a way, I think, of trying to come to terms with it.

Back to the problem of finding special writers—writers with a unique voice. I assume that writing is like singing, in a way. Most every famous singer's voice is unlike anyone else's voice. If it is the same, they can forget it. Is that what you're looking for, a voice in a writer?

Exactly. A friend of mine wanted to write and she would show me scenes she had written and I said to her, "You're not writing in your own voice.

You're writing in my voice, you're trying to write in my voice." I said, "You have your very own voice, find that." That's what she went ahead and did and she's a successful writer now.

Are there times when you can't find your voice?

No. But I know that there are some things that I can't do, that I can't write. If you told me that I would have an on-the-air commitment for 44 episodes about a baseball team, there's no way in the world that I could write that. I wouldn't want to write it. I wouldn't know how these people talk, I don't know who they are. I couldn't do it.

But what about Benson? *What did you know about a governor's office?*

I never wrote it. I created it. He was a spin-off.

How do you create a new idea for a sitcom? How do you sketch it out?

You pitch it. Paul, Tony, and I sit down. With *Soap*, I said I wanted to do a show that did not end every week, which gave me a tremendous luxury as a writer. Because I didn't have to squeeze a story into 23 minutes, which is a brutal form when you think about it. When you are confined to 23 minutes, everything has to go towards the plot. Not to tell a story every week gave me a chance to write scenes that didn't just advance the plot but were just good talk. And, that's where I think I did my very best work.

I said to Paul and Tony that I wanted to do a continuing saga, a soap opera. We talked about it. We'd talk about characters and then I'd go off and I'd think about more characters and draw character sketches.

Do you just write a page on who the person is?

For me, yeah. For me to be able to write somebody, I have to be able to hear them. Sometimes I will imagine an actor's voice and then I will be able to write them. It's a way for me to hear the dialogue. The characters I've had the most trouble with are the characters I can't identify with at all and I can't even find an actor who I could imagine saying the words.

Is it harder for you to write a man?

It's generally easier for me to write women. But the film I'm writing now is about three men. I wrote about 30 pages and I gave Paul the scene to read. I said, "Is this the way men talk when they are alone?" Because there is no way that I could know what men talk about when they're alone. He read the scene and said, "Absolutely. Right on the money."

Are there rules of writing that you follow and that you lay down for your writers?

For me, as I said, I'm a creative deserter so I've stayed away. I was around for the first 13 episodes of *Golden Girls* and then I left. But if I were to look in now, I'd probably say it's getting too jokey. Too jokey, too unreal. Those are general notes. Let's do some more of the reality thing. On *Golden Girls* or any of our shows, we like to do real stuff. In other words, there is always room for a show that is a little bit wacky, but not every week. Our shows have a mix of comedy and seriousness. To me that's the best kind of writing, and it's very hard to get. *Golden Girls* does some terrific schtick. They really do. We have a wonderful writing staff. I certainly don't want to say anything bad. But I would like to see more reality in the show, a little bit more meat. But, the show's doing beautifully. It is incredibly well received and loved. So you don't want to mess around with it all that much.

Matt Groening

MATT GROENING

Matt Groening (pronounced gray-ning) is the creator of *The Simpsons*. After college, and after a series of dead-end jobs, Groening began drawing the alienated rabbits that would populate his breakthrough, underground comic strip, *Life in Hell*. *Life in Hell* gained wider distribution, and in 1987 caught the attention of James Brooks (with Allan Burns, one of the creators of *The Mary Tyler Moore Show*). Brooks started working with Groening to create short vignettes of *The Simpsons* for *The Tracey Ullman Show*. Full-length episodes would come with the show's launch on Fox in December of 1989. The program is still going strong all these years later, airs in over 100 countries around the world, and at last count had won 16 Emmys.

The Simpsons overshadows most every other television program in its biting satire of American life. The show appeals to children and adults alike and has revolutionized how commercial television thinks of animation. Without *The Simpsons* it's hard to imagine *Beavis and Butthead* or *King of the Hill* or a slew of other programs. In 1999, Groening launched his second animated program, *Futurama*.

The Simpsons has been taken quite seriously by critics and academics. One book, *The Gospel According to the Simpsons*, argues for the fundamental moral and religious message conveyed by the program. Another, *The Simpsons and Philosophy: The D'oh! of Homer*, analyzes the cultural, philosophical and political meaning of the program.

We learn in the interview how Groening's alienated experiences in school served as an important source for *The Simpsons*. We also learn how an animated program is created—how the dialogue is first taped in a recording studio and the drawings made later, in Korea, to match the sound.

I interviewed Groening in his offices on the Paramount lot in 1991 during the second year of *The Simpsons*, not long after Bart Simpson had been turned into a Macy's Thanksgiving Day Parade balloon. Groening seemed unfazed. He was struck by what he had accomplished but it hadn't gone to his head. This might be one of the reasons he's still turning out terrific programs years later.

I read that one of your school teachers had phoned you and remembered that you hadn't been a "good listener."

Yeah. That was on my report card. She had given me an "N"—needs improvement.

Is Bart Simpson at all like you?

Bart really isn't me. I joke about it in interviews sometimes because it's an easy answer, but he's more a combination of me and some of my dumber friends.

Santa's Little Helper, Bart, Lisa, Maggie, Marge, and Homer Simpson (l-r).

It does sound like you had some difficulty in school.

I was in an almost constant battle with authority, but my battle was conscious. Bart doesn't know what his rebellion is about. I think I had an inkling of what my rebellion was about.

What was it about?

I was bored, and that seemed unnecessary. There was way too much busy work. There were arbitrary punishments and humiliation on an almost constant basis. And a lot of what we were taught was not only questionable, it was obviously untrue.

A lot of the other students probably bought what they were taught. Why didn't you?

Part of it was my background. My father was a filmmaker and cartoonist and we had lots of books and magazines and films around. My mother is funny and clever, and we were praised in my family for being verbally quick, which was what got me whacked on the head by teachers. My parents were very supportive of my deviations from the norm.

How early did you start cartooning?

There isn't a time in school that I don't remember drawing. It's how I kept my mind occupied. Stuff was confiscated, as they put it, and torn up by the teachers. My friends also drew cartoons. We were a little rambunctious, but at least we weren't dead in our seats the way a lot of other kids were. They punished creativity. What I've ended up doing as an adult has been in spite of school because every step of the way I felt that my aspirations were criticized. I was told they were frivolous.

Bart Simpson

At least they gave you something to rebel against.

I would have found something else to get annoyed about. But definitely the struggles and the rebellion I experienced growing up are a main part of my creative output. It's part of my comic strip. It's part of *The Simpsons*.

I've read that as a kid you were reading a World War II P.O.W. book that reminded you of 4th grade.

I was in the 4th grade and I read this book called *Escape from Polvitz*. You had these oppressive guards who kept you from going out of the classroom, or your prison cells, and we were forbidden by the school to cross the street and go to the candy store during lunch time. The principal stood in his office with binoculars, so we'd sneak down to the basement of school, tiptoe past the boiler, and go out of this utility tunnel and circle around two blocks below the school and this hill to sneak in the back door of the candy store. It was very dramatic!

Where did you grow up?

I was born in Portland, Oregon, in 1954. That's where I grew up.

Do you have brothers or sisters?

I have an older sister and an older brother and two younger sisters.

I was a precocious kid. I went to my first antiwar demonstration in 1966 when I was 12 years old. I wanted to see what all the commotion was about, and I was fascinated by ideas about progressive education and put them to the test when it came time to go to college.

Where was that?

I went to Evergreen State College in Olympia, Washington. It's a state school that has no grades and no required courses. It was amazing to me because by the time I finished high school I thought that there would be no institution I would ever be loyal to because they were all corrupt and full of bureaucrats and stuff.

What was the first thing you ever published?

My very first piece was in 1962 in *Jack & Jill* magazine when I was eight. It was a "finish the short story" contest. The story was about a little kid who wanted to be a ghost for Halloween. He put a sheet over his head and went up into the attic and bumped his head on the beam in the attic and said, "Now I know what I want to be" and then you were to finish the story. They printed a number of winners. The other kids said Little Billy wanted to be a cowboy, or a truck driver. In mine the kid hit his head and died. The force of the blow killed him and they boarded up the attic.

When did you start drawing your alienated rabbits?

I drew rabbits in high school and then I continued to draw them in college. When I moved to Los Angeles in 1977 after graduating from college I started drawing a little comic book called *Life in Hell* in which I described my misadventures with bad jobs and so on.

How good is your cartooning in your opinion?

Well, I'm probably more critical of them than anybody, but I do have a sense of clarity which a lot of underground cartoonists don't have.

You make it look simple.

That's one of the appeals of my stuff. It's inviting to people, it's friendly to the reader. It's not mystifying. The artist is not a virtuoso artist.

How did you get started doing Life in Hell?

I had a series of really lousy jobs when I moved to Los Angeles. At first, I just did it for my own amusement. I came to Los Angeles because I had this idea about doing creative work in Hollywood. I had worked on a college newspaper and had enjoyed doing everything from typing up classified ads to composing headlines. It didn't matter, it was all part of the process. I wanted to work in journalism and I was hoping that there would be some sort of underground press left in Los Angeles, but there wasn't really. They went out of business simultaneously with my arrival.

The counterculture was dying.

The counterculture was *dead*. Then came the rise of alternative news weeklies, the *LA Weekly* and the *Los Angeles Reader*. I wrote freelance articles, concentrating mostly on rock music. Wrote about all sorts of weird bands with names like Severed Heads and The Ugly Janitors of America. Some even weirder than that. At the same time I was doing my weekly comic strip for the *Los Angeles Reader*, starting in 1980.

How hard did you push to get The Simpsons *off the ground? Was the concept in your head much earlier?*

Since the time I was a kid I was a fan of animation, in particular *Rocky & Bullwinkle*. I thought all of the Jay Ward and Bill Scott cartoons were really well written, with great voices and great music. I thought if I ever got a chance to try my hand at it I would really enjoy it. I didn't have the patience to do the animation myself, but I knew that I wanted to do design and write it. So from time to time I would pitch ideas. I would finagle an appointment with some producer at some studio and I'd try to tell him my idea. I got nowhere.

The very first meeting I had was right next to Paramount studios. When it came time to go to the meeting I walked over there, but the guard wouldn't let me on the lot because I wasn't in a car. Like I was a nut. And I said, "I live right over there." He didn't believe me so I had to go back and get my car.

I met with this guy. He shook my hand and said, "I just want you to know I'm a completely duplicitous asshole and nothing I say can be believed." Those were his exact words. "Now, what are your ideas?"

He swatted away every single idea I had. I would naively try the same thing over and over again. I'd say, "I think there's room on television for a prime time cartoon that appeals to kids and adults, not exactly the same as, but using as a role model, *Rocky & Bullwinkle*. A cartoon with very poor animation, but with great writing, great voices and great music." Invariably, they said that that cartoon was a failure. It only appealed to smart kids. "I want something that will appeal to the three-year-olds," they'd say.

So how did things get started?

What happened was that a woman named Polly Platt became aware of my stuff. She is a movie designer who had worked with James Brooks on *Terms of Endearment*. She liked my cartoons, showed my stuff to James Brooks, and brought him a piece of my original art. My girlfriend at the time, whom I later married, Debra Caplan, was managing my career and was syndicating my comic strip. They liked my stuff. I was too shy to go over to Paramount and meet him myself. Debra was always talking to these people.

Debra published my first book, *Love is Hell*, and then *Work is Hell*, and then we got picked up by Pantheon Books and I was doing just fine.

Did you meet Debra through the strip?

Debra worked at the *Los Angeles Reader* where I was an editor, writer, and cartoonist. She sold ads. We knew each other for a number of years before we started going out together.

At what point did you know you were going to get a shot at television?

Brooks moved Gracie Films from Paramount over to Fox and started working on the Tracey Ullman show for the Fox network. He called me up. We had lunch. Originally the idea was to do *Life in Hell* as a short cartoon for *The Tracey Ullman Show*. The format changed from a 2-minute cartoon each week to four 15-second cartoons.

Then I found out that Fox demanded to own whatever I did. I had been working on *Life in Hell* for several years by this time and I felt I shouldn't give it up for TV cartoons, so I made up *The Simpsons*.

My introduction to television was idyllic because Brooks had done some of the most memorable shows in TV history and he's got enough clout to make his artistic vision work. He made it so I didn't have to meet with any network people ever about content. He's executive producer along with me and Sam Simon.

How quickly did The Simpsons *gel in your mind?*

I needed to come up with an idea really quickly. In the back of my mind was the idea of doing something that might possibly end up spinning off into its own TV show, so I created a family which I thought would lend itself to a lot of different kinds of stories. In high school I had written a novel, a sort of a very sour *Catcher in the Rye*, self pitying, adolescent novel starring Bart Simpson as a very troubled teenager. I took that family and transferred it, made them younger, and then drew. It took about 15 minutes to design the characters the first time out.

Were they all the same characters that we now know and love?

Yes, but they've been transformed.

Why didn't you leave Bart as an adolescent?

TV does children really badly, and I thought there was room for something different. Teenagers are already running rampant on television, but kids are done very unrealistically in sitcoms. Sometimes, a particular character gels with an audience and becomes the star.

Was Bart at the center all along?

Yeah. The rest of the Simpsons in my original conception were in a struggle to be normal and Bart was the one who thought that being normal was boring.

How much has Brooks helped you to learn how to tell a story in 22 minutes?

In terms of writing, it's been the greatest learning experience in my life. I've learned more about structure, storytelling, and pacing. Everything is a writing problem to be solved, so even though these cartoons were very simple in dialogue it was a matter of learning how to tell a story and keep people interested.

Brooks was a great mentor because he had ambitions for the show which were even loftier than anything I could articulate. I intuitively felt the things that he said. The way the show was going to work was to have moments of emotional reality. Our goal was to make people forget that they were watching a cartoon. To go with a real emotion with a cartoon effect. And it worked.

There are moments when Homer is abject, depressed, and you see it in his eyes and it's quite poignant. I don't know if that's unprecedented in cartoons, but I certainly hadn't seen much of it before. Is it hard to get that effect?

It's a collaborative effort in order to get these effects across. It's working with great writers. Brooks contributes many memorable lines. Sam Simon, the other executive producer, is brilliant and quick.

Three of our five directors started out being the original animators on *The Tracey Ullman Show*. They've drawn the characters over and over again enough to know them. Most traditional cartoonists convey emotion by extreme exaggeration, and what I try to do is have my characters start out looking grotesque but there's an open quality to the line, and by shifting the shape of the eyeball just slightly you can completely alter the mood of the character. I learned this from a book called *How to Cartoon the Head and Figure* by Jack Hamm, which says in lesson number one: draw an oval, draw two dots, and draw a slash for the mouth.

There was a clear design to the characters which lends itself to the acting and then the animators make the characters act, working with great recorded lines from the actors.

Doh!

It's a constant struggle, but we get effects that are beyond my wildest dreams and stuff that lets me create beyond belief.

What problems do you have to stay on top of?

Keeping the characters on model, looking the same from shot to shot, from show to show. Most of my characters appear in three-quarter profile and maintain whatever emotional impact they have best from that angle. I very rarely draw characters straight on, and when I do I never hold it. It's an effort to convince the animators to draw them in three-quarter profile.

Do you know why that works psychologically?

It's because they're flat drawings in an animation that we're trying to bring to life. It's an illusion.

Are there many cartoonists who do this too, or do you do it more?

I try to take advantage of my limitations. I do good limited work.

How does the production process get started?

At the beginning of the season all the writers get together in a fancy rented hotel suite. We spend a day or two just throwing out ideas. A series of harried secretaries scribble down everybody's words and then these are typed down as notes. Story ideas are fleshed out in other meetings and different writers go off and write the scripts. They come back, the scripts are written, rewritten, rewritten again, and then we have what is called the table reading, where all the actors get together and sit at a table and read.

Just like a sitcom?

Exactly like a sitcom.

The approach is heavily influenced by James Brooks.

Definitely, the writing for most animation on television is an afterthought. It's one guy cranking out stuff, which is why cartoons on TV are so bad.

After the table draft the writers go away for a day or two, furiously having scribbled notes during the reading as to what works and what doesn't work. Then we rewrite the script one more time and then on the day we record the show, the actors get together one more time. They run through the script and then leave anywhere from 15 minutes to 4 hours, and we rewrite based on that day's reading.

Next we sit down and record the show in the recording studio. The actors stand in a semicircle with microphones and music stands and read the scripts. We go from scene to scene. They interact with each other and we do several takes to get the kinds of performances that we want. Actors ad lib stuff and we change things and rewrite it. Simultaneously with the recording the script is sent to the animation studio and a director and a storyboard artist sit down and visualize the script. The script is written in standard television form.

So, when Julie Kavner does the voice for Marge, she doesn't know how it's going to be drawn at all. She provides an intonation that even the writer didn't put in.

Exactly. And they pull jokes out of thin air. Traditionally, cartoons have looked for a consistently "up" tone. In fact, we've used people who do cartoon voices and we generally have to say "Bring it down, bring it down," because cartoons are always up, up, up. Everything's "Hey! Here we go!" We want real acting instead.

We do storyboards. We have about 40 speaking parts per show, much higher than a regular sitcom. We have special character designers and background designers. I also design characters and alter characters. By now it's a fairly smooth process.

I get the glory on the show but it's a collaborative process. A lot of people don't get any credit at all. The storyboard is about 120 pages long and our scripts vary from 40 to 60 pages. Once that's approved, the animation is filmed. It's basically a film storyboard: an outline of pencil drawings that don't move but which are synched to the dialogue soundtrack. We have a vague idea of how the show is going to look.

Then the whole thing is sent to Korea and about four months later we get back color film and we watch a rough cut of it and we call for re-takes where characters heads fly off or where the synch is off. We edit the show and spot music. The show has a full orchestra accompanying it; it's not just a synthesizer. That's recorded right across the street here. And then we put in the sound effects and finish up the show about a day or two before air.

We started out with 5 animators and now have about 80. The expense of animation is such that if the show were done completely here it would be too expensive. This is the only way to make the show work. All the creative decisions are made here. The ink and paint and the actual filming of it are done in Korea.

Are the production costs at all close to what a sitcom would be?

It's about equivalent. We don't have any costumes or sets, but its offset by other costs.

The problem with the show is that it's too successful for it's own good. Fox took a big chance by committing to 13 episodes without a pilot, based on the *Tracey Ullman* cartoons. Then when the show went on the air, *The Simpsons* took off immediately. It'd only been on the air a little over a year and they ordered more shows immediately, but it takes us 6 months to do a single show.

You must be thinking of a spin-off.

We've talked about spinning off the show. I have a few ideas for spinning off the show. It could happen. And I have lots of other ideas for other animated shows.

Might you spread yourself too thin or lose quality?

It's not so much the quality that I'm worried about, because I think I can maintain the quality. The idea is to keep having fun. That's what I'm interested in, keeping the fun going. I have some other ideas I'd like to try out. I'd love to see my *Life in Hell* characters on the air. I'm not going to sell them to somebody else, I have to own them.

There's a similarity between you and David Lynch of Twin Peaks *in that both of you came from the underground and have made it in the mainstream.*

I think the history of pop culture, at least since I've been a kid, is about co-opting hipness. Something is far out and then gets sucked into the mainstream. MTV is full of film techniques that were outrageous and avant-garde, and now everybody's gotten used to that fast cutting.

My underground pals and I used to sit around and talk about sneaking into the media, trying to see how far we could push our ideas. Often, the stance of the oddball artist is antimainstream because it's soul killing and represents compromise. Instead of thinking in those terms, I've embraced it and tried to see how far I could make my stuff go.

You don't think you've had to compromise very much?

You give up something on one level and you gain back a lot more on a different level.

What do you think you've given up?

Back in the early days of my comic strip I would not allow any compromise. Any word that occurred to me, I would use. Any profanity. And then I made a conscious effort to not use profanity because it kept me out of some daily papers. Now, with *Life in Hell*, I'm in a little over 300 papers.

Did you have any compunction the first few times you censored yourself?

Yes, but then I've also never called myself an artist. I've always said I'm a commercial artist. Being commercial is part of it. It's the nature of the endeavor.

One of the things that intrigues me about your show is that it would be difficult to do this kind of satire in another medium. It wouldn't work.

One of the things that always appealed to me about animation is the ability to take short cuts with storytelling. You can compress the story and you can have emotional things turn much faster. You can do satirical things, and because it's a medium which is considered frivolous and for kids, you can sneak up behind people and pull the rug out from under them. It's really a blast.

In that regard, does it surprise you to have the former secretary of education critique the show? You've had T-shirts banned. Some adults are actually threatened by your cartoon characters.

The Simpsons pose for a family portrait.

No, it doesn't surprise me. There's always someone out there willing and eager to be offended.

Actually, I'm not sure how I feel about a kid wearing a T-shirt to school that says "I'm an underachiever" on it.

What the T-shirt says is "Bart Simpson, 'underachiever' and proud of it." No kid calls him or herself an underachiever. It's a label that's stuck on kids by adults. It's a way of programming kids for failure. Bart just embraces it because that's part of his rebellious attitude.

Some people argue that some kids are going to think it's okay to be a goofball.

Which is the worst lesson? Teaching a kid that a T-shirt may encourage you to be a goofball, or banning the T-shirt, saying it's more important than an idea being banned?

Where does the word "hell" appear?

On the T-shirt that says, "I'm Bart Simpson, who the hell are you?" It is cocky, sarcastic, willfully obnoxious, and reflects in a very mild way what kids are really like. Kids really do use the word hell and worse on the playground everyday.

But if everyone started saying "fuck" and "shit" on television kids would assume that that language was tolerable.

Well that may be so, but then the war is lost if the use of profanity is going to cause a deterioration in the culture. It's lost, because it's everywhere. Part of *The Simpsons* is to reflect that. One of the reasons that *The Simpsons* is appealing, and troublesome to some people, is that in a medium that is characterized by lousy storytelling, and condescending moral values, *The*

Simpsons is refreshing because it's slightly more close to reality. It does reflect in a mild way the way that people talk and it does say to people, "you are not alone" if you feel different. If you do not identify with what you see on television, *The Simpsons* says there are other people just like you.

When Homer chases Bart, there is the implication that if he gets a hold of him, he's going to inflict some sort of physical punishment. Indeed, he's been shown strangling Bart. Do you think those scenes could ever concern a child, as some might be so young as to naively think that there was approval or acceptance of such behavior on the part of a parent?

Child abuse is one of the recurring themes of *The Simpsons* and it's something that I think about a lot because we're dealing with a dysfunctional family, but one that is not completely evil. They love each other, but they also hurt each other a lot. We're also trying to do a show that's funny. I don't want to trivialize child abuse, but I also want to reflect it.

Conceivably, you could have Marge tell Homer that hitting Bart isn't inappropriate.

One of the things that I always say to the writers and to the animators is that *The Simpsons* should not enjoy their own insensitivity and cruelty. Everything they do is ruled by the impulse of the moment. There's a lot of very cruel humor on television and in the movies. *The Simpsons* portrays cruelty and insensitivity but we don't linger on it and we don't enjoy our own cruelty. The point of the chasing is not the sadistic satisfaction of hurting someone else. It's about someone who is not able to control his own anger. It's a complicated issue. It troubles me because I'm very opposed to child abuse. I deal with it in a much more thoughtful way in my comic strip. I did a comic book called *Childhood is Hell*. I like to think of the Simpsons as bad examples.

What would happen if Homer found himself with his hand over Bart in one episode and then flashed back to when his father did that and he says, "Oh no! I'm doing the same thing!"

As the show has proven to be more popular we get increasing pressure to tell good messages, to tell people not to drink and drive, to tell people not to litter, to tell people not to drop out of school. We think one of the reasons the show is popular is because it doesn't fall into the trap of preaching to people about the way they should behave. The Simpsons are bad examples. They do not behave the way people should behave. We give people credit for being able to tell the difference. Cartoons are characterized as a kiddie medium and kids are not trusted to delineate between good behavior and bad behavior. I personally think that kids appreciate the fact that they're not being condescended to.

One characteristic of child abuse is reliving it again and again. I think one of the things *The Simpsons* does is relive it for people in a vicarious way, in a palatable way, in this silly cartoon. In real life, an insanely raging father chasing a kid half his size through the house would not be funny.

The Simpsons *rarely misses an opportunity to mock popular culture.*

There are other forms of abuse.

Yes. Homer represses Marge. Talk about abuse—what about emotional abuse of Lisa? Lisa is a genius and the family is not even aware of it. They're squelching her. There are constant examples of the way people shouldn't be. All the gory figures on the show are corrupt or stupid. We're fairly even handed in our disdain for the way people behave.

But there is no character with any distinctiveness who hasn't gotten some sort of negative reaction. We had a bartender offer the police some pretzels and they say, "Sorry, we're on duty. But a couple of beers would be nice." We got some outraged letters from police.

There's also things that are depressing about *The Simpsons*. Homer works at a dead end job, and he's causing untold harm to the environment on a weekly basis.

There's a fairly clear statement that you are trying to make about nuclear energy.

It's a sacred cow in many ways. It's fun to make fun of. Those moments when Homer tosses around one of those radioactive particles that falls out into the street might actually have more resonance, it might actually motivate people to be wary about nuclear power, more than most other messages they see.

But I want to be modest here. I don't know if television changes anybody's mind. I think it may just give comfort to people you might agree with and there's a possible shifting of mood a little bit to one direction or another, but the goal of the show is not to do that. It's to entertain. It just happens to be that the best entertainment has a very strong point of view. My point of view happens to be something that doesn't get on TV very much.

Let's talk a little about the experience of becoming famous.

One of the good things is that it's not my face up there, so I can walk down the street and not be bothered, more than once or twice a day. Maybe in a restaurant. And then it's just fine. On that level, the attention is really enjoyable.

But there's so much work. I'm not basking in a hammock, drinking a coconut drink and saying, "Ah, fame." Because the work doesn't go away—it's still here. The most surprising thing about the attention is how isolating it can be with friends, who are put off for one reason or another. It's not even so much envy, although there's some envy with some people. It's a feeling that because of the attention I get I must have changed and I must not want to deal with them anymore, that they don't count anymore. I've questioned a few of them and they say they've imagined that I'm too busy for them, or they say, "I don't want you to think that I'm trying to get something from you."

So, simple social interaction has changed to an extent with a few people and I was surprised that it did. That's isolating and sad. But, most of it's really great.

Have you had the experience of thinking for a moment, "Is this really happening?"

There is part of me that still can't believe it. But there's a part of me that doesn't blink an eye at some of the more amazing stuff that's happened. But every so often something symbolic blows my mind. Like I went to New York for the Macy's Thanksgiving Parade and saw the giant Bart Simpson balloon coming around the corner and that was definitely a dream like experience. Seeing Bart Simpson on the cover of *Time* magazine was just numbing. Bart's been on the cover of every magazine and by the time he got on the cover of *Time*, which is symbolic in our culture, I didn't know what to think.

The bootleg T-shirts have been one of the wildest aspects of the whole Simpson phenomenon for me. There's a certain amount of conscious engineering of everything else that has to do with the success of the show. The bootleg T-shirts, with black Bart—that's something that couldn't be engineered, it's a spontaneous eruption.

Have you been asked to speak at any colleges?

Sure, lots. I don't do it more often because it just takes up too much time. I could go around the country nonstop for the next several years, I'm sure, and speak from college to college. It would be very easy to truck around the country with a couple of videotapes under my arm, answer questions and talk about the show.

Do people try and pitch you story ideas? Are you at all receptive to receiving them?

People try and pitch story ideas all the time, and, no, I'm not receptive. Any plot outline of a *Simpsons* show in the barest details could be good or could be great. Anybody could come up with that. It's the execution that counts.

What you're trying to do is do something as quickly and efficiently as possible, and we have a bunch of people who are really well paid and do what they do very well, so we're not looking for outside stuff.

One of the alleged myths of American culture is that money is going to make you happy. Does it make you happy?

There is no good answer to give. Any answer that somebody who has money gives just makes me want to punch them in the mouth.

It's very nice being comfortable because you can turn your attention to other problems, and it's much more interesting to turn your attention to abstract creative problems. On the other hand, that's been the story of my life. I used to live in a cockroach-infested crummy Hollywood apartment and didn't balance my checkbook and could barely get the rent paid and stuff and I was still as uncorrupted by money. I don't care about it. It's nice to make my family comfortable.

But of course, money doesn't buy you happiness. The great thing about being comfortable and having the money is being able to choose

Edward Zwick

Marshall Herskovitz

your destiny and not have to worry about little stuff. So that's really good. It's nice to be able to contribute to charities that you appreciate and political causes. There's not much gratification in throwing your money down the drain for hopeless political causes.

What are your primary political causes?

Let me put it this way. When you're perceived as having money there is a constant stream of people trying to get you to contribute money. What I have tried to do is support things directly rather than large bureaucratic groups. There are certain fantasies that I had in the old days when I didn't have any money as far as creative projects that I wanted to do or finance, and it would be interesting to see if I get the opportunity to do those things.

It must have run through your mind that there's some symmetry between you and Walt Disney. Do you think about him? Or a Simpsonsland?

This has been the most amazing year of my life. I had fairly grandiose dreams that . . . if they didn't happen they didn't happen, and they happened beyond my wildest dreams. So I hesitate to rule things out, but, yeah, Disney was one of my heroes growing up. I hope I don't make some of the same mistakes that Disney made.

As far as politics?

Yeah.

Well, he started a good school, California Institute for the Arts (CIA).

Yeah, that's where many of our animators come from.

EDWARD ZWICK AND MARSHALL HERSKOVITZ

Edward Zwick and Marshall Herskovitz comprise one of the most innovative writing, directing, and production teams in television. They are unusual in that they successfully move back and forth between film and television. In television, they are best known for the award-winning *thirtysomething*, which ran from 1987 to 1991 on ABC.

More recently, they produced *Once and Again*, a near sequel to *thirtysomething*. The stylistic similarities are unmistakable as they were with *My So-Called Life* and *Relativity*, their other two series. Zwick and Herskovitz fit the description of auteurs about as well as anyone in television.

An everyday naturalism is one of the hallmarks of their style. The story lines are not so much about a specific plot and its resolution as about an evocation of the characters' inner lives. Instead of telling a story about how a character loses his small company, they are more interested in telling the story of what it *feels* like to lose one's company and how the loss echoes through the rest of the character's life.

Their clever use of indirection in storytelling is captured in our discussion: how they made the skeletal framework of their storytelling invisible by letting scenes appear to be about one thing when the important twists of the plot arise in surprising and novel ways. The story of how they came up with the idea for *thirtysomething*, and how they pitched it to the network tells us how television programs are sometimes launched. We learn how the everyday realism of scenes, especially those shot in the kitchen of Michael and Hope Steadman's home, were meticulously brought to life.

Zwick and Herskovitz met at the American Film Institute and focused on directing and writing. Their first important work together was a TV movie, *Special Bulletin*, which won two Emmys, a Writer's Guild Award, and the Humanitas Prize. Herskovitz wrote it and Zwick directed it. They also both wrote for *Family*. When they decided to form a production company, they named it The Bedford Falls Company, as they both greatly admired Frank Capra's storytelling style in *It's a Wonderful Life*.

Zwick and Herskovitz's film successes are many. Zwick directed *About Last Night . . .* , *Glory, Courage Under Fire, Legends of the Fall*, and *The Siege*, coproduced *Shakespeare in Love*, and coproduced, with Herskovitz, both *Traffic* and *I Am Sam*. Herskovitz's directing credits include *Jack the Bear* and *Dangerous Beauty*. They have also won Academy Awards, Emmys, Peabodies, and Directors Guild Awards. In 1993, Zwick was awarded the Franklin J. Schaffner Alumni Medal of the American Film Institute.

I met with Zwick and Herskovitz in their production offices on the Universal Studios lot, toward the end of their *thirtysomething* run. Interviewing them was fun. Burt Prelutsky writing in the January/February 2000 issue of *Emmy* wrote that:

> It should be stated that, aside from a court reporter, nobody could possibly hope to faithfully reproduce an interview with the guys. Rare is the sentence that either one begins that isn't finished by the other. They are constantly completing one another's thoughts. It is done so respectfully that no umbrage is ever taken. They function like jazz musicians who, only occasionally, allow the other his solo. In person, they make perfect sense; in print, it would drive you nuts. So, in the following, understand that attribution is based solely on which of them began the sentence.

My experience was not dissimilar. Early on, we talk about the nature of their relationship and how dialogue in *thirtysomething* resembles how they work off of each other in conversation. They settled down after horsing around the first few minutes, and I was able to work with the transcription. I think it holds up.

✫　✫　✫

I'd like to get a little bio from each of you.

Herskovitz: Ed is from Winnetka, Illinois.

OK. That works. You can tell each others' life story.

Herskovitz: Ed went to Harvard. He worked for *Rolling Stone* and *The New Republic* and got a Rockefeller Grant, which allowed him to spend a year in France. Basically, he just kind of hung around and chased girls and had a good time.

What was his area of study at Harvard?

Herskovitz: English. Magna. Was it Magna?
Zwick: Summa in English, thank you.
Herskovitz: Summa in English. OK, pardon me. When he came back to the United States he went to the American Film Institute.

That's where you two met. Ed, what was Marshall's childhood like and where did he matriculate?

Zwick: He's the youngest of three brothers and his lifelong pursuit has been an attempt to overcome that particular liability. Becoming a director and being able to tell everyone what to do is the fulfillment of that.
Herskovitz: It's true. Comes from no other basis.
Zwick: He has no aesthetic or particular narrative wellspring. He was raised outside of Philadelphia, went to a progressive private school run by people who had sort of been blacklisted.
Herskovitz: They were public school teachers who were Communist party members who had been thrown out of the system in the early 1950s.

You strike me as being quite competitive with each other. What are you most competitive about?

Zwick: A better question would be, "What are you *not* competitive about?" We abuse each other mutually. Ironically, we somehow manage to be equally competitive and very deferential. I think we accede to each other's passion constantly.
Herskovitz: I think we have a deep respect for the power and danger of competition. We know how to put it aside because competition can kill you. We accede to each other's areas of superiority and don't compete in those areas, but it is because both of us are essentially very competitive that we are able to be very honest and realistic about those impulses.

The ultimate compliment one can give the other is to say very simply, "I'm jealous" because it's something rarely admitted and only admitted when it's really true.

It's as if you're describing a very good marriage.

Herskovitz: And the sex is good.
Zwick: And the sex is great.
Herskovitz: It is like a marriage, although certainly both of us have other friendships, and we have marriages that are very strong

and complicated. There is a way in which this relationship for us is an island. There is a kind of honesty between us and a tenure that is hard to find elsewhere.

The way you guys are interacting right now, really quickly and in an interwoven, seamless way, is something frequently seen in thirtysomething.

Zwick: That comes from the fact that there is a partnership and a friendship that is at the center of it.

Herskovitz: But I think you're also talking about the texture of the show. The *way* people talk. That has as much to do with the people we respect as filmmakers, going 60 years back, and the kind of examples they set.

Capra no doubt.

Herskovitz: Capra is a great one. [Howard Hawks'] *His Girl Friday* had everybody talk twice as fast as normal.

Zwick: Self-mocking, circumlocution, repetition. There are a lot of practitioners of that in the theater.

Herskovitz: It's also the Marx Brothers and Robert Altman.

Thirtysomething *was a breakthrough show. How was it conceived and how was it pitched?*

Herskovitz: Basically, it was a half-assed notion I had while we were trying to come up with ideas for television shows.

Zwick: *You* had?

Herskovitz: Yes. We keep having this argument. This is the one idea we've ever had that was mine. I give him every other one and he argues with me about this one.

Zwick: You're actually going to try and claim that you came up with the idea for this whole show?

Herskovitz: I said we should do a show about people of our generation because our generation is not represented on television, except on *Saturday Night Live*. I said, "We are the most influential generation and why are we not represented on television?" If we did something that would appeal to this generation it would probably succeed.

Zwick: Except the way it was said was nowhere near as articulate as that.

Herskovitz: Oh, shut up! Let me go with my version.

Zwick: This is interesting though, because it bespeaks a way in which we *do* work.

Herskovitz: I said that and you dismissed it.

Zwick: On the contrary. *You* said, "Why is there no one in television that looks like us? Or feels like us?"

Herskovitz: But I went further than that. You just didn't hear me.

The next day we were sitting in the living room with his wife, and we were supposed to go into ABC the next day to pitch ideas for television series. We had, I think, six of them. Didn't really like any of them, and I brought up this notion again that we should be doing something about our generation. It was Ed's wife, Liberty [Godshall], who kind of responded to that.

Zwick: Her idea was to personalize it. She said, "Oh, look. There's one of our friends who is having problems in their marriage, there's another one who's dealing with the birth of children, and another one the death of parents."

I said, "Well, why don't we just do that? We can do that."

Herskovitz: It was Liberty who said, "Well, what about this friend? You could do a story about that." And I said, "But what's the context of the show? Is it people sitting around a living room like this?" And then, that's when we began to feel that we were on to something, because we said *look* how we're sitting.

Zwick: I was upside down in a chair. And she was perched on something. Marshall was lying on the floor.

Herskovitz: Right. I said, "This is what you don't see on television."

Zwick: This is natural.

How much further did you take it before you walked into ABC the next day?

Herskovitz: The amazing thing is we sat down very quickly and we came up with some characters, just ideas of characters which changed later. And we came up with some types of stories we might want to tell, some types of dilemmas.

Zwick: I do remember that we said we might lower the theatrical stakes in order to heighten the neurotic ones. And that the drama of character might replace the drama of car chases.

Herskovitz: Right. In fact, one of the earliest things we said was that we wouldn't do an episode where Hope gets breast cancer. We would do an episode where one of the characters knows somebody else who has cancer and has anxiety about it. Because that's the corner of life we were more interested in exploring.

Who did you pitch it to?

Herskovitz: We pitched it to Chad Hoffman and Marie Sorie at ABC, and I think Stephanie Tuttle was in the room too.

Zwick: Chad at that time was 34 years old. Marie was pregnant, in her early 30s. Stephanie the same. I mean, it was a group of people of similar sensibility and age.

Did someone stumble accidentally upon the show's title in conversation, "She's thirtysomething, I guess."

Herskovitz: Oh no. We were working on the pilot. I said, "Ed, what should we call this?" Ed said, "Let's call it '*thirtysomething*.'" I said, "Oh, okay. That's good." And that was the extent of the conversation, and that's literally how long it lasted. We wanted something that would seem spoken because the word, the overheard phrase, was very much the currency of this show. It was something that was observed closely. It was life observed.

I can imagine someone at the network saying, "Wait a second, this title is all wrong."

Zwick: Everyone! Everyone! They despised it!

Herskovitz: They hated it.

Zwick: They despised it and up until the eleventh hour they were telling us to change it.

Herskovitz: When they were about to pick it up as a series we got a call saying, "They will pick it up if you change the name."

What were some of their ideas for names?

Herskovitz: Well, the name they wanted was "Grownups," which was owned by Jules Pfeiffer, and he refused to relinquish it, thank God.

Zwick: The point is we were unbending.

Baby boomers seem to have this sense of their being the first adults, the first people, to ever live through adult life or have children. It's something that is

The cast of thirtysomething

captured in thirtysomething. *We're much more youth-oriented than previous generations. Does that strike a resonant chord with you?*

Herskovitz: That's something we wrote in the pilot, and also in our first descriptions of the show. We even joked saying, "because we're the first generation ever to have children, ever to hold down a job."

In 1946, I think all our parents got together and said, "Let's have lots of kids and give them everything they want so they'll be totally messed up and unable to cope with real life."

Do you think previous generations just sort of slogged through adulthood in a much more accepting way, and all of their angst or neurosis was much more private?

Herskovitz: I've been doing some reading and discovered this in the people that came of age in the 1920s—right after World War I—a very similar sense that this was a new world, that all the rules were gone, that they were the first to ever live. They were the first to do a lot of things at that time, especially in the arts. In reality, many generations prior have thought that they were unique.

Zwick: The other idea with *thirtysomething* was that we would not have a template. Shows would vary wildly from one another.

Was that part of your pitch as well?

Herskovitz: Yes. We told them that. No specific form.

How did the name Bedford Falls develop for the company? How does that mesh with the show?

Herskovitz: When we fell in love with *It's a Wonderful Life*, it was not a film that was talked about very much. It embodied for us certain central aspects of filmmaking, the craft. To me, it is still the best movie ever made. Perhaps some would find that silly, but I could talk for hours about why.

It is true that every scene in It's a Wonderful Life *contributes to the final result. Every single element contributes to the story.*

Herskovitz: That's right.

Zwick: Its fabric is so tightly woven.

Herskovitz: It's a piece of storytelling. There's never been anything that's equal to it. It's remarkable. Really remarkable.

Would you agree that there often isn't this kind of attention to story these days?

Herskovitz: It is a form of laziness today and it's institutionalized laziness. People don't really understand how hard you gotta work.

We had the benefit of two teachers at AFI who were cruel and relentless in their desire to reveal to us what the truth is of making film. They both believed that film itself is relentless, always moving forward, and it always must justify its existence. It can never be self-indulgent. It instilled in us the discipline of filling things up, and how you need to make scenes pay off.

In thirtysomething, *you put out, nearly every week, a better quality script, in my opinion, than many theatrical films.*

Zwick: I'm very proud of the scripts we do. It's about ideas, and it's about structure—the laying out of scenes and what happens in each scene. The shape of a piece, the arc of a story. Only in the leanest, and most rigid structure can you then have the flights of naturalistic behavior observed, and digressive funny moments.

Imagine a Christmas tree, if you will, full of beautiful, extraordinary ornaments and lights and branches and needles, and *that's* what you see. When you walk in a room *that's* what you appreciate of the tree. You do not see, nor do you particularly care about the base and the branches on which it is hung, but without it . . .

Herskovitz: It wouldn't move you.

Zwick: It wouldn't move you, and in fact it wouldn't stand.

How invisible is the structure, the armature?

Herskovitz: We try to make it invisible. We try to cover our tracks.

Zwick: Especially in an obligatory scene.

You have some exposition to accomplish. You have to get it told that Nancy has learned that her cancer is worse. You've got this obligatory scene, so how do you cover your tracks?

Zwick: It's a scene that presumes to be about something else or it's a scene . . .

Herskovitz: That has something funny happen in the beginning of it . . .

Zwick: Or something contradictory happens while the other thing is happening.

How far ahead are things scripted out? How many weeks ahead are you working?

Zwick: Less as the season carries on. In the beginning we might begin with seven or eight scripts already written, and by the end of the year we're living hand to mouth.

Herskovitz: We like a script to be finished by the time shooting starts. We're working from a draft that's pretty much finished while we're in our week of prep before an episode starts. We will get the basic working draft a week before we start shooting, do re-writes during that week, then shoot, then take two to three weeks to do post-production on the show, and then it will air.

How far in advance do you have scenarios written?

Herskovitz: At the beginning of each year Ed and I sit down, and plan out the stories for the year. We say, this is going to happen to Nancy this year,

Timothy Busfield, Patricia Wettig, Ken Olin, and Mel Harris (l-r).

this is what's going to happen to Michael, this is what's going to happen to Gary. We go through each of the characters and we come up with a kind of an arc. Then we try to break down how many episodes it will take to tell each story. We finally come up with a list of 22 shows—this, basically, is the show where *this* is going to happen. This is the show where *that's* going to happen. Sometimes we realize, "Oh God, we gave that a *whole* show and we could have done it in one act." Or, "Oh God, we gave *that* a whole show, but we need two shows to do it." It eventually works out.

One of the more obvious comparisons in terms of this long scenario is to soap opera. Do you see any symmetry there yourself?

Herskovitz: Soaps are character driven, but also incident driven. Soap opera is driven by the external relationships and the twists and turns of the relationships. They use up a lot of incident in order to tell the story. So and so is sleeping with so and so, and that's found out. Then there's scandal, then they're fired. Whereas we will take an entire season to have a character meet another character, fall in love with that character, move in with that character, and then find out that that character is not such a great guy, and fall out of love with that character. We will take an incredible amount of time.

Zwick: Or if there is an incident of some real plot significance, the death of a parent, that will have resonance over months. The loss of a business became a linchpin for an entire season.

My guess is that there are certain writers who tend to get assigned certain characters. I would think that someone writes Melissa better than Michael.

Zwick: No. Characters have not been the preserve of certain writers, nor have plots.

Is any of the dialogue improvised?

Herskovitz: None. Zero.

Do the actors have input into the writing?

Herskovitz: Well, let me put it this way. The actors have been welcomed into this process in a way that they're not on other shows, but it's within certain very defined limits. We find that our actors are incredibly good troubleshooters, and that when they have a problem with a scene, they're always right—there's something wrong with the scene. They're saying, essentially, "I don't know how to act this, I can't find the truth in this." Our job then is to make it work for them.

In addition to the convincing naturalism of the show is the incredible blocking and camera work. Sometimes you have scenes where people are passing through, often in a kitchen, food's getting cooked and someone's coming in and the camera is following all of it with no edits.

Zwick: I'm glad you noticed it because in years of dealing with the film studio they've never understood why it takes us longer than most shows to shoot. That's exactly why.

Herskovitz: We basically do in the neighborhood of 16 setups a day, which is much less than other television shows.

Describe what a setup is.

Herskovitz: A setup means setting up the camera and lighting that shot. It's basically a shot. A setup.

Zwick: We're trying to do fewer setups and have more things happen within each setup.

How many days are you shooting?

Herskovitz: We shoot eight days for every episode.

Zwick: Five working days during the week and three in the next week.

Is there a story you could tell about the blocking? How laborious one scene was to shoot? One of those kitchen scenes?

Herskovitz: When we did the pilot there was a scene in the kitchen with five of the characters and a dog. I knew what I wanted, I had just never done a scene like this. We rehearsed the scene for three hours, and it was all about the business. She's cooking this, and he's going over there and we were getting so confused, none of us had ever done this before.

I could imagine an actor getting a little bugged after a while, saying, "Look it doesn't matter if the spaghetti doesn't go in the pot just so and then the dog barks."

Herskovitz: On the contrary. The actors are zealots. They want the food to be real, the props to be real, they get very upset if they have to fake. They'll do it, because they're professionals, but they would much prefer doing the real thing. The punchline is that what took us five hours to shoot these actors can now do in minutes because they're so used to it and they understand it.

And the poor prop crew learned very early that when we're in the kitchen, they gotta have everything right there to do anything. They have to have all the real food, all the real utensils, in doubles and triples and quadruples, so that if this person suddenly wants to make eggs we could do it.

Is there any other show that does anything like that?

Herskovitz: I doubt it. It's possible. Not to the extent we do it.

Increasingly, you've generated directors from your own ensemble; some programs bring a director in from the outside. How hard is that to bring about?

Zwick: We have had a number of directors from the outside and we have had 21 people direct for the *first* time on the show, many of them from the outside. We always have a period of observation for someone. They spend about a week up here, with us, watching cuts. And then they will spend a lot of time on the set, in dailies, watching the cuts

Can I assume that the character name "Michael Steadman" is like "Marcus Welby" and "Willy Loman." Steadman is no accident. He's at the center of the show and more stable than Elliot. The steady man.

Zwick: There may be some deep psychological Freudian slip, but it was not intentional.

How hard is it to do a scene where two characters are laughing uproariously? I've seen this in a recent episode. This seems absolutely natural, and I assume it somehow is. How do you get that effect?

Herskovitz: The magic of actors. That's what they do.

Do they start cold?

Zwick: No. I'll tell you how they did that. People began, without the cameras rolling, to tell the filthiest, most vile joke that they knew. In fact, only when they got themselves in such a state of hilarity did we roll the cameras and get the dialogue.

One wonders if you'll ever have an ensemble like this again. Thirtysomething *is going to be very hard to top.*

Zwick: What will be hardest to top will be the synergy, the coming together. And the artistic freedom that we have been given, the license.

Could it go another five or six years?

> Zwick: No, not at all.
> Herskovitz: You can't do this forever.

You would never get to "fortysomething"?

> Herskovitz: No, we won't. We talked about coming back on a sporadic basis.
> Zwick: Seven years from now or 10 years from now.

Return to Gilligan's Island.

> Herskovitz: Right.

There have been two critical academic articles about the show. About the "hegemony" of thirtysomething.

> Herskovitz: Really?
> Zwick: The hegemony of *thirtysomething*?

The hegemony of certain kinds of role depictions.

> Herskovitz: What are they in?

It's a journal called Critical Studies in Mass Communication.

> Zwick: Hee hee hee hee hee!
> Herskovitz: Oh, great. I love it.

One of the critiques that they make is that the show "valorizes" marriage, that all of the women who are not married, want to be married, and that their lives are unfulfilled unless they are married. Moreover, all of the women, except for Gary's wife, are basically at home and kind of working on the side. Yet, there are a great percentage of American women who are working full time. You don't have that kind of character depicted. And then when Gary's wife wants to take a full-time job, the marriage explodes.

> Zwick: We do not believe that women have to be in the home. It just happens that we believe that these two women *would* be. The reason that the character that plays Gary's wife, that that marriage has exploded, was necessitated by an actress's availability and the inability to afford to bring her on as a series regular when we already had a budget that was strained.
> Herskovitz: The point is that we do not presume to say that this show is a model for what society should be. These are just these characters. They represent themselves and their experiences.

It is also claimed that the unmarried people in the cast are like children and often depicted like children.

> Herskovitz: We also do that to the married people.
> Zwick: Anything that is summoned up from the personal is going to reflect some aspect of psychology or belief or values that are themselves

personal. And so the fact that they might find them not politically correct, or programmatic, or following some scriptures of a more acceptable political guideline is inevitable.

LARRY DAVID

Larry David cocreated *Seinfeld* with Jerry Seinfeld. In 2002, in its 50-year look back at television milestones, *TV Guide* ranked *Seinfeld* the number one program in the history of the medium. In the opinion of some, Larry David was the critical creative factor behind the show.

After college, David tried improv and stand-up comedy. Later, he wrote and performed in the much overlooked *Fridays*, a *Saturday Night Live*–like comedy program that aired on ABC in the late 1970s and early 1980s. For those who remember the show, David stood out in sketches playing a rabbi secret agent and imitating Larry Fine of the Three Stooges. In those days, his hair stood up in long curls. Another *Fridays* regular was Michael Richards.

David met Jerry Seinfeld years before while doing stand-up. Asked to create a concept for a situation comedy, Seinfeld had a hunch that David was the person to help him. The rest is history. At this writing, *Seinfeld* has been seen in an estimated 90 countries around the world.

David left the series after its seventh year; after his departure, the program lost some of its freshness. The viewer often notices the laugh track in some of those episodes—a sure sign that what you are watching isn't funny, that you've seen it before, or that the writers and actors are just going through the motions. David was coaxed back to write the finale.

Both Seinfeld and David were at the top of the annual earnings list in entertainment when *Seinfeld* was sold into syndication. David's percentage was an estimated $264 million, just under what Seinfeld received.

I met with David at Castle Rock's studios in Santa Monica, in an editing suite where he was putting the final touches on *Sour Grapes*, his first feature film. David's newest comic venture, in which he also stars, is *Curb Your Enthusiasm* for HBO. From the title of these two works, one knows that Larry David is still close to his angst. In the interview, we learn that he is happier than when he was poor, but that he's not entirely comfortable either.

✯ ✯ ✯

What might you have been doing when you were much younger that is similar to what you do now?

I used to make up all of my book reports.

Where did you grow up?

I grew up in Brooklyn. My father was in the clothing business. He worked for a manufacturer of suits and sportcoats.

Larry David

Like Jerry's father.

Yeah, except on the show he sold raincoats. That's where we got that. My mother worked for the bureau of child guidance.

Where did you go to college? What was your ambition then?

University of Maryland, history major. My ambition was to avoid manual labor, which literally made me cry. Any time I lifted anything over 10 pounds I would become hysterical.

I got out of college in 1970. It was a very depressing period of my life. I had a series of odd jobs. I was a private chauffeur, a taxi driver, and a paralegal, with a lot of unemployment in between all of those. My mother sent me to a psychiatrist; thought there was something wrong with me. Just like George's mother sent him to a psychiatrist. Then one night in New York I went to the Improv, a comedy club in New York. I thought that seemed like something I could do. I was so naive I thought I could get up and do it that night. After all, you're just talking. It seemed easy. Of course it was anything but.

Four years later the producers from *Fridays* came in and saw me and I got that job. First I just got hired as an actor, but I was writing my own material. Then, after 13 shows, they gave me writing credit and I was put on the staff.

Fridays was never given the credit it deserved. There was a period where, at least in my opinion, it was better than Saturday Night Live *back when* SNL *was still very good. I know that's where you met Michael Richards. Is there any thought of taking those things out of the vault and reselling them into syndication?*

I hope not.

How do we get you from Fridays *to* Seinfeld?

I moved back to New York in 1984 and I got a job as a writer on *Saturday Night Live*. I did that show for a year and then I got back into stand-up full time.

I met Jerry in 1976. We weren't really close friends, but whenever we saw each other in the clubs we always had very stimulating, funny conversations. The subjects most people never discuss because they're too trivial and insignificant is what we loved to talk about.

One night in 1988 he told me that NBC had some interest in him. He had read a screenplay of mine a few years earlier that he liked and he was always a fan of my stand-up.

The initial idea for the show was that it would be a one-camera, filmed show, no audience. It was about how a comedian comes up with his material. So we would follow him around for a day and whatever he experienced that particular day would become his stand-up that night. It really *was* about nothing. We pitched it to Brandon Tartikoff. Warren Littlefield was there.

Jerry and I started talking about this in November of 1988. One night before we shared a cab to the westside, we stopped off in a grocery store and we were talking about the products. It was the kind of dialogue you never hear on TV, or in the movies for that matter. Then at some point I said, "You see, this is what the show should be." That was the germ of it. We didn't know at the beginning what it would be about, but we knew we weren't going to emphasize story. It was going to be more of a rambling thing, more of a slice of life than story driven. We did the pilot in April of 1989 and it aired shortly thereafter.

You started with Jerry. How easy or difficult was the casting of the other three?

Jason Alexander auditioned on tape for the show from New York and I literally saw no more than ten seconds of it and I said, "This is it, shut it off, we got him!" He was working from the pilot script. Julia Louis-Dreyfus I knew from *Saturday Night Live* the year that I was on the show. Invariably, whenever I gave her a part in any of my sketches, she always nailed it. I never had to give her a note, so I knew that she would be great for the part. And Michael, of course, I knew from *Fridays*. The character he brought to it was much broader than we had intended but he was too funny to pass up.

One of the things a veteran Seinfeld *watcher appreciates is how intricately interwoven the plots often are, and how interdependent everything is. When did it occur to you to do that?*

It happened in the episode called "The Busboy." It was maybe our tenth show. I was in Larry Charles' office and we were talking about the ending. Elaine's boyfriend had missed his plane to Seattle and was coming up to Jerry's apartment, and in a completely unrelated story the busboy was also coming up at the same time. And we thought it would be funny if they got in a fight in the hall. So that was the first time two separate stories ever connected. And then once that happened I thought, "Hey, this is great," and it became a conscious thing to try and weave these stories together and it became fun to do it and very challenging.

Do you ever think you went too far with it?

You could point to a story or two where maybe it was a stretch here or there, but for the most part there's these lights bulbs going off.

The surprise element is very important. It rarely played as contrived. It must have been very hard to do, so the audience doesn't see it coming.

Predictability was definitely something we always wanted to avoid. You'll notice we never did any shows where two of the characters stopped talking to each other, because you knew they would eventually make up. We were very determined to try and do ideas that not only had not been done before but that no one else could do.

The cast of Seinfeld: *Michael Richards, Julia Louis-Dreyfus, Jason Alexander, and Jerry Seinfeld(l-r).*

Tell me about the writing staff on Seinfeld.

In the first four seasons there were hardly any writers at all. The first season we had two writers, and one left. Then we hired three more. It wasn't like a normal sitcom those first four or five years. It made it harder for me because I had to write more shows, more first drafts. There weren't a lot of writers generating first drafts. I tapered off as we added more and more people to the staff.

How many hours per week were you writing at the height?

We never worked too late during the week. Unless we were actually filming where we had to be out late, or unless it was a show night, I was home by 7:30 at the latest. We did a lot of work on the weekends, from 9:00 in the morning till 6:00. We didn't have a writer's room, and I think that reduced the amount of hours. Jerry and I did the rewriting in the office on the CBS-MTM lot in Studio City.

Why did you leave the show?

I did it starting in 1989, through 1996. I just wanted to try something else, really. There was no falling out at all. No Yoko Ono. I put a lot of pressure on myself. I remember whenever a season ended. I would think, "How can we do it again?" But we always did.

Where do you think your comedy comes from?

I don't know but obviously at some point very early on something went wrong—terribly wrong. I also grew up in an apartment building in Brooklyn where people were always screaming at each other. Anger is much funnier than passivity. I'm able to express my thoughts a lot easier than George.

Speaking of George, did you have your heart broken many times and have difficulties with women?

Of course. My whole life. Never being able to interpret what they meant, always making the wrong decision. Remember that "opposite show?" I always did the wrong thing, never knew what to say.

Why were you so stumblingly bad at it?

I was just unbelievably shy and scared of them. That idiotic message that George left on the answering machine—that's my dating history in a nutshell.

How many Emmys has the show won?

I feel the show has been under-rewarded. We won one Emmy for best show, two writing Emmys, Michael's won three Emmys, Julia's won one, Jason hasn't won any, which is a crime.

Do you own a piece of the show?

Oh yeah. I had a very good agent and did well by him.

Has money made you happy?

It doesn't change your disposition—you just transfer your worries and concerns to other areas. I don't feel like I'm happier than when I didn't have a lot of money, because now instead of worrying about money I worry about something else. Now I can worry about my health more.

But I used to have a lot of hostility towards the rich, definitely. I'm sure I've become a person I would have hated 10 years ago.

Do you ever think about buying a place in the south of France and just letting your hair grow long?

Larry David with Julia Louis-Dreyfus, playing herself on Curb Your Enthusiasm.

Impossible. I would be bored to death. Anyways, what's so special about the south of France? Maybe people in the south of France dream about coming to New York.

Do you love your work?

Occasionally I love the finished product.

The work that you do. Does it feel *like work?*

It doesn't really feel like it, no.

When does it feel like work?

Beginning a script is always the hardest. Just getting it going, getting it started. Getting to that point where you say to yourself, I've got a story here.

What was the production schedule like on Seinfeld?

We would do two shows and take a week off. We would finish a show on a Tuesday or Wednesday. On Thursday we would get the story for the next show.

You have a staff of writers and they're all working separately on shows at different stages. We'd take a look at a board and decide what to do next. On Thursday morning, if we just finished a show on Wednesday, we would read the next script and get to work on it and by the end of Thursday we'd have the story all beat out. We'd write it Friday and Saturday and read it on Sunday. It would get filmed on Wednesday.

Would you always be on the set when it was being filmed?

Always.

Did the directors change much?

We only had two directors for the show. For the first couple of seasons we had one director and then we changed after the fourth or fifth year.

What's involved in getting a character right?

When you have so many episodes to do, sometimes the story takes precedence over what you would normally expect the character to do. For example, we did one show very early on where Kramer was kind of tough, and he went into somebody's house and grabbed him and tried to get back some statue or something, but he was kind of a tough guy. And then a few years ago we did a show where we had these two sort of gay ruffians and they frightened him and Jerry. Okay, so you could say, "How can he be this tough guy in one episode and this scaredy-cat in the other?" So you could complain and say, "Well, it's out of character for him to do that." But it could happen. It's happened to me personally where I threatened someone, if you could imagine that. But generally I'm frightened to death. Anyway, you have to make allowances for things like that because ultimately the story is more important.

Many people know the shows extremely well. Is that fun for you?

I love talking to fans of the show, people who really know their stuff. I'm constantly amazed at how much people know about the show.

It's become such a part of the culture.

There was a time when ESPN would do their hockey highlights and if the goalie made a good save the announcer would go, "No soup for you." I get a big kick out of things like that.

What do you look back on about the show?

My fondest memories of the show are working in the room with Jerry and writing some of these episodes—just the laughs that we had and how we'd break each other up. We always kept a tape recorder going. There were no rules, but we always told each other if we didn't like something. The working relationship was as good as you can get.

How long have you been married?

Five years. I have two kids.

After you left the show, did you ever get a great idea and want to call Jerry with it?

I did get ideas, but now I just write them in my notebook and hope I can use them for something else.

ALLAN BURNS

Allan Burns' start in life and in television wasn't easy. After his father died when he was 9, he was shipped off to a military school. He was fired after one month in his first writing job, coming up with gags for *Truth or Consequences*. To make a living he turned to writing greeting cards.

Then, with the cartooning talent he had developed as a child, he began working in animation with Jay Ward, the creator of *Rocky and His Friends*. Burns went on to invent Captain Crunch for Quaker Oats, and later, *George of the Jungle*. Then, he and his partner came up with *The Munsters*. Later he did some writing for *The Smothers Brothers Show, He and She*, and *Get Smart*, and then hooked up with James Brooks when he was writing *Room 222*.

It was the beginning of an extraordinarily successful and significant partnership which lasted 12 years as Brooks and Burns created *The Mary Tyler Moore Show*, and later, *Rhoda* and *Lou Grant*. Brooks and Burns are often credited with breaking new ground in creating the model for a new kind of situation comedy with a single, independent, working woman at the center of the program.

At one point, Burns had three successful programs on the air at once and nearly lost his health as a result. Burns has won six Emmys for his writing and received an Oscar nomination for *A Little Romance*.

Burns discusses the discipline of comedy writing and the difficulty getting directors and executives to understand his brand of humor. I first interviewed Allan Burns in the late 1980s and then again in the late 1990s.

I came from a family that would never have approved of my going into show business. Somebody from a "good family" wouldn't get into a messy business like this.

My father was a lawyer, who died when I was 9 and I was sent off to military school for three years. My brother was a lot older and was at the Naval Academy. My sister was ten years older and married; I was the baby at home and my uncles were afraid of what was going to happen to me if I got too much motherly affection, so I was shipped off to military school. It was a traumatic experience.

Allan Burns

How quickly after you lost your father did you go?

Immediately. Within months.

In a way, you lost both your parents.

In a manner of speaking. And in my mind I would plot how to run away from there. That place was really something out of Oliver Twist—one of those rough military schools. Corporal punishment was administered by the older students. They were allowed to belt you across your bare butt with sabres. It would raise welts that would last a month.

Mostly these were a bunch of kids who were troubled: rich kids whose parents didn't want to deal with them. There were a lot of unhappy misfits there. But after the initial adjustment I got used to it. Even grew to like it. I suppose you can get to like anything.

After three years, my mother, God bless her, for reasons having to do with my brother being stationed by the Navy in Honolulu, schlepped us from Baltimore to Honolulu. Talk about culture shock. But good culture shock. Still I was uprooted and alone. I didn't know a soul.

Humor didn't help you?

I wasn't a cut-up. Never have been. I'm not now. My humor comes out in my work and I'm not even sure how that happens. I never know just where it comes from. It's a spooky process that I don't want to investigate too closely for fear it will somehow go away.

I had always had a certain artistic ability. In high school I did a cartoon strip in the local paper, *The Honolulu Star Bulletin*. All the best comedy writers come from Honolulu, you know. It's a hotbed of comedy writers. Forget what you've heard about New York.

Well, Hawaii's such a tough environment to grow up in.

You know, the hostility of it and everything. Plus the bad climate. So naturally you have to fend off all that stuff with humor. I'd always gotten straight As in creative writing. And I did manage to get my rocks off doing those cartoons. I would get patted on the head for it, but architecture school was what I was supposed to be headed toward. Being a dutiful kid, I went into that at the University of Oregon.

I lasted in architecture for about a year. I'm the most right-brained person I know and I just never had any ability at all with numbers. I thought that maybe I could make it in commercial art so I came down to L.A. to go to art school. That summer, I got a job at NBC as a page and absolutely fell in love with the business. I said to myself: "This is what I want to do, I don't want to ever do anything else."

I was a page on old shows like the Steve Allen *Tonight Show*, *The George Gobel Show*, *The Jonathan Winters Show*, and *The Colgate Comedy Hour*. I just wanted to be around it and to watch the rehearsals. Let it sink in. Then I'd go home every night and pound out my spec monologues that I was sure I'd sell to those shows. But I didn't.

I'd show them to producers, and every once in a while someone would take enough of an interest in me to keep me going. My material showed promise, but it was pretty crude. I was a page for a few years. Then I found out about this thing that Sylvester "Pat" Weaver, the great innovative president of NBC developed, called The Comedy Writer Development Program. They announced it and must have gotten 30,000 submissions. They were up to their ears in submissions.

One day, they called me up and I thought they were going to let me in. I'm the happiest guy in the world, but instead they offered me a job paying $125 a week screening other people's stuff. Talk about discouraging, but it paid more than the $75 a week I was making as a page. They would put these writers on staff as junior writers on shows to let them learn from professional writers. Not a bad idea. As a matter of fact, it's something people tend to do in a sort of ad hoc way today. Garry Marshall used to do it a lot on his shows; he'd hire promising writers, take them under his wing, and let them develop. Some very successful comedy writers learned under Garry's tutelage.

Anyway, I never got a job that way, but I finally did get a job writing gags for *Truth or Consequences*. A disaster. I lasted about a month, got fired. I was awful. The show was slapstick, dumbheaded stuff. I couldn't do it.

I was jobless again so I fell back on my cartooning. I started freelancing, doing contemporary greeting cards. Did that for maybe three years. Then I went into doing animated commercials on a freelance basis. I got into the animation business with Jay Ward who created Bullwinkle and Rocky and Dudley Doright [from *The Bullwinkle Show*]. I wrote and drew some of that stuff. Mostly wrote.

The first thing I ever created myself was Captain Crunch. The Quaker Oats people sent me a box of cereal and said, "Name this," and we did a whole campaign around it. Thirty-five years later it's still going strong— and all I ever made from it was my $217 a week salary and a $1,000 bonus.

I also developed other new stuff. *George of the Jungle* was something I came up with there. And then I met my first partner, whose name was Chris Hayward. He and I sort of tunneled out of there together. We went from doing cartoons to television sitcoms that were really cartoons, like *The Munsters* and all that crap.

Chris and I created *The Munsters* and it was nearly stolen from us by Universal. Although it was our idea, we never wrote a single episode— which was just as well because I thought the show was pretty stupid. Then we did the first *Smothers Brothers Show*, the one that was unsuccessful, the one where Tom played an angel. From that we went to *He and She*, starring Richard Benjamin and Paula Prentiss, the first TV comedy show I was really proud to have written, then on to *Get Smart*.

I was about 30 and had just gotten married. Chris and I had a pretty good run, three or four years together, but then we split up after *Get Smart*

Allan Burns, Walter Cronkite, Jim Brooks, and Ed Weinberger (l-r) on the set of The Mary Tyler Moore Show. *Walter Cronkite, long the most trusted man in America and anchor of the CBS Evening News, played himself in this episode.*

because I wanted to write movies and he didn't. I went off and started free-lancing again and I did some work writing *Room 222* for my friend, Jim Brooks. Jim had created that show and he got me to write some episodes.

Grant Tinker had this idea that we should team up to create a show for Mary. He'd sold the idea of a Mary Tyler Moore series to CBS and that precipitated what was to become the best twelve years of my life.

Following Mary *was* Rhoda?

Then *Lou Grant*. And we also did a show with Paul Sand called *Friends and Lovers*. One year we had three shows on the air simultaneously. I was on the verge of suicide. It was the worst year of my life. I thought I was going to die. My wife was so worried about me. I had back and neck pains. There was no way I could delegate. We just didn't know how to let other people take charge.

One wonders how Norman Lear did it?

He knew how to delegate. Norman would know how to come in and simply read the script, watch rehearsals, tell the writers what to do, what he thought, and go on to the next show.

Putting a trance on Mary.

But we were going crazy. We were trying to totally produce all the shows, to be in on all the story conferences, to do all the rewrites, and to be there when every show was shot. We were shooting *Rhoda* and *Friends and Lovers* on the same night, on the same lot, literally bicycling between sound stages to do it.

During *Lou Grant*, I wrote a movie called *A Little Romance* with Laurence Olivier and Diane Lane, directed by the great George Roy Hill, who'd directed *Butch Cassidy and the Sundance Kid* and *The Sting*, among others. It was a wonderful learning experience.

You got an Oscar nomination for that?

Yeah. But then I wrote *Butch and Sundance: The Early Days, Part I*. It was what they called the "prequel." It didn't work at all. You can't do a successful western where the audience already knows the heroes are going to live at the end.

How does a comedy writer do his work?

First, you don't try to analyze where it's coming from. There's always that fear that you'll find out and poof! it will be gone. I'm a guy who doesn't seem like a funny person, but things come out of my fingertips that constantly amaze and surprise me. Neil Simon has said the same thing about his writing, that he'll read something he's written and feel like it was written by somebody else.

You feel as if you're a channel for something.

Like there's something that's floating around out there and somehow it comes out through you. It sounds a little pretentious to say that, because it's a little like saying, "Well, I have this God-given gift or something." I just feel that you hook into something that you don't quite understand.

My approach is to write everyday regardless of whether it's coming or not. I found that if I wait for it to come, it's not going to. But if I start to write, even if it's crap, I can go back and fix it, and usually find something funny in it. It's like that story about the kid who's shoveling through a roomful of horse shit, saying: "There's gotta be a pony in here somewhere."

I work best in the morning. There are times, though, when I'm on such a roll that I can't stop. I've written a first draft screenplay in three weeks, working from 8:00 in the morning to 8:00 at night. It was just rolling out.

I remember reading somewhere that Hemingway said he would quit when he was still hot, when he felt like he knew exactly where he was going. In other words, don't write yourself out. Leave another bullet in the chamber. And the next day when you pick it up, it's there and you already know where you're going.

I always quit before I've exhausted what I have to say. I find that it helps me to bridge the gap, carry me into the next scene. It's hard to do that sometimes, though. You really have got to put on the brakes, because you find yourself saying, "If I just do two more pages I'm gonna finish this scene."

You need to come in the next day and say, "Okay, I know what the next line's gonna be." And the next line takes you to the next line which takes you to the next line. And you're off again.

If you create good, full characters, they take over. And sometimes this amazing thing happens that you find yourself being touched by what your characters are doing. Being angered by them, being amused by them, sometimes even being turned on by them. I take very little credit for that stuff because I feel like it is coming from somewhere else.

Once in a while something you write will connect accidentally with something else you've done in the same script. You've set something up early and somehow it comes back up and you think, "Boy, how clever of me." But it wasn't you. It's just been laying there waiting for you and it makes it look like you're more clever than you really are. You can then go back and take that and lay it in earlier and really look smart. Make the most of those happy accidents—that's my advice. And take bows for them. Who's gonna know?

Can we talk about creative criticisms from network executives?

There are bright people and there are not so bright people. We had a lot of trouble getting *The Mary Tyler Moore Show* started. Jim and I had wanted to make it a show about a divorcee and they simply wouldn't let us. They recited chapter and verse about why the American public wouldn't accept divorce on television. How dumb was that? But they were firm about it.

There is very seldom the desire, on the part of the programming executives, to do something really original on TV. They'd rather you copy something that somebody else has been successful with. But they want *that* to look original. And if you give them something really innovative it just scares the shit out of them. It doesn't have anything to do with their lack of intelligence; it has to do with fear.

Of losing their jobs?

Yeah. Those people are under such pressure all the time. They're under much more pressure than we are. Yet *they* have the power to put your show on or not. You go in to see those people and they all have that look of quiet desperation in their eyes. They're always on the verge of being fired 'cause they're not the number one in the Nielsens. They're thinking, "Can this show help bail us out? I'd love to do something really different and really original but please God don't let it be too different or too original." Because what if it fails?

It's funny. After the *Mary* show was a success we couldn't find anybody over there at CBS who didn't say they loved it from day one. But they didn't. They just hated it and us, because we were two weird guys who didn't know how to write three jokes per page.

They didn't know how to read our scripts because none of them had jokes in them. Our comedy came out of characters rather than out of the punch lines. We just wrote to please ourselves. We had our own rhythms and senses of humor and we'd hear the way people talked and I think we were accurate about it. But they'd read our stuff and say this doesn't read like . . .

This doesn't read like The Munsters.

Or *The Beverly Hillbillies*. Our style was naturalistic, for one thing, and they didn't get that. I remember early on in the first year of Mary's show we had a successful director named Jerry Paris, who came in to direct. Not many, as it turned out, because he just didn't get us. The first time he directed for us, it was a script I'd written. Jerry came to me before the cast reading and said, "You know, this isn't funny. What am I supposed to do with it?"

We should note that Jerry Paris directed The Dick Van Dyke Show *and also played Mary Tyler Moore and Dick Van Dyke's next door neighbor, Jerry Helper, the dentist, married to Millie.*

And did a good job for them. So we read the script aloud and everybody in our cast and staff seemed to like it around the table and Jerry says, "Wait a minute! Aren't we going to fix this?" I said, "Jerry, let them start to rehearse it." All week long he was pestering us, asking where the jokes were.

How do you hold on to your vision when someone like that is trying to change it?

Just stick to your guns and know that you could be right. I said, "I think we know the characters better than you, Jerry." The end result was that we shot the show and the studio audience adored it. And Jerry turned around and said, "Son of a bitch, you were right." The audience was more familiar with the characters than *he* was.

What other network objections did you hear with the Mary *show?*

There was one show where they called up and said, "This is just awful, you've got to come in and talk about this script." It was a show about Rhoda and her mother. Her mother had come out from New York to visit and Rhoda refuses to see her. "They're gonna hate Rhoda," they said.

We had a whole scene in it, about how television sitcoms had screwed up Rhoda's life. That when she was a kid, she'd thought her family's life should be like *Ozzie and Harriet.* When you grow up, you think that your life is all fucked up and that everybody else is normal because of what you see on television. So we got a call, a guy from CBS saying, "You can't shoot this show. I forbid it."

We called Grant Tinker and said, "They're telling us we can't shoot the show." He said, "What's wrong with it? I love it." Grant said to go ahead and shoot the show despite their order not to, so we did. He was able to do that because he had made a deal with CBS where he was taking the losses himself on his shows. He and Mary had gone to the bank, raised a lot of money and were covering the deficits. So he had extra leverage. They literally couldn't tell us that we couldn't shoot the show. The most they could do was advise us strongly. So we shot it. And Jim and I won our first Emmy for it. Lucky for Jim and me. Not a lot of producers have guys backing them up the way Grant backed us.

Didn't you hear from Harriet Nelson?

Yes. Harriet Nelson was upset that Rhoda said *Ozzie and Harriet* had screwed up Rhoda's life. She didn't understand what we were driving at either. But the audience did. After the show we got all these letters saying, "I felt like I was the only person who felt that way." We had hooked into what people felt and in sitcomland, they weren't dealing with that.

But we weren't doing a *sitcom* in the traditional sense. I've always objected to that term in describing the kinds of shows that we were doing. Because they aren't based on situational comedy. They're really *character* comedy. "Sitcom" is where Lucy gets her left toe caught in a bowling ball. Carl Reiner, in *The Dick Van Dyke Show*, started the trend toward character comedy. We just picked up on it.

I'm curious, in the Mary *show, did Mr. Grant's name come from Grant Tinker? Or was that just a coincidence?*

Oh no, that was very deliberate.

Cast and staff of Rhoda *(Burns standing, second from right).*

What does it feel like when you have a hit show that you've created and good ratings are coming in and everybody's talking about the show?

Good, of course, but never for very long because you simply don't have time to relax and enjoy it. You're so busy trying to get next week's show done; you're always fighting to keep ahead. You don't feel like you're doing anything "classic." I still have a hard time accepting that word in connection with anything I've done.

We knew we were doing pretty good work most of the time, but boy, there'd be those weeks when it was just drudgery. Jim and I always felt if over 50 percent of the shows we did were ones we really liked, we were ahead of the game. And if there were 10 shows out of your season that you thought were really excellent, that was great. And you always knew there were going to be two or three absolute turkeys every year.

No one gets every show to be great.

In a given season of 22 shows you've done the equivalent of five one-and-one-half hour movies. How many people can write five movies a year, much less make them good? It's just the sheer volume of it and the pressure on you to get it out every week.

Sometimes you get an idea and you just know it's wonderful and that it's gonna fly. But American television isn't like the BBC, where you wait to put a show on when you've gotten it right. And they only do six or eight episodes a season at that. We're turning it out every week whether the muse strikes us or not. You don't always have a hot idea, but you've got to put your head down and keep going.

Since we talked back in the 1980s, you've had more experience working in film. How is writing for film different than writing for television?

As the director George Roy Hill said to me on my first draft of a movie screenplay, "you're trying too hard to pull the viewers in." He said "don't forget these people have spent five bucks and their asses are in the seats, it's gonna take a lot for them to get up and walk out." You can take your time, whereas in television you gotta grab them. You can develop the characters.

Still, the writer in movies has little or no power. There are very few who have the power to really have it their way. And those people are generally writer-directors. Like Jim Brooks. He can do what he wants, and he still sometimes has problems with the studios.

What changes in the industry in the last 10 to 15 years would you point to as being most significant?

There are too damn many networks right now. WB, Fox. The talent pool was stretched critically before that. It's always been very hard to staff up your show. Now, with the addition of three more networks, plus Show-time, plus HBO, USA, where in the hell are you gonna get the writers and producers to do this? That's what's wrong with the quality. I think there just aren't enough writers.

It's also trying to cast a good comedic lead who's young and good looking. Those people are hard to find.

They've always been hard to find. Historically, it's the leading man. Never hard at all to find funny, attractive leading women.

Do you think that part of the reason is that the young, male, attractive funny leads cross over to film?

Absolutely. Is Ben Affleck gonna do television? And if they have succeeded in television, their agent is saying, "No, no, no, you've got to get into the movie business, that's where you're going to make the big money." Although if the agency packages the show right, they're going to make a lot more money on television than they could make off of their actor being in a film.

But to an actor it's still more prestigious to be in a movie.

Absolutely. But television is the most civilized way for an actor to work. Especially doing comedy. They have relatively short hours, compared to movie hours, which can go 12 to 14 hours a day.

But if you're in a successful series, it's a lot of pressure.

No, it's not. Nah.

The actors would tell you otherwise.

The actors. They're full of shit. It's the best gig for an actor. The producers are the ones doing all the grunt work. They only have to come to work at 9:00 in the morning. They do four days a week, if that. Then there are really lazy people, like Cosby, who comes in to work two and a half days a week or something like that. I mean, my God, they've got it made.

It sounds like you think that there is more bad stuff than ever.

Right, that's right. There's probably as much good stuff as there was, maybe a little less because of writers getting pulled away from the good shows.

What happens now, is, somebody spends a year or two writing *Friends*—he's just been writing, he's never produced, but they call him a producer, because his agent has blackmailed the studio to call him a producer. There's a proliferation of credit. It's silly.

You've got a half-hour show with eight producers on it. Stupid. All they're doing is writing scripts, sitting in on script conferences, in these rooms with a bunch of other people, banging out these stories. The show's popular for a few years, and then these agents go out and sell the writer who's had two years experience on *Friends* or *Everybody Loves Raymond*, and they say, "My guy is tired of that, he needs more." And they make a huge development deal for him at Fox or something like that, but this guy is not anywhere ready to produce at that point. I wrote for years before I ever got a producer credit, and by the time I did I really was producing, I really knew how to produce. These guys don't know how to do it.

Why don't the production companies and the networks figure that out? It's not hard for them to find out that the guy has never really produced.

I don't think they want to know. Most of the network development people, the executives, do they really know what producing is? I don't think they really know, or care. And yes, you would think that they'd ask those questions, but they don't. My agent, who is a major agent for television—he is the head of ICM Television—says they're always promoting up these people with very little experience and that's the problem.

This group writing concept I just loathe. When we were doing the *Mary* show, of course, all the first ones were all Jim Brooks' and my image, and we wrote a lot of the scripts in the first year or two. We had a vision, and we knew our characters, what they do, what they wouldn't do. Now, it's not unusual for a situation comedy to have 12, 14 writers on staff. What kind of vision do you get from a group like that? You don't. You can't.

I had a very discouraging experience a couple of years ago. I was asked to consult on a show that had been on the air for three years but it was in trouble. It had started out sort of promisingly in its first year, and they sort of got in trouble. And I was asked to come in and help for about five weeks to help them break stories for an upcoming year.

I went in and was amazed at the way it was done, how sloppily the stories were prepared. There was this gang effort, with literally 10 or 12 people around the table, all pitching ideas that were being put into a computer by a writer's assistant. They were working on a story line, for example, and everybody was pitching, and it would take three or four days, and people would be walking in and out and getting lunch and food, and coming back in. I left at the end of one day to come back to find out that they had abandoned the story that they'd been working on all day for something else because they were having difficulty with this idea. And it was so sloppy, and people were talking about everything else other than what they should have been, they weren't really concentrating on the effort. People were talking about other shows.

The Writer's Guild Foundation, of which I am vice president, had three days of panels a few years back with all types of writers in the business, a lot executives, and directors, studio people, and network people. One panel was called "Throw Another Writer on the Fire," and it was about that mindset—that if we're not happy with the script and we can't articulate how we feel about it, let's just hire another writer and let that writer see if they can solve what we perceive to be the problem, even though *we* can't articulate the problem.

There is a lack of discipline and an abandonment of responsibility.

Yes.

Executive committees spread responsibilities, but you can't make artistic decisions by committee.

There is some security in numbers. *M*A*S*H* was a great show because Larry Gelbart had an image and knew what the show was and stayed with that show for years.

When you say that the talent pool is getting thin, there are, at the same time, a lot of people trying to get into the business.

I don't know the answer to that. It took me a very long time to break in. There is a certain amount of luck involved. I know a couple of good writers out there whose work I've read who haven't been able to crack it, who have contacted me for one reason or another—a couple of writers just out of the USC writing program, who I think have a real gift. I've tried to help them get an agent, and I haven't been able to do it. I don't know why. Without an agent you really can't get in.

Will the agent read their stuff on your recommendation?

Sometimes, but more often than not I am very disappointed to find out that all they do is give it to a junior agent at the agency. They're too busy, so they give it to somebody else to read, and the other person may not be that good. I think it's very tough to read comedy and get it, to understand it, on the page. I have never written jokes. My humor, for example, comes out of characters in situations. Those kinds of things are not readily apparent in a quick read.

There probably is a lot of undiscovered talent.

I know there are many good writers out there who are frustrated because they can't break in. And there are many untalented people who *are* working. And I don't get that. You'd think they'd get discovered, but they get covered up in these group efforts. As they say, if you're part of a writing team it's really hard to read somebody's script from a series and have any sense that they actually wrote it themselves because you know there have been other hands involved. So you just don't know.

CHAPTER 5

A Different Kind of Writer

Here are four writers who work in different formats: TV movies, drama, soap opera, and comedy.

Though she also produces, Arla Sorkin Manson is a writer and has a writer's sensibilities. Because she tells us a lot about the problems that television writers encounter, I decided to have her lead off this section. She knows how writers, producers, and executives interact and gives us a list of executives' pet peeves. Manson also provides insight into recent changes in the business that have altered the playing field for everyone concerned.

T. S. Cook started out telling scary campfire stories to his Boy Scout troop. Today, he specializes in suspense movies and has written for a number of dramatic series. He is also known for doing a lot of technical research on movies, which is one of the reasons he was asked to help write *The China Syndrome*. From Cook, we learn about the life of a freelance writer and how the business operates. Cook, like Manson, is especially good at listing the unwritten rules and demands that studios and networks place on the TV movie writer. Producers and directors often pressure writers to hurry up the story and reveal more of the story's premise earlier than the writer would like, and they often emphasize action over dialogue. As Cook notes in the interview,

> Directors do this all the time. They have a tendency to skip over the dialogue to get to the action. Because that's the way they're trained in TV. They're not really trained to work with actors. They're trained to do set-ups to get on to the next piece of action. There is no rehearsal time. You shoot the rehearsal. There's no taking people aside and working on the lines for a few days.

Both Cook and the next interviewee, Jean Rouverol, also discuss the industry's discrimination against older writers.

Rouverol's personal story is fascinating. There aren't many people in Hollywood who have written soap operas *and* been a victim of the

187

Arla Sorkin Manson

Hollywood blacklist. With her family, Rouverol fled the United States to Mexico so that she and her husband, writer Hugo Butler, could escape a government subpoena to name names to the House Un-American Activities Committee (HUAC). As a young woman, Rouverol was an actress and played opposite W. C. Fields and Gene Autry. She later became a writer of books, magazine articles, and soap operas. After talking about the blacklist, we focus on how soap operas are written following a scenario created by others. Her interview might be read in combination with Agnes Nixon's in Chapter 3.

Bob Ellison is a comedy "punch-up" writer. He's in demand when a comedy pilot is being written and the producers believe a handful of additional funny lines might make the difference between the network ordering episodes for production and the program dying a quick death with the pilot. The financial difference is nothing to sneeze at: a net loss for the production company versus as much as $500 million down the line if the pilot is turned into a series that is eventually sold into syndication. "In comedy," says Ellison, "every word has a weight to it. Every word has a value to it."

ARLA SORKIN MANSON

Arla Sorkin Manson and I first met in 1987, then again in 2001—shortly after September 11, to be exact. Ms. Manson helps us understand the changes that have taken place in television over the intervening years. (Those interested in such changes might read this interview alongside those of Lee Rich, Ray Solley, Bruce Sallan, and T. S. Cook.)

Ms. Manson is a writer, writer-producer, and an award-winning documentarian. She has written pilots for each of the three main networks. She has also served as a production executive or coproducer on Broadway. In 1995, she coproduced, with her husband David Manson, *Original Sins*, a TV movie for CBS. More recently, her production company, Sarabande, produced *The Wedding Dress* with Tyne Daly and Neil Patrick Harris.

Ms. Sorkin is upbeat, very straightforward, and especially savvy about the nature of interpersonal conflicts in the business. We learn what drives deals and what kinds of stories network executives won't even consider. She tells us how to make collaborative relationships work, about fostering creativity, especially in writers, and about the value of sticking to one's guns in television.

What I wanted to do as a child was be Brenda Starr. I wanted to be an investigative reporter because I watched *Superman* when I was younger. You know, Lois Lane. It all looked exciting.

I was in a transitional generation in the mid-1960s. I didn't know whether my future would be as a wife and mother or as a working woman. It wasn't articulated until the women's movement came along.

I went to Northwestern and studied English and creative writing. I took a journalism degree and got teaching credentials and tried teaching for six months and found it wasn't for me. I was 21 and I wound up going to a television station, Channel 4, in Chicago. I got into documentary filmmaking and did a number of award winning documentaries.

After I finished the documentaries, I wrote with a partner for five years. We had some very good deals together. We made, like many people, a bit of money but didn't get anything produced. I know of one team that made $600,000 in partnership writing screenplays, and had nothing produced. The object is to get it made. Financial success in this business is not the only measure. But it is one of the real ironies that you can live well and never have a screen credit.

After my partner and I broke up I wasn't sure I could get work as a screenwriter on my own, because in Hollywood when you are writing with a partner, the minute the partnership breaks up, they assume it was the other guy who had the talent.

Can we talk about network executives? Executives who make decisions to put a lot of money into a television show obviously don't want to make a mistake. Is it their tendency to find ways to say no?

I couldn't agree more. Also, some have such low opinions of themselves. They don't actually do anything but find other people. I'm not saying everyone, there are some very good people. But some have such little confidence in themselves, that they don't know a good thing when they see it.

I'll tell you a story. This happened with an executive at ABC. A producer came to pitch a story. The executive said that he liked it a lot. He asked, "Who would you get to write it?" The producer says, "Well, you'd need somebody like Oscar Wilde." The executive suggests that he try to get Wilde to write it. The producer had to decide whether to make the guy look stupid and lose the deal by saying, "By the way, he died over 80 years ago."

I also think that certain executives who make judgments are not concerned with the actual material. They are concerned with the trappings and packaging because marketing is such a strong orientation. Marketing is what they know how to do and while the script is really the most important thing, it becomes the weakest.

They also let marketing dictate casting decisions, even when that's been disproved over and over again in Hollywood. Somebody did a master's thesis on this idea of the bankability of stars. They found there was more bankability in a consistent writing/directing team than in a star. Every bankable, major mega box office star has had bad failures. Stars will "open" a movie, but they will not hold a piece of shit for too long.

I don't believe, however, that it's different from 400 years ago when people with money were making artistic determinations. They have always been removed from the process and don't always make the right choices.

There will always be a conflict between money and art. It is a more dramatic conflict in film and television because it is so expensive. The people that have the kind of money to make possible a film or TV show are removed from the process and that creates conflict.

I'm one of those people who has sat on both sides of the desk. I was a vice president and west coast head of a film company. It helps in the selling and it's a perspective that few writer's ever get. Writers need to really understand what a development person goes through.

What are some of the rules and maxims that you hear from network and studio executives about what elements a script should or should not have to be successful?

"Don't bring me a coal miner's story." "Anthology shows will never work." *The Millionaire* and *The Twilight Zone* were anthology shows.

Anthologies "won't work" because you don't have continuing characters and the public doesn't want to see too many strange faces on TV. PBS did a focus group study some years ago and many of the people they talked to said that they didn't like PBS dramas and Masterpiece Theater *because they didn't know the actors. So Richard Chamberlain ends up in one TV mini-series after another.*

Oh, I know. Chamberlain's popularity, his TV Q's, are real high. In fact, I'll tell you a funny story. When *The Simon Weisenthal Story* was in development at HBO we were sitting around one night and someone joked that the promotional campaign would say: "Richard Chamberlain *is* Simon Weisenthal." The joke, of course, was that Weisenthal is a little old bald man.

Another maxim is that "Only beginner writers use flashbacks. A person who uses flashbacks doesn't know how to write exposition." This is what they think. Also, "Don't use voice-over narration. It's boring, it won't move the film." It's immediately identified with weak exposition. It's thought to be artsy fartsy. And if it's artsy fartsy it's going to die commercially. It takes it out of the commercial mainstream. Voice over narration such as in Woody Allen's narration of *Radio Days*, would be unacceptable. Any kind of split structure is rejected. "They'll never be able to follow it."

Split structure means what?

The device that was used in *The French Lieutenant's Woman* and in *The Strawberry Statement*. There was a forward story and a backstory.

Most executives also want the story to cut in too soon, to the detriment of character development. They want to go straight to the plot. They want to start the movie with the climax of the movie. Writers are also often told that they start the movie too early, too far back in the character's history.

They want action immediately. But, if you start the movie at level 10, where are you going to go? In television, they feel they have to hit that peak in the first 25 minutes in order to hold the audience at the first commercial break. They have no commercials for 25 minutes in a movie for TV and then they start breaking it up. They want the viewer to be stuck in it.

Executives will also say, "Let's get to the chase." Here's a phrase— "Dumb it down." or "Can you make the characters dumb? It is too intelligent." I've been told this on my writing a couple of times. "I think it's a little smart for the room. You are addressing a crowd above the audience's intelligence level. The concepts are too intelligent. You're dealing with too much subtlety."

What you're telling me is that some executives see the screenplay largely in terms of plot and in the most skeletal kind of way.

There's a very good reason for that. Plot is easier to hold onto and understand for someone who is not a writer. Writer's really need to understand that so that they don't get so angry at the executives and learn how to work around it.

Writers want to talk in terms of theme. That's the main element missing in most movies. Without a theme, the real dramatic premise is lost. Unless you are faithful to the theme, you don't have a movie. You may have a string of events, but you don't have a story. *The Hustler*, which was the prequel to *The Color of Money*, was very thematic. It was about illusion and reality. It was about winning and losing. In contrast, what was *The Color of Money* about? It was not thematic.

Executives are not trained to be writers. They are thinking, "Where am I going to get the thing that's going to look like the other successful things that I've seen?" The trap with network executives is that they are comfortable with this little mechanical structure. Anything that goes against it becomes too uncomfortable. They are comfortable with seven acts and they try to mechanize a process which is really not mechanizable. The percentage of network executives that are dealing with movies who do that is fairly high. And the ones that know how not to do it leave being an executive very quickly. They get burned out and they want to go into independent production. They don't want to get stuck with the network. They don't want to do the sequel to *F Troop* just because it's a network business obligation.

In defense of the executives, the job is not doable. An executive's day starts at six in the morning when they read the script that they should have read over the weekend. Then they run out to breakfast. Then they get into the office and they start addressing the phone calls that they didn't return earlier. This is how they live everyday.

Then they may have two meetings, then more phone calls, then they toodle to lunch. Then they come back and have more phone calls until their afternoon meeting. Then they have more phone calls and another meeting. Then they have more phone calls, go meet for drinks, then they have dinner.

An executive's job is to be at parties to find out what's going on, to meet the new people who are coming into town, to be out there. Seven days a week, 50 hours a day. You never have a chance to rest and you cannot do all the work. You cannot do it physically. And then the corporate politics become impossible. You've got seven executives fighting each other for the best projects and backstabbing. They can work from morning to night, seven days a week and still not do the job.

You cannot see everything, know everyone, know every piece of new talent, read everything, and still deal with the projects you have in development. It is not humanly possible. They are the most overworked, put upon, loved and hated people in Hollywood. A lot of them really want to do good work but they get stuck with garbage. Their job is to make ice cream out of shit.

If they're really good and they really care about quality, they're going to get burned out and they'll want out and want the time to work on those projects that they care about and have passion about instead of having a full plate of stuff they don't want.

Could American commercial TV deliver higher quality and still get the same ratings?

H. L. Mencken said you can never go broke underestimating the taste of the American people. Still, I continue to believe that the public does want quality and would watch quality. You can continue to turn out crap and you'll make money on it. But I also believe that you won't make any less money if you would merely condition the audience to accept better material. I think the audience is conditioned from a very young age.

There've been good and successful things on TV: *Special Bulletin, Who Will Love My Children?, Something About Amelia, Adam.* A good many of the crummy programs that go on actually started out trying to be that good but they get broken down in the process.

You also have MTV which has largely affected the concept of what an integrated piece of work is, because it's nonintegrated work. It's an idea here, an idea there. The value of laboriously integrated work is gone and that comes from lack of exposure to reading. You have executives nowadays who have grown up on that stuff making artistic choices. Their thinking processes are different. What we have now is the first generation of TV baby TV executives. They're removed from any sense of family history, ties, continuity.

I'm still an optimist, though. There will still be periods of bounty where groups of good things come out. I think there will always be people working for quality and I think that there will always be a collaborative, huge unpredictable system that mitigates against that quality at times. But good stuff will break through if people are willing to fight for it.

There's another important thing. The old guys who ran the studios were immigrants who had a sense of family, and who understood the difficulties of making a living. A lot of them had been poor and experienced the difficulties of building themselves up into something. In contrast, many of the people making decisions these days came right out of some eastern school. Some of the executives are people who went from an upper middle class home into an upper middle class school into an upper middle class job. They remain children in that they are still consuming members of society. They are buyers, not sellers, and they have never gone through the struggle. They don't tap into that aspect of American life that builds intestinal fortitude. So they miss it when they see it in the script and they think it's indulgent on the part of the writer.

There is also so much miscommunication, so many bruised egos, and so little tolerance. In television, you are largely dealing with strangers at the outset. You are constantly with people you don't know very well. Clear communication falls apart and people lose sight of the common goal which is to make the thing good.

Eventually you find people you can work with. I've now got four or five very good producers and directors that I can work with. If I have a new idea, where will I go with that idea? Where I feel safe. Where I think someone knows my intrinsic worth so that what goes on is not about our personalities. It's about the work. With people you know you get rid of that entire area of paranoia and you can work on a more intimate level. It produces better work. It becomes positively collaborative because it comes out of trust and I think that it's very hard to do that when the executives shift all the time. The jobs are, as I said, burnout jobs.

Let's talk about editors for a moment.

They are the unsung heroes. Often they help a TV movie. They are in the middle of the director and the producer, who are often at odds. The editor is working and the producer walks in at night and says, "Change it this way" and the director walks in and says, "Change it another way." Editors get a lot of directors who didn't cover properly when shooting so they can't cut together property. Or it's a beginning director and he doesn't start the scene on an action. He doesn't have anybody in motion or he doesn't overlap from the previous shot. Or worse than that he starts from an awkward position and there's no way to cut it. The editor can change the momentum of the film greatly. The editor is the guy who puts the pace on, and many times it's the editor's ideas but the director gets credit for them.

Let's shift and talk about the writers.

Here's the problem with the writers. I think that a lot of writers like to see themselves as creative wiggos and it's a childish thing. They assume somehow that understanding the business aspects would impede their creativity. They say, "I don't do that." They refuse to understand that many of the executives they're dealing with really have no power at all. They *can't* say yes. They attribute more power to this person and then get furious with them when they can't deliver.

Some take no responsibility when they write under contract and feel no obligation to the person paying them. They often refuse to accept that. When they agree to write something, they don't understand that they took money in exchange for total creative control. They allowed someone into the process. If they wanted complete control over the script, they should have written it on spec. Executives would like writers to be more open.

When writers do write a spec script, they transact too fast. They don't realize how much power they have before they sell if somebody wants their script. They sell away their rights too quickly without understanding what they're doing. They don't ask the right questions. Does this producer have a reputation for buying up an original screenplay and sticking another writer on it? Does this producer have a reputation for screwing people?

A lot of writers go into a meeting with a producer and they can't even say who they'd like to see star in what they've written. They just think about the story. I think that when you're in a medium that's dependent on casting, you need to turn the cap a little and do a little of the other guy's work, or at least be able to talk their language. The writers limit themselves by saying, "Well, I just write. I'm just a downtrodden writer."

This idea of the poor persecuted writer is something I really detest. Is the writer in the project half for creativity and half for the money? Are you in the project purely for the money? Understand what you're doing when you're doing it. It will avoid a lot of problems. Also, understand the position the executive is in. Is this executive on the way out?

The project I am doing right now, I was supposed to start six weeks ago. I knew my executive on this project was going to get fired and I didn't want to pitch my story to him, have him pay me to go off and write, and know that he'd leave his job and I would be left with a lame duck script. So I stalled. My intention is to try to get it made and involve the new executive in the project. In order to do that I waited for the new executive to come in. This was a choice I made. It makes my job less profitable because I don't make any money by waiting. It's taken me years to understand all this.

If you're a writer and you hear something coming from an executive that you think is totally crocked, you don't say, "Well, that's a pile of junk." You can't be that way. They should simply say to them, "That's a possibility. Let me see if I can do that," or, "Well, that's a valid idea, but I'm not sure I can make that work," or, "I can try." And then go off and do what you want because 10 weeks later when you turn it in, they don't remember the material. They remember the confrontation but not the material. Now that's a simple political ploy, but it can get you a lot. It's a simple ego thing. You need to simply validate the other guy's position.

Nearly 15 years have passed since we first talked. How has the industry changed?

It's changed enormously. The vertical integration of companies means that one, large parent company holds many, many media outlets. The management has a style, and that style starts to filter into the different companies.

Producers—the sellers—have to pick carefully where they are going to try to sell a project because NBC is going to buy a very different kind of show from what CBS is going to buy.

Some of the syndication markets that were in place in the late 1980s have dried up. The relative proportion of comedy to drama has also changed enormously. Dramas are very expensive to produce, although NBC had a minor resurgence with *ER*. And that helped lead them to do *The West Wing*.

Could you explain how vertical integration has changed how you operate and the rest of the decision making process in television? These changes are also partly the result of the Communications Act of 1996.

Whereas before, 15 years ago, when I sold a show to an executive, that executive was the next person in line to the person who decided on the programming. That executive had an enormous influence on what went onto the schedule. *Now*, when you sell to an executive, although they talk to the decision-makers, the decision-makers have three more people in between. And the networks are starting to package in the way the movie studios did.

There's an old adage that "Stars don't make television, television makes stars." And I think that that still holds true because the nature of someone who's going to come in your living room every week is different from the nature of someone that you go to see in the theater, and that can drive an opening weekend for a film.

The networks are now starting to hinge their programming on promotable, packageable elements. You find Richard Dreyfuss, for example, this season in *The Education of Max Bickford* getting the primo slot on CBS, the one that follows *60 Minutes*, and that has a tried-and-true audience. And they programmed it with an older protagonist for what they know is an older, in-place audience. Also networks now make huge overall holding deals.

What do you mean by an overall holding deal?

They hold the talent. They promise the talent a series deal. Or they'll pay the talent $1 million to hold them. They'll guarantee the stars of their series certain movies. So when we make a movie now for television, we often are asked very strongly to put in someone who's a lead on one of their series. They lay off their commitment onto the independent producers who are supplying the network. And there aren't as many of them anymore because networks have also taken back the ownership of many of their programs. Before, the networks weren't allowed to own the majority of their programs. The studios owned them.

Can you lay out how you believe the financial-syndication ("fin-syn") rules changed the playing field?

There was anti-trust legislation that went into place in 1961 because the three networks were perceived to have 98 percent of the viewing audience. And at that time there were only three networks. So, in 1961, there was concern that heavy penetration to 98 percent of the homes in the country would be monopolistic and would threaten free speech. There was anti-trust legislation that said that the exhibitor (i.e., the network) could not own all of its programming while penetrating most of the homes in the country.

The idea was that the independents that supplied the programming would, in fact, own the negative, and would be free to distribute it to the rest of the world after it aired two times on the network. The network had purchased, in fact, two runs from Twentieth Century Fox, or from Universal, and under those rules, the network did not pay for the entire cost of the program. Then the independent studios could get these enormous amounts of money selling it into syndication to independent chains of networks, selling it into syndication not only in the United States but also overseas.

In some ways this was similar to the breakup of the old movie studio control of theaters.

Yes, it's not unlike the legislation that prevented the studios from owning the stars *and* also owning distribution. That legislation in the feature business separated distribution from production.

In some cities you can still find a theater called The Paramount or The Roxy or The RKO. At one time, those theaters were owned and operated by the very same company that was putting the material up on the screens in those theaters.

And in the late 1980s, you started seeing a proliferation of reality shows like *Unsolved Mysteries, Missing Persons, America's Most Wanted.* Because they were able to make those shows for exactly what the network gave them to run them and they didn't have to put large deficits in.

Then, all of a sudden *ER* hit and the networks and the studios together were willing to take the risk to do a little more expensive programming again. And there were quite a few dramas again. Now, networks like NBC insist that studios must partner with them on any series that they have on the air. They have an ownership position in everything they're airing. ABC buys almost all of its development from Touchstone Television. Only a portion of its development is purchased from other studios.

What I'm hearing you say is that even when they're buying outside their own shop to have something developed that, in the case of ABC, they're going really only to one shop.

They're going to many fewer shops.

Whereas 15 years ago ABC or NBC were getting material from five or six differ-ent studios.

> That's right. They are also keeping shows on their air that they otherwise would've canceled due to minimal ratings because they have an ownership position in them. They'll keep shows on the air now that normally would never have been kept on the air because they want to get enough episodes—you need at least 66 episodes to put something into syndication. To run them five days a week, they need enough episodes to be able to do that.

Can you provide an example of a show with only fair ratings that has survived longer due to these new arrangements?

> *Profiler.* I don't believe that that show would've stayed on the air. Or *Family Law.* Of course, you don't need as high a rating as you used to need, because nobody gets a 35 share anymore.
>
> Let me add one more thing that has really changed. Because of the new deals that are being cut, there are a great many more feature writers that come into television that don't do well because they can't write on a weekly basis. They can maybe write a script over a period of two years, but they can't really develop a compelling script in a week. Or they lack the narrative skills on a weekly basis to be able to generate that kind of project.

So they're making a deal with the network where they're getting a shot at writ-ing network television.

> They get huge deals.

It sounds as if you're also saying that the vertical integration that's occurred in combination with the fin-syn rules has made it so that even fewer players can break through and get something on air.

> Absolutely. And also, with *Millionaire* and *Survivor*, it eats into writing opportunities.

It sounds like you're also saying that vertical integration has resulted in . . .

> A lack of diversity in the product. And a proliferation of nonwriting show runners. And there are any number of writers who don't want to write with a nonwriting show runner but one who can manage the per-sonalities, get the material out on a weekly basis.

The term show runner is used synonymously with producer now, yes?

> Show runner is an executive producer.

Steven Bochco, then, is a show runner.

> Oh, yes. Very much so. David Kelley is the show runner on his shows.

You really have to know a lot about the business to do your work. It's very complicated.

> It is harder to advance now than it was then. It's harder to become a show runner. The networks used to rely, for every movie for television,

almost every single one, on outside suppliers. Two years ago NBC said, "We're not buying from any outside suppliers." And, look at the nature of the movies they're putting out now. Movies for television are just about dead. Now they're looking to do musicals and things with a built-in audience. Excuse the pun but it's a penetration problem. They can't find their audience anymore. Networks used to rely on a core, dependable spate of series television that would grab a viewer and keep them there all night.

But this has been changing ever since most everyone got remote controls.

And now I would add digital cable, I would add satellite cable, and I would definitely add TiVo. I think that you haven't heard the last of TiVo yet, because for me as a viewer, I can pick the shows I want, get 'em down, watch them, and not watch the commercials. I can watch an hour show in 45 minutes.

There are so many changes. The economics have changed, the marketplace has changed and then the law changed. And when you put all three of them together, you're facing a different selection process.

How have all these changes affected writers who don't get very involved directly in production?

Systematic rollback of prices. To the degree that they control the marketplace, they will not pay what they used to pay.

So, relatively speaking, the typical writer is making less?

Even the typical, very successful writer is making less. There are a handful that are still making the unbelievable amounts that nobody would believe on the planet. But even the experienced working writers who were on shows and might have gotten another overall deal from a studio or something, those people are out on the street. And there are more personal managers who are now producers of television. The manager of a star becomes a producer of a television show. That takes money out of the budget of the show. That takes money away from the writing pool.

What would you say to someone who thinks he or she has a flair for and likes the idea of writing for television—they're in New York or they're in the midwest— and they're coming out to Los Angeles and trying their hand, versus what you would have told them 15 years ago? Or would you tell them anything different?

I would still say the same thing, only I think I would say it to a greater degree. Don't be influenced by trying to imitate. Try to find a voice as a writer. Don't watch so much television that you forget to read what's really good writing because in the end, good television is driven by good writing. It really is.

More and more all we can sell is franchise shows, 'cause that's all they understand. Cop and medical are the most common.

But there's hope. During the Vietnam War and during times of great crisis, great drama has emerged. We were in a very complacent place until a few years ago and before September 11. I was to have pitched a certain kind of show to NBC. They called since September 11 and said, "You know, we're changing." The hope is that the themes will be bigger because bigger things are on people's mind. What it means to be human, what it means to have a family, what it means to be in love.

From great crisis comes great drama. Instead of just reporting the news, I think there will be people out there with more to say about the nature of existence. And I hope that it will come out even in comedy. You can deal with quite serious themes in a very humorous way. I don't mean that everything has to be dealt with as major melodrama. But I think that there should be more substantive things on people's minds.

Let's talk more about writers and how much they need to know about the business.

They don't have to get involved in the business side of it, but they *should* understand who's controlling things. How do you tell if you're getting good representation or bad? What's wrong with understanding how the people you sell to think? Writers should ask themselves, "Am I doing this project because I need a job?"

In my view, the people who fail commercially with something of quality abide. You should be sure that what you put down on the page is something you can stand by. Don't get railroaded too badly. This is why understanding these relationships *is* a part of your job. Making an executive your ally and not your adversary, and not looking at them as a bad parent but as someone on your team, is a very important lesson to learn. It's imperative that you learn ways to ameliorate their concerns while holding fast to your vision. And to find ways to elegantly meet a compromise that doesn't wholly compromise the intent of the piece because then you wind up with nothing.

Tell me about your recent TV movie, The Wedding Dress.

I think it's a good project. First of all, it is an optimistic show that was in development for six years. It took a year for the network executive to read it. We kept saying, "Give it back to us, we'd like to take it elsewhere." They kept saying, "No, no, we like it, we like it." This was someone else's writing, but I was the executive producer on it. We developed it from scratch with the writer on this.

So it's a Sarabande production?

This is a Sarabande production, but we developed it. I executive produced it. I was on location in Vancouver for two-and-one-half months. *The Wedding Dress* is optimistic. It talks about possibilities. It talks about a wedding dress that transcends race, age, economic status, racial types. It's light. It's not the deepest drama in the world, but it's optimistic.

I have written a pilot for every single network. I have been able to sell pilots. I've written a pilot every year for five years. And when you consider that ABC only buys 25 pilots in a season, and NBC only bought 20 last year, CBS buys more, that's an accomplishment in and of itself.

As you know, there are many people in TV who make very good money writing pilots but find that it can be heartbreaking after a while not to have them produced beyond the pilot.

Oh yeah, it'll kill ya'. Not to get on the air. You come up against disappointment, and you will be disappointed, because most of what you do will never see the light of day.

People hear about the Spielbergs and that, but you don't hear about what happens to most folks. The reason I keep working, even though a lot of times I haven't been as lucky as other people, is that I've had good work to show. And I continually worked whenever I've wanted to work and I've continually sold projects because people like my work. Whether or not they get made. Even if it hasn't gotten made, you can make a feature out of it, you can recombine the script, you can redo the characters in another form. Do you know how many years David Chase toiled in the field before he got *The Sopranos* on the air?

It always comes down to, do I quit or do I keep going? And if I keep going, I don't worry about what happens.

You're saying you've got to enjoy the work enough because even if the money is quite frequently rewarding, that you have to be, at heart, a writer.

I think that whenever I hear somebody say they want to be a famous so and so, I say what I used to say to my child and what I would still say to any of them: Do you want to *be* or do you want to *do*? If you want to *do*, you'll be in a lot better shape. If you want to *be*, that can be very illusive.

Do what you love to do. And the money will follow somehow, some way.

And if there isn't enough money, at least you're happy with what you're doing.

Honor the work that you do. Make sure you're proud of what you're working on. I know a guy who's finally an A-list director in Hollywood. He's been in Hollywood for 30 years. He was a producer first. He came to Hollywood intending to direct. He finally got a huge, big box office movie, although the things he had done before had never really been very successful.

When he came to Hollywood, he wanted a certain kind of job to land for himself. He was 24 years old, and he worked for nine months neutering cats in an animal hospital until he landed the *right* job.

So, I would say, you know, take a look at that. That's a good example. And it's been a process over many years, for him to get to where he is. But, the point is, before he ever entered, he was very careful. Even though he was neutering cats, he held out for what felt right. Don't just settle because you really need the dough. Because if you're smart enough to write, you're smart enough to do something that will pay the rent.

T. S. Cook

Your production company, Sarabande—where does the word come from?

Sarabande was a naughty dance in England in the sixteenth century. It was something that was not supposed to be performed because it had suggestive connotations. And eventually it became a courtly dance and got accepted. And the most famous Sarabande was the theme for the Kubrick movie *Barry Lyndon.*

It's a dance in the rhythm of a Sarabande. Just like there are waltzes and there are mazurkas . . . the piece of music is a Sarabande . . . it's by Hayden.

Your husband, David Manson, produced Nothing Sacred. *In some funny way was* Nothing Sacred *a Sarabande?*

A little bit. It's something that amused us.

And it's sort of naughty.

Something bad became something accepted.

T. S. COOK

T. S. (Tom) Cook started off in television trying to write an episode of *Gunsmoke.* He slaved over the script for months, then submitted it the same day the program was cancelled after a 25-year run. But it helped him get an agent.

His first television writing credit was for an episode for *Baretta.* He then went on to *Project U.F.O., The Paper Chase,* and *Airwolf.* Since then he has worked almost exclusively in "long form," largely television movies, but his best known writing credit is for *The China Syndrome,* which won the Writer's Guild Award for best screenplay adaptation. He specializes in suspense, adventure, and crime stories such as *The Tuskegee Airmen, Red Flag—The Ultimate Game, NightBreaker, Out of the Darkness,* and *Scared Straight—Another Story,* all of which have won awards. Other titles include *Forgotten Evil, Texas Justice,* and *High Desert Kill.*

We met first in the late 1980s at the Sunset-Gower studios, where Cook was renting writing space, and caught up once again in the late 1990s. Cook is a large, burly man, a colorful storyteller with a no-nonsense attitude and a keen sense of what matters most in writing and in television. In the interview we learn of the ups and downs of freelance television writing as well as some of the industry's rules for long-form television writing—such as the memorable, "Movies on water lose money." We also discuss how the business has changed over the last decade and the problem of age discrimination in Hollywood.

☆ ☆ ☆

When did you first start telling stories?

When I was a young boy we sat around a campfire in Boy Scouts telling ghost stories. I had a good memory and I used to read these things like *True Weird Mysteries* and then I'd recite them around the campfire.

I've always admired storytellers. In so-called primitive cultures, the storyteller, the person that remembered the stories, is revered more so than anyone in the tribe. They would rather lose their hunters than their storytellers.

I got a B.A. in English from Denison University in Ohio. Then I worked in Chicago editing course material for LaSalle Extension University. Maybe you've seen our matchbooks—careers in air conditioning and refrigeration. That was a way of making some money. They weren't about to hire an English major from Denison to edit novels. Then I got accepted to the writer's workshop at Iowa and went there for two years. I met my wife there. She's a novelist. A mystery writer.

My writing heroes are not William Goldman or George Roy Hill or any of the standard show business heroes. I consider them to be interesting talents, but the real major talents that I admire are William Styron, John Updike, Fitzgerald.

Anyway, I got my master's at Iowa with a finished novel but I found myself delivering pizzas for a living and decided that if I really wanted to have a family and be a mensch that I should go someplace that I could actually make a living telling stories.

I came out here and spent a couple of years pounding around doing odd jobs, living off whatever I could get. Odd jobs, editing, freelancing and so forth. I worked for a while in the defense industry as a technical editor, designing and writing up manuals to be translated into Farsi so the Shah and his boys could get their planes started. All of those books are probably being used as toilet paper in contemporary Iran. I also did some editorial work for the Center for the Study of Democratic Institutions in Santa Barbara. And I spent a lot of time watching TV, watching the current shows, watching who the characters were and how the stories developed.

Where did you get your first break?

Universal. *Baretta.* I had acquired an agent. He'd read some of my stuff and thought that it could sell. I'd written an episode for *Gunsmoke.* A very good one, I thought, about an early form of opium addiction. Drug addiction in the Old West. I spent several months crafting this piece of work down to the point where it just shone. The day I sent it in to the producer was the day they canceled *Gunsmoke*—after 25 years. Writing for an existing show is one way to get started, if you have the discipline to learn the technique.

Then I wrote a script for *Baretta* and had better timing. It was on his desk the day the series got picked up for another nine episodes.

What was a writer paid then for a first sale?

In those days it was about 10K.

You must have felt pretty good.

Yeah, because I was working for this war contractor, I'll call him, and was making about 20K a year doing that. This was 50 percent of my salary. I took my wife out to a real nice dinner and bought, what was for me at that time, a great bottle of champagne. Popped the cork to the ceiling and had a great time. But I had to go to work the next day. I did a couple more episodes of *Baretta* in 1975.

My agent then got me an interview to do a rewrite on *China Syndrome*. I was hired to do that job.

Isn't that unusual? All you'd done was Baretta *to that point.*

I had written spec scripts for movies of the week and a feature. One of the reasons I was hired is because it was an enormously complicated technical movie dealing with nuclear energy and had to be absolutely researched down to the nuts and bolts. Since I was working with a technical editor, I think that background helped.

You seem to have a penchant for research.

Things that I know about intimately are very limited, so if I'm gonna write convincingly about other things, I have to do research. I really disapprove of writers who think they can walk into a project, read a couple of articles out of *People* magazine, and fake the rest of it. It shows.

There are different breeds of TV and movie writers. Some have a literary background, they've actually studied writing. The other breed that has come along are film school writers. These people also don't have a literary background. They have a film background. The school of human behavior and psychology in film is thin compared to what's available in literature.

Is television a business before it's an art form?

It certainly is. That is the essential frustration. But I would hope that writers as a class would want to write at the top of their form.

If you can imitate something and do it well, even do it poorly, you feed into the audience's sense of comfort and sense of familiarity. There are people who are willing to do that but it doesn't push the envelope at all. It's a chicken or egg situation. Which should improve first, the taste of the audience or the product? Stories develop along the same franchises as ever.

What do you mean by a franchise?

Private eye shows, medical shows, and comedies. A show is a franchise when the main character has a reason or license to get involved in other people's lives every week. Consequently you have *The Fugitive*. Actually, *The Fugitive* was an offbeat franchise. It's not that he got involved in others lives every week, it's that they got involved with him. If you're going to do a weekly TV show which is 22 episodes a year, in order to be able to tell that many stories, you have to have a franchise.

The problem is that the audience has become comfortable with certain franchises. I can name them on one hand: cop, medical, newspaper, hospitals, and PI. Those are the franchises that the audience is comfortable with, that they know. So those are the franchises they get. There is not a whole lot of energy at the networks at the development level to even listen to new concepts to new franchises. If you pitch something new, the reaction is, "Gee, that's *strange*, that's *unusual*." My sense is that it's not strange or unusual, it's fresh and original.

I developed a concept for a series. A guy living in the middle of San Francisco Bay. He lives on an island at the base of the Bay Bridge. The premise is that a sea chest is discovered on the island that says that Sir Francis Drake deeded the island to his ancestors long ago. So he says to the city, you either take this bridge off my island or I'm going to take you to court. It eventually evolves that he becomes an independent principality in the middle of San Francisco Bay. It's a *new* franchise. I have a big list of things that can possibly happen. He can trade with independent nations as an independent person. He can be a neutral ground for warring drug factions and mafia factions. He can do all kinds of things ad hoc that the city cannot do.

There's something you really haven't seen before. I'm not saying that it would make a hit series; I think it could do well if written with the right, sly approach, very clever plot lines, good surrounding characters. The reaction from the network—"Gee, that's unusual."

A phone call came in earlier, someone telling you about something he doesn't like that you wrote. What was going on?

When you do a TV movie, which is what this is, there are several factors involved. You write the script and during that period, called the development phase, only the writer gets paid. The producers don't get paid during development. If you're a small independent producer, you don't make money unless you get something going. Which is why it's hard to be a small independent.

I turned in a first draft on this project. The producer and I saw eye to eye but it was my job to answer some of the director's questions. I did a second draft which was intended to answer their questions without ruining the simple fabric of the main story, which is the story the network bought. Now he's telling me the studio loves it, that they have every confidence in it and they're going to send it in to the network but I made a few errors that, although small, really stand out conceptually. These were things that we all agreed on. So nothing he said really upset me.

This particular guy is an old pro so I have great respect for him. But sometimes you get people coming out of film school and in some cases business school because of contacts with friends or a certain polish, going to the right parties or whatever. They manage to get into development and work their way up the ladder. There are good ones and bad ones.

That's what writers always talk about when we get together because essentially, if you go into a room with a writer or director and you're one of these development people, you are in an inferior position even though you are the boss. Essentially, you're the only person with no marketable skills. What *are* their skills? Their skills are being able to read, which some of them can do, and being able to try to figure out what their boss wants. The writer and director have skills. The producer is an entrepreneur and businessman. He has skills. So it creates, in a lot of cases, an inferiority complex which manifests itself in nastiness. They do have respect for how hard a writer's life is. And a lot of them know that what we get paid for is not putting words on paper, but for taking abuse.

It's a hard job physically to be in the development position, so they go off into independent production and they leave the network with a one-picture commitment: "We will make one of your pictures that you bring to us in the next year." Now, sometimes these people go away and are never heard from again because they don't have the skills. So they start bringing stories to their replacements and suddenly, and I would love to be a fly on the wall in these meetings, they begin to see what it is that other people were having to deal with from them.

Are there unwritten rules that you can't violate in television writing?

You may not do stories for movies of the week that deal with show business or TV. You can make a miniseries about the movie industry. In the long form, if you get Valerie Bertinelli or somebody like that and it was written by Judith Krantz, then it's OK. Long series are all based on books that are presold and have a presold audience.

There is also a tendency among executives at all the networks to want to see the whole premise in the first act. They make it impossible to follow a rational, satisfying plot line.

It's also supposed to be the kiss of death to do a show in which there is a musical background to the story. Like, "Simon & Simon befriend a rock singer and help her through a crisis." This is a particularly prevalent attitude at Universal, where they don't like to see shows where a cast member is also a singer and will do a musical number. They don't think that fits in well with an action show.

Another is, "Movies on water lose money." Because when you're under the water, it's all the same color. And the networks want colors to change and move around a lot. Blue gets boring after awhile. TV is also a moral medium, so in a show in which a psychopathic killer is shown, it is not permissible to deal with the character in any sympathetic way.

Like the comic book code. Can a criminal get away with a crime?

Not very often. They can occasionally. If you're talking about going in to pitch something, I don't think anyone would go in and say this is a story about a criminal who gets away with it. That would be instantly rejected.

Movies of the week are written in seven acts. Does the action have to rise after every commercial break?

There has to be something that leads you out of the story. Something emotional. It gets to be second nature.

Sometimes it helps in terms of structure. Makes it easier. You do have to find certain kinds of "act-outs." There's one in this thing I'm working on now which is a downer act-out. The wife is having problems with the husband. She says, "I'm no wife to you at all. I wish I could help you more but I can't." It's very sad. It's Christmas day and it fades out. The executive said, "What a downer. There's no way we can do this." I said, "You're wrong. It's an emotional highpoint for these characters. They're admitting things to themselves. If you're talking about a male/female audience, the women will turn right back into it."

Executives prefer, "FREEZE!" In a cop show they want the guns pointing. That's the classic act-out.

Do you ever hear anything about reducing talking heads, or "you've got a piece of dialogue that is too long?"

Yes, they say that. "This goes on for a long time." "We have to cut this up." "Can we open it up?" "Put this someplace else." "Put this scene in that." They're always concerned that it seems too long and the people will be bored with what's going on. "There's too much dialogue." Directors do this all the time. They have a tendency to skip over the dialogue to get to the action. Because that's the way they're trained in TV. They're not really trained to work with actors. They're trained to do setups to get on to the next piece of action. There is no rehearsal time. You shoot the rehearsal. There's no taking people aside and working on the lines for a few days.

What are some of your rules?

There are things that I will not do. I will not write shows that are an excuse to show people getting blown away. I don't like shows that glorify handguns. Sex is fine. But I want to do sex in a realistic way, not a cutesy-poo, sheets and shoulders thing. I don't like shows that show the sex act or the violent act without showing the consequences. I tell myself, "Life's too short to get involved with things that don't have a point that I agree with." So if it doesn't have a point, if it's just another show about something or other, I won't do it.

What do you and your writer friends talk about when you get together?

Problems working with directors. Problems with getting the network to read the material in any timely fashion. Sometimes it takes longer for them to read it than it takes for us to write it.

What percentage of the movies that you have written have been produced?

Sixty to seventy percent for movies of the week. Features is way down.

There's a widely held notion that the pace of the medium has sped up.

Yes, the public is beginning to think in terms of little sound bites. The TV age has finally had an impact on people's psychology. We think

15 minutes is about the most anyone can concentrate on a subject these days.

How often do you hear that kind of thing in the industry?

All over the place. But hearing people talk about it and hearing concern are two different things. A lot of people think it's OK and don't care about it. I think it's not to be desired and could be disastrous. I worked with a director recently. I gave him a script and I don't think he read it. After I had written the script for the next story meeting, he wanted me to give him an outline of what was in it.

I deal in three basic arenas as a writer: series TV, movies of the week, and features. And you see a wide range of what directors do. In series they come in and keep the actors from bumping into each other. Movies of the week, they come in, assess the script, they might even rehearse with the actors a little and ask for a few things that will help them shoot it. They're an important part of the package, but it's basically the producer who's in charge with the TV project. In features, directors are king, the director is your God, directors can do anything they want. In features the director can change a line, recast a part, can do virtually anything he or she wants to do and writers are treated like second class citizens. Perhaps even barred from the production. Older writers are not being hired and it's ironic because writers get better as they get older.

How do you get new projects to work on?

You develop relationships with executives who work their way up the line and when people bring them projects and they say, "It's a good idea, let's find a good writer," the producer says, "Who's a good writer?" and they say, "Call Tom Cook and see if he's available." One thing leads to another.

When we met 12 years ago, you made the statement that television is a business before it's an art form. Has that changed at all in the last decade?

It has become even more true in recent years. Television was always a business. Don't get me wrong. But there was in earlier years, perhaps as short as 5 to 8 years ago, a sense that at least at the networks, that they had a public responsibility. That they would do shows that perhaps weren't always ratings makers. Because there was a desire to discuss this issue or to do this piece of drama. It is really now a bottom-line business much more across the board. It's now being driven far more by ratings. Competition for ratings points has become ferocious. And from a writer's marketing point of view, when you come up with an idea, you better know the one place where it's going to go.

How have ABC, NBC, and CBS, the big three, changed in terms of what they might buy from a writer like you?

They're really specialized now. There are two kinds of movies that CBS does right now. There's their Sunday movie, which follows *Touched by an Angel,* which is a big stars, big production, classy, Hallmark sort of movie. Then on Tuesday night, it's a basic thriller—woman in jeopardy, stalker, whatever.

Characterize NBC and ABC.

NBC does very few two-hours. When they do, they are primarily thrillers. They do a lot of multi-part things. ABC is only doing seven movies this year, when they would have done 20 or so in the past. And most of them, not all of those, are going through Disney. And they're not really after a broad market at all, they're after the demographic niche.

They don't consider themselves to be the full-service, broad service, broadcasting entities that they did 10 years ago?

No. They are not the big tents that they used to be.

So even with more buyers, from the writer's point of view, it sounds as if it is a tougher environment?

I think that it is tougher. And when they're making half the number of movies at the networks that they used to, that makes it hard to get a job.

To play the devil's advocate, a lot of people would say, "There are so many more opportunities, there are so many more channels, there's so much more stuff getting produced, whether it's episodic or not, that just the pure number of hours of fictional or other kinds of entertainment has increased." But that doesn't speak to your specific interests and needs in terms of the writing that you do.

This is true. There are more outlets, and I try to market to all of them. I've worked for every cable outlet except for Showtime. HBO, TNT, TBS.

That's tough on you because you're always dealing with different people and slightly different systems.

Well, I don't mind that so much, but these are all specialist places. So, there is a USA kind of movie. There is a Showtime kind of movie, and you have to write to that format. And Showtime and HBO are trying desperately to make themselves look different from the networks. Their idea is that we make little movies here. We don't make TV movies. So, if you're a guy like me who's 50 something years old and has a string of TV movie network credits as long as his arm, you're suspect when you walk in. So there's a kind of discrimination—both age and career discrimination—which is hard to overcome, but I have.

From the industry's point of view, the audience is getting more good entertainment, more material, diversity, lots of places to go. The audience now has 60 to 70 channels, 24 hours a day. How would you respond to that?

That's true, but then you know, Bruce Springsteen wrote a song. "Fifty-seven channels and nothing on." And a lot of people spend their lives flipping through channels, looking for something to grab their interest.

There's a real dissatisfaction with the television wasteland that's out there. It's been called a wasteland before, but it truly is now.

Why is there more niche marketing in television today?

They're all after the same demographic. They're all after the same audience. The 18 to 35-year-olds, who they believe spend every last dollar in this country.

Since the networks can now own their own negatives, there's much more money in having a series being successful than a TV movie of the week. We're talking billions of dollars of difference. Is that what's motivating this change?

Part of it, yeah.

Revisiting the fin-syn rule, was it a good thing to let the networks start owning more of their own product?

Yes and no. It did move out of the business a lot of really talented, independent producers. Having the networks own all of their own properties, and developing everything without the serious input of that other producer's taste and voice, I think tends to make it a little less diverse.

On the other hand, it's good for writers because the method of doing business used to be that writers could not go in to the networks directly and pitch stories, they had to have a producer attached. And the producer was the one who set up the meetings, and the producer was the one who presented the story and was attached as the owner. Now, the networks don't want writers to come in with producers. It complicates the issue. So now, they are inviting writers to come in and pitch to them directly. If they like it, they buy it and we're in business. It's good and bad.

Before, how did the compensation work for someone writing television movies of the week?

In the earlier days, it used to be that you were paid on commencement, you were paid when you turned in the story, you were paid when you turned in the first draft, and then you were paid when you did one of two revisions.

This is probably through most of the 1980s?

Up to the mid- to late 1980s. After the '88 strike, it began to change. For one thing, it suddenly became two polishes and a revision, instead of one polish and a revision. So, there was an extra step worked in there.

You said the competition was ferocious. I don't know if you would have used that word 12 years ago, but other people did. But some people make it sound like it was a walk in the park in the late 1980s relative to now.

If someone who was writing dramatic episodes, like *Simon & Simon* type of stuff, if they were saying 12, 10, 8 years ago, "It's ferocious," they would have been right. Because later, the episodic arena underwent a "consolidation."

Are you saying that because of the power of certain so-called auteurs like a David Kelley or a Bochco, who probably are pretty damned good to their staffs and writers and producers, that that's consolidated things somewhat, the writer is better protected?

To a lucky few who are working, yes. But there is, for example, in the Writer's Guild, a committee called the Freelance Writer's Committee. It has been struggling for the last 10 years to try and increase the number of freelance assignments in dramatic programs and sitcoms. It used to be that people could come in and write an episode of a sitcom—now this was admittedly 20 years ago. Ten years ago, when I was doing episodic, you could come in and write an episode of *Baretta*, write an episode of *Simon & Simon*, come in from the outside, watch the show, listen, come in to pitch a story idea and that would get you the assignment. But the nature of television was changed by Bochco and others. They have a more stable staff now.

So we've had an evolution in series work, in dramatic hour series work from lots of freelancers and a small staff looking over them to a larger staff of writers who write all the episodes—that's what Bochco did about 10 years ago. Now it's evolved again to where you have one show runner, Kelley or Sorkin, writing everything. It's a remarkable feat that they do it. And I think that Kelley does a reasonably good job, but those very people who were once the insiders in the Bochco era, the 10 lucky people who were on staff at the show, are now complaining that they don't get the chance to write anything because one guy is writing it.

They're still getting paid though?

Well, they're getting paid to some degree, but they're not being writers. They're there to come up with ideas to feed ideas. This is the way I understand that Sorkin works—he wants people to come up with bits and ideas and characters.

Well, that makes sense. Pat Caddell, Dee Dee Myers, and Larry O'Brien who work on The West Wing *were not writers but they all worked at close range in the White House for years. They might not be writing full stories or dialogue but Sorkin can, and so they feed him with these interesting things that happened, characters, situations, and little details.*

The primary question that a lot of us ask ourselves these days is whether what happened to the freelance writer in episodic over the last 10 years is going to happen to the freelance writer in long-form.

So, on the one hand, people say, "No, it's cyclical. The pendulum will swing back and long-form will once again be one of the triad, it will be respected again, you'll be able to do good work on television." The pessimists say, "We're going the way of the dinosaurs."

I would tend to be pessimistic, too. What's going to change the economics of it? If you look at a successful episodic program that sells into syndication for $200 million, and the networks can now own a piece of that, why are they gonna get all hot for TV movies of the week unless they can find a way to syndicate that? Tell me more about the problem of age discrimination against writers.

It's difficult to talk about because it's all in specifics. No one admits to age discrimination. At one point, the guild thought it had caught an executive, because a feature executive at one of the studios was quoted in a big meeting as saying, "Don't bring me any of these gray beards in here." There was talk of the guild taking some kind of legal action. If he had said black people or Filipinos, he would be on trial right now.

In the movie *Bowfinger*, Steve Martin plays a producer. And at one point in the film, someone on the phone asks him how old he is, and he says, "Well, I could be 39, or 42. I could be 45, but I'm not 50." The line is, "They smell 50 in this town"—which is a great line. And that's actually to some degree true. The irony of it is that probably as writers, you're really hitting your stride when you're 50.

Were they as concerned 12 years ago about a writer's age?

Yes.

So that hasn't changed.

It has changed in one degree. In one big, important way. I don't think that 12 or 15 years ago that the demographics were as important to the broadcasters as were the raw ratings, and this leads to people thinking that you need someone young to write for a younger demographic.

Thankfully, writers are the only people who can solve their age problem—unlike actresses who have a really tough time. We can write our way out of the problem. If you write a very hip, young story, they can't deny the fact that you've got the chops to do it.

If you're a writer and you want to make money in television, where would you start your career today?

I wouldn't say that long-form television is the place to start your career these days. I wouldn't go into television.

Where would you go?

I'd write features, low-budget features.

Jean Rouveral holding her book, Refugees from Hollywood.

JEAN ROUVEROL

Jean Rouverol is among the most interesting people in Hollywood: a television soap opera writer hounded out of the country by the Hollywood blacklist. Rouverol tells a harrowing story of how in 1951, she and her family, along with Dalton Trumbo's family, fled the United States to Mexico to keep one step ahead of a subpoena that would have forced her and her husband, Hugo Butler, to testify or go to jail. Trumbo was himself afraid of having to return to prison. The Butlers stayed in Mexico for 10 years.

Ironically, one would be hard-pressed to find an American family that has produced more wholesome, mainstream American entertainment. During the blacklist, Ms. Rouverol wrote *Autumn Leaves* with her husband, both using pseudonyms. Hugo Butler also wrote *The Adventures of Robinson Crusoe* using the pseudonym Philip Ansell Roll, cowriting with Luis Buñuel. Before the blacklist, he wrote *Lassie Come Home, The Adventures of Huckleberry Finn,* and *A Christmas Carol.* Years later, their son, Michael Butler, wrote the screenplays for *Air Force One* and Clint Eastwood's *Pale Rider.* Her mother wrote the play that served as the basis for the Andy Hardy series with Mickey Rooney. Her father-in-law, Frank Butler, received an Oscar for writing *Going My Way* and wrote some of the "Road" pictures for Bob Hope and Bing Crosby.

Rouverol, now 87, started as an actress in 1933, and once played opposite W. C. Fields. She reveals that Fields carried a thesaurus with him to hone his lines and that he *did* hate children. (Some of her credits from that period spelled her name Rouveral.)

Rouverol stopped acting and began writing movies, books, magazine articles, and beginning in 1969, soap operas. In the interview, we learn how soap operas have changed, how they are structured, and how they are written. Rouverol's interview nicely compliments Agnes Nixon's in The Pioneers Chapter 3.

Rouverol is active in writer's issues with the Writer's Guild of America, continuing her penchant for social action. She says about entertainment products, "When people say there's free enterprise and there's no censorship in the United States, the fact is that market forces effectively govern everything that is produced." Rouverol also reports, as do others, that older writers are often discriminated against. And she takes a solid writers's swipe at auteur theory.

Jean Rouverol has lived an extraordinary life. Her memoir, *Refugees from Hollywood: A Journal of the Blacklist Years,* was published in 2000.

My mother was a playwright and wrote the play that was the basis for the Andy Hardy series. She was also a play broker. She would bring plays home, and I would read them as a child. During idle times, I was putting on extemporaneous plays.

At 17, I got a film contract as an actress. It was 1933. I was terribly young for my age. I had a small nervous breakdown and my mother pulled me out of the cast. It was for the lead in *Eight Girls and a Boat* at Paramount. Then I played the ingenue lead as W. C. Fields' daughter in *It's a Gift*, and a schizophrenic in *Private Worlds*. I played little parts in big pictures and big parts in little pictures. I was the first girl Gene Autry ever kissed in his westerns. I had a number of leads in westerns.

Your son, Michael Butler, has written a number of westerns, including Pale Rider *for Clint Eastwood.*

Michael is the third generation of writers. Michael's grandfather was Frank Butler, who wrote most of the "Road" pictures. He got an Academy Award for *Going My Way* and was briefly the head of Paramount.

What was your first writing job?

I got my junior writer's job with Paramount in 1940, by which time I was pregnant with Michael. I also sold a string of novellas to *McCall's.*

My husband, Hugo, was at Metro. He had already graduated from the junior writing department. I wrote several movies, none of them big.

W. C. Fields, Kathleen Howard, Jean Rouverol, and Julian Madison (l–r) from the 1934 movie, It's a Gift.

So Young, So Bad was a movie about delinquent girls. Harold Hecht took our names off of a film called *The First Year*. Frank Capra directed it. I wrote a lot under the table, down in Mexico while we were blacklisted.

Why were you blacklisted?

For our politics. There were friendly witnesses who cooperated with the committee [HUAC]. They had the same politics as we did, but they got off the hook by naming everyone they ever met at a meeting.

How many people were blacklisted?

Something like 250. Because the studios were sued constantly by people who had suffered from the blacklist, they insisted that there was no list but what they did was go by the names in *Red Channels*, the names that

As an ingénue, opposite James Ellison, second in the Hopalong Cassidy *series, 1935.*

had been mentioned before HUAC, the House Un-American Activities Committee.

All our best friends went to jail—Dalton Trumbo and Ring Lardner for contempt of Congress. They wouldn't answer questions. They were sentenced for a year and got out with a month off for good behavior.

Were you and your husband ever asked to testify?

They would have liked us to. My husband was named by a lot of people. I was only named by one.

I imagine that some readers may not know how acceptable it was to be interested in Communist politics, in the 1930s. It was fashionable in some circles.

It was. And the best and the brightest got themselves involved. It was partly a matter of showing that you weren't as frivolous as the rest of Hollywood. You were trying to better the world. It was like working in the nuclear freeze movement now, except that we knew that there could be repercussions.

Hugo and I decided to go to Mexico. If we hadn't, we would have been served with subpoenas to testify. If we had testified, we would have been forced to name names. You cannot refuse under the Fifth Amendment.

We had been on the lam in California, moving from house to house, for months. We were all afraid. Under the McCarren Act, the government had the right to intern "potential spies or savages."

So we moved to Ensenada. We loved it. I wouldn't change a moment of it. We felt like some curious kind of pioneer. And we were periodically terrified.

Hugo went down first. We had to stop moving around, especially because the kids were in school. Mike was 10, his sister was 8½ and we didn't want to louse up their school year. Now how middle-class can you get?

What are your politics now?

I am a pretty good New Dealer. From 1956 on it was very hard to be a Communist because Russia was doing things that we did not like at all— the invasion of Hungary and Czechoslovakia. We voted for the Democrats. Voting Communist would have seemed like a wasted vote.

We drove down to Mexico with the Trumbo family in November of 1951 in three cars and a trailer. And their dog and our cat and their three children and our four children. We made a long hegira because Dalton Trumbo didn't want to go back to jail. He did not like it. We got to Mexico in December of '51, and we were there for just about 10 years.

We began to do a little writing under the table. Bob Aldrich had always been a friend of ours. He wanted a cheap screenplay. This was '54 maybe. He had read one of my slick stories, a novella in *McCall's*.

So I did the screenplay for him. Hugo quarterbacked me. It was released with the name of a friend of ours for whom we gave a quarter of our earnings. That came out as *Autumn Leaves* with Joan Crawford and Cliff Robertson.

In 1960 we went to Italy. I collaborated with my father on *The Miracle*. Hugo had a job with Aldrich on *Sodom and Gomorrah*. While in Mexico, Hugo wrote *Robinson Crusoe* with William Wellman. We put the kids in an English school in Rome. I became an Anglophile. They were so bloody broad minded compared to the Americans at that moment in history. They hated friendly witnesses because finking and tattling in England are among the worst things that a person can do.

When did you start writing soap operas?

I wrote several books first—a gothic called *Storm Wind Rising* and two young adult biographies on Pancho Villa and Benito Juarez. Actually, I wrote books every time I lost a soap job.

I got my first soap job in about 1969 and that was on something called *Bright Promise* with Dana Andrews. I got that job from a guy that I had been in college with. He called and said that he had several headwriters as clients and he thought that soap writing was right up my alley because of my slick writing experience. Then I got a job in the early '70s on *Search For Tomorrow*, which is the oldest soap on the air.

In those days the headwriter wrote the outlines for each day's action. An outline could be anything from just a couple of pages to, nowadays, they go to almost 30 pages for one program. Ordinarily they are shorter than that, 15 to 20 pages.

Sounds like an awful long outline for a half hour or hour of programming. Wouldn't the script itself run a page per minute, 60 pages for an hour?

They run about 80 pages because they want to be able to cut.

Do the networks see scripts ahead of time?

There is so little time to write, to correct, and to have it go through all the offices of the network that have to approve it and to get it to the actors in time for them to learn it. They are supposed to have it a week before but they don't necessarily.

They shoot over the space of one day, never more. Sometimes half-hour shows will shoot over a half of a day.

There is a sort of musical chairs with headwriters. If your headwriter likes you, you will stay with him or her as long as they're on that show. When he leaves, you generally leave. I was never a headwriter on a show. I was an associate writer.

Then I went to work on *Guiding Light* and I was there for four years. Then we all moved over to *As the World Turns*, for two and a half years. Three of the shows that I had worked on were Procter & Gamble shows. They were the owners and producers. The true soap opera.

Did you always get a screen credit?

There isn't a daily credit on soap. It has to be no less often than the director is going to get. And the Director's Guild realizes that it averages out at about two and a half times a week.

I have been on the last three negotiating committees of the guild. We have negotiated our minimal basic agreement, making sure that soap opera writers got a better deal than they had been. We used to be the most anonymous people in the whole world.

What are some of the techniques necessary for writing soaps?

You have to monitor the show for about a month. You don't get paid for that.

An actor that is successful on a soap has built up an enormous following and you learn to write to the sound of that particular actor. A soap actor isn't expected to be changing at all. He is what he is and he stays that way, and that is what the audience likes. So you write to that character.

You might monitor a show for a month, but what is fascinating to me is that there are some viewers who have been following the same character on certain soaps for more than 20 years. There is a whole history of the character that the writer cannot possibly know about—that a character had a child by another character and so on. The longtime viewer may know things about the character that you don't know as the writer. How do you deal with that? Do they have a character history that they give you?

They don't have a character history, but there are books that give the major points of all the back stories. You have to know what the subtext of any scene is. You have to know what that character is feeling, no matter what he is saying, because of the relationships in the past.

Do you bring the back story out in new expository scenes to inform the new viewer?

Since they started taping the shows and electronic editing became a reality, it became possible to cut in flashbacks, and they do. An associate writer who has to turn out 65 to 80 pages a week loves being able to use a flashback.

Where are most of the scripts produced?

Most of them are produced in New York. Both *Guiding Light* and *As the World Turns* are produced back east, but our headwriter was out here in L.A. We sent our scripts to Santa Barbara, where our headwriters were living, they corrected them, and sent the correct versions to Procter & Gamble in Cincinnati. It cost a fortune.

As a writer you are absolutely responsible for having that script in on time. You usually get the outline on a Saturday; you have to start immediately to do your writing, and you have to leave time for rewriting.

How's a soap writer paid?

By the script. If extensive rewrites are demanded, they have to pay for rewrites, but if you follow the outline it is your responsibility to have it pretty much within the parameters set for you, and if it's so bad that they cannot use it, you're pretty much off the show.

Have you ever tried to create a soap opera?

No. They only commission a soap opera when they see time coming available on a network. It is very rare.

One fascinating aspect is that you send your script out to New York and then turn on your TV and watch what you wrote a few weeks later. That must be exciting in one way, seeing it produced so rapidly.

Oh, yes. And you self-criticize. There is nothing like watching your own show to see what you have done wrong.

So there is a lot of learning on the job.

Enormous learning on the job. And there is a different lead time among the different soaps. Some producers like to have about six or seven weeks between sending out the breakdowns and the time it is taped. It's usually taped a week before it is aired. Then it is broadcast from New York and picked up and taped at the various centers across the country and rebroadcast at whatever time.

The headwriter does the long range projection, breaks it down into 13-week segments which are known as cycles. Writers' contracts are issued in cycles. They also have to give the actors months of notice for vacations and layoffs.

If a major character wanted to leave, how much notice would he or she have to give?

As much as possible. If you are faced with an actor leaving a show, a popular actor, you can do one of three things. You can write him out temporarily, you can kill him off, or you can replace him.

Sometimes when a new headwriter comes on a show he won't like some of the supplementary characters introduced by the last headwriter, and he'll kill a whole bunch of them. This is known as "sending the car off the cliff."

What things do you need to have happen in each episode?

Well, in an hour show you need flocks of story and storylines. You need six or seven storylines, and you need to be concentrating on four, all at the same time, and these storylines have to be intertwined, so it is an enormously complex job to be a headwriter.

Do soap headwriters try to get into writing for sitcoms or dramatic series? I would think that the money would be better.

For headwriters the big money is anything from $200,000 a year to a million.

But the people who write and produce a nighttime soap like Dallas *are making gobs of money because those shows are syndicated. What is scale for an associate writer?*

On an hour show, probably about $2,800 a script [2003 dollars]. A script he spent a week writing. If you are doing a half hour show, then it is around $1,500 a week. Up till recently I was paying 10 percent to the agent. Because all my kids were gone, I was being taxed a third. I was receiving less than half of my salary every week.

To hold the audience's interest, what do you have to do, so people won't hit the remote?

It is different with soaps. The vast majority of the viewers of a soap are more or less hooked on that soap so you don't have to worry about losing them in a flash as you do in nighttime TV.

You do try to end each scene of each act with something that is a little bit arresting. Tension. It has to have tension. But if it looks as though its prolonged, you're dead.

Headwriters are also limited. You'd think that they'd have absolute freedom, but they are limited by the number of sets that have been built. They can't invent sets unless they know they're going to use them. Remember, the watchword of soap writing is economy. Daytime soaps support the networks. Nighttime episodic TV does not go into profit until syndication.

How do you manage to get one scene to flow into the next?

You use devices. John and Mary, before their scene ends, will mention the people in the next scene, casually. Or you'll use a camera device, like John slams down the telephone, cut to the telephone being held by somebody else. You use devices like that to keep it from being choppy.

Are most soap writers women?

It's mostly men in the rest of TV. There are more women writing soap than nighttime, because of the female audience. Only lately have they built up the male audience to 20 percent. To aim for the youth audience, on *As the World Turns* they were starting to write a lot of sci-fi stories. I just hated them. That totally destroyed it for me. It breaks the genre.

We had a homicidal maniacal dwarf. We had one scene with a giant venus fly trap. You know, you can't take the genre seriously when it goes into this stuff.

What do you say to those who would say that you can't take the genre seriously, period.

I'm comfortable with soaps. I could easily earn a living writing romance novels, you know, the Signet Romances. But I hate them. But I also won't do nighttime episodic. I'm not inventive enough. A nighttime episodic writer has to go into a show and pitch four or five stories at once. Every time he pitches, they sit there and listen to him and say, "Well we've done that," or "We don't like that, but we like that one," or "We don't like any of them." It takes me a long time to evolve a story, from scratch. So it's a relief to be given a structure.

And you've got the characters already developed?

That's right. I like writing to character, but the challenge to me is to turn an outline into something that is credible and identifiable, that presents things that people watching have been through, so they might say, "Oh God, yes, they're talking about me." I love doing that.

How else have soaps changed?

Besides infusing sex, they began going for melodrama and moving so fast that you didn't have time to develop emotional relationships. I began hearing from people who had been watching soaps for years that they couldn't watch them anymore. Because you didn't care, you stopped caring. They began using so many antiheroes and antiheroines. They carried the notion of the flawed hero too far.

How are you instructed to actually put sex into a scene?

Oh, that's always in the outline. Sometimes you're only told what happens, or what the general feeling is.

You give scenes as much subtext and texture as you can find in the backstory. You give it as much conflict as you can because there's conflict in everything, and it sometimes isn't just between two people but it's between a person and himself.

You give it mood. All these things should be put in by the associate writer. At the same time, you can't take any liberties with the story development without checking with your headwriter or with the breakdown writer.

Have you had any difficulty writing the sex scenes to spec?

Well, I have six kids. So I was never without contact with the next generation down. The one area that does change is the slang, the idioms. But basic relationships don't change.

Are there other changes you can point to?

When I first started writing soap back in '69, none of the women wore slacks. They all wore dresses, and this was a Procter & Gamble decision.

The viewpoint on the two coasts is far more liberal than it is in middle America. Middle America is resisting some of this stuff. I did some talk shows when my book came out. The major complaint from callers was that, "I can't let my children watch soap opera anymore." I don't watch it myself unless I'm going to be writing it, unless I know I've got a sample script coming up or something, 'cause it's a terrible time-killer.

But you're creating this material, and in effect you seem to be saying, "I don't want to waste my time with it." Is there a conflict there?

My feeling is that good soap, like good any-other-kind-of-writing, enlightens the viewer about the human condition. There is way too little soap opera living up to its potential. Soap opera has the potential to follow character changes, and the interplay of character and situation, more than any other genre.

And it's marvelous when it happens. When a wonderful flawed character is created and you watch him and the pressures and the tensions, that's marvelous. There's a character named John Dixon on *As the World Turns*, who is a thoroughly unlovable man. It's like watching Lucifer. He's the guy who louses everything up for everybody, and yet he's pathetic.

If you can say something about human beings that makes it worth watching, then it's worth it.

In some ways I think of soap opera as actually being closer to real life, especially in its pacing.

I think it is a lot more real than sitcom. I just hate sitcom. I think the laugh track is vulgar, unless it's done awfully well. And sitcom has less to say about the human condition, I think, than daytime.

What would you say if someone said that they think that soap operas are the most conservative material on television?

Well that's imposed on them pretty much by Procter & Gamble, and sometimes the networks. Mary McCall once said that the law in soap operas is, "Get your heroine behind the eight ball and keep her there." That's pretty much the way it is.

There's also an odd situation that arose in an effort to get to the youth market. With motion pictures kids go back multiple times. That's why there is such an enormous market for pictures targeted for the high school audience. The soap producers feel that once they hook a kid, a teenager, they've got 'em for life. This was their philosophy and certainly P&G's.

Harding Mays, who wrote *Another World* for years, was very upset when P&G told him they were going for the youth audience. He said that he didn't think that young people had lived long enough to acquire enough experience for their lives to resonate in an interesting manner.

And they started importing 21-and 23-year-old executives. One of the best television writers in the business told a story executive on *Golden Girls* that he wanted to come in and pitch a story. He was 55. "Oh, I don't know, Dick, we've already got our gray," he said.

Older writers are discriminated against.

The Writer's Guild had a study completed by some statisticians that showed a plummet in the employment of writers over 40. One of my best friends in the business is now a widow, she is 72; but she cowrote *Backstairs at the White House.* She's a quality movie-of-the-week type writer. She was interviewed by a 24-year-old story editor, who said, "Could you write a love scene?" What are the assumptions behind that question?

Are writers mistreated in other ways?

They are in terms of being rewritten. Read William Goldman's *Adventures in the Skin Trade*. He says that if you try to get all your satisfaction by writing for movies and television, you'll die. It'll just break your heart. He said if you don't have another way of writing which will preserve your integrity, you'll die. Very few people don't get rewritten.

Why are you so involved in Writer's Guild Issues?

Well it's a translation of my need for social action. What better area than your union? What more do I know about?

The writer is abused in several ways, especially in terms of industry-wide recognition of his contribution. You've heard of the auteur theory. Well this is driving writers crazy, because they know bloody well that they are the authors of those movies. Very few directors work with their writers on a script. By and large, directors have preempted the creative position in terms of their self-definition. And there are 200 million people who think that actors extemporize their lines. Occasionally they do, but not very often.

Now W. C. Fields, in the movie that I worked with him on, carried a thesaurus under his arm to hone the line. He was a drunk, too, but drunk or sober, he was such craftsman. He would tool those lines. Only once in a while would he improvise. He also literally did hate kids.

Now, in England, the writer is always on the set. Always. Never on the set here. The writer hasn't been on the set since the end of the big studio days. The writers were usually under contract and were in an office and could be quickly called down if there was a need for rewrite on the set. That never happens now. It's the director who does it or the actor does it.

I think on the whole, that human relationships are going down the drain. It's a catastrophic statement and I shouldn't make it. In soap opera, and I think certainly in nighttime episodic, the wealth, the riches of human relationships are being lost to a need for rapid montage, for sensationalism, and for the quick impact to sell. When people say there's free enterprise and there's no censorship in the United States, the fact is that market forces effectively govern everything that is produced.

Bob Ellison

BOB ELLISON

Many comedy writers in Hollywood consider Bob Ellison to be one of the top, if not *the* top, script consultants—or "punch-up" writers—in the business. Ellison is one of a small handful of highly paid script doctors who are brought in to write new gags, help in overall structure, and just plain improve or "punch-up" a script wherever possible. His services are most in demand in the final writing stages of the all-important comedy pilot. Even a few additional funny lines can make the difference between a pilot being given a commitment for 6 to 13 episodes and having a shot at a long run and eventual syndication, or sinking like a stone in the ocean. The difference can be worth hundreds of millions of dollars. No wonder the punch-up writer is well compensated.

Ellison's beginnings in comedy go back to his days as a big band trumpeter when he began writing material for nightclub comics. He then graduated to write for Dom DeLuise, Alan King, Steve Allen, Dean Martin, and Jackie Gleason before launching into his career in situation comedy. His credits read like a hit list of television comedy: *The Mary Tyler Moore Show, The Bob Newhart Show, WKRP in Cincinnati, Rhoda, Valerie, Cheers,* and more recently, *All Fired Up.*

I was forced to be a funny kid. I came from a broken home. My brother was five years older than me and had to take care of me against his wishes. He wanted to be off with the older kids telling jokes. I figured the way to break into this circle was if I could be funny.

What I wanted to be was a musician. I went to the High School of the Performing Arts in New York. As soon as I got out of school I was on the road with bands. I became a musician and was working nightclubs playing trumpet. I began to write stand-up material for comics in nightclubs while I was performing as a musician. I found out that I could charge for my comedy writing and I bought myself a typewriter with the money that I charged. I once charged $68.30. I had priced a typewriter at Macy's for that amount.

I went to school with Dom DeLuise. When his career started taking off he asked for some help with some material and I wrote some things for him. I began writing for all the stand-up comics in New York—Pat Henry, London Lee, Alan King. Once Dom DeLuise started to take off in 1968, I was called out here to work on a special with him. I made an impression, I guess. I came back the following year to do *The Steve Allen Comedy Hour* and then *The Dean Martin Show.*

Ed Weinberger called in 1975 and asked if I'd be interested in doing a script for *The Mary Tyler Moore Show.* They liked what I did and I stayed on for two years as the story editor on the show. I wrote fifteen *Mary* scripts. When that went off, I stayed at MTM and produced *The Betty White Show* and *Rhoda.*

I then left to go to Lorimar and then to Paramount, where I pro-
duced *Angie*. I was allowed to leave and go over and do rewrite nights on
The Bob Newhart Show. While at Lorimar, I worked on the pilot for
WKRP, helping out, punching it up.

I left Lorimar and then they called me back to help out on the pilot
of *Valerie*. That took off and did real well. Then I was exclusive to Paramount and working on *Cheers*.

*I've heard that you are widely considered to be the top comedy script consultant
in the industry. Would that be accurate?*

One of them, certainly.

How many are there?

Not too many. Three or four.

What's the bottom line in writing for television?

It's just a matter of keeping the people entertained until the next commercial. That's what you're there for. You have to keep them. Don't lose them.

*Tell me how script consulting works. What are some of the things you are re-
sponsible for? What's involved in punching up a script?*

If you're a consultant on a show, you should be doing more than just
punching up a script. A consultant is a guy who comes in with a fresh
eye after the show has gone through several stages. You see what's in
trouble, what needs to be fixed. They used to call me the Manny Mota of
comedy. He was a pinch hitter for the Dodgers. When you're in trouble,
call Manny.

You are supposed to come in and basically help to make it work better. That's what it boils down to. Sometimes you'll come in on the final
run to get it into the best possible shape and there are still things that
aren't working. You need a blackout here. This isn't working, that isn't
working.

There are other facets to it that no one even considers. Think about
the guys who have worked on the show. They've gotten it into what they
think is the best possible shape it can be in. They go to the table and they
read it. All of a sudden, it's not working. The writers have given their all
to the script. Things don't work on the stage and they'll come back and
they will be dejected. That's normal. Everybody has been through that.
While you are in there, helping to make the show better, at the same
time, you can—and this is important—lift the spirits of the other writers. You keep the room alive. You don't want someone to say, "How
about this?" and you say, "No. That stinks" or something. 'Cause that
means you get quiet in the room.

The group is going to be in that office a long time. They are going to
order out some kind of a dinner for the night and they're going to be
there till 2:00 in the morning, 3:00 in the morning, 4:00 in the morning.

How hard is it to work under those conditions?

You have to be professional. Most people are. Sometimes it's great. I mean you can't ask for a better business to be in than going in a room with a lot of funny people and making people laugh. You also have to know when to stop and say, "This is it for the evening. Let's come back early tomorrow, fresh, and we will have a whole new perspective."

Do you still attend these sessions into the middle of the night?

Fortunately, I haven't because the groups I've been working with are so good.

You're especially called in on pilots, yes?

Sure. On pilots they do that all the time. It's such a lucrative payoff if you can sell a pilot that producers are willing to put in whatever bucks are necessary to get the thing off the ground. You will hire anybody you can to come in and help make the thing work.

You can understand how important it is for a studio to get a show on the air. There's a lot of bucks down the line when they sell them into syndication. God only knows how many millions they are making. They wouldn't pay you this money if they could get their cousins to do it. That's what it boils down to.

It's a very open process. Many times a producer will call and say, "Come in, we're having the rewrite tonight," or "We're having a run through, come to the stage," or "We would like you to come and do three, four days, and work on the entire pilot."

I don't know if I work harder at it than other people, but I do work at it. I try to get the script ahead of time and make my notes and observations before I see the show at a run through so that sometimes they'll say, "We've got a problem here," and I can say, "Got the picture already. Don't worry about it."

Many people are unable to read a script and envision it.

I think that's important. But after a while it comes. You can hear singles, doubles, triples, home runs when you are reading.

I am lucky that I work with the people that I like and admire. I have a great deal of respect for most of the people in the business. I know how hard it is to knock out 22 shows a season and do that year in and year out. To do it with a certain amount of quality is very difficult. It does eat up a lot of talent on television. When you add all those hours together, it is a tremendous job that television writers are doing. If the show's good, then they've really done a hell of a job.

How do comedy writers work? Do most people sit at a desk?

No. Anywhere. People stroll. You pace. You sit here, you sit there. It's collaborative. People in a room on rewrite night.

Do you use a computer?

No, I don't. I use a yellow pad and I like to walk around, sit at the kitchen table, sit at the pool, sit on the terrace. I can take a pad and pen with me. Someone else types it or I'll type it myself. I'll do the fine tuning on the typewriter or sometimes I like to dictate. I have a court stenographer. I can dictate to her as fast as I can talk. Then I start to put it into a form.

I haven't seen a funny script come out of a word processor, I must say. It's good for speed but I don't think it's good for quality. I know a lot of guys who do great work on old, nonelectric standard typewriters. A word processor is okay for hour shows, soap operas, or something like that. In comedy, every word has a weight to it. Every word has a value to it.

CHAPTER 6

A Different Kind of Producer

Television isn't confined to the weekly drama or comedy series. There are also musical specials, movies, game shows, documentaries, and special events to produce, just to name a few. Political parties even hire television producers to produce their national conventions and inaugural events.

How these programs and events are conceptualized and created is fascinating, especially because we hear so little about them in the academic literature, trades, and popular media that cover the industry. Like the producers of comedy and drama series, some of the producers of these programs and events can also be said to have a personal style.

Gary Smith, for example, is one of television's top designers, and produces musical specials and other special events programming with a style that audiences recognize. He made a mark with his distinctive set designs for *Hullabaloo* in the 1960s, and went on to become the preferred producer of musical performers like Judy Garland, Frank Sinatra, Barbra Streisand, Bette Midler, and Paul McCartney. He has also designed and produced special events like the Emmy and American Film Institute Awards and Liberty Weekend. With his partner, he has won a record 24 Emmys. Smith was among the very first television designers to help a major political party produce its national convention.

Marty Pasetta has also produced major political events, specials, and award shows and is the only person to have produced the Emmys, the Grammys, and the Academy Awards, not to mention Elvis and the Pope. He is also known for his game show designs, especially *Wheel of Fortune*, and in his interview we learn in some detail how he designed the program to attract and hold the audience's attention.

Dave Bell works in an entirely different format: television documentaries, usually for HBO. His tough documentaries evince a personal style; like his programs, he is blunt, especially about the rougher aspects of production and the business side of the industry. Bell tells us how the

Gary Smith with Stevie Wonder

collaborative process in television can often turn something of substance into something vapid.

Bruce Sallan specializes in television movies, first as an executive at ABC, then with independent production companies. He has been on both sides of the table in deals, as a buyer at the network and a seller in independent production. He explains industry mantras, such as, "Movies on water lose money." I particularly like his story of how, as a vice president at ABC, he got producers to tighten up their pitches of TV movies:

> I used to have an egg timer, a five-minute timer on my desk. . . . When someone would come in and say, "Tell me how I can sell to you," I would take the egg timer and say, "See this," and turn it over. "If I don't know everything about that movie in five minutes or less, you haven't done a good job pitching it to me. . . . How am I going to sell it?"

I interviewed all four producers in the late 1980s and talked with Smith, Bell, and Sallan again in the late 1990s and 2000. The double interviews help us see how the industry changed over that decade.

GARY SMITH

For over 35 years, Gary Smith and Dwight Hemion have run the leading television special event production company in Hollywood. Smith-Hemion has won an unprecedented 24 Emmys. Their abbreviated credits list runs 51 pages.

Smith flunked out of high school and struggled through his last year of college; after much effort he left without completing his degree. Like Einstein and Edison, who each had their problems with conventional school, Smith proved a genius of theatrical and television set design. He started out as a paint boy in a design studio washing brushes and tin cans, came to Broadway, and rose to the top of his craft.

Smith is as much a designer as a producer. He created *Hullabaloo* in 1965, breaking new ground in the presentation of rock music on television. With Hemion, he produced "Baryshnikov on Broadway" and Emmy-winning salutes to George Gershwin, Irving Berlin, and Richard Rodgers. His distinctive spare and modern designs for musical specials for Judy Garland, Sammy Davis, Jr., Harry Belafonte, Frank Sinatra, Elvis Presley, Neil Diamond, Ben Vereen, Paul McCartney, Bette Midler, and Barbra Streisand still live in the memories of many who saw them decades earlier.

Smith's production company is also where people go when they need an experienced television creator to help them stage a presidential inauguration, a national political convention, or "ABC 2000," the network's 23 hours of programming covering the end of the twentieth century, for which Smith-Hemion won an Emmy and a Peabody. Their credits include the bicentennial of the U.S. Constitution, Liberty Weekend, and the 100th anniversary of

American film: "100 Years, 100 Stars." Since forming The Gary Smith Company, Smith has been involved in looks back at television history, producing the "I Love Lucy 50th Anniversary Special" and the "Mary Tyler Moore Reunion" for CBS.

Gary Smith's is a unique vantage point. We spoke twice, once in the late 1980s and again in 1999 as he was preparing to produce "ABC 2000."

✩   ✩   ✩

So tell me your life-story.

My family background is fairly artistic—my uncle is Harry Abrams of Abrams Art Books, the very classy coffee table books. I was definitely exposed to that kind of lifestyle. We were middle class people, living in Queens, born in Brooklyn, grew up in Forest Hills, both parents worked. But there was always classical music in our house; my parents were very involved in artistic things.

My father was in the dress business. My grandfather died when I was 10 or 11 and was the drama critic for a Jewish paper in New York. My mother tells stories of taking me, when she was a theater enthusiast, and me sitting on the knee of Maury Schwartz and some of the great actors of the Second Avenue Theater in those days. So that might have been where the seeds were planted. In high school I did little drawings. I wouldn't draw figures or people, but architectural and environmental things. I enjoyed play productions in high school and got involved designing the scenery. I started to get bitten by the theater bug.

I am an only child and both my parents worked, so I had a lot of free time. I stopped filling those afternoons with baseball, football, and stuff like that in my junior year of high school. I quit all those teams and took a job in New York City at a scenic studio. I was a paint boy. I washed brushes and tin cans. But I was allowed to do a little bit of drawing after the place closed. I didn't have a plan. I really am a day-to-day guy. I am pretty well organized and I've learned to structure my life, but I don't really live by it. Ask me what my objective is for the future, I'll let you know tomorrow. Anyway, I got involved painting scenery for shows like *Top Banana* and *Guys and Dolls*. I really got hooked.

I was not a very good high school student and decided not to go to college, but my parents thought that was real important. I found out that Carnegie Tech, Carnegie Mellon now, was the place one could go to learn scenic design. I applied. In fact, I found out that a man named Woodman Thomson who had been one of the early scenic designers in the theater in this country had been a teacher at Tech. I arranged for an interview with him so I could get a letter of recommendation, because technically I had flunked out of high school. I got a general diploma out of high school, not an academic diploma. I'm not a terribly good student. I'm very self-educated. I only know what I need to know.

I'm not very good at a lot of things. I still have problems with verbs and adjectives.

Tech accepted me because I had a very good portfolio. Not too many college students come in having worked professionally on Broadway shows, even as a paint boy. They said, "Gee, this kid doesn't just want to be an actor." I was the first student at Carnegie to design a major production as a sophomore. Usually only a senior got to do it, sometimes a junior. As a sophomore, I stayed up nights doing all the sketches for the next show. I took them to the woman who was going to be directing, and said, "What do you think?" She took them to the faculty and said, "Here's a kid on his own who went and did this and they're wonderful." So they let me design it.

I did the whole four years at Carnegie. Most kids don't. The enrollment in drama was about 200 freshman year, and only 26 would graduate. They fall out of theater when they realize how much work it is, or how little talent they have. I think it's mostly disillusionment, lack of ability, and much more work than anybody ever really wants.

The head of the drama department called me in at the beginning of my senior year and said, "Look Gary, you flunked English, you have to make that up. You flunked history. You make sure you get that B in those academic subjects." He said, "Even if you have to give up a little bit of time on your designing, get these things passed." To make a long story short, I ended up having to cut some scenic design classes in order to get my thesis done and my scenic design instructor flunked me. I ended up not getting my degree. The students petitioned. They knew I was one of the best students.

I left Pittsburgh in a storm, came to New York, and took the scenic design test that everybody always says you'll never pass the first time. You take it to be able to join the United Scenic Artists Guild Union. You take an exam that lasts over a three-day period. You pull out of a hat the name of a production. Overnight, lined up in hotels at tables, you design the lighting, the costumes, the sets, and all of the sketches, ground plans, the elevations. You also had to show that you were fiscally and technically responsible, and creative. They can tell by the way you design that you know what you're doing. They look at your sense of design, your technique, even your engineering capabilities.

Which one did you pick out of the hat?

Lady Windermere's Fan. Far from my style. I read it that night. Not only did I pass that exam the first time out—one of 12 people of the 200 who took the test—but I got a letter telling me I scored the highest.

Do you remember how you felt?

I felt especially terrific because this is all on the heels of the problem at Carnegie and I had said to myself, "I'll show them." I got a job and the other students in my class did not. The other two kids in my scenic design class did not pass the exam that year; they passed subsequent years. I went around to the networks and I got a job right away as a designer, and that really started me in my career. So from designing *Lady Windermere's Fan,* my first job was designing a huge-sized Geritol bottle for a commercial at CBS.

I quickly went from the menial task of being a staff designer at CBS to doing a soap opera set and then to a summer replacement series called the *Andy Williams Show,* 1958. It was quite a set. Norman Jewison was the director. I was the art director. It was a terrific, hot staff. We started a look on television variety which was the opposite of window dressing scenery. It was clean cut, white backgrounds, and the *idea* was the thing, not just scenery, not just window dressing.

Scenery became an integral part of an idea in presenting a number. It meant taking a huge roll of paper, for one example, and a silhouette against a white sky and kicking that roll like toilet paper. It came running down towards you, towards the camera, and then it was just a simple musical line. All of a sudden when the paper came down, the singer sang "Look Down that Lonesome Road." The *idea* was the thing for me. At the same time I got involved in graphics, and using *words* a lot in scenery.

My last thing at CBS was a terrific special we did with Harry Belafonte. Belafonte called everybody in. He's very articulate and bright, sensitive and artistic about everything he does. He said there's no scenery on the special, there's just singing and music. I felt kind of silly. Why was I there? I went up to him and said, "Scenery doesn't have to be what you traditionally imagine as scenery. The roots of a tree are scenery. A barbwire fence and a pig pen with people sitting up on beams with ragged wire." His face lit up. He was expecting a traditional designer.

Had this kind of thing been done in TV before?

No, not too much.

To what degree would you say you were responsible for innovating this spare trend in scenic design in television?

I've been told that. If you recall, shortly after this was a show with Judy Garland which used a lot of light bulbs. I was the first person to use electric light bulbs to make a lot of scenery. Remember the big wall, that ended up spelling her name in lights? I was using words and side boards. I'd find old Broadway painted signs, real signs from marquees, and actually take the letters and lay them on the floor. Abstract things. We were going to do Gene Kelly and "Singin' in the Rain" on the show. Do you know what the set was for that at the Ziegfield Theater? The word "precipitation" in huge letters around the whole thing. *That's* an idea.

I left CBS after the Belafonte show. I was making my $280 a week right out of college in 1958, which was fabulous. Somebody said they were looking for a designer and a new breed of staff on *The Perry Como*

Show. There's a guy named Dwight Hemion that's going to be the director, Lester Gottlieb was going to produce. Gottlieb had been very helpful to me. He was the executive at CBS who said, "Let Gary design *The Big Record.*" *The Big Record* was a big musical, nighttime Patti Page show. I was only 22 years old. So Lester put me with Dwight. He put us all together. We did the Como show for three years. I got an Emmy as an art director. I think Dwight got an Emmy as director of that show. It became a very, very popular show.

At Perry's request a spot might just be this black and white platform with a music stand and microphone and a single red rose in a vase. It became a trademark. And we used a lot of lettering styles. I left that show after three years to move to California. I knew I wanted to move up. I said I'll do whichever show I can also be the associate producer on, because I do more than scenery.

I started designing and was associate producer with Judy Garland in 1963. CBS then came to me and said, "We want you to produce the Judy Garland series." She *was* really difficult to work with, there's no secret about that. My approach was pure business with her. I was not the kind of person who could sit at her house until 4:00 in the morning. I had just recently married, had my first child, the second was on its way, yet I had to sometimes go to the house at midnight.

Gary Smith receiving one of his 24 Emmys.

With Nathan Lane at the Tony Awards. Smith frequently produced the Tonys.

Judy Garland was not the kind of star or performer who was meant for a weekly television series. And the network could be difficult, too. There used to be dictums that came down from CBS executives. "She should do no talking at all, only sing songs." That didn't work, so then they'd say, "Let her talk more, she's kind of cute."

I did 20-odd shows with her. Then I was out of work for a few months and then produced a couple of *Bell Telephone Hour*s. I was just trying to establish myself. Then I created a show called *Hullabaloo*, the first kind of contemporary rock music show that also used stars. That show really kind of launched me. It became a very innovative, contemporary musical show out of New York. I met a lot of people doing it and got a lot of notoriety at 27 years old. The best thing about it was that I also met the woman I am currently married to.

Hullabaloo lasted for two years. Shortly after that, Dwight and I ran into one another. He had gone on to do Sinatra and Streisand. We met one night, and I think it was Dwight that suggested that we do our work together. We both think alike, we're both very visually oriented.

We liked each other, we had great respect for each other. He knew my nature. I am very aggressive. I really kind of technically run the company. I am very active at making the deals and the concepts. I hire people, get involved on the floor. I'm a workaholic. I get very involved, get my hands dirty. Dwight loves to direct. He's the most brilliant director.

He loves to sit in the control room, work with the lighting and camera people, without having to worry about all the other bullshit that goes on in doing a show: dealing with the network, dealing with the sponsor. I do all of that stuff basically. But he lets me. When somebody says, "Well, let's call Gary," it doesn't bother him. There are no ego conflicts. We've been together 32 years—a long time for a marriage like this. We're proud of what we've been able to achieve. He really is a great check for me, because I will sometimes react to something emotionally.

Do you know how many Emmys you've won as an individual, or do you win them together?

Both. Dwight has more because he's also the director. Smith-Hemion has 24 Emmys. We always say it that way, but he has many more than that.

What makes a Smith-Hemion production unique?

They always say, "I can recognize it." I can't give you it very specifically, but I will give it to you philosophically. The show comes from here. I'm pointing to my stomach. I'm not pointing to my eye or my brain. If it doesn't work here, it doesn't work. This part, eyes and brain, are relatively easy. You can work at this, this is craft, this is technique. I am now pointing at eyes and brain. This can be learned. I don't think things in the gut can be learned. I think this is intuitive. Somebody asks, "What does a producer do?" I say I'm really a psychologist.

What are some of the ways you put that into practice?

There are two main kinds of specials that we do. There is either the individual special: "The Neil Diamond Show," "The Ben Vereen Show," Paul McCartney, "The Bette Midler Show" or there was "Liberty Weekend," or there's the Emmys. There are either concept specials or personality specials.

When we do personality specials, I spend a good 10 to 14 hours just talking to that person. When we did Sammy Davis' one-man show, I went to visit him in Vegas, and I lived there for three days and talked to him about his whole life. I read his book, and I really got the essence of what he's afraid of and how he started.

It's like what you just did with me. You do the same thing. You said, "I want to hear your life story first." When I talk about somebody's life and they throw in the things that they liked, or they were afraid of, what impressed them, motivated them, I hang on to those things.

I'll give you a good example. When we did Ben Vereen's special, Ben talked about his beginnings. He said, "I remember when I was a kid, there was this candy store in the neighborhood that we used as a hangout. I didn't know I was going to be a dancer, but there was an old tree stump, this huge tree somebody had cut down in front of the store. That was our stage. We used to do our little shtick on that stage. Everybody would jump on the tree and they would do a little number."

I said, "In other words, your first stage was this tree trunk outside? It's also interesting that you did *Roots*. There's a real double meaning in that." We ended up calling the special: "Ben Vereen: His Roots." Roots just having been on the air the year before. *Brilliant*. So obvious. It just seemed so simple. He *gave* me that idea.

The home base for that show was a bunch of kids sitting on a stoop out in limbo, and in front of the stoop was this huge old tree. It's very Jewish. When I explain it to other Jews, they just nod their head and they say I know what you mean—going back to your roots, going back to your beginnings, using the natural things from your life to build on.

I also believe in being extremely truthful. I'll sometimes use that to effect, like one little funny anecdote on the show we did with Sammy. The show was just called "Sammy." He talked a lot with his father on the show, and how when he first walked out on the stage, he was this little kid in his father's vaudeville act with the Will Master Trio, touring the black vaudeville circuit. As the years went by, he became the headliner.

When it came time in Sammy's TV special for the finale, I had his father introduce him. The line his father was going to say was, "Now, the Will Master Trio, minus two." I said, "Dad, just say that line three times in a row," because I knew it would get better each time. The first time he would be nervous. I said, "Ready? I'm not even going to cue you. Just take a beat in between." So he says it three times and then he says, "It ain't going to get no better than that." I kept that in and I used all three. It was so charming, *so* terrific.

I like things being what they are. It is what it is.

What do you watch on television?

I don't watch that much television. I watch 90 percent sports, the other 5 percent is movies, and the other 5 percent might be the kind of things we do occasionally, award shows, things like that. I don't tend to respond to these obvious bullshit kinds of shows that don't ring very truthful.

What is it that makes them untruthful?

I don't know. I run into trouble when you ask me to analyze. I'm not a great analyzer. I can speak from my heart. Maybe that's an ego thing I have, but I find it difficult intellectualizing and verbalizing, very awkward. I don't answer those kind of questions.

Are you reluctant to comment because you don't want to step on anybody's toes?

That might be true. No. I would rather pick a genre. There was a whole period of time where television variety became childish: Andy Williams, Sonny and Cher, the Osmonds. I didn't like that.

I am criticized for being obtuse, obscure with things that I do. My answer is: sometimes, I don't care. As long as I know that we're right. I don't like to play down to people's intelligence. I like to give the audience the benefit of the doubt. I've made some mistakes that way. I've been too subtle. I like to give the public credit. And if it means losing a percentage of them who may not catch on or get the real impact of what we're doing, I'm sorry, that's the way I go.

I'll give you an example. We did a show called the "75th Anniversary of the Screen Actor's Guild." First of all, I didn't want it to be a Hollywood show. I wanted people to identify with the actors. There were people at the network who said, "No. Glitz is the answer. Hollywood! We bought the Screen Actor's Guild show because we wanted it to be full of Hollywood like 'Night of a Hundred Stars.'" But I said, "It's a union! Do you know the average actor's salary is only $322 a year? Not Tom Selleck's." We started the show with a song called "Here's My Union Card." I am an actor, here's my card. We wrote the song and it was performed by 12 actors. Not only Ralph Bellamy and little Emmanuel Lewis but a guy in a wheelchair, a character lady, a stunt guy and Ed Asner— he was president of the union then. The concept was one that all of America could relate to.

You said earlier that some variety programs were childish.

Like children's shows. They dress everybody up in funny costumes. Remember Andy Williams? They put Andy on at 7:30. They had a bear, funny costumes. They made Andy do a lot of sketches.

Could you talk a little about the U.S. Constitution and what you did on that?

We were brought in by the city of Philadelphia to be the exclusive packagers of the bicentennial special. We not only produced, we were asked to create all the television packaging relating to the Constitution. It was a huge celebration of the Constitution with performers, political figures, the president was there. I wanted it to be meaningful, I wanted it to relate to the Constitution. I just didn't want a bunch of dancing people in a variety show. So I had to find appropriate material that dealt with the Constitution and dealt with the issues of the Constitution, from drama, from music, from film, from Broadway.

You've won a lot of awards. Is that important to people at the network?

I have been told by network executives, "We're not interested in the awards, we're interested only in the ratings."

How much is the quality of American television hurt by the emphasis on ratings?

A lot. As long as television is an advertising medium, it'll be that way. It's always going to be that way. It's become more and more that way in terms of bottom line delivery, meaning cost per thousand.

We did a show for three years called *Television Academy Hall of Fame.* I was very proud to be involved with it from its inception—a show that inducted a nice cross-section of seven distinguished people and used a lot of historical background material. The show never performed well in the ratings. NBC decided it wasn't picking up the show. It went off the air because it didn't deliver enough audience.

Witness the vulgar talk shows we have on today. There's a lot of programming that is only on the air because it gets big ratings, much more so than years ago. That's at the network level. I don't think that's true at the cable level. Cable has less concern about that specific program's ratings. They still care about subscription and viewership.

We do an awful lot of things for the Disney Channel, for example. We created a show called the *Disney Teacher Awards* and we're doing our ninth year of that, where we honor teachers. Michael Eisner said he wanted us all to be proud of the fact that we can pay tribute to teachers the same way stars and actors are paid tribute to on awards shows. It's a very expensive show for a small network like Disney, so somebody said maybe we should offer this to a major network. But the network tried to alter the concept so much, in terms of de-emphasizing the teachers and putting more emphasis on the stars and the presenters and how to showcase that show, that Disney and Eisner said, "It's not worth it. We would be compromising the show too much. Let's keep it on the Disney Channel."

It's a fairly nice example of how a cable channel can maintain the integrity of a program, because they look at that program as part of their overall structure as opposed to what audience they're delivering between 9:00 and 11:00 on any given night.

Cable has given the creative person so many more opportunities. If it wasn't good for a network, it might be good for cable. At the same time, there's obviously less money. It's all spread out, so we're forced to do things a little more economically because the audience base is smaller.

You said it's always going to be that way. Is it possible that better quality could be produced and you could still get ratings?

I believe that we could exercise some influence—not dictate or change people's taste. We have the time to make them aware that something is good. Shows need a chance to grow on you, to grow on an audience.

After years of working in TV, would you say that the tastes of the public have changed?

I would subscribe a little bit to that theory, but I think it's entirely possible that we have been guilty in playing a part in reducing the taste level or reducing the expectations of what things can really be. Although I will also tell you that I am very proud of what television has done in the television movie field compared to what theatrical films have done. I think that the opposite is true there. I think television movies address themselves to issues and social problems and tackle a lot of things that theatrical films won't. Theatrical films are supposed to be the real art form. That's bullshit. I think television films can take tremendous credit and the industry deserves a tremendous amount of credit for raising the taste standards and the expectations of what should be dealt with in subject matter for drama in television.

Is there pressure on people like yourself to keep segments of film and tape shorter and shorter?

It's one of those dictums we get. One of them is the fact that things have to be done in 20-second bites, so the audience is constantly titillated. I'm not sure that that's wrong. That is a fairly valid point—in order to keep people interested, there's a sense of energy.

There's another truth: you can't use original music. You must only use music that the audience is familiar with. And I happen to agree. I understand that when I hear a song for the first time I don't respond to it as emotionally. Still, I tend to think rules are to be interpreted. Not to be totally observed regardless.

We don't listen that well anymore. We need to be stimulated. I'm not a big fan of music videos because I think they lack in emotion. They don't move me. I think some of the effects are wonderful. Occasionally I see a music video that really is a complete drama: beginning, middle, and end.

You had input on the 1984 Olympics in Los Angeles.

Yeah, I introduced David Wolper to some very key people. He called me to ask who were the best people to work with. He didn't know of a good scenic designer, a good art director for that kind of show, a good lighting director. At one point, he did call me and ask me to produce the closing ceremonies for the Olympics. I wasn't available.

You have been the *producer who has been involved in more of these very large entertainment and news events than any other individual. What events have given you the greatest satisfaction?*

"Baryshnikov on Broadway," Paul McCartney's first television special when he left The Beatles. They *became* events. Those were pure entertainment shows.

I've been extremely proud of producing the Democratic National Convention over the last 12 years—not to produce the *television show,* but to produce the *convention,* to help determine the look of the last three conventions. The more and more the networks started to diminish the amount of time that they would give the conventions, the more and more crucial it became to make the best use out of the limited amount of time that the networks were giving to us. And I've done three presidential inaugural galas: one for Reagan that Sinatra was the executive producer on, and I was the executive producer on Clinton's two inaugural galas.

How does it feel to be called upon to produce these programs and events that the whole nation, or world, is tuned in to on each of these historic occasions?

I get caught up in it. We got caught up in "Liberty Weekend." When we did "Liberty Weekend," it wasn't just another show, and I give Wolper a lot of credit for instilling that feeling. We all made sure that the show wasn't a television show and *was* a celebration. The work we did on the Constitution was first a genuine celebration of the event that had meaningful ideas about it, and *then* it was a television show.

We at least put those things in the proper order. Certainly, when you do those kinds of shows that have that kind of national impact, you're dealing with a lot of people's feelings about it, and you also have to state it in a fairly nonpartisan, nonpolitical ground. The easiest thing is to jump into a Hollywood formula.

How well can you envision the work ahead of time? Hitchcock used to say he wished he didn't have to go out on the set because he had it all in his mind.

I can picture pretty well. We've been doing it a long time. We're not that surprised, but that doesn't mean that everything is purely predictable—don't get me wrong. Many times we think something's going to work great, and it falls a little flat or we're worried about something, and it plays better than we thought. Generally speaking, I think I'm able to kind of see it and feel it.

What are you doing for ABC for their millennium coverage?

I've been brought in by ABC News to be the executive producer of their 23 hours of millennium coverage. This involves organizing the worldwide coverage that will be available to us through a consortium of 60 foreign countries and their individual broadcasters.

What is it that you can do that ABC News cannot do for themselves?

We are looking at a day that is unique and special in the life of the world. In addition to the entertaining aspects of what's going on, whether it's a presentation by various countries or up close and personal stories that relate to the millennium, we're doing 23 hours, so there is a lot of pure entertainment. It's all part of the mix. It's a combination of merging entertainment elements and historical news elements.

What's the best way to grab and hold the attention of the viewer?

I'd like to believe that the best way to hold a viewer is to involve them emotionally. But, I'm afraid that the success of MTV and the obvious statistical support for the fact that the eye needs to be stimulated much more than the ear has weighted things toward the visual instead of the emotional.

You're in your mid-60s. Any thoughts of retirement?

I'll be 65 at my next birthday. I'll play baseball at Dodgers Stadium this coming Saturday. We play Hollywood stars night. People like Billy Crystal and Tom Selleck. I've been the catcher all my life. And even at my age I still go behind the plate and Tony Danza is the pitcher. It's probably my fantasy day of all time.

So there are no plans to retire.

Not right now, in fact we're moving full speed ahead. There are moments where I feel that I'd like to, to be honest, but so far there aren't any plans.

MARTY PASETTA

Marty Pasetta began working in local television at K60-TV in San Francisco in 1951 as a stage manager and producer for Jack LaLane, *The Les Crane Show* (later *ABC's Nightlife*), and for the famous stripper Gypsy Rose Lee, who had one of the earliest talk shows in television. After 16 years, Pasetta moved to Los Angeles. Since that time he has become one of the most successful producers and designers of continuing programs such as *Wheel of Fortune* and specials such as the Academy Awards, the Emmys, and the Grammys. Marty Pasetta is the only person to have produced all three awards programs. And probably no one else can say that he has produced both Elvis and the Pope.

Other stars for whom he produced specials include Glen Campbell, Andy Williams, the Everly Brothers, Bing Crosby, Stevie Wonder, the Smothers Brothers, Frank Sinatra, George Burns, and Carol Burnett. He has produced both President Carter's and President Reagan's inaugural balls, as well as galas at the Kennedy Center.

We discuss the planning that went into *Wheel of Fortune*, which he designed 40 years ago; how the design of the board and its lighting and the amount of time it takes each letter to be turned are critical to holding the audience's attention. His other game show designs include *Celebrity Sweepstakes, Name That Tune,* and *Love Connection.* We also discuss how the attention span of the public has changed. The interview was conducted in the late 1980s at his offices in Los Angeles. Pasetta is very businesslike and intense and speaks very quickly.

In school I did plays and totally fell in love with theatre. In high school I did all the lighting and staging. I went to school with Bing Crosby's kid, Gary, and we would do shows together 'cause we were friends. I went into lighting 'cause I liked the technical side. I'm not an outspoken person or one who likes to be in front of the lights.

I started in television in 1951, June 10 to be exact. I took a summer job at KGO-TV, the ABC affiliate in San Francisco, when television first hit on the West Coast. I became so enamored with it that I didn't go back to college.

My parents were upset and didn't speak to me for about two years. I eventually was at KGO for about 16 years. I started as a stage manager. Eventually I was executive producer and started a formula that was

Marty Pasetta

copied at all the ABC owned and operated stations. I had about 12 producers and directors under me when I left. I started Jack LaLane up there and *The Les Crane Show.*

Why did you decide to move to Hollywood?

I was doing the *Gypsy Rose Lee Show* and I got mad at her. She was really most difficult and temperamental. I finally had had it, slammed the door, called her a bitch, and said good-bye to KGO. I walked out after 16 years, cold turkey. I just couldn't handle it anymore.

I went home. We had three babies. I was two weeks away from vacation and they wouldn't give me my vacation money and that hurt because we only had $500 at the time. My wife went out and bought a $1.98 bottle of champagne and we celebrated. I got into the car, drove to Los Angeles, and we've been down here 25 years now.

I called some ABC friends in L.A. and became an associate producer on a new daytime talk show called *Dateline Hollywood.* Then ABC immediately pushed me into another show called *Temptation.* The Smothers Brothers saw that, liked it, and asked if I would come over and direct *The Summer Smothers Brothers Show.* That's what started me in nighttime television. Then I came in as a director on a summer series starring Glen Campbell that spawned his regular series, which I also started. I also did the Andy Williams series and the Everly Brothers series. And I did the last season of the regular Smothers Brothers—the one where we did a lot of innovative, wild and creative things. We won all kinds of awards.

Then I started to do some things for Bing Crosby. I did about 10 years of all his specials. NBC liked it and they said, "Would you come in and do the Oscars?" They said, "We want to make it really happen." That first year we did a big opening number with Joel Grey. It was a big show.

I started the Grammys on TV. I've produced and written the Grammys for eight years, The American Film Institute's show for eight years, the Emmys for two years. I'm the only person who has done all three major award shows that exist on the air.

We've also done the Cerebral Palsy Telethon for 10 years. We also do a lot of event specials. Stevie Wonder. We did the Martin Luther King special. It was gigantic.

Most people who know your name outside the industry associate you with the Academy Awards. What other things do you do?

I do maybe 12, 14, 16 specials a year. I did the first satellite show that was ever done. That was with Elvis Presley from Hawaii. I also did President Carter's inaugural and Reagan's inaugural. The balls and the big gala at Kennedy Center. At Reagan's, I had 52 cameras.

I don't do parades and I don't do speeches. I also do a lot of game shows and game show pilots. I design them. I had nine game show series on at one time. Right now I have one that's been on for 26 years, *Wheel of Fortune.* I get paid twice a day for that.

You designed the set for Wheel of Fortune?

I designed the show. The show *is* the set. I designed the camera shots, the dialogue, everything. And *Celebrity Sweepstakes, Name That Tune, Love Connection*, and *Catch Phrase.*

I'm a show doctor. And my name does not go on the credits. I keep my name off. It dilutes my position as far as nighttime goes. See, I am one of the very few people that has crossed the borderline that goes into daytime. Most of the people who do nighttime shows do not do daytime and vice-versa.

How many Emmys have you won?

None. I have been nominated maybe 18 or 19 times. I've won a lot of other awards, but not any Emmys. I've also done specials with Sinatra when he retired and he came back ["Old Blue Eyes Is Back"]. I've done Carol Burnett. Mostly the musical variety kinds of shows.

We also have a foreign company. We do a lot of work in Europe. We produce and direct shows for the French and the Germans. We did "George Burns in Paris" for Showtime. I did *Caesar's Palace,* a two-hour show live for Showtime. I did the "Supernight of the Superbowl." I directed the Pope here at Universal Amphitheater. So, we have our fingers into a lot of different areas.

What makes a show work?

When you design a particular show you design it for a particular audience. An audience is defined by a certain age group or defined by a taste. And as long as you address that and you do it in an entertaining and not a demeaning manner, you will hold them. There are many cases when television is an instructional medium, but even when it is instructional or documentarian, you always must entertain.

What do you say to people who are critical of entertainment values creeping into news production?

Taste works hand-in-hand with that. You're certainly not going to have dancing chorus girls on a newscast. But everything does not have to be morbid. You can entertain by showing a lighter side of something.

When you offend an audience, you have lacked good taste. You can offend them by one word, a look, an item of clothing, a set. Anything can offend somebody. You can't condescend to an audience. You must always respect your audience. There has to be a purpose to what you're doing, otherwise you're wasting valuable air time.

If you don't have good taste yourself or surround yourself with people who do, then you're not a good businessperson and you're not a good producer. Something offensive will be spotted relatively quickly by the network and by the buyers. They can be offended *once*—one time you're OK. The second time, you're history.

Are there people in the industry who don't respect the audience?

Most definitely. They'll do something for sensationalism and a fast buck or a rating point. I'm not gonna point fingers and I'm not going to identify anyone.

What about pacing? How crucial is that?

Well, every producer thinks about pacing in a different manner. I tend to be a little bit more show-bizzy than some of the other producers. The audience has an attention span that dwindles by the day. Because there is so much choice out there and with music videos, the pace has gotten to be so fast, that the audience expects pace in all aspects.

You can't keep doing a show the way you did it 10 years ago because you'd have time pass you by. Their attention span won't allow it because they'll be gone. You can't do a Carol Burnett show, for example, today and expect to have the same response. It would never sustain the audience.

How do you know how to pace a program?

There is no school. You can't teach pacing. You either feel it or know what will hold attention. You can't read that in a book.

When I edit a show, I edit every line, every cut, every dissolve. Every frame is my edit. An editor doesn't do anything other than what I ask him to do. I do not sit in a room and have an editor show it to me. I don't function like that. I have my fingers in all aspects of a show, from the designing of the set, to lighting, to costumes, to lines, to music cues. I'm into every music cue. I sit in the booth and say, "Circle out those trumpets over there, I want to add this music cue." I have musical knowledge. So I have a feeling of pace. I also work with the choreographers. We work as a creative team. I try to surround myself with people who are open and are open to me. It's not a dictatorship. It's an open conversation.

You talked about the attention span of the public dwindling by the day. Does the responsibility lie with the medium itself?

Oh I totally think so. Because I think there are so many choices now. Twenty to thirty years ago, they had three channels. Now they've got 33 channels, 24 hours a day. What do you expect? With today's competition you can lose an audience very rapidly since they've got a remote control in their hand.

It puts tremendous pressure on us. The competition is staggering. And the cost factors do go up. It's harder to do a show with a profitable margin. You can't do everything with deficit financing.

When you say that the attention span is dwindling by the day, how literally do you mean that?

I mean that literally, I really do. If you don't hold their attention that dial goes click. And it's too easy to click. They don't have to get up out of their chair anymore. They can hit that remote button and that hurts us considerably. The technology has hurt the programmer. If they don't like something, before they would sit with it because they were too lazy to get up and walk across the room.

This is a different kind of generation. It starts with the fast beat of the music. The whole lifestyle is speeded up and that just becomes infectious. Many of them today unfortunately can't even do homework without music blasting and to me that would be a definite distraction in my day and age. But not in today's age. They truly handle it. It truly would be more distracting if it wasn't there. It's a whole different lifestyle.

Is holding the viewer's attention the bottom line for you or is it only part of what you're doing?

You have to hold their attention, but once you've got their attention and they're gonna stay with you, they'd better like what they see. So it's a two-fold situation. Once you have their attention, you'd better have something designed that they feel they can participate in. They need to

Pat Sajak and Vanna White on the set of Wheel of Fortune.

get personally involved and feel that they're not a dummy, feel they're not spoken down to. So if you can accomplish all of that and still have a laugh or two, and make it pay off, and make it have pace, make it build to a finale, and all that happens in the time span you have, you have a winning situation.

In a program like Wheel of Fortune *there are a whole lot of things going on that might intrigue people. One is the question of the answer to the puzzle.*

That is the key. It starts there. It's a puzzle. People can look at that and they can think about that.

Notice how much time that puzzle is actually on the tube. All of that has been well thought out. And it was also well thought out that we had a real person go across with letters. That's all my design. The flashes, the colors, the time it takes her to turn the letters. All that was my design. And the time for the person at home to study it.

Then there's a greed factor. Even if the contestant knows the answer, they're gonna turn to greed to see how much money they can build up until they go bankrupt. So there's also the gambling aspect.

It seems to me that one of the reasons that you're successful in what you do, particularly the Oscars broadcast, is that when I hear how fast you talk, it tells me that when you're in the booth you can make rapid-fire decisions.

It's true. I have a sixth or seventh sense and I do speak fast. I do think fast. Hopefully I make proper decisions. Obviously I make enough that I'm invited back. The Oscars is probably the largest television show in the world every year. It has over one-and-a-half billion viewers. There's nothing in the world that comes close to it.

What are the challenges for you in producing the Oscars? Every year, regardless of how well you do it, someone says it takes too long.

The press is not remembered if it says nice things. They're only remembered if they say nasty things. And so they want to glom onto their own name being attached to the criticism. "Did you hear or read what so-and-so said?"

When we do the Emmys, we're dealing with three hours of people that the audience all know. They're household names because they see them day in and day out for a year. And every award is a star-laden situation. And that's true for the Grammys as well. I've done all these shows.

With the Oscars you have, out of hundreds of awards, only, maximum, if you have a good year, six awards that the audience might relate to: director, actor, actress, supporting actress, supporting actor, best picture. That is it. And if the people have not seen that picture, they cannot relate to those people in any way, shape, or form, and an audience can't relate to a lot of technical awards.

It's a three-hour horse race. There are many different divisions of that horse race, and that's what it is all about. All the rest is tap dancing.

Dave Bell with his Emmy for Do You Remember Love?

That is why to hold a viewer's attention on the Oscars is the most gigantic challenge in the world. And that is why we always use different devices to try and make it a little different here and a little different there.

Could the program ever be limited to the 10 to 12 essential awards?

The Academy takes the position that every Oscar is an equal Oscar and is to be given its equal due. Of course the network would love to have them take off some of that stuff. The Academy is divided because they see the ratings problem. But as far as the show ever being in trouble— never. All three networks would give anything for it.

A lot of other award shows are taped a month ahead of time and then they're in the editing room for a month. The Oscars aren't. We are live, we have one take. These country music awards things, they're on camera for seven days. We're on camera for three days. We only have the theater for a week and the complexities of this show are so staggering and enormous. Nine mobile vans, a crew of 450, 19 camera positions. We have 26 tape machines. It's like taking a Broadway show on the road where you get two months to break things in, and time to work out the technical problems. But we have three days to do all of that.

The Academy Awards presentation is different from most TV because the film industry still has a certain special glamor about it that the television industry doesn't have. The television industry wants to brush up against that, yes?

That is correct. Movies span the world. Everybody is in on it because the movies play in the smallest suburbs of Africa. I mean every place in the world. And Hollywood is Mecca. Hollywood is the Mecca of the movie industry in the world. There is no other place like it and there never will be.

DAVE BELL

Dave Bell owns a production company, Dave Bell and Associates, and is known for his hard-hitting documentaries with arresting titles such as *Five American Guns, Skinheads: Soldiers of the Race War, Asylum, Sex and the American Teenager, Toxic Time Bomb, Transplant,* and *Hooker.* Ironically, his most successful venture has been the Emmy and Peabody Award–winning television movie *Do You Remember Love?*, a sensitive portrait of a woman suffering from Alzheimer's disease starring Joanne Woodward. While he occasionally still sells his programs to the broadcast networks, his main customers these days are cable companies, especially HBO.

Bell is one of the most opinionated and candid creative people I've spoken with in television. He is highly critical of public television's content and its business practices. He believes that the collaborative process in television often turns the vision of an individual creator from a tasty textured rye bread into unnourishing white bread.

Bell wisely points out that everyone's first job in television—or any other industry—is to keep his or her job and not make waves. This also explains why so much television is redundant and derivative. He also discusses why simple television stories get produced while more subtle or complicated scripts are often not developed.

Bell and I first met at his headquarters near Studio City in 1987. We caught up again in 1999.

☆   ☆   ☆

Tell me a little about your background and how you got started in television.

I went to a tiny little high school in a tiny little town in Northeastern Ohio. They said I had a good math ability. I'd like to meet the guy who designs those tests that tell people what abilities they have. Maybe I have a math ability. I had no interest in it whatsoever.

I went to Hiram College in Ohio specifically because they had a showboat that went up and down the Ohio River, and I thought that would be a lot of fun. I was on it for three years.

Back in the day, Dave Bell taught himself to shoot and edit film. Here he's shooting in East Berlin, without a permit, since he's "merely a tourist."

I got totally involved in theater and I thought I was going to be a theater director, until I got out of college and discovered what an awful job that was in terms of income. There are only probably 25 or 30 people who make a living out of directing professional theater and probably about a 1,000 more that direct some kind of regional theater who make a subsistence level living out of it, and that's it. It's the same for actors. I thought for a while I might be an actor, but I got out of acting almost before I got into it because other people kept telling me what to do. I decided I was smarter than them by and large.

Anyway, I decided to go into television. This was in the mid-1950s, and television was just getting started. But I couldn't get a job in TV so I went in the army. After that I went to Syracuse University, specifically to get a master's degree in communications—a one-year crash course in television. In those days, they could teach you all you needed to know in 10 months. It was a hell of a good course, and I got the best grades of anybody in the class because I was interested in it.

The head of the department at Syracuse, who didn't have any idea of whether I had a creative bone in my body, got called from ABC for his most creative student to come down to Baltimore to be the producer-writer of a show called *Johns Hopkins Science Review*. I thought I would go into dramatic television but the Johns Hopkins show was a wonderful experience and was, of course, reality television. One of the first on the air. It was on ABC on Sunday afternoons. I did that for two years.

The executive producer canceled it because negative pressures were developing—television was becoming, even then, more unionized and advertiser-driven and becoming much less thoughtful and less challenging. From there, I went to Buffalo to put on an educational television program. I hated public broadcasting, hated educational television, and I hated Buffalo.

Why did you hate educational television?

Because it was boring. Jesus Christ it was boring. I've spent my whole life with academics, and the only problem with academics, as a general rule, is that they don't have to produce. Consequently, they will put up with levels of boredom that no other single profession will. I have probably more Ph.D. friends than anyone you'll interview outside of educational television. Most of them don't deny what I say. I got a telegram one night from a friend of mine who had just struggled through a Ph.D., through years and years of fooling with the damn thing, and the telegram said, "I got my Ph.D. Thank god I'll never have to read another book." I think that's a telling statement.

Educational television is basically a failed process in this country. It's disgraceful. Congress set up this whole system but allowed no way of funding it. Consequently, it will always be the poor sister. The failure with the audience is probably the principal thing that bothers me. It has totally failed to attract the attention of the bulk of the public.

Given what you do now, it sounds as if the Johns Hopkins experience was very formative for you.

There's no doubt about that. Ironically, one of the reasons why I didn't go to law school is that a good lawyer told me that my law career would be dictated entirely by the first job I got. So if I got a job with a firm that did a lot of accounting law, I would be an accounting lawyer. And I thought to myself, "Screw that. I am not interested in that at all." Ironically, the same goddamn thing happened in television. It probably would in any profession.

I often say, "I got stuck with reality programming." I don't mean that in a derogatory way because, basically, it gave me a very strong foothold on reality which most television producers don't have. One of the reasons that dramatic television programming is very often paper-thin and uncomplicated is that the producers, directors, and writers, or all three, manage not to actually see what they are covering, and the work is not truly reflective of real life. But if you spend a lot of time in prisons and schools and other failed social institutions you get a very quick and very thorough grounding in the reality of life. As a result, when you read a script, which is total fiction, you can measure how close it is to reality.

Can you describe some of your shows that illustrate what you try to accomplish in your documentaries?

Shoot/Don't Shoot was the story of five police who for one reason or another, shot somebody. And it went into the background of what their situation was, and what the circumstances were of the shooting and how they felt about it afterwards.

I felt that there wasn't a clear perception among the public about how police feel after a shooting. We showed that film at a screening at the Writer's Guild Theater and there was a discussion afterwards. The discussants were from the National Rifle Association and the Anti-Hand Gun lobby. Interestingly enough, both groups liked the film. I was amazed that both groups liked it. Both of them thought that the film got *their* message across. That just floored me.

Another show was called *Death on Death Row*. That basically was an hour which was spent inside death row at an Arizona Prison, and what it was like to be there.

We did *Sweet Sixteen and Pregnant*, which followed four girls, in different circumstances, who found themselves pregnant. It was a really touching film.

We also did one called *Hard Time*, again in a maximum security prison. I'm real interested in prisons. Then we did one called *Combat in the Classroom*, which wasn't a great film, but I think was real interesting because it emphasized some of the problems of the schools.

You infuse a lot of dramatic value in the reality programming that you produce.

That's right. I've always felt that the purpose of television is to entertain. It doesn't have any other purpose. If television doesn't entertain, it's not watched. This is not to say that everything has to be *Wheel of Fortune*. Of course, all I have to do is look at the numbers, the grosses, and I can say that I wish I had a small piece of *Wheel of Fortune*. I might actually go out on some occasion and attempt to get a *Wheel of Fortune*–type show started. I can assure you, I would never work on it long, but I would try to get one started. I find the creative process to be intriguing irrespective of what you're creating.

Apart from the bottom line you do seem to have a social agenda in your programs.

I do have some social aims. I think the best entertainment is involving and I don't think that people get involved in things that aren't provoking. Unless you get them in the gut, you don't get them at all.

It's hard because the commercial interests get very nervous about things that have social relevance. They are afraid that they're not going to be entertaining. They are afraid that some pressure group will complain. A lot of them will tell you that they aren't affected by pressure, but that's bullshit. They're all affected by it and by all the crazies in the world who can get 25 people to write letters.

It's better in cable. Cable people are less influenced by the outside world. I tend to be uncompromising on a lot of stuff, and maybe one of the reasons I don't sell anymore than I do, is that people know that I don't want to compromise. I just lost a deal on something I was interested in called *The Plight of Women*.

Actually, it surprises me that I'm interested in it. Why the hell should I care about that? But I look around at women executives in this business, and I think to myself, "These dames have a tough time." They either have to take on all the trappings of a man, which they do badly, or they suffer in one way or another because this is basically a male chauvinist country. This industry is like a concentration camp as far as women are concerned.

Can you elaborate on the forces that work against more interesting and provocative programs?

Let me give you my theory, and this theory holds true for any kind of television, any kind of medium whatsoever. A person creates an idea that I call rye bread. It is tasty, it is tough, it is thick, it is textured. From that point on, everybody that that person comes in contact with will turn it into white bread. It doesn't matter whether it's a network, PBS, or an advertiser. That's what happens, and the person who has the vision has to keep it rye bread. It's the nature of human beings and the nature of compromise. Every time there is a compromise, the rye bread gets a little whiter.

Also, you have to understand that virtually everybody at one point or another covers his ass. His *job* is to cover his ass. His first job is to keep his job. That's it! And the way you keep your job, in most middle positions, in any industry, is to not make waves. You aren't going to be fired for maintaining the status quo. You aren't going to be fired for hiring the very best writer, even if the poor son of a bitch is ready to die—even if the guy doesn't give a goddamn about the project.

It's the same reason that business people often do market research or that doctors run extra tests. If something fails, your boss can't say that you didn't do market research, nor can a patient sue you for malpractice.

That's right, it's an ass-covering process.

Has the pace of TV sped up and is TV less inclined to go into depth?

That's true. The faster the cuts come, the more it looks the same. There isn't time to differentiate what the information is before you've gone to something else.

McLuhan is coming true. McLuhan was wrong about a cool medium and all that bullshit. But yes, form is superseding content.

The attention spans for most material are getting shorter. It's another way of saying that more information can be grasped quicker by the public. This is not saying that if you present a subject dramatically, entertainingly and in depth, that the audience won't watch it—they will.

I think it depends on what kind of program they are watching. If you are watching an access program—7:30, a *Two on the Town* or *Eye on LA* kind of program—things go by so fast that you can't see anything. Part of the reason for that is that they almost subliminally flash the tits and ass by, particularly during the sweeps. Every goddamn one of these Channel 7 programs during the sweeps had girls in bathing suits on topless beaches and bottomless beaches and total no bathing suit beaches, and the cuts were real short. You could see tits and ass in the thing, if you never blinked.

Is the audience being sufficiently challenged by TV?

To a great extent, the audience has not been challenged. I don't think the PBS audience has been challenged either. I could name PBS programs—*American Playhouse, Nova,* and *National Geographic*—that are good. But see, there's not much adrenalin running through PBS. That's the basic problem with it. They don't have enough of the Channel 7 mentality when it comes to promotion. British accents just don't make it. All the drama comes from England, except for *American Playhouse.*

Basically, the superstructure of PBS is sinking it. Individual stations do whatever they want. There is no *network.* There is no continuity of programming. There is hardly any programming at all that runs at 8:00 p.m. Wednesday, all across the country on PBS stations.

You think it would be better if it were more standardized and had more of a commercial aim?

Absolutely. The technical parts of it should be more standardized. Eight o'clock Wednesday night, you ought to be able to tune in and know you're going to see *American Playhouse*. You can't get national publicity for programs that aren't national. The government ought to support it and the commercial interests ought to support it and I think there ought to be some commercials. In some European countries, all the commercials run at one time at the top of the hour.

Let's go back to something you said earlier about injecting sex into TV programs. Do you have any problem with what the industry does both in programs and in promotions when they are teasing the public with sex to boost ratings?

Not a bit. I'm very much in favor of sex.

Do you have children?

Sure, two boys and two girls. All grown. As far as kids, I've read a lot of these studies, and stuff is constantly coming out about television's effect on kids, and I'm sure it has an effect on kids. I think though, that we underestimate the intelligence of our kids. Just like we underestimate the native intelligence of the adult television audience. The kids are a hell of a lot smarter than the researchers who are doing the research, by and large. Kids differentiate real war and play war; television from real life. "That's television, this is life. That daddy in that sitcom is stupid. My daddy is not stupid. That kid runs that family on that sitcom. I don't run my family."

Are there things that you think work best to hold an audience?

I have no idea what works. I produce programs that *I* would watch. Real simple. If I'm really hard up, need some bucks, I might do a program or two that I wouldn't watch, just because somebody wants me to do it.

I'm not a real smart guy. Let's just start with that. I grew up in a little teeny town in Ohio. I had a real mediocre education. I am an average Joe. I was lucky to go to Syracuse and then Johns Hopkins and that's really to a great extent where I got my education. I think I'm just kind of middle American in my tastes, and I've always just had the feeling that if it entertains me, it will entertain everybody.

I've been fooled occasionally. Stuff that entertains me doesn't entertain everybody, and stuff that I think is kind of mediocre, that we've done, sometimes gets great numbers. But basically, I don't know how any television producer can tell you that they understand the audience. If anybody understood the audience, they would be the president of the network.

You receive feedback in various ways. Are there sources of feedback that you take more seriously than others?

I read all the reviews. You can learn from reviews, there's no doubt about it. One of the things you learn is how many crappy reviewers there are around the country. *They* have short attention spans. It's also interesting to read reviews from various parts of the country and how differently things are perceived.

Do you think much about how people view TV? Do you think about what they're doing at home?

Oh, they probably watch it about like I do—casually. Somebody called TV a talking lap. It's kind of like a noisy friend who you can occasionally turn off and who occasionally says something smart that you want to listen to, and most of the time it's just prattling on like your mother or somebody.

What do you need to put into a program to make a person pay attention to it?

You're looking for a formula for entertainment success, and one of the wonderful things about this business is that there is no formula for entertainment success. If there was, and some guy had it, there would be only one company producing programs.

There must be general rules.

Well, everybody in a drama has to be their own character. They should be non-cliché, if at all possible, unless they're written as a cliché. Every

Bell with Danny Glover in Glover's directorial debut. Bell is dressed to look like Clark Gable for a role in his Showtime movie, Just a Dream.

character ought to be fresh. This is drama 101. Every character ought to react as that character reacts, not as the playwright, or the producer, or somebody else wants him to react. If you've got a message, the message should grow out of the drama. It should not be superimposed.

Do you believe that the audience has some control, either directly, or indirectly over what they get to see? Some people say that ultimately, this is a very democratic medium because of the rating system—"People vote every night," they say.

There is a certain amount of truth to that. All people think that it could be better, including the people that are doing it, but it's a question of how to make it better, and the dollars are diminishing. Television is the most important communications medium in the country and I think it's important that it get things right. I am appalled at how superficial the news broadcasts are.

I'm a print-oriented person and I read the paper every morning and at night. You read a story in any mediocre newspaper and it's better than you get on CBS news. You get more information out of it. To tell you the truth, I think Ted Turner is the way of the future. Ted is crazy, I think, a little bit. I don't say that derogatorily at all. I think that the guy is a creative genius in many ways. Both financially, which is very rare, and artistically. He's also ballsy as hell, which I love and he will do things

With two of the stars from Nadia, *the story of the Olympic gymnast, Nadia Comaneci. When it aired,* Nadia *got the highest rating ever achieved by a syndicated movie.*

because he wants to do them. He's done a biography of every state, for Christ's sake. That's an idea that went out in the 1950s. Nobody's going to do that. The Goodwill Games in the Soviet Union, while it was a disaster financially, was a damn good idea. CNN is a real broad, diverse, information source. You can tune it in anytime, and within an hour, you can catch up with the news, in more depth than you get on the commercial networks. You also get a lot of features, most of which are pretty goddamn well produced.

You mentioned earlier that you were going to significantly change your mode of business operation. Does this say something about the way the industry is changing?

Actually, I think to some extent it is bringing this company more in line with the way the industry has been operating for a long time. We will now function with a core of creative and business people who will run the company and when a project comes along, hire freelance, creative people to do the project. I've always resisted doing that because I've felt that you lose a great deal of synergistic effect without a group of people who always work together. However, the other side of the coin is that when you get a bunch of people and you bring them up with you and you all achieve a certain plateau, synergy tends to diminish anyway as egos grow. Also, the need for individual recognition transcends the desire to make sure that all of your coworkers and associates are totally in sync with you. I saw that happening in the company.

It's also much more economical to operate with the freelancers.

Yes, very much more. It also gives me more freedom. I've had good people leave my company because the company couldn't move as quickly as they could. The more people you get, the slower they are going to move. It came to the point where I couldn't move as fast as I wanted to.

The delivery systems have changed as well: VCRs, cable, satellite dishes. The trend is toward greater and greater audience control.

The real trend is that America watches things that are entertaining and does not watch things that aren't. And that is a trend that has been around ever since the first curtain went up on the first theater. It's real goddamn simple. If something is just riveting, and fascinating, and if you can do a 100-hour mini-series that has got every single element just right, everybody is going to watch 100 hours of that mini-series, including me. They are not going to watch *Casanova*. When you don't see any tits, you don't see ass, you don't see anything that *Casanova* was noted for, why in God's name would anybody watch it, I ask you?

I watched 20 minutes of it and it was just a bore. And most mini-series are, because they've got a four-hour idea and they make an eight-hour mini-series? Or a two-hour, and they make a four-hour. Most television movies are a one-hour idea.

I could tell you why that is, incidentally. Stand by for a revelation: Why are so many television movies bad? Why are they so simplistic? Why are they so straight-line? Why are they so uncomplicated? Why are the characters so cliché?

The answer is because television executives are stretched thin. Television executives read 8, 10 scripts on a weekend, read them in the car, read them on airplanes, read them on boats, read them every goddamn place except sitting down in a nice quiet spot. As soon as you give them a complicated script, they lose track. They have had three phone calls, they've had a drink, they've played some tennis in the middle, and they have lost track of where that argument is going.

Another explanation would be that a lot of these things are sold on the basis of what people in the industry refer to as "high concept." You've got a concept and you know up front how you're going to position it in the market, how you're going to advertise it. It may get picked up based on an attractive title, sometimes before there is anything even written. Does it concern you that you must reduce your concept for a movie or documentary to four or six words?

The show develops the concept. The purpose of a title is to attract an audience, that's the only purpose a title has, in my view. If you can call something, *Combat in the Classroom*, which was an attractive title, based on the ratings, you can spend 99 percent of your time in that program dealing with problems in education that had nothing to do with violence in the classroom. That's O.K. with me. That particular program did deal with combat in the classroom, as it happens, but it wouldn't have bothered me a damn bit if it hadn't.

Nowadays, "reality television" is the mantra in the industry. You were ahead of the pack on this, developing reality TV and documentaries two decades before the trend started.

I was certainly at the forefront of what is now called "reality television" and many days in looking at television as it is today I think I was one of the people who helped create a monster. I am especially unfond of virtually all of reality television.

There is a lot of manipulation of the audience to get you to quickly sympathize with certain people in many of these programs, the kind of material that 20/20 and Dateline do constantly. They'll intentionally leave out critical information to the very end to make sure that they've held the audience.

I agree. There is no doubt that narrative is carefully structured to as much as possible enhance the interest level of the viewers. If that requires leaving facts out until the end, then that is what is done. I don't have a problem with that, as long as all of the pertinent facts are given. My objection to virtually all reality programming today—I won't even call it documentary—is that it tells you what you're going to see, tells you what you're seeing, and it tells you what you saw. Anybody with a

Bruce Sallan (r) standing with actor Nils Alan Stewart in the NBC movie, The Jesse Ventura Story.

double-digit IQ is going to be able to get it and anybody with a triple-digit IQ is, if they are the least bit aware of what the hell is going on, going to turn it off.

HBO, in my view, is the only sanctuary that I know of, for intelligent documentaries. They are the only place that doesn't have somebody droning on about what the hell this thing is all about.

You'd like to be more subtle and indirect.

I'd like to be involved and allow the audience to do a little thinking on their own. HBO is a sanctuary for vérité documentaries and even HBO doesn't do very many.

What are some of the HBO documentaries you've done in recent years?

Skinheads: Soldiers of the Race War. I did another one called *Asylum,* which is about everyone who populates a state institution for the criminally insane. Also, *Transplant,* which I particularly liked. It followed organs from one donor to five or six different recipients. Heart went one place, liver went someplace else, each kidney went someplace. Both *Asylum* and *Skinheads* were exceptionally well received.

BRUCE SALLAN

My interviews with Bruce Sallan reveal how the American television industry changed in the 1990s. In listening to Sallan at two times—while at IndieProd in the late 1980s and again in 1999 as president of Davis Entertainment—we see how the change in the "fin-syn" (financial syndication) rule and mergers and vertical integration within the media industries substantially altered the day-to-day business of television production.

Sallan's move from vice-president for movies at ABC to an executive position at IndieProd, an independent production company, was typical of the career path for many successful television executives in the 1970s and 80s. Sallan's departure from ABC was part of the pre-fin-syn "brain drain" when network executives were constantly moving to independent production.

While at ABC, Sallan was associated with the productions of *The Day After* and *Golda* and functioned like a mini-mogul. After five years at IndieProd, Sallan went to Lee Rich Productions, where he produced reunion shows of *The Waltons* and *Dallas.* Then he was briefly with Brandon Tartikoff at New World Television. In the interview, Sallan reminisces about the much-admired Tartikoff and his untimely death.

Sallan explains television movie production from the point of view of both a buyer at the network and a seller at a production company. We learn how program and movie concepts are pitched and bought. His story of how he came up with the idea for *California Girls* while at ABC is one of my favorites, as is his joke about the insurmountable budget problems of producing a very particular sort of television movie in New York.

Most striking is how Sallan believes the industry has been hurt by increased financial competition. Some of his view may be sour grapes, but he is not alone in feeling that the industry has become more competitive and less enjoyable.

I grew up in Los Angeles and graduated high school at 16 because I skipped twice. Then I skipped around colleges because I was restless. I spent my first year at U.C. San Diego. Then I went to Antioch that summer. It didn't work out and I went back to San Diego in the fall. Then I went five straight semesters and took winter off and went skiing all winter.

I studied film in college. Took my first film class as a freshman at UCSD. Then I went to U.C. Santa Cruz and was in charge of all the film societies on campus. I came back to Los Angeles when I was 19 and took the next year off, not knowing what I wanted to do. At that point I thought I might like to be in the motion picture business. I didn't even know what development was, which is what I do now.

I worked for the post office, went to Europe, skied another winter, and decided to go to UCLA's Graduate School of Business in a program called Management of the Arts. They had a National Endowment for the Arts internship from which I hoped to gain entree to a studio. To support myself I also got a job at a tennis club. I played competitive tennis in high school and college.

At the tennis club, I met a producer, Jerry Isenberg. He offered me a job which I converted into my internship for my master's. He had an MBA from Harvard and felt the MBA was a very useful thing in this business. He owned a small TV production company. This was in 1975. I finished my degree and started working with him.

I learned what development was and what producing was. He was a terrific mentor. I became his assistant and started developing my own ideas and trying to sell them. I was affiliated with him for six years during which I was promoted from assistant to director of development to VP of development. During the six years, I was an associate producer, co-producer, producer, or exec-producer on 10 to 15 projects that were made. Mostly TV movies and a few pilots.

We did a series of movies called *Having Babies* which were landmark films of the mid-1970s that dealt with couples having babies. It turned into a series with Susan Sullivan as the doctor. I started the "Golda Project" on Golda Meir. It was my approach. My idea. I sold it. I did a three-hour called *Berlin Tunnel*. Another really fine film we did was called *Act of Love* with Mickey Rourke and Ron Howard. I also did *Ski Lift to Death*—a favorite of mine.

I decided I wanted to work at ABC in the movie department. My perception as a seller was that it was the most exciting movie department. It was the freest and it would be the place I'd fit in most.

Aside from your background in film, do you have a background in literature or drama?

I don't think I'm well-read enough. Just for my own security I'd like to be a little more knowledgeable. I will often find myself in a discussion with people who may make a reference to Shakespeare and I never really read much Shakespeare.

I was a voracious reader as a kid. I read all the classics and pop-classics. Edgar Allan Poe, Dickens, famous popular reading of the ages. Twain, Tom Sawyer, *Last of the Mohicans*. I loved that kind of stuff. Also, all kinds of popular novels, James Bond, etc.

Do you have a sense of what makes a story work, about structure and narrative style?

I think I do. I think I just learned that through experience. I think I'm a very good editor. That's one of the things I do best. I think a movie is interesting if the character changes or grows or is affected by what goes on during the course of the movie. If the person is exactly the same at the end as at the beginning, then it's less interesting. They haven't gone through much growth or change. In the TV movie, I think that's what you want to show. How a family survives a rape or a loss of a child.

Tell me about your time at ABC.

What I learned, more than anything else, was something that didn't come natural to me—politics in relationships. The entertainment business is 99 percent based on networking and 1 percent based on talent and good ideas. Maybe it 95 to 5 among executives and producers. Since it didn't come natural to me to go out and politic, a job at the network would force it to happen. I got the job at ABC because I was friendly with the then-current VP of movies, Stu Samuels. I worked under him. I was one of three executive producers. A year and a half later he left and I was promoted. I was VP for two-and-a-half years and made 75 movies. Among them, *The Day After, Something About Amelia,* and *Consenting Adult.*

Why did you leave?

Lots of internal changes occurred when Capital Cities took over ABC. I felt I was very underpaid. My predecessor was making over $200,000, his predecessor was making $175,000, and I was making about $130,000. I wanted a substantial amount more if I was going to stay, plus commitments, which they weren't giving any more.

I wanted too much money and they wanted too much time. They asked me to stay but they wanted a two-to-three-year guarantee and

I really didn't want to stay longer than a year and I wanted a substantial increase. So, I joined IndieProd because it seemed to be the proper marriage for me. They were partnered with Phoenix Entertainment for television in the world. It's like a mini-studio. I'm president of TV.

How much more money can one make by being an independent producer and selling television movies to a network?

I'm not at this level yet, but a friend of mine is a producer and has his own production company and has made over $1 million a year for the last six years, making two to three TV movies a year.

You said networking was very important.

It's a good thing if you know the right people. Bad if you don't.

Does it mean that talented people with good ideas don't get heard because they're not in that circle?

I think that's absolutely true. Certain people with certain strong relationships with certain buyers continually make products and get deals when they're not turning out any quality. There are certain writers and directors who have friends in high places and who continue to work and a lot of newer people are not even tried.

As a producer, probably the most important people to me are the agencies and agents. The agents control the talent that have the ideas or the packaging ability that will make an idea come alive.

How hard do you have to work at networking?

That's a choice you make. I made a choice that I could only do so much of it and as a result, my upward potential in this business has a governor on it, so to speak. If the best you can get in this business is a 10, the best I'll ever get is an 8 because I've chosen not to go the distance to make it to 10. That choice is one that I make willingly and with comfort because in this business I can be a very rich, successful man working at level 8. The difference between $1 million and $1.4 million isn't worth it.

What would you have to do differently to go from 8 to 10?

I don't like to eat breakfast at meetings. People who are going for that extra two points will have breakfast meetings almost every day of the week. They will meet people for drinks almost every day of the week.

I tend to work out after work. I maintain certain friends since childhood that can do me no good. I truly make time for my friends and family. I don't have my own family—I mean my parents or the family of whatever girl I may be involved with at the time. That takes a certain amount of time. In contrast, I know any number of people who have consciously chosen to put their social and family life aside in the pursuit of success and I don't think that's necessary to reach the level of success that I'm going for.

Let's talk about the networks and how they make decisions. Could they make better decisions?

I certainly think so. I'd also say that given the amount of programming that's made, the haste and rush and financial restrictions that are attached to it, there's a remarkable amount of terrific TV. I believed that when I was at the networks and I believe it as a supplier. I believe, pound for pound, there is more quality, more thought in TV than there is in features. You give me any week's *TV Guide* and I will show you any number of terrific things to watch every night of the week.

What people forget about TV is that it's a business, not a charitable foundation. It's not a public service. If *The Dukes of Hazzard* gets a 40 share a week, that means a lot of people are watching it and they're liking it.

What do you look for when someone comes in with a new project?

I was looking for different things when I was at the network versus now. When I was at the network, I was looking for projects that I thought combined ratings potential with quality, more accent on the former. I also wanted balance—a certain kind of quality show to look well rounded.

Who would you want to look well rounded to?

Mostly my upper management. There was a great pride in the movies we made at ABC. We always made the fewest number of movies, but always made the greatest impact. I remember one year I was there, we made 19 movies to the combined 80 of the other networks but we had over half the Emmy nominations.

You said that one of your considerations when looking at a project was ratings. What rules did you live by in order to get ratings?

The truth is you fly by the seat of your pants. There *are* certain assumptions we make. For example, westerns and sci-fi don't work for ratings, as a rule. You'd also try to have a female deal because women strongly control TV sets. There's research to support this. Women have more influence in the family over what to watch. There's also a certain kind of feeling in a program needed for a certain night. For a Sunday night movie you want a bigger, broader based movie whereas Monday night can be more of a domestic sort of movie. I also cared a lot about having stars because I thought that would help get ratings. The last year I bought projects with Dolly Parton, Audrey Hepburn, and Liz Taylor.

As a supplier and as a network executive there were certain things I didn't want to do. I would not do pictures about mass murders or terrorists. This is Bruce Sallan's sense of morality. I didn't want to glorify or encourage those people in any way. It made me crazy that people at CBS would do the Ted Bundy story and NBC did a story about Charlie Manson.

You said westerns and sci-fi wouldn't work. What else doesn't work?

Stories that are too soft. That means a very sweet, lovable story about a runaway kid that falls in love with a hobo. It won't work because it doesn't have a broad enough appeal. Such a story is hard to capsulate in eight seconds or less for promotion purposes. A TV movie, unlike a TV series, is sold two ways: 80 to 90 percent of its sell is from on-air promos. The other 10 to 20 percent is print, either ads or press. That's why you need a star. You have to grab the audience and you only have one chance to do so.

I am a businessman. I'm in business. Other than the moral problems I would have doing mass murders and terrorists, I will develop and try to sell things that I'm not interested in on a personal level.

California Girls

In a way you could be more morally straight and narrow at the network than you can be now.

Right. I still maintain my sense of morality but I can't afford to be quite as picky. We are a business. I may not love a particular project, but if I could sell it and as long as it has some sense of value, I might do it. I try to find in every project a sense of value.

How does an idea for a script for a movie of the week come to you?

They come from every source imaginable: agents, writers, news, my own head. As an example, take a movie I did at ABC—this is one of the things about my former job I miss. I drove to work one beautiful day, my convertible top was down, the radio was on. I was enjoying the outside and driving to work and on the radio comes an old Beach boys song, "California Girls." I'm singing along to the song and I suddenly thought, "I'm going to buy that song and make a movie called *California Girls.*" It's a hook, it's a title, it gives a mood. I didn't know what the movie would be about. I drove into the parking lot, I was VP at the time. I talked to my assistant, Chad Hoffman, and said I want to do a movie called *California Girls.* Check on the rights and come up with an approach. Fourteen months later, we aired a movie called *California Girls*, with Zsa Zsa Gabor, Martin Mull, and Robby Benson, with the original Beach Boys song as the title song.

What did it cost for the rights?

It was $25,000 to use it the one time.

When people pitch ideas to you, what makes a good pitch and what makes a pitch bad?

It's all about making me interested. I used to have an egg timer, a five-minute timer on my desk. I didn't literally do this but when someone would come in and say, "Tell me how I can sell to you," I would take the egg timer and say, "See this," and turn it over. "If I don't know everything about that movie in five minutes or less, you haven't done a good job pitching it to me. That doesn't mean we can't go on talking about it, but if I don't know in the first three to five minutes what that movie's about, how am I going to sell it? Who am I appealing to?"

Did you care where you heard a pitch?

As a network exec, I much preferred it in my office because I feel a meal is a social environment. At lunch, let's talk about business in general. I work very hard all day long. I want a break in the day. Then, come to my office and we'll spend 15 to 20 minutes concentrated, uninterrupted time.

What else happens in pitch sessions?

Anything you can imagine. I tried to sell a show once that CBS finally made, called *Zoo Vets.* It was about a wild animal vet. The writer and

I took a black spotted leopard to the pitch to NBC. We cleared it with everyone except the executive whom we were pitching to because we wanted to surprise him. As we brought the cat into the network everybody was jumping out of their offices.

I just thought, they hear hundreds of pitches over the course of the development season, and they all start to run together. How do you make yours stand out? There've even been strippers that have been brought to the network.

But it can backfire. The network exec was so nervous that this woman was going to take off her clothes, that he never focused on the show. The black spotted leopard, as great an idea as it was, backfired because the network executive we were pitching had a deathly fear of cats. So he was petrified the whole meeting. He did not say anything. He did not hear a word. He was sweating with fear. Animals are sometimes attracted to where the most fear is and this animal was let loose in the room and started licking him.

When you were at the network, did your superiors restrict your ability to do your job?

Yes, but I was very fortunate. I didn't have too many experiences like that. There was one experience that really caused me a lot of grief, where a project that I was developing was killed for political reasons to favor a friend of upper management who had a similar project at another network. I was not allowed to do our project that was in the same genre. That project aired on another network and beat ABC badly. That made me crazy. That's a classic example of the 95 to 5 percent. Something that blatant is pretty rare.

Or take Aaron Spelling's deal at ABC. It was clearly favoritism. You could argue that there was good and bad that came from the extraordinary size of commitment, money, and obligation that ABC gave to one producer. Is that favoritism? Is that good? Who knows.

What attraction is there to produce a series?

The attraction is purely financial. *The Cosby Show* was worth more money than any theatrical event, TV movie, or play in the history of entertainment. It was worth $500 to 800 million. That's the bottom line.

If I develop a series idea and I bring in a writer-producer and we sell it to the network and make it a hit, it's got to have 66 episodes. Three whole seasons. At that point, all the principals involved stand to make a great deal of money if they own a piece of the show. But if I'm a studio exec, VP of development, and I'm responsible for *Miami Vice* and even if it's my idea, I will see nothing more than a bonus at the end of the year, or a raise. The only people that get a piece are the owners, the risk takers.

In the case of *The Cosby Show*, you have Carsey-Werner. The two of them are former ABC execs and they own a piece of that show, 25 percent or some number. After distribution fees and everything else, let's say there's $300 million left over. They're going to get $75 million of that, or some number that's very considerable.

Are there people working in television who are primarily interested in money rather than because they like being involved in the industry?

I don't know anybody who's in it just for the big bucks, myself included. I really feel privileged and lucky to be doing what I do. I enjoy it a lot of the time. It's a very unstructured business that allows all sorts of freedoms without too many corporate constraints.

Just look at how I'm dressed. I'm wearing a pair of designer blue jeans with two-year-old dirty running shoes with no socks and an oxford shirt with rolled up sleeves, and that's it. I don't have a jacket or tie. And Dan Melnick, who's a major independent film producer and who's my boss and runs this company, will come in and not look at me and say, "Why aren't you wearing socks?" Because probably he's not wearing them either.

Even at the network I rarely wore a tie. That seems like a silly thing, but I could be individualistic. I didn't have to conform. It's not like a Japanese conglomerate where everyone tries to look the same. It's almost the reverse. You're rewarded for your differences. It's encouraged. Probably less so at the networks these days now that they're owned by GE and Cap Cities.

I can wake up in the morning and go, "I don't feel like going to work today." As long as the bottom line is successful, as long as Dan is seeing that we're doing a lot of stuff, I could just call in sick, or not even call in sick. Just say, "I'm not up to it today. I'm going to stay home and read." Nobody cares as long as you get it done. You don't punch a clock.

People also move around *very* quickly. My first job was with Jerry Isenberg at Paramount. The head of production and feature films was Robert Evans, who held the industry record for the longest duration as a senior VP of Worldwide Production at the studio. Somebody told me that, so I wondered how long: It was something like six-and-a-half years. When I was promoted to VP of movies at ABC, I knew there had been four or five people before me who had that job. The longest any of them held it was three years. I had to figure that I would be at that job probably no more than two to four years, which turned out to be true.

By and large, do you think that's a good thing that there's that much movement or do you think that so much movement means there's less coherence?

I think the latter is true. There tends to be a heavy ego investment in one's own projects so new people throw out the previous regime's developments or don't take them seriously. As a result, companies lose a lot of money and time. Agents, producers and suppliers then have to redevelop all their relationships. It is very common for a new regime to be less supportive of existing products of a previous regime and to allow them to either languish or go away in favor of their own projects.

Let's talk for a moment about the reasons that an executive at the network will turn things down. He or she will be saying "no" to many more projects than saying "yes." What percentage?

I'd say 99 out of 100 times. In my department at ABC I wouldn't hear all 100. A lot of them were passed on at a lower level because executives working for me would know there were certain ones they shouldn't even show me. So I'd say 9 out of 10.

But I always felt an obligation to try to give a good reason. I worked on being considerate in how I passed on somebody's idea when I was at the network. There are two or three reasons I always felt were the safest and the easiest to understand. If they were ever applicable, I would try to use them.

One: I have a competing project that touches on the same area. There's no argument for that. It's not fair to the producer who's developing it.

Two: Sometimes I was pitched ideas that had already been tried at another network and didn't work and tarnished the ability to do that type of project. Or it's either in development somewhere else or it's been done somewhere else. The first two I thought were real clean.

The third reason I tried to use didn't always work. I'd say, "It doesn't have the right demographics." It always sounded like bullshit. Finally I would say, "I'm just not responding to it. It's just not something that touches me and I just don't like it." At least it would be honest.

Couldn't you say to the writer, if it were true, "Look, I don't think this is one of your best efforts."

I would never say that because they presumably came in believing in it and thinking strongly. They would say, "Bruce, what do you really think? Am I on the right track?" I don't feel it is my place to answer that. I chose to be diplomatic and say we're not looking for that kind of thing right now. The most successful writers in the business have many, many unproduced scripts. The best directors in the business don't make good movies every time. So to say to somebody that your previous work is good and this one isn't is nonproductive because maybe the next one's going to be great. It just doesn't accomplish anything.

Is it conceivable that a writer might actually want to hear some constructive criticism?

Not from a buyer, because you're born to be hated when you're in that job. Because you're always saying "no." I'll give you an example: In my current job, I had an idea for a TV movie and I wanted to get a particular actress committed to it before I went to the network. This particular actress is managed by her husband. So we set up a meeting with her husband to present the idea before we even brought it to the network. A woman who works for me and a writer that had the idea were going to go to this meeting. I couldn't make it. So they went and started presenting the idea. In the course of the conversation, my name came up. This husband-manager went into a tirade about what an asshole I was. He explained to the people that work with me that I passed on a project he cared about when I was at ABC. I never met the man or talked to the man but I may have passed on his project. Something may have been communicated back to him by someone along the way that touched him wrong. But he condemned me without a hearing, without meeting me. Who knows why I really passed. I offended a lot of people in that job just because I said no. It all comes back to haunt you. What comes around goes around.

A writer told me about being turned down on a script about submarines and a shipwreck on a desert island. The network said they didn't want it because "movies on water lose money."

"Movies on water are expensive to make" is really the right answer. To hear it after the script has been written is really a pretty shitty cop-out. If you're not going to make it because you can't afford to make it, then don't put it in development in the first place. Yes, it's a fact. Movies on water are expensive and drawn out.

Can you think of other rules like that?

Period pictures are difficult and expensive. Sci-fi is expensive. Kids, dogs, and animals are expensive. Also time consuming. Winter is expensive. New York's expensive. The joke is to do a New York period piece about a kid and his dog in the winter.

Very funny. What about stories about ethnic minorities?

There's no overt prejudice against doing stories about minorities, but there certainly is a practical one. If 75 percent of the public is white and 25 percent is not, you're not going to want to do the majority of your projects that are with nonwhites.

Let's turn to a different topic. Is there a "brain drain" at the networks?

I think a long-term problem the networks have had, which they have not yet completely corrected but are trying to, is they haven't made it a place where you get compensated commensurate with your work. It is unbelievable the number of major executives that started at ABC that left to pursue other interests and went on to extraordinary success. I can name 8 to 10 ABC alumni off the top of my head: Barry Diller, Michael Eisner, Leonard Goldberg, Dan Mellman, Len Hills, Stu Samuels, Bruce Sallan, Jerry Isenberg, Marcy Carsey, Tom Werner.

By implication, if a person's really good, ought they be in a network job for only a few years?

If a person's real good, they probably won't stay in a network job for long because the outside temptations are too great. If you're a network

VP, you're going to make between $90 to 175 thousand. If you go to run a production company or be a producer you will make considerably more than that. The big difference is you profit from success on the outside. You also have the risk of failure. But if you're Tom Werner and Marcy Carsey and you form your own production company and you get a Cosby, you're going to get $75 million. Whoever was the VP of comedy at the time the show was developed at NBC and worked on the pilot and said to Tartikoff, "Let's buy that show," they were making $140,000 the year they did that. The next year they were making $150,000 because there was only a 6 percent ceiling on raises allowed that year.

Still, a network job is great. It was glorious to be in the job I had. I was a mini–Louis Mayer, Harry Cohn, Warner Bros. That's what I did. I was responsible for 100 scripts a year in development, 20 to 25 movies a year getting made, and I had just about full and total autonomy and control over the whole operation. I do miss it.

At the network you had power. Now you have to pitch stories to your replacement at ABC. I guess it becomes a question of what you want more.

My mother understands my job now because it says "Produced by Bruce Sallan." Before, it didn't say my name. I would go, "Mom, that's my movie. I developed it." She says, "Where's your name? Aunt Ruth in Detroit doesn't understand." I'd say, "Mom, it was my idea. I came up with it. *California Girls.* I came up with that idea." She asks, "Who's Bob Goodwin? He produced it." I tell her "He's the producer *I* hired to do it."

Now it says "Executive Producer, Bruce Sallan." I'm being a little facetious in my description. But it mattered to me to get credit for what I did and you don't get that in an executive job.

How secure are network executive positions?

I don't think there's any security in a network job. Particularly at ABC and NBC. CBS has no contracts. As a result, a lot of network people take the conservative route and don't take chances. Some have overstayed their welcome in certain departments and are tired.

Could you ever see yourself going back to the network?

You don't ever go back, almost never. I did have a nicer lifestyle at the network than I do now because I could complete a day's work in my network job. I can never complete a day's work in my current job. At the network, I could return everybody's phone call, read all the scripts that were in development, and basically be on top of things. When you're running a production company, you never have enough scripts in development, there's always someone else you should be talking to or meeting with. There's always eight things you should be reading.

When you're developing a TV movie, screenwriters tell me they have to be written in seven acts and that network executives tell them to develop more plot and exposition in the first 25 minutes to get the audience hooked.

I have a different opinion. There is a common feeling that you have to hook the audience in the first act or they'll turn away. I always contended that wasn't true. I had the research department do a study on this.

I had them take 10 movies on regularly scheduled nights, a regular movie on a regular night, on each network for three seasons and track the half-hour ratings. That was 90 movies for three years on three networks. Four half-hour measurements. In 90 cases in three years, there wasn't one number that was less than the previous half-hour.

In the last couple years, I have noticed an occasional case where a movie will have less viewship at the end than the beginning. At that time, it had not happened ever. What that means is that if a movie started at a 15 share, it would end up at 18. I think if it's good drama and you care about the people and characters, it doesn't have to have a heavy plot.

I think making a good TV movie, series, or feature film is one of the most incredibly difficult things imaginable. When it turns out right, it's a combination of so many factors that includes luck, the right people, the right timing. It isn't just writing either. How good would the *The Sting* have been if the music was terrible? How good would *Saturday Night Fever* have been if the Bee Gees hadn't done the score?

My favorite example is *Cosby*. This is the capriciousness of the business. Imagine me going to pitch an idea for a series about a black family: "Dad is a pediatrician, Mom is a lawyer, and there's three kids. There's this little black girl that is so adorable you won't believe it. Another girl is 16 and about to go to college, and then there is a wiseass 14-year-old. We might do a whole story about the tooth fairy. Or we'll do a whole story about what happens if the cat got lost. Isn't that brilliant?"

I would have been thrown out of the office. *Cosby* happened because of Bill Cosby and they got a good writer and producer. Bill Cosby in the right vehicle at the right time. Was the idea brilliant? No. It was the execution, the timing, the good fortune.

We last talked over 10 years ago. I know you were with Lee Rich for a time, after IndieProd. How did you get to New World?

Brandon Tartikoff offered me the job running New World Television under him. I was responsible for all television movies and all the drama series. Brandon Tartikoff! This was his last job before it got bought out and then he had eight months to a one year period before he died.

Many people in television loved Brandon Tartikoff and he has been much mourned since his death.

He was a genuinely good guy. He had a level of enthusiasm that was inextinguishable. No matter what was going on, no matter how he'd get beaten down, he couldn't wait to get back into the game. But the New World experience and the betrayals that he and all of us experienced there were too much. People manipulated the division solely for their gain, building a company all as a show to manipulate the company, to have a certain appearance of value, to be sold. Welcome to America.

So Brandon brought me aboard with all this enthusiasm and optimism of building something special and for me I thought, "Wow, this will be the first time I join a company that has money and it wants you to really build something."

Do you think that the problems at New World contributed to the decline of Tartikoff's health?

Well, there is a debate among his friends. I feel very strongly that it did. Other friends of his believe that's what kept him alive, that his devotion and his excitement over show biz allowed him a distraction.

Let me tell you a Brandon story. This was a few months after he was bought out at New World and got this very substantial amount of money. I was still there, kind of caught in the morass of the buyout, but I knew I was gonna be leaving. I ran into him at a party and we had not really talked since he had left.

Before that we had exchanged a lot of e-mails, the files of which I saved. I wrote that I was thinking about leaving the business and maybe do something in the charitable world and I'm sick of it all. He wrote me back an e-mail. He was furious with me. "You're too young, you have too much to offer, you're too smart. You know, when you're 60, you can go do whatever. I've seen you in meetings, you're born to be in the business." It was flattering and wonderful, but it was really about *him.*

He was not ill; as far as he knew, he'd beaten it once and for all. So we run into each other at the party. I ask him why he doesn't take the family and do a trip around the world or something? "Why don't you take a break?" And he said, "I can't." He could not stop working because he was either addicted, he loved it too much, or was afraid to leave for whatever reason, some combination. And it was a really frightening experience because I really loved this man, he's a really good man, and I knew what he just lived through—not the health stuff, just the horrible business experience at New World. And he was not gonna miss a season. And he wasn't thinking he was dying at that point. It was about his commitment.

What did you do at New World that you were pleased with?

A family show called *Second Noah* that had a two-year run on ABC. It has a certain meaning to make something like that because TV has really disintegrated into a lot of crap. And that one I am especially proud of.

What was Second Noah *about?*

Second Noah was about a couple who couldn't have kids and adopted "strays," and had a blended family of different ethnic and racial backgrounds—for that matter, health backgrounds—of eight kids and a whole bunch of animals. Hence the name *Second Noah*, like a new Noah's Ark. We shot it down in Florida, and with the cooperation of Busch Gardens, we used their animals and their facilities. And it was a really lovely show.

How has the industry changed since we last talked in the late 1980s?

It's changed, I think, hugely. I'm not personally 100 percent sure if the filter that I have of now being 45 years old with a couple young kids is affecting how I look at things. But among my contemporaries in the business, and even more specifically, among those that have made television movies a primary focus of their career—meaning my peers, people in their 40s and 50s—nobody thinks it's fun anymore. Nobody. It's absolutely not fun. Competitive and cutthroat instead.

Two things have happened that have affected me, which is why I am very seriously wondering how much longer I will be here. Number one is the consolidation and corporitization of the business, the whole idea of synergy and all that, where you have ABC and Disney. That process has affected the way in which business gets done.

The television movie business evolved and grew with independent producers that financed their own movies, owned them, and were really like mini-studios. Little moguls with $1 to 2 million TV movies. Two guys would run a little company and they'd make two, three, four, five movies a year, and between them, they'd make well over $1 million a year. They have a little company of 6 or 8 or 10 employees. That was the business. There were three or four networks you went to (you had three originally, then Fox, then HBO, and then TNT), and of course now there's like 20 to 22.

Number two is that they repealed the financial syndication, or "fin-syn" rule, which allowed the networks to own their programming. Before fin-syn, networks could own very few of their own negatives, and that's where the money is—in the later syndication as reruns of successful series television and movies. So, it was relaxed, and they now can own as much as they want and that destroyed the way we used to do business.

The networks said, "We want to make a movie, but we also want to own it. You are just gonna work for a fee." So instead of having the upside of making a million or more dollars to a movie we might now make from $150,000 to $300–350,000 per movie.

There used to be a brain drain from networks to independent production because that's where the greater money, freedom, and independence was.

Now people at the networks hang on to their jobs kicking and screaming because there is no place to go. The independence in that world is shrinking. And the network executives aren't having a lot of fun either because the cutbacks as a result of all the consolidation mean they have more and more work to do.

The Day After

Is it less rewarding too, that even if you get something on the air, the audience is smaller?

When I ran *The Day After*, when I ran movies on ABC, it was the highest rated movie in the history of television. That share will never ever be beaten because of all these changes and the cable channels. When people ask me what I've done recently I tend to not want to tell them because I'm embarrassed. They won't recognize the titles.

It is truly more like a business now, where you feel like you're cranking out product?

Yeah, and there's very little personal reward. Also, because of all of these competitive cable outlets that now make TV movies, even the critical attention that you used to get with a TV movie for CBS or NBC or ABC, no longer happens. All the critical attention goes to the cable outlets. And all the feature people, because their business has been going through downsizing, are now slumming in television. So the TV producers and TV directors that are working now, not only will they not own their product anymore, but now they're competing with all these feature people who want to play in television.

What about from the audience perspective?

The audience perspective couldn't be better.

So you don't like working in your niche of television anymore?

Many people who I talk to say it's over. There's two analogies that I use. One, is I'm making horseshoes right after Henry Ford has introduced the Model-T. Or, I own a mom and pop store right down the street from a Wal-Mart. I'll get a little business, but mostly they're gonna just drive right by me and go to Wal-Mart. Wal-Mart is the network, the cable outlets, all of them.

The audience has more diversity of product, though.

Sure. I'm a shopper, too. Using the Wal-Mart analogy, I'd rather go to Wal-Mart or Costco and buy things cheaper than go to a mom and pop store that supports some little guy and his family.

The other thing is that human graces are falling by the way side. There's a level of rudeness in the process. If I have three lunches scheduled in a week, I can assume two of them will be cancelled, usually the day of. Phone calls—forget it. Answers in a timely manner—forget it. The network executives stay there longer; they don't think they can leave so they're not looking to make friends.

A lot of people would say the media have themselves contributed to a general decline in civility in society. As a parent and as a person in the industry, how do you respond to the idea that some of this decline is related to the product that Hollywood puts out?

I think there's absolutely no question whatsoever. But you see, I am an endangered species in Hollywood, one that is more blacklisted than any other minority could ever be—I'm a conservative. And Hollywood is run, literally, by the liberal establishment to such a huge degree that if you have conservative values and/or do something really horrible, like vote Republican, you are almost literally out of a job. In fact, among my few conservative friends in the business, you don't talk about it.

But people on the left have kids and care about the culture. Don't you think it's the commercial forces that result in a lot of questionable material, not the politics of the producers?

They blame the forces, they don't blame themselves. Very few take any real responsibility for Quentin Tarantino's movies or *South Park,* or any of the other crap that's out there. Or the music.

I think the worst culprit in the media is news. I think television news demeans our society more than anything else that's out there. Do you realize how we were assaulted for a year with all the Clinton bullshit about oral sex on the 6:00 news?

Television, as bad as I think it is, is better than film, and film is better than music. Music is the lowest of the lowest of the lowest.

I'm talking about the grace of life, the kindnesses.

CHAPTER 7

Two Directors

Although the director is clearly very important in film, he is often relatively unimportant in television. Indeed, many television shows have different directors nearly every week. As a result, television actors often report that they do *a lot* of self-direction. A few television directors even have been known to arrive on a set never having read the script. It's rare, but it happens, more often in comedy than in drama.

Given the television director's reduced creative role, it's easy to see why television, certainly series television, is considered a producer's medium. Television directors have little opportunity to put their stamp on an individual program. Indeed, they are encouraged *not* to put a stamp on a program; it ought not to stand out as different from the series work already established.

The director is expected to fit well within the machine of television production and to *not* change things, to adhere to the producer's overriding vision of the program. In John Ravage's 1978 book *Television: The Director's Viewpoint*, directors lament how little creativity they can exert within this system of production:

> Directors find they must sacrifice a careful and insightful style in favor of satisfying the producer's wants. . . . Most directors have learned to cope by accepting the occupation for what it is, and they try to work within it. Many others sublimate their creativity into other considerations; they learn to "get involved" with the minimal human values present in the scripts on which they must work; they search for meanings not readily apparent in the original scripts; they attempt to create interest and vitality by an artful edit or a sly expression, tucked away where the producer's inquiring eye might miss it. (pp. 9–10)

But there are important exceptions to this general view of television directors. Many of the episodes of *Soap, The Mary Tyler Moore Show,* and *The Cosby Show* were directed by Jay Sandrich—one of the reasons I wanted to interview him. Both Sandrich and the producers with whom he works prefer

Jay Sandrich with Bill Cosby on the set of The Cosby Show.

to have him stay with the same program for many episodes, particularly in its first season, because he brings an authority and wisdom to the set that makes a real difference with the players and the program.

TV-movie director Walter Grauman directed the pilots and all of the first two seasons of *The Fugitive* and *The Streets of San Francisco*. Producer Quinn Martin, well known for his identifiable style, wanted a very consistent look and feel for his programs, and Walter Grauman helped him achieve this.

As a rule most episodes of a drama will be directed by a different director. Occasionally one director will direct multiple episodes, but very rarely will one director work an entire season. Grauman and Sandrich, unlike many of their colleagues, have been given the opportunity to serve as a critical creative force in series television, which is why their insights are included in *Creating Television*.

JAY SANDRICH

Jay Sandrich is without rival as a director of television comedy. He was the premier television comedy director for much of the 1970s and 1980s, directing the first two years of *The Mary Tyler Moore Show*, *Soap*, and *The Cosby Show*.

In those years, when a production company would produce the all-critical pilot of a new program in an effort to sell it to the network, it was often Sandrich who was asked to direct. He served in this role for the pilots of *Newhart*, *Phyllis*, *The Golden Girls*, and *WKRP in Cincinnati*, among others. His other credits include many of the most memorable and classic comedy programs over four of television's five decades: *I Love Lucy*, *December Bride*, *The Danny Thomas Show*, *The Andy Griffith Show* (as a producer), *Get Smart*, *The Dick Van Dyke Show*, and *Rhoda*.

Sandrich has won four Emmy awards, two for *The Cosby Show* and two for *The Mary Tyler Moore Show*. His discussion here tells us a good deal about how he believes a television comedy director should work, which clearly has a great deal to do with people skills. And people are still turning to him: In 2002 he handled the television direction for the Broadway revival of Clare Booth Luce's *The Women*, which aired on PBS.

We first met in the late 1980s, when Sandrich was still directing *The Cosby Show*. His office was at GTG Entertainment in Culver City where he was partnered with Grant Tinker. Ten years later, we caught up again to see how his views on the industry had changed.

☆ ☆ ☆

I'm one of those people that used nepotism to its fullest extent. I was born and raised in this business. My father was a director, Mark Sandrich. He directed the Astaire–Rogers pictures. He passed away when I was 13, so

I was never really able to use the knowledge that he had. I wasn't particularly interested in the business, but when it came time for me to go to college, like most college students, I didn't have any idea what I wanted to do. My father had been in the business, so I thought, "Why not?"

I never particularly wanted to be a director. I went to UCLA and majored in theater arts and motion pictures. I was in ROTC and went in the army just after Korea ended. When I got out I realized that television was the medium where you could work and stay at home. Back then every feature film was shot somewhere around the world on location, and I had a small child and a wife. I decided that I would go into television.

I applied to the place that appealed to me the most, which was Desilu. I loved their comedies. The man in charge of production and who was hiring assistant directors was one of my father's assistants. Obviously, I got the job working on *I Love Lucy* and later, *December Bride*.

Eventually, I became first assistant director on *I Love Lucy*. Then I worked on *The Danny Thomas Show* for about five years with Sheldon Leonard. They let me direct two shows. It was the first chance I had to direct. I was 26. Then I was an associate producer on the pilot of *Get Smart*. Leonard Stern was the producer. He was wonderful in allowing me to move up from assistant director.

When *Get Smart* was sold as a series I became the producer but I quickly realized that I liked directing more than producing. When the series *He and She* with Dick Benjamin and Paula Prentiss got started, Leonard Stern asked me if I would like to produce it. I said, "No, I would rather direct." So I became the director of *He and She*. That was my first full time directing where I was really earning a living as a director.

One of the things I didn't like as a producer was that I would wake up at 4:00 in the morning with all these problems I had to solve. As a director, I never wake up in the middle of the night, because I know in the morning when I get there with the cast, we're going to do the best we can and the group effort will solve it. As a producer I would know how to fix problems but I couldn't fix them. As a director, I can go to the writers and say, "This doesn't work," and 9 times out of 10, they'll come back with wonderful stuff.

After *He and She* finished, I spent a couple years doing assignments here and there. Then I worked on about five or six of Bill Cosby's show where he was a basketball coach [*The Bill Cosby Show*] and did the first five shows of *The Mary Tyler Moore Show*. I had been the assistant on *The Dick Van Dyke Show*, and that's where I first met Grant and Mary. Over the course of the seven years of that show, I did two-thirds of them.

While I was at *MTM*, I directed the pilot for *Newhart*, *Phyllis*, and *WKRP in Cincinnati*, and about four or five other shows. Then I went and did the first two years of *Soap* for Witt-Thomas. *Soap* was the first time I committed to a show. I did all of them. It was unusually complicated so they couldn't bring in different directors each week like most shows. Then I left after two years to do a Neil Simon movie, *Seems Like Old Times*, with Goldie Hawn and Chevy Chase. I found out that I really enjoyed television more than I did pictures. I came back to do another series for Witt-Thomas called, *It Takes Two* with Patty Duke-Astin and Richard Crenna. I did about 13 of those.

Television then went through a very low period in terms of comedy for about four or five years. For a year, I just did a couple of shows. A couple of *Night Courts* and a pilot. Then the Bill Cosby presentation came up.

I was doing two pilots, one with Ed Asner and Eileen Brennan called, *Off the Rack*, and immediately following that I was supposed to do this 10-minute presentation for *The Cosby Show*. It was not a full show, it was just a presentation. The network had already bought six shows of *Cosby*, with no premise. Basically, it was just the idea that it was a father and mother and the kids. They didn't know when they were going to slot it. They just wanted to see the chemistry. I accepted to direct without a script, which I usually won't do. But, number one, it was with Bill, and number two, it was never going to go on the air.

It turned out to be one of the most wonderful presentations that anybody had ever done. So they decided instead of six, they were going to order 13 episodes and put it all on in the fall. The rest is just history.

I directed all of them the first two years. Part of the problem for me was that the show was in New York, and I don't like New York. I did not like spending all winter in New York.

Now I have joined Grant and his company. I work in development and direct pilots. But Grant understood my loyalty and love for *The Cosby Show* and understood that I was not emotionally capable of giving it up while the show was still going on. Now if there's an episode I really feel like doing, I will direct it. Oh, I also did the pilot to *The Golden Girls*.

Did your father have any influence on your work?

He did musicals and comedy, but I really have not been influenced by any of it. Some of his pictures I've never even seen. He did, *Top Hat*, which to me is a wonderful picture.

I went into this business essentially because I had to earn a living. I got into the Director's Guild earlier than I planned because up until then, sons of members were automatically taken in the guild. I got a call my senior year in college from somebody who said, "Listen, they're going to change the rules, so if you want to get in, get in now."

As an assistant director I spent time working three-camera comedy shows in front of audiences. I liked that much more than doing outdoor adventures or westerns. I was the assistant director on the original *Untouchables*, and I found I hated being on a set. It was dark. You had to deal with gunshots and blood and there was nothing that appealed to me. I liked being on a stage and laughing. But it was very hard doing comedy. I didn't know that at the time, but comedy is much more difficult to do.

I was fortunate that my first job was on the *I Love Lucy* show, watching a master like Lucy at work. I was fortunate to be surrounded by the top people in television comedy. I learned from them, and as I became a director I was smart enough to realize that the director was only as good as the written word. Again, I was fortunate to work with Buck Henry and Susan Harris, Allan Burns and Jim Brooks, and the people I'm working with now on *The Cosby Show*. John Marcus will eventually be considered one of the top television writers.

How much of a hand do you have in the writing?

I don't personally write, but I do have an awful lot of input on *The Cosby Show*, more than I did on *The Mary Tyler Moore Show*. Bill and I have a really wonderful working relationship and a lot of mutual respect.

You mentioned a little while ago the poor state of television comedy some years back. How does that happen? You'll recall that people were running around saying that the situation comedy was dead.

The people who were saying that were network executives. None of those executives are still there. Grant Tinker really was the savior of the sitcom as far as everybody in this industry was concerned.

If you look at the comedy shows that were on the air when Grant went in, *Cheers* was about it. There was not one other show that an adult could sit and watch. ABC shows were all aimed at kids, CBS didn't have any comedies, and NBC shows were pretty pathetic. Grant came in with the philosophy of the *MTM Show*, which was that you create a good show, you create a show that's interesting, with well-rounded people, and leave it there, and audiences will find it. *Cheers* and *Family Ties* were there, but Cosby just gave an impetus to the other networks to go and find comedy again.

How can there be people in network positions making executive-level decisions who could think that the situation comedy was dead?

How can there be? Because whoever hires them was hiring people who were essentially people who went by statistics and demographics.

MBAs?

Right, or they came out of research. In my career, *He and She* was a great disappointment. It was a show that we all loved, and it was really doing quite well, but not by network standards. Somebody in the research department said that the show would never get over a 30 share. It was stuck right there at 29 share. So they moved *Green Acres* in its time slot. That's the reason we were canceled.

The week after we were canceled, we went up to 34 share, and it just kept growing. The following season they came back and said, "Let's put the show back together." It was too late.

My feeling about television is that there's got to be something for everyone. If you're really a service to the public, you have to have shows that a small percentage of the public watches and have shows for a large percentage. But what has happened in the past 10 years as ratings have become so important is that television's become much more of a commercial money manufacturer than it has been a service to the American public.

The enormous irony to me is that ultimately, they can have their ratings too if they just . . .

Well, Grant proved that. One of the reasons, by the way, that we all love Grant and everybody wants to work with him, is that Grant is a great sharer of credit. He picks the right people and has an influence on the way people think and act. And he trusts his people, and they're not afraid to make mistakes. When Fred Silverman was completely in charge of the situation and didn't have anybody to discuss things with, he would pull shows off after three weeks.

In my own career, I owe a lot to Fred, because he put on *Soap* and it was a big, innovative show. But Grant would find shows and say, "I think this show is well-made. I think this show has potential. I think the producers are producing well, and the acting is good, and the directing is good. Let's leave it on. It will find an audience."

Can we talk for a moment about Emmys?

It bothered me on *Soap* that I didn't win, because it was one of the most complicated, technical shows. Plus, it had such a large number of viewers. But I was more upset that Susan Harris never even got nominated for anything for the writing on *Soap*, nor on *Golden Girls*. You get to the point where you realize that awards are nice but they don't mean anything.

Is it difficult working with writers?

Sometimes writers won't listen. There have been a couple of occasions where I have said to the writer, "You really don't need me. Because if you're not going to listen to what I am saying, or listen to my thoughts, you don't need me. It's a waste of all our time—why don't you just work with somebody else."

One of the most pleasurable experiences I have had with a writer, ever, was working with Neil Simon. It was just a joy. You'd say to Neil, "I think there's a problem here," and he'd say, "Yeah, I agree. I'll fix it."

Really talented writers are willing to listen to other ideas. That's the same way it was with Jim Brooks and Allan Burns, and Susan Harris. Bill Cosby is the same way. You can go to Bill and say, "Bill, it just doesn't work," and he'd say, "Okay, fine."

I mean, they're so good at what they do and they know that there's another eye, and once they respect your opinion, they listen. There are times I'll go to Bill and say, "I don't think it works," and he'll say, "No, that's what I want to say. That's what I want to communicate." And I'll say, "Okay." Or I will go to him and say, "This is what we're saying with this scene. Is this what you want to say?" And he'll say, "No, I want to say so and so." Sometimes it's very clear to a character what they're saying, but it's not reaching the audience. And that, I think, is the director's job: to be the audience and say, "I don't understand what you're trying to say here." It's got to be very clear, what you're trying to communicate.

How seriously do you take the views of TV critics?

None of them understand why a show works or doesn't work. Unless they've been there. Everyone in the business who reads Tom Shales' writing has great respect for him. He's a bright, intelligent, interested man. But, I don't know whether he really understands the inner workings of a show.

While we're talking about critics, let me say this, and it's going to sound immodest. *The Cosby Show* has had a tremendous influence on America, and from everything I've heard, it's had a great influence in foreign countries about the way they look at American life. For a long while, all America was exporting was *Dallas* and *Dynasty*: people were rich, angry, cheating, and conniving. Cosby's being exported now. I was talking to somebody from Norway the other day and apparently the country literally stops for *The Cosby Show*. In South Africa, we've heard it's number one with both the blacks and the whites, which is surprising.

Somebody came from Australia and said that it's the number one show in Australia. What they respond to is a mother and father who love each other and talk to their kids, and kids that are decent and a family unit. It doesn't matter whether critics like the show or not. The public has found the show. We went all out against *Magnum, P.I.*, which the year before was number three, and nobody gave us a chance.

People no longer talk about it as a black family. People talk about it as if it's a family. We just went down to shoot in Atlanta, we were shooting at Spellman College, and the love that we got from the people down there is unbelievable. And in many ways, this show has represented the black population. Not in the same ways that *Good Times* and *Amen* did. Those shows represented a lower economic level, or a less educated group. These are wealthy, successful, educated, caring human beings, and they also are black. And it's done a wonderful thing: whites start realizing, "Wait a minute, I love that family so much and they're black—maybe they're really nice."

We don't make racial statements. Bill's racial statement is, "I'm here. I'm a black person, I'm a black American, and that's all I am. I've got the same problems, the same families, the same strong qualities," and that is a very positive statement to make.

So, what I started to say is that whether the critics like it or not doesn't matter, the audience will find it.

In some ways when you work on a show like Cosby, *does it become a family?*

Oh, does it! I mean we were so blessed in casting. It's risky when you cast a 4-year old and a 13, I mean Theo, Malcolm Jamal Warner, is now 16, but he was 13 when we cast him. Tempestt was, I think, 7. And they're all growing up into such terrific people. I mean, when you cast you say, "Okay, they're good actors." But you have no idea what they're going to be like as human beings.

What was the cast's experience like on The Mary Tyler Moore Show?

It really was a family. I don't know if you remember, but the last show they all get fired and they say good-bye to each other. Well if you don't think we and the actors and the audience were crying real tears . . . The weeks preceding it we couldn't talk about it. We experienced such separation anxiety. I still talk to Ed a lot, I still see Mary whenever I can. Betty, of course, I see a good deal. It was a very dear family.

Since we last talked, you've worked again with Neil Simon, this time on London Suite. *How would you compare directing a comedy film to directing television comedy?*

The cast was Kelsey Grammar, Michael Richards, Julia Louis-Dreyfus and Richard Mulligan. Just a wonderful cast. But I found that the work was just too slow. I'm just somebody who has a faster tempo in my head and I had to get back to television.

You're on the same movie for three to six months versus doing a TV half-hour every week?

Right, and not only that, I really like the pace of television and movies take a long time.

There is a lot of "hurry up and wait"?

A lot. And I'm not a perfectionist. I believe, for the most part, comedy works best in front of an audience. I really love the type of television shows I do when you work, five, six hours a day of concentrated work, not sitting around. Then, the day of the show, you turn it over to the actors and they do it and you still have your input on what works and doesn't work and you start a new project the next day. It's really rewarding, rather than working on one project for three months and then spending months in the editing room.

Television comedy is an interesting hybrid. It's like theater in the sense that you get to know the cast really well, but once the director generally finishes with the play he or she might come back every three and six months to fine-tune it, but you're doing this week in and week out.

It's definitely like theater, except that in theater they develop things much more slowly, as they do in feature films. In television you pretty well have to develop it right now. Yes, you have three days to rehearse and then two more days of rehearsal and shooting, but you don't have a lot of time to think about the characters.

The night of the show, you do retakes and you talk to the actors, so it's not quite like the staged performance, where you get it how you like it and walk away. You have your input, but the actors bring wonderful things when there's an audience there. The pace and speed of television interest me. A lot of fine directors really like to do things over and over and over until till they get them just the way they want them. I'm not a control person—that's probably part of it.

On *Mary Tyler Moore* we once worked with a fine stage actor who had not done a lot of camera work and when the five days were over, he came to me and said, "I'm so sick of how I wasted the first three days. I really didn't dig deeply enough. I got up in front of the audience and realized I should have done more work." But when you do it every week, you sort of learn how to do it.

There are also film actors who could never survive in weekly television.

It takes amazing ability when an audience is there to react differently on the spot. I've worked with some very good dramatic actors who just can't get laughs.

Has the job of TV director changed at all in recent years?

Today what happens is, because of network pressures, the networks quickly take writers who've maybe had one season on one show and make them producers. The producers are taking over much of the function of the directors.

What is the television director's function?

A good director can walk on to a show, no matter how big the star is and who the writers are, and have his input. He will stage the show, talk to the actors, he will direct them, he will put the cameras where he thinks is best.

In the Mary *show and other classics, it seems that the camera placements are pretty well set week to week. If you had a new director come in, there is no way they could put a camera in a substantially different place.*

It isn't just where you put the cameras, it's how you shoot, what you want the audience to see. I personally like a lot of reaction shots. When somebody's talking I like to get how the other person reacts. Other directors will play shots always on the person talking. It's how you stage it, how you shoot it. I will stage differently than another director, and therefore, it will be shot differently.

What has changed technically, say, since The Mary Tyler Moore Show?

Number one, we didn't use zoom lenses back then—we only used three cameras. Today, every show uses four cameras and has zoom lenses, so you have a lot more mobility in your shots today than you did then.

In those days, the story was important and you tried to find reality. Today, I think, it's much more sketchy and broad and sexual, and not necessarily witty. I think the art of writing is deteriorating because that's what the sponsors what. The sponsors don't really care if anybody over 35 or 40 watches the show, so there is a less sophisticated audience and the shows become less sophisticated.

What are the main forces that have affected the industry over these last 10 years?

Several differences. Number one, in the old days, the ratings would basically come out only once a week. Also, today, product is aimed basically at young people. Also, if you look at who owns the networks now, they are all large corporations and it's very different.

In the 1970s and 80s, producers of shows had experience, they'd been on staff, they'd watched how shows were being run, they knew how a show worked. Today, in a lot of cases, somebody is right of college, works on one show for a season that's a big hit and they are producing their own show so they've never really had a chance to learn what a director does.

Your greatest consistent success was probably the Mary *show.*

Well, *Cosby* . . .

From the critics' point of view, the Mary *show was probably* . . .

Well, again, you don't do shows for critics. I think *The Cosby Show* had an enormous impact on America at the time, and it had an enormous impact on television, and I couldn't really care less what the critics thought and felt about it.

I think you're right about *Mary* being the more critical success. But I think *Cosby* had a great, great *impact* on American television. Everything in life, I think, is based on timing. You have to remember that with *Cosby* there was no show where children were treated with any intelligence, and no show that had shown a black family as successful and not along the lines of the earlier black shows. It had a great influence on its time, as *Mary* had a great influence on its time. But, then, from my point of view, *Soap* was also a tremendously important show for *its* time.

Which show did you like doing the most?

The *Mary* show was the first time I had been on a show that really was working and had wonderful writing. But *The Cosby Show* was the first time I had done a show that had really a major impact, and Bill and I had a wonderful working relationship. I really loved working with Bill.

I look at *Soap*, and I've never been as challenged because every day you would do a different type of conflict. But I can't rate one over the other; they were all wonderful shows.

What percentage of the Cosby *shows did you direct?*

Well, I did the first three years, and then I would go back, like once a month or something. It was done in New York and I came back to California and then I just would go back periodically because I just missed it. I came back to California to join Grant Tinker and company.

What happened at GTG? It only lasted four to five years.

We never did any really wonderful comedies. We just weren't able at that time to compete with the money that the popular comedy writers were getting. There was so much money being given to writers then. There were a couple of writers we came very close to getting but we couldn't offer them features. One of them ended up going to Disney and had a great career; the other one went to Columbia.

So they wanted to get into feature film writing, not into TV comedy writing.

Well, they wanted to do both. At GTG, we did do one show for NBC that was called *Baywatch* and ours was slightly less babe-oriented. It was a show that was sort of supposed to be like *Hill Street Blues*, but on the beach. NBC got it and sort of turned it into a monster of the week, crisis of the week show, and then cancelled it after one season. And after a couple of years, the guys who created it came back to Grant and asked if they could buy it back and he gave it to them. Same characters, same cast.

Can you comment on Seinfeld?

Everybody I know and respect adored it. It never got me because I cannot deal, week after week after week, with selfish people. I feel, seriously, that television has to have something for me to like about the characters, and although I never questioned that it was funny, it just wasn't my style.

The first show I really worked on that reached me greatly was as associate producer on *The Andy Griffith Show*. And I used to see these shows where Andy would relate to his son and I would say, "Darn it, I wish I had thought of that." I could have reacted that way as a father. And maybe it was cornball, but there were really interesting human relationships. *Mary* dealt with men and women and the workplace and yes, hopefully it was funny, but we also would a lot of times . . .

You would illuminate something.

Yes.

Seinfeld *may also has some instructive effects, but perhaps not intentionally.*

Well, you asked me if I watched the show. You didn't ask me if I *appreciated* it. Believe me, I never wondered why *Seinfeld* was so popular. I just personally didn't watch it very often. If somebody asked me if I'd do *Seinfeld*, I probably would have done it. But there were certain times, like when George's girlfriend died, I found I couldn't go on liking this guy.

Why is television different for you from other media?

Number one, I find it terrible that the networks are putting on adult shows at 8:00. *Friends* is obviously a very funny show but in my opinion, that 6 or 7 or 8-year-olds are watching *Friends* is a problem. I feel this about television because it comes into the home, because it's a weekly show. A television series gets audiences believing in these people, and I hope the audience starts finding a certain sense of values in some of these shows.

Do you see possibilities that, for you, television could get better again?

I just feel that what's happened is that shows are aimed too much at young people. We might get a little more philosophy of life because life is not just jobs and girlfriends or boyfriends.

Walter Grauman

WALTER GRAUMAN

Former World War II B-25 pilot Walter Grauman compares directing to flying a plane. And he flew quite a few: over 20 TV movies of the week and 7 features, most notably *Lady in a Cage* with Olivia de Haviland. The pilot analogy is a good one and helps Grauman convey what it *feels* like to direct action and suspense drama.

In series television, Grauman worked closely with Quinn Martin, directing the pilots and the first two years of *The Fugitive* and *The Streets of San Francisco*, the pilot for *Barnaby Jones*, and episodes of *The Untouchables*. He also directed episodes of *Murder, She Wrote* from 1984 to 1996.

Before he became a director, Grauman struggled as a commercial pilot and a real estate broker. He began in the movie business in the late 1940s, first selling popcorn and candy at theaters. Then he became an apprentice publicist for motion picture exhibitors. Sometimes when the movie theater owners would visit Hollywood, they would put pressure on Grauman to help them find women. Many years later, one of Grauman's TV movies, this one based on a true story, was *Vice Queen of the Sunset Strip*, an idea inspired by his experiences as a publicist.

Grauman is straight and to the point. He holds few illusions about his work as a director. He tells us what directing television action and suspense involves and what it demands.

☆ ☆ ☆

I was born and raised in Milwaukee. My mother was ill so we moved to Tucson. My father was a motion picture exhibitor. He had a chain of 13 theaters in the midwest. Every Saturday and Sunday my friends and I would go to the movies for nothing. I was very popular on weekends and came to equate entertainment with being liked.

During the war I was a pilot in the air corps, in Europe, flying B-25s. I came out of the service in 1945 and got a job as an apprentice publicist from a man who was the president of Universal Studios, who many years before had managed one of my father's theatres in the midwest.

Years later I produced and directed a TV movie for CBS called *Vice Queen of the Sunset Strip*. The idea for this story started back when I was doing the apprentice publicist job.

One of my principal functions was to take motion picture exhibitors who were visiting Los Angeles and show them the studios. One consistent thing happened. The exhibitors were middle-aged guys who were younger than I am right now, but they seemed like old kooks to me. They would always say, "Hey kid. You gotta girl you can fix me up with?" They thought this was the land of honey. The broads would be lying on the street corners waiting for them. They were always trying to get me to find girls. It would drive me crazy. I was 22 or 23 years old.

They were asking you to "pimp" for them.

Exactly. I sure as hell wasn't going to try and fix them up with any of my girlfriends. I went to a guy named Clark Ramsey, who later became one of the presidents of Metro. He was the head of advertising and publicity. I said, "These guys are driving me crazy. What am I going to do?" He gave me a telephone number.

It was for a madam here in town who had a hundred and sixty call girls working for her. *She* was the vice queen of the Sunset Strip. She was paying off the police, political figures, as well as motion picture celebrities, and servicing half of Hollywood. When they would ask, I would give them the number. "If you are willing to pay for it, I'm sure you can get a girl," I'd tell them.

Some years ago, I read a newspaper article about that period of time and I thought, "Shit, that would make a great TV movie." I dreamed it up. I went to a writer friend and said, "Let's develop it and try to sell it to one of the networks as a TV movie of the week." Which is exactly what we did.

Have you come up with the concept for TV movies very often?

Quite a few times. I like to direct *and* produce. I don't think I'm a particularly good writer. I can write, but I don't call myself a writer. I do have a published book of short plays, which I wrote many years ago.

Take me back to your first directing job and your entry into television.

I did lots of things before I started directing. I had a commercial pilot's license. I was a real estate broker, which I hated. I went into the candy and popcorn business and had visions of becoming the king of popcorn in the theater business. But I was so goddamn naive I didn't realize that this was a giant business. While I was buying popcorn by the 10-pound bag the companies were buying them by the freight car. Then I became a literary agent to a friend.

I got married. For a wedding present in 1949, my in-laws gave us a TV set. I was looking for work and I was watching TV one night with my wife. There was a local television show on—Rita LeRoy. "Christ, if this is entertainment," I thought, "I can do better than that."

My wife said, "Why don't you?" I dreamed up an idea, and I called it *Lights, Camera, Action.* It was a talent showcase for young actors and actresses. I went to a cousin of my wife's and asked her if she would be my partner. I went to another man I knew and asked him if he wanted to be my partner and the MC. He had been a Shubert operatic star many years before, and an agent, and knew everybody in the city. I put together a little package. I pounded the pavement and sold this half-hour show to the local NBC station. I wrote, produced, and directed along with my cousin.

It was on two years. What I really liked was the excitement and pressure of directing. It was the closest thing to flying that I had experienced. This was live TV. It was a tremendous, exhilarating, thrilling thing.

With Gene Hackman (l) and George C. Scott on location for East Side, West Side. *George C. Scott starred as a young social worker navigating the New York slums. Innovative for the 1963–64 season, critics admired* East Side, West Side*'s early, gritty social realism. Nearly amazing that the subjects of child abuse, crime, welfare, aging, and drug addiction saw any airtime against the backdrop of happier, colorful programs of the day.*

In a live TV booth you are dealing with five cameras and instantaneous editing decisions, punching up one camera and then the other. Actually, there were a lot of very fine directors who were pilots during the war. Delbert Mann and Virgil Vogel were both B-17 pilots.

Then I got a job as an assistant director from the local NBC station. As a staff director I did everything from football games to musicals to the 11:00 news to cooking shows. Kids shows, comedy, I don't know what. But that gets pretty dull after a while. How many spaghetti cooking shows can you do? Or 11:00 news? I realized that I really liked drama. I got myself transferred to the network and started as a stage manager on the *Lux Video Theatre*, which was a dramatic show. I drove everybody crazy asking them to direct. Finally, I got a chance to direct *Matinee Theater*. It was a different hour show every day. I ended up directing 81 of those hours over a three-year period.

How many TV movies of the week have you now directed?

About 20. I've done seven features. A big WWII flying picture called *633 Squadron*, shot in England. I also directed *Lady in a Cage*.

Quinn Martin and I were very close. I did the pilots and the first two years of *The Fugitive* and *Streets of San Francisco*. For Quinn Martin I also did a bunch of other pilots. *The New Breed, Barnaby Jones, Manhunter*, and *Most Wanted*. Other TV movies include *To Race the Wind* and a five-hour version of *Valley of the Dolls*. I've miniseries such as *Bare Essence*, and *Outrage* with Robert Preston and Burgess Meredith. I also did *Naked City*.

With David Janssen (Dr. Richard Kimball) shooting the pilot for The Fugitive, *1963. Quinn Martin entrusted Grauman, time and again, to capture the landmark style and imprint of each Quinn Martin Production he directed.*

What does a director do?

Once you have a script the director becomes the equivalent to the pilot on an airplane or the captain of the ship. He makes all of the decisions, really. He has the final authority to say, "Yes, I like these people as actors," or, "No, I don't want them."

The director takes the written material and gives it dimension. I read a piece of material and as I read it I will stage it, both in my head and on paper. I visualize a set and/or a location.

A writer says a character walks into a Babylonian castle. I want to visualize what that castle looks like. I even sketch them out. I take a piece of paper and pencil with my script and I'll draw four walls and I'll put the door there, camera on the left wall. I'll put a sofa here next to the fireplace. Then I find a location that matches the way I want a scene to play. I've staged the whole picture in my head before I ever shoot the first foot.

The writing also demands that characters relate in some specific way to each other. The director visualizes how to put these people into relationships that help to interpret the writing.

Giving direction to Michael Douglas and Karl Malden (r) on The Streets of San Francisco, *from the 2-hour movie pilot, 1972. Another Quinn Martin Production.*

The result of not preparing is cost, incredible wastes of time, effort, and energy and very often a floundering ship in which everybody has an opinion and nobody has authority. I can't, nor will I, work that way.

You want to work with people whom you respect and with whom you have rapport. And the written word is the bible. The script dictates whether a character is a 300-pound dwarf or a 6-foot leading man.

In TV do you screen test actors?

For the lead in a series you would. You look at their past work, you meet them, you get a sense of their ability, and you have a gut instinct.

Another thing that I do is see that the sets are constructed the way I want them. I approve the wardrobe. I deal with any special makeup problems. This is all in accord with each department head.

Do you have someone assisting you in picking your department heads?

Yes. That's also where experience comes in. The unit production manager will suggest people that he or she has worked with. Possibly an assistant director will help. You draw from the experiences of all these people.

The assistant director is a critically important person to a director, because almost all of the physical aspects of a production filter through the first assistant. Otherwise the director becomes so overwhelmed with detail that he or she begins to lose sight of the bigger picture.

How many assistant directors might there be on a TV movie?

There is first assistant, second assistant, and quite often a third assistant. There will be a fourth person if you have problem scenes. To me the most important thing a director does is to create the physical concept of the film and then sees to it that it is executed and shot according to that concept. That's why the position is called "director."

Sounds a little like running a war.

Well it is. I was shooting a four-hour miniseries with Wayne Rogers, written by Irwin Shaw. It was called *Top of the Hill.* I was shooting in Lake Placid, just prior to the 1980 Olympics. It was all about bobsledding and winter sports. One day I was shooting out in the snow and it was 40 degrees below zero. I had six cameras going on the 90-meter ski jump, plus a helicopter. I was having the time of my life, hollering and running from one spot to another. It's as exciting as hell. Wayne Rogers, who is my good friend, said "For Christ's sake you're not a director, you're General Patton." You said it is akin to a war and in a way it is. It's the logistics and movement of men and material.

When you finish directing a film are you exhausted?

Every director is tired afterwards. But it's fun and a challenge instead of a stressful, torturing fear. That is why I enjoy directing.

Pilot Walter Grauman standing with his B-25. Later, Grauman would direct TV pilots.

I understand that if a director comes to the set and doesn't know clearly what he or she wants to do, the crew can sense it in an instant.

They'll let him drown. They don't tear him to shreds. They'll just let him drown. The director better damn well, even if he doesn't know what he's doing, he better make them believe he knows what he is doing. Or they'll just let him sink in quicksand. If they really know that you know what you are doing, most crews will break their asses for you. Because they enjoy it.

You're saying that crews are professional. It's not like some people think, that everybody is snorting cocaine out here?

Not at all. I'm going to tell you the truth. And I've been around a long goddamn time. I guess they snort coke someplace, but I have never seen with my own eyes, and I swear before God as my witness, I have never seen any drug use on a set. I've suspected occasionally that somebody is high. I've seen people drink, but that is usually on the performing end of it, not the crew. They are terribly conscientious, hardworking, and intelligent people.

How much better could TV movies of the week be if you had more time and fewer financial pressures?

I don't think it makes a lot of difference. The majority of my films can be done as well and as efficiently within the given boundaries of budget and length of time. I'm not sure that more time doesn't mean more self-indulgence and less efficiency. It can become a kind of masturbation, if you want to use that word in your book, in which everybody is gratifying their egos.

Time and economic constraints keep you on your toes in a good way?

Yes. In a very good way. It forces you to come in and do your best with alacrity.

You've shot features and had more time. I would think you might prefer that.

No. *Lady in a Cage* I shot in 16 days. *633 Squadron,* which was a marvelous flying story with Cliff Robertson, that took me 40 days.

Are there problems in the industry that particularly concern you?

There are too many inexperienced people from networks and production companies who feel they have to make noise. They seem to need to justify that they've got a job and that they are getting paid. They say, "Heh, I'm not contributing. I could lose my job." It's all bullshit and you and I know it and everybody else knows it. It's self-protective interference.

How have you seen things change in the last 20 years?

I've seen more of these same interfering people. Layer upon layer upon layer upon layer. Until it becomes an enervating chore just to hold onto an original concept. It's just an unwieldy bureaucracy. It begins to mushroom. You have to go through these people as diplomatically and diligently as you can to the true decisionmakers.

Some say that the American public's attention span is growing shorter, and that this is related to TV and film.

I think that there may be some validity to that. The abbreviated form of storytelling, whether its TV or *Reader's Digest* or *People Magazine* or *Time*, is on the rise. It's compress, compress, and compress.

Still, it is mandatory as a director that you have a sense of timing and find the most efficient way to get your audience involved. You're not going to keep them long. They're not going to sit there. They're not a captive in a theatre. They haven't paid $5.

Which came first, the chicken or the egg? I think that TV reflects the American public's desire. I don't think all TV shapes the attention span. It does shape it in news a great deal and in advertising, but so did *Life* magazine and so does every published form in which advertising is used.

Some countries have all the ads at the top of the show and at the end. What do you think of that?

I think it would be great, if you could do it. I don't know if it would be economically feasible. It is difficult to tell a story with commercials. That's why you have to use "hooks" at the end of each act, six of them in a two-hour movie. They have to be manufactured so the audience will come back after three minutes and a station break. I would love to see no commercial breaks and if you could convince somebody, that would be not only marvelous, but a miracle.

Any final comments?

I don't want to do trash. Nor do most of the people I know want to cater to pornography, sadomasochism, or anything else. I don't like all that shit. I really don't like it. The longer I've been in this business the less use I have for the titillation of the audience.

You see it in the cross-fertilization of programming and news, which I find very distasteful. It has no place in the news. A girl with big tits is covered in the news program because it is going to help advertise a soap opera on the same station coming tomorrow.

CHAPTER 8

The Actors

As viewers, we come back each week to see what Jerry, Kramer, George, and Elaine will do; or what repartee will fly between Tony and Janice Soprano, Lou Grant and Mary Richards, or The Fonz and Richie Cunningham. We enjoy these characters as much as we do, in part, because they have become so familiar to us.

As soon as Kramer or Norton crashes through Jerry or Ralph's apartment door (without knocking) we know something about what might occur and what foibles mark each character. Kramer and Norton are so familiar to their neighbors that they can enter unannounced. And just as they are familiar to Jerry and Ralph, so too are they familiar to us. Jerry and Ralph respond to their antics much as we do, and for an instant, they are also members of the audience. *We* are in our living room, *they* in theirs. We experience much of this unconsciously but it helps us identify further with the characters.

Cheers used a similar device, with the other characters calling out "Norm" each time he entered the bar. And the show's theme song, "Where Everybody Knows Your Name," reinforced the concept. The audience likes such programs not only because the characters are familiar, but also because the characters are so familiar to each other. We feel like *we're* part of Cheers—the bar and the show. In television, there is often an especially intimate merging of audience and character.

There are stock characters in Italian commedia dell'arte, in Japanese Kabuki, and in vaudeville and the American melodrama and minstrel shows; they are not a new invention by any means. However, the same person inhabiting the same character each week to the extent seen in the early years of American film, radio, and television *is* noteworthy and a critical factor in television's commercial success around the world.

Viewers like knowing the characters in their favorite programs (Kubey, 2000, 2002). Indeed, it is instructive to watch very early episodes of a long-running situation comedy to see how much the characters and performances have evolved since the beginning. Very early *Mary Tyler Moore Show* episodes, for example, don't feature the more developed and precise characterizations that we know from later episodes. The same is unmistakable in early *Seinfeld* episodes. Jerry's character is different, less mannered. Jason Alexander tells us that he didn't understand the George Costanza character until somewhere between the fifth and tenth episodes. He began by playing George as if he were Woody Allen; on learning that the character was based on Larry David, the show's cocreator, Alexander began to play George differently.

Only when a program achieves the special blend of creativity that emerges when a good ensemble of actors comes together with a good set of writers does it develop a consistent feel of its own—especially in situation comedy performed before a live audience. Yes, the writers and producers provided the basic components for the eventual gestalt of the program, but virtually no program has all the elements working in perfect harmony at the beginning. It takes time for the characters to grow and become more real in their interactions with each other and for chemistry to develop with the live audience. This is among the reasons that a wise producer will often choose to have the same director in place at least until a show finds its legs—if it ever does. By watching the actors in rehearsal and performance, the writers also begin to observe nuances in each actor and character that can be developed for subsequent episodes.

In television, we are less aware of the actor's performance than in film. This is because of the regularity and familiarity—the everydayness—of television and the way we watch in the intimate confines of our homes and bedrooms. In television, we are more apt to forget that the players are actors. Indeed, television actors are much more accustomed than are movie actors to being addressed in public by their character's name. In television we talk about what Kramer, Hope, or Sipowicz did last night. We less frequently say what Michael Richards, Mel Harris, or Dennis Franz did.

Of course, this close identification of the actor with a particular role is why a long running hit on television can typecast and severely limit an actor's career options. Dustin Hoffman and Gwyneth Paltrow keep playing different roles. But for many, Henry Winkler will *always* be The Fonz. And Jason Alexander may always be George—at least on television. None of the *Seinfeld* ensemble may ever escape the characters they so indelibly inscribed.

Alfred Hitchcock referred to actors as cattle. But we learn from Henry Winkler that the television actor, particularly in a situation comedy, is not given much direction by the director. Winkler emphasizes how much a television actor must be prepared to direct himself. Jason Alexander reports that the *Seinfeld* cast frequently directed each other as does Aida Turturro of *The Sopranos.*

Betty White explains why an actor must listen carefully in each performance so as to react authentically "in the moment." An actor can't permit the delivery of a line to become set in rehearsals, but must react *as the character* as spontaneously as possible to the particular line reading the other actor has just given, lest the performance seem wooden and unbelievable.

This helps explain the less-developed characterizations in early sitcom episodes. The actors haven't learned precisely how to play off of each other because each character has yet to be fully formed.

Actors train and prepare differently. Betty White is a natural actress who's never taken a lesson. Jason Alexander, like Winkler, studied formally for many years. We see in each interview how actors think about their roles and apply their talent and skill.

Actors also bring a great deal of themselves to the characters they play and, in a continuing character especially, their personalities and habits influence their performance and what the writers write for them. Henry Winkler and "The Fonz" both have the habit of giving very direct and knowing advice to others. Ed Asner incorporates his constant vacillation between aloofness and warm charm in his portrayal of Lou Grant. Aida Turturro, on the other hand, plays Janice Soprano, Tony Soprano's difficult sister, as complex and flawed a character as the medium has known. Turturro doesn't always view her performances in movies and television, feeling uncomfortable when roles bear too close a resemblance to her real life. But in the case of *The Sopranos*, the character is so far removed from who she is, Turturro feels comfortable watching herself play Janice.

We shift gears with Paul Petersen and learn about the experiences of a child actor. He was fired from *The Mickey Mouse Club* at age nine. He then became familiar to millions of Americans over the eight years he played Jeff Stone on *The Donna Reed Show*. Later, his career would crash, and so would his private life.

Petersen founded, and now leads, A Minor Consideration, a group of over 500 former child celebrities who share a concern for how young people can be abused when fame, success, and the stresses of a professional career come too early in life. Petersen opens our eyes to much we might not otherwise have known about celebrity. (The interview in Chapter 9 with Jay Bernstein, who was in the business of creating celebrities, is similarly revealing.)

For Petersen, celebrity had its dangers. He is not alone. Henry Winkler was a dyslexic kid and struggled in school before eventually becoming a household name. Being The Fonz gave him a swelled head.

> By itself, my car started to turn itself into a Rolls Royce dealership. It would just turn off Sunset Boulevard into a Rolls Royce dealership and I had no control. It starts to overtake you. And you must exert great will power not to allow it to do so.
>
> Also, when you become a celebrity, you immediately become a public figure. People adore you. People expect you to become an authority on stuff you had no idea about 10 minutes ago and you start to replace all the homework you never did with cotton. So you're actually living on no structure whatsoever. You start to believe that you are more than you are. And when the reality hits that you are still the same guy, everything starts to shake and fall down.

Ed Asner, Betty White, and Aida Turturro also comment on the power and pleasure of celebrity. As we see in this section, first and foremost, actors are people.

Ed Asner

ED ASNER

Ed Asner may be the most honored American television actor in the medium's history. His seven Emmys set a record. He's versatile, as adept in serious drama as in comedy, his deep, resonant voice marking every role he occupies. In the early days of television he was usually cast as a villain and appeared in such classic programs as *Naked City* (as a regular), *Route 66, The Fugitive, The Outer Limits, Gunsmoke,* and *The Virginian.* He played feature roles in two of television's most acclaimed miniseries, *Roots* and *Rich Man, Poor Man.*

Ed Asner began occupying his best known role, the gruff WJM news director Lou Grant, on *The Mary Tyler Moore Show* in 1970, and went on to fashion one of the best loved television characters in the history of the medium. He later took the title role in the one-hour dramatic program *Lou Grant,* playing the character for a total of 12 years. He appeared as a regular character in a number of less successful television series, including *Bronx Zoo* and *The Closer,* as well as taking on roles in programs like *Ellen, Dharma & Greg,* and *The Practice.* Most recently he played the title role in the Italian miniseries *Pope John XXIII.*

Asner became president of the Screen Actor's Guild in 1981 and served for two terms through 1985. During that time he publicly challenged the Reagan Administration's policies in Central America; shortly thereafter, CBS cancelled *Lou Grant* (see also Daniel, 1996). We discuss the complicated mixture of the entertainment industry, acting, and national politics in the interview.

Asner has performed in plays on and off Broadway, in 14 feature films, and in 24 movies for television and miniseries. In addition to his Emmys, he has received five Golden Globe Awards, and in 2002 received the Screen Actor's Guild Lifetime Achievement Award.

For the first minutes of our first meeting, at his offices in Studio City, Asner avoided eye contact, choosing to rummage through the bottom right hand drawer of his desk while I explained what I wanted to cover in the interview. The experience seemed familiar. I had seen him do this before. He remained aloof, subjecting me to the same treatment that Mary Richards regularly experienced when entering Mr. Grant's office to talk about a problem. Before long he stopped searching the drawer and warmed up quite a lot and I saw the other side of both Asner and Lou Grant. We met twice, once in the late 1980s and again in the late 1990s. I've combined the two interviews here. I began by asking him about his childhood and his beginnings in theater.

From the earliest I loved to get on stage. I was always delighted to participate in the religious plays in Sunday School or in the Friday night songs at temple, trying to belt louder than any of the other kids and generally succeeding. Of course, I was always very careful never to volunteer to act. Terribly unmacho. Then, if called on, I would try to act the shit out of it. And that carried on into high school.

There were five kids in our family, three boys and two girls. I was the youngest. And I think some of the acting desire that I always had was the result of being low man on the totem pole. Not only with the family, but with a huge ring of cousins. I was looking for my place in the sun by participating in the singing and in the plays.

My father was a taciturn man, but when aroused, a bellower. My brothers were loud. We were not an introverted family. My father was a junk man. He started off when he first came to Kansas City with a pony and a wagon.

I was an acquisitor in high school. I wanted as many awards as I could lay my hands on. I wanted to get my Thespian Club pin so I did a walk-on in my second year. But I never felt I had the appearance to be an actor. But I had a great voice. In my senior year I took a radio class. I could conjure up all kinds of images with radio.

Then I went on to the University of Chicago. I wanted to get out of Kansas City. I had some vague idea about studying political science and I was attracted by Chicago's vaunted position at that time.

It was announced there was going to be a closed-circuit radio station and I asked one of my roommates if I ought to try out. As a joke they gave me the *Song of Songs* as a birthday gift, so I read from that. Well, their jaws just dropped to the floor in amazement that their roommate, whom they thought was a jock, could give such sensitive readings.

I became hooked and did any plays that came along. My school work went to hell. By February of '49 I dropped out. I went in the army for two years and just before I got out, Paul Sills asked me to come back to Chicago to do plays and make fifty to sixty dollars a week.

Then I went on to New York for five-and-a-half years. When I got to New York, radio was dying and blending in with TV, but one of the greatest thrills of my life was doing the *Eternal Life Radio Show* with the greatest voices in radio.

I finally did a Broadway show and found it to be laughable, amateurish, and ridiculous. The thought of going through that very often made me most uneasy. So I was searching and was open to do anything to avoid that kind of thing.

I had begun working on *Route 66* and then was hired to do "Busty" on *Naked City*. Later I went on to do *Hamlet* with Ellis Rabb at Princeton. Some time later, *Naked City* was running short of product and was shooting two shows back to back. They had me come out to California to reprise my earlier character.

I wanted to be flown out on a private jet. I did not want to go to California until I had become a lion on Broadway. But in the course of talking to people in Hollywood I fell victim to the siren song. I was strongly encouraged to move out, got an agent, phoned my wife and said I wanted to move out. She was not pleased. Wives fear California.

Principal Players, The Mary Tyler Moore Show.

Women feel safe in New York. The culture, the clubs, and the theater . . . . We pulled into town on Memorial Day and started making the rounds with my agent. We got a little pad up in the hills. She's still up in the hills.

What other things were you doing before The Mary Tyler Moore Show *came along?*

In '63, I was first costar on *Slattery's People* with Dick Crenna. After the first 13 episodes I asked out of it and they were decent enough to let me out. I continued to freelance, trying to work my way up both in terms of TV and trying to snag whatever movies I could get. Then, in 1968 and 1969, everything seemed to begin drying up for me. I stopped getting jobs. My income fell.

My agent tried to explain that that happens sometimes—the well dries up and you can't do a lot about it. We had just moved into a new house and had payments up the wazoo. I was very worried. I thought at one point I was going to have to walk away from the house.

Then in '69 out of the clear blue, Wally Grauman gave me a couple of pictures. So that turned into my best year. At the beginning of '70 I was asked to read for *Mary Tyler Moore.*

I have always felt that dry period was very good for me because I had experienced the fright and the fear of a decreasing income and then my

"Oh, Mr. Grant." Asner with Mary Tyler Moore.

confidence was restored the following year by my best year ever. So I had experienced the good and the bad.

It sounds as if you had played little comedy on TV before that. I would think the casting directors for the Mary *show might have been concerned with you playing Lou Grant.*

I had always been good at comedy. They liked the audition reading a lot. In trying to double-check for themselves, they turned to Ethel Wynant, vice president for talent, who had had me do a small comic role on a CBS special. They asked, "Can Ed Asner do comedy?" She said, "He can do anything."

Do you believe there are actors who have a wider range than you?

I don't think so. But I think people would have a difficult time believing me as a weak character, and an acting teacher in town was telling my daughter that he thought people didn't want to let go of thinking of me as Lou Grant, making it difficult for them to accept me as other characters.

Like most major stars, you have an agent, a publicist, and a personal manager. Have you resisted some of these accoutrements of stardom?

It used to be worse. There was a time when I had bodyguards and a political advisor because people said I had to have somebody to keep me from getting my dick in the door all the time.

Linda Kelsey, Jack Bannon, and Ed Asner, in Lou Grant

Since you brought it up, do you regret that Lou Grant *might have been cancelled because of your political activity?*

Of course I do. It was a criminal act. But do I regret whatever I did to bring that about? No, I don't regret that.

Because of your political activity you may have prevented some people involved in the show from making many millions of dollars from Lou Grant. *Has that ever bothered you?*

Yes, especially in regard to the people who did not work after that. That was my first concern and I had guilt. Regarding syndication, I most certainly suffered as did the other people since I hold a piece of *Lou Grant*. But all my previous life in show business I had watched my mouth politically. I had no idea of the repercussions that would occur.

I had gone to Washington to announce the formation of Medical Aid for El Salvador. We made a statement to President Reagan and Secretary of State Haig, that "our enemies are not your enemies," as they conceived El Salvador.

The other side made enormous capital and twisted what I had said. Many people were made to think I was giving union money. I was president of the Screen Actor's Guild at the time. Charlton Heston pushed the idea that I had not properly clarified that I was not speaking for the union. During the course of the affair, and I'll never forget this, three sponsors wanted to pull out. Kimberly Clark, Vidal Sassoon, and Cadbury, I am told.

Principal players, Lou Grant

A Mr. and Mrs. Bollack wrote to me, showing me a copy of a letter they had gotten. They had written to Kimberly Clark saying, "Because of your support of Ed Asner and your sponsorship of *Lou Grant*, we are going to be buying all of your products from now on." They got back a formula letter from this twit who handled their PR: "Thank you for your letter. We are pleased to tell you that we are cancelling all of our advertising."

It was unfair. The viewers didn't give a shit. They liked the show. Two thousand people marched outside CBS for Christ's sake. And I'm sure a great many letters came in. The second clincher in that thing was a letter from the president of Vidal Sassoon, a Mr. Solomon, who wrote to the President of CBS and said, "Can't you shut him up?"

If I had known right then and there before I had left for Washington that they were going to cancel the show if I opened my mouth, I would have thought about it. Bill Zimmerman, the man who engineered the creation of medical aid, told me much later that he didn't watch TV. He had thought we were number one and couldn't be cancelled. And in terms of intellectuality, we were. He thought they couldn't get to me.

It sounds as if there were others besides yourself who wanted to exploit the Lou Grant persona.

Everybody wanted to exploit him. They had me be spokesman during the actors' strike of 1980 because of the fact that I was facile in front of the camera and because of *Lou Grant.*

To my mind, the problem was that people confused you with Lou Grant and with the president of the Screen Actor's Guild. The president of GM or the president of the United States often have to confine their public image to one role. It becomes very confusing to people if they do otherwise.

Does Joseph Coors do that?

Well he isn't confused with a television character, he's not elected, and he owns his own company. I think that the reason you got yourself caught in a windmill was that it's very easy to see how people confused Lou Grant, the president of SAG, and Ed Asner. It was hard back then to know where Lou Grant ended and Ed Asner started.

Had I known what would ensue I probably wouldn't have gotten involved. But at the same time, all my performing life I had kept my mouth shut politically except for the ACLU and stuff like that. I laid low during Vietnam because there were so many people out there doing it. I wasn't needed and I wasn't a big enough name. I wanted to expunge the constipation of silence that I had to live with under all those years of not venting my true emotion.

After the controversy had started, and after the shit was hitting the fan and there were death threats on my life, Allan Burns and two other producers on *Lou Grant* came into my dressing room to ask me to stop what I was doing. One of them said, "I think there are two ways to make a point in this life; one is in the way Lou Grant was doing it and one is the way you're doing it, and I think our way is better, with Lou Grant." And I was willing to grant all that, but they were demonstrating their own naiveté by thinking I, in any way, could stop it. I repeat, there were death threats. You never believe death threats but some people thought they were legitimate. I got a bodyguard and the cops wandered around.

Changing topics, how good do you think American TV is? Is there a dearth of talent?

It's amazing it's as good as it is. It's unfair to compare it to *Masterpiece Theatre*, the product of the finest actors in the tight little island, with government underwriting, with Mobil Oil paying them a fortune to eventually bring it over here. It's all very good stiff upper lip stuff.

But this country is enormously talented. You'll find plenty of Britons who have vast respect for American acting talent and I'm sure the same can be said for writing talent as well.

If only we had state participation and support for great projects. This country is so unused to civic and national endeavors and when they're done, they tend to get some artsy fartsy person in charge who is out of touch and more often than not they screw it up. So you need a longstanding tradition and we constantly fight against longstanding traditions in this country. I also love to play with the idea whether we wouldn't be better off in this country if we had just one network. The networks are so busy emulating and counterprogramming against each other that I think all too often it makes it even more difficult to produce quality.

As for talent, people far more talented than I have never enjoyed one-tenth of the success that I've enjoyed. When Ronald Reagan was President of the Screen Actor's Guild there were 8,000 members. When I was President, there were 58,000.

So talent doesn't always rise to the top then?

Of course not. No. It's so much luck. Being animally persistent is another way of looking at it. Being a grunt and saying, "I can do it, I can do it. Give me the job. I'll walk across the stage." The bone is thrown and I'll somehow blunder across the stage.

What is it like to become a household name?

The deification of stars doesn't go on anymore. The stars themselves have become so much more sophisticated in withdrawing. They insist on their privacy. I try to be as discreet as possible and to be as normal as possible. It's not that hard to do. Only once in a while does it become panicky. I'm at an age now where it's very safe. I don't generate much interest in little kids and teenagers. I'm not an Adonis.

How much have you enjoyed it?

Robert Redford went into Chicago, I believe it was, and wanted to be able to move around freely without any hang-ups. I guess he was given a beard and moustache and makeup and a hat and an un-Redford type coat. He moved around all day and nobody recognized him. I was told that he didn't care for it, he didn't like it.

I love the power and the rewards that being a star can generate. I love being seated at a restaurant. I love being able to get theater tickets when I want them. When you go to certain places you can expect them to recognize you. And you might be disappointed when that doesn't happen. On the other hand, you mentally prepare yourself for Europe.

But, I'll never forget when I was asked to come to Barcelona and appear on a talk show there. A huge collection of kids surrounded me. They knew who I was. One kid is bouncing his soccer ball, 10 or 12 years old. He elects to be their spokesman. What does he say? "Why was *Lou Grant* cancelled?!" It was so funny. The way he asked it, he knew something was rotten in Denmark.

When you go abroad, there are countries where Lou Grant *has not been seen. Do you go through that Redford experience and find that you don't like being Joe Blow again?*

Oh I miss it. Sure. I like to be able to be greeted warmly with a smile. I just started up with a new cleaners near my house. There was a young, pretty girl in there. And I'd bring the stuff in and she treated me very nicely, but I knew she didn't know me from Adam. Around the fifth time, someone either told her or she had seen me on the tube. The whole attitude changed. I'm not talking about adulation, I'm just talking about *smiling* into your face.

It was as if it almost hurt that she didn't recognize and smile at you.

There are no cautionary ways or means of slapping yourself into appropriate consciousness.

Is it an actor's problem or everyone's problem that you aren't happy enough with yourself to withstand her lack of recognition?

No, I think you're turning us into bent monsters, unnecessarily. If you're having this and this [*Asner slowly caresses and strokes his face*] and you don't get it anymore . . . I don't care who you are, you're going to miss it. It's a wonderful, wonderful god-sent feeling to have people demonstrating that they *like* you. Not saying you're gorgeous, adorable, a great human being, just, "Hi, how are you, nice to see you."

As for actors, I think they are entertaining people. I think they are generally intelligent, well-read, and quite catholic in their knowledge.

I read a capsule description someplace that actors were unfinished human beings, that they were attempting to finish the job through their art. It was a brutal, goddamned thing. Many of us are not happy. I am not. . . . I don't think I am a happy person. My therapists have said—at least, one of them said—that I felt such an emptiness inside that I was busy attempting to stimulate and breathe on the outside sufficient for the inside. So, maybe if I felt happier, I wouldn't need the strokes.

Betty White

BETTY WHITE

Betty White is one of the most familiar faces on American television and has been for 50 years since *Life With Elizabeth* was first launched locally in Los Angeles in 1952, and then syndicated in 1953. At that very early point in her career *TV Guide* lauded her as an attractive and wholesome "girl-next-door" type, a new candidate for "America's Sweetheart."

Betty White was born in Oak Park, Illinois, in 1922. Her family later moved to California where she graduated from Beverly Hills High School.

She is best known for her roles as Sue Ann Nivens for the last four years of *The Mary Tyler Moore Show*, and for her seven years as Rose Nylund on *The Golden Girls*. For each of these roles, White played the character's personality attributes to absurd extremes—the sugary-sweet, man-hungry television hostess of WJM-TV's *Happy Homemaker Show* in the *Mary* show and as a naive, space cadet in *The Golden Girls*.

She received supporting actress Emmy awards in 1975 and 1976 for *The Mary Tyler Moore Show*, and another in 1986 for Outstanding Lead Actress in a Comedy Series for *The Golden Girls*. In 1990 she won The American Comedy Awards' Lifetime Achievement Award, and in 1996 was inducted into the Academy of Television Arts and Sciences' Hall of Fame.

Betty White has never had an acting lesson, yet her advice to actors is clear:

> If you're thinking how to play it, you're in deep trouble. You better not be thinking that. You better be listening because every time the other person reads a line, he's going to give it to you a little differently, so you better react to *that*. . . .
>
> There's only one "acting line" and that's your first line. The rest is all "reacting," and if you don't listen to the other actors and you're only busy with your own performance, you might as well do it in front of a mirror and be out to lunch.

I met with White during the second year of *The Golden Girls*. We talked in the living room of her classic *Leave it to Beaver*–style home in Beverly Hills—exactly the sort of home one would imagine her in. The coffee table that sat between us was covered with glass animal sculptures. Ms. White has long been a committed advocate for animals.

I was an only child. My mother was a housewife. My father was with a company that made flood lights for ballparks and athletic stadiums. Their primary things were traffic signals and explosion-proof fittings for the navy.

As a child, I was going to be a big writer. I wrote the graduation play in grammar school and as any red-blooded American girl would do, I wrote myself in as the lead. I realized how much fun it was to be up on the stage. That was my first brush with anything in show business.

But I'm still writing and I'm still acting. I have one book on pets and I have another, *Betty White in Person*, that's a series of short essays on a variety of subjects. It's about my views on anger, guilt, widowhood, marriage, laughter, grief, fear. That kind of thing.

I went on to high school and got the lead in the senior graduation play. Then I went to Bliss Haven Little Theater where you paid $50 a month for the experience of working in plays. I got my first raise in the second month—they said I could work for nothing. I didn't have to pay them $50 anymore. So I felt like my career was launched.

I broke my dad's heart when I opted not to go to college, but I wanted to get out into the world. I was so lucky to have parents who were completely supportive. Next, I did a couple of little singing jobs for KLAC in Los Angeles and then a local game show opened called *Grab Your Phone*. It was three girls on a panel and an MC. We were on once a week. The girls got $5 a show, except I got $10.

I was not to tell anybody I was getting $10 a week because I was ad-libbing with the MC. They figured that took a little more doing than just answering the phone and writing down the numbers. I always suspected that the other girls were getting $20 and I wasn't supposed to tell them I was getting $10.

A man named Al Jarvis saw me on that and invited me to be his girl Friday. He was starting a show that went five and a half hours a day, six days a week. Everything was live. The first week he was a disc jockey and we played records. But the audience went nuts because they didn't know what we were talking about while the records were playing. So we "deep sixed" the records and just talked and interviewed people. Anybody who came through town was on our show and anybody who knocked on a certain door at the studio was on camera when we opened the door. I eventually inherited the show.

You were "yourself" on the show?

Oh, it was strictly into the camera. I was also doing a variety show at night. This was 1951. Six days a week on camera and five and a half hours a day wasn't enough. So at night, one hour a week, we would do a variety show. First prize for contestants was a week's engagement on the daytime show. I would do a couple of songs with sketches.

We'd always do one sketch on a married couple. We got so much reaction to it that the owner of the station called us in and asked us what we thought about making a half-hour situation comedy out of it. At that point I didn't think anything we were doing would sustain for a half hour. The story was funny for only about five, six, seven minutes. So we would do three incidents. Incident number one in the life of Elizabeth, incident number two, and we'd jump around in time, which was a wonderful format that we'd owned for years and years. Eventually we did 195 of those. The show was called *Life with Elizabeth*. They broke them up and they were running for years as reruns. In fact, I think we're still

Betty White (far left) in the final episode of The Mary Tyler Moore Show.

on in Germany and Australia. There's a movement afoot here to resurrect the old shows.

Meantime, I began commenting on the Rose Parade, which I did for 20 years. Macy's parade I did for 10.

It wasn't until the fourth year of The Mary Tyler Moore Show *that you were cast as a regular character. Do you know why they brought you in? What were they looking for?*

They wanted an icky, sweet, yucky, sickening television type. A "Betty White" type. The casting director at CBS said, "Why don't you get Betty?" They said, "We can't do that because Betty and Mary are best friends and if Betty came in and didn't get the part it might be awkward." But of course it wouldn't have been awkward because that's the way the business works. They finally interviewed 12 girls and couldn't find anybody, so they said, "What the hell!" They didn't call me in for an audition. They just called me and asked if I'd do the show. I was thrilled to pieces.

I called Mary and said, "Guess who's going to do your show next week?" And she said, "Who?" I said, "Me," and she said, "Oh no you're not—I have veto power." She was kidding.

We had all been such close friends. We had sweated out the pilot with them and had been at the pilot, and we would sweat it out at each opening season. Allen always rigged up some little number with flowers at the opening of a new season. [Ms. White's husband, Allen Ludden, was well known to audiences from the 1950s through the 1970s, usually as a game show host on the *College Bowl* or *Password*. Grant Tinker mentions Ludden in his interview.] Allen and Grant had gone back many years. Grant brought Allen down from Hartford, Connecticut, to New York to do the College Bowl on radio. And then they were just best friends forever.

I went over and did the show and in two weeks I was back again. I never did more than 12 in a 22-episode year, but somehow, Sue Ann got identified with the show as one of the regulars.

It was a lovely experience, and it was such a classic to be associated with. Then to go into something like *Golden Girls* is just like getting hit by lightning twice.

Who was Sue Ann Nivens and what made her tick?

She was the neighborhood nymphomaniac. She was the best home economist in the world, but in her mind, she was a devastating sexboat. She was a very lonely, frightened lady. I never believed a word she bragged about, but boy, she just killed everybody.

Have you ever had any formal acting training?

No. I think sometimes that can get in the way. I have no ambitions to do stage. I have turned down more Broadway shows than you have any idea. The "big screen" isn't interested in me nor am I in it. I would do summer stock. I did *The King and I* eight times.

With summer stock you can go in for three weeks and then you can come home.

I did not want to live in New York and I can't imagine anything more deadly than doing the same show night in, night out. I'm not that kind of an actress.

Television is a medium where you are only talking to two or three people, ever, at a time. If there are more than two or three people in a room they are not listening to you, they are talking to each other. So it is a real one-on-one situation. It's a medium that I love. If I have something to say, I can look right in the camera and I can say it. In films, you're at their mercy. It's hurry up and wait. With television, you get there, you get the job done, and you get off. And you can move onto something new and different.

How do you prepare your role for each episode on Golden Girls?

We all go in and read the script on Monday morning for the first time. If it still has a lot of work to be done by the writers, we start on the scenes that won't be worked on a lot. Tuesday morning we can begin to put the whole thing on its feet. Tuesday afternoon, we run through for the writers. Wednesday night we'd do a really heavy "writers' run through." So they work Wednesday night, all night. Thursday we get a new script with all the input in it. Then we camera block, and on Friday, we tape the first show, break for dinner, and then tape the evening show. We keep getting new pages, sometimes between shows on Friday. We do it in front of two different audiences so that we can use what works and drop what doesn't work.

How hard is it to work with rewrites? You learn the lines, and then you have to learn new lines on top of them.

I don't see very well to read idiot cards, even on commercials and things like that. I memorize everything, so memorizing is no problem. I happen to have a rather photographic eye. I memorize visually. It's become a conditioned reflex.

Allen, my husband, worked absolutely in reverse. He could look at a thing forever and not get it, but if you read him a line, he'd remember it and retain it. So it's easy for me. It's tough for the stage ladies. It was really tough for Estelle at first because she had never done television.

Do you think there's enough rehearsal time in television?

Never. But what I love about it is that very effect of not having had a chance to research your character and really experiment with the depths of it. We're not doing *War and Peace*; we're doing a light situation comedy for entertainment. It keeps you on your toes and it keeps you stretching every minute because you know you don't have a lot of time. You do your best at every run-through.

This is going to sound like a dumb question, but what does an actor actually do?

I don't have a lot of fancy language because I never studied acting, but I have certainly paid my dues over all these years. You try each time you go through a scene to make it as natural as you can. Sometimes it's difficult if there's something about the script that is not natural or goes against your grain. But if you really concentrate on it, you can put those words in your mouth and make them come as close to home as you can.

What are you thinking when you're waiting for your cue and a line is coming to you?

If you're thinking how to play it, you're in deep trouble. You better not be thinking that. You better be listening because every time the other person reads a line, he's going to give it to you a little differently, so you better react to *that*. Somebody may change a preposition on you, or they may phrase it just one word off, and if you just do your line, it won't work and it won't fit. You may be dying a thousand deaths inside, trying to remember your lines, particularly if you've got a difficult scene. You might be scrounging like mad, with minimal rehearsal and a lot of words, but you can't let it go beyond you. It can't show or you're in trouble.

There's only one "acting line" and that's your first line. The rest is all "reacting," and if you don't listen to the other actors and you're only

Bea Arthur and Betty White

busy with your own performance, you might as well do it in front of a mirror and be out to lunch.

When you get the script, do you make notations?

Everybody is superstitious. I never touch my script, I just learn it that way. We keep getting new pages and new scripts, and if I were to rely on those notes, and those notes are suddenly taken away, in my mind, I'm thinking, "Now what did I write on that other page?" So I don't do that. Rue and others outline their lines. We've got bright colored pencils and they fight over who's going to have what color.

How much have directors helped you in your shows?

They run the whole show and the less obtrusive they are, the better. All week long, they let us experiment. I've been blessed on *Golden Girls* and on *Mary Tyler Moore* working with complete pros who come in prepared and ready to work.

Directors are most concerned with the cameras and their placement. He's pretty confident with the actors so it's his job to be sure to get what we do on camera. If he doesn't get the cameras right, or if he doesn't have you placed right, you can do your best performance, and it's lost to the camera. That's his primary function.

Why do you think you've been popular with so many people for so long?

Because they got to know me as myself. I'm sure if Sue Ann Nivens had been the first job I had ever had, they would think of me as Sue Ann Nivens for the rest of my life. But because they have known me in so many contexts and on so many shows where I'm talking directly to the camera and to them, they know I can't lie to them. You really can't lie to the television camera.

Some people like you, some don't. Now, I'm sure there's a world of people out there who can't stand me, but fortunately there are enough people who do to keep me working. I've never done anything highly controversial on any side of the ledger. I've played it pretty much down the middle and I've kept my sense of humor.

I've worked with animals all my life. As Allen used to say, television was my hobby. Animals were my work. I'm sure there are a lot of people out there who like animals, so they know I like animals, so they like me.

Still, I'm sure a great deal of the public isn't aware of your interest in animals.

Well, a great deal of the public is. I keep such a high profile working for them, that if you like me at all, or have followed me, if you're any kind of a Betty White fan, that goes with the territory.

Let's talk about this business of being famous and recognized. Is there a downside to it?

You can't move about quite as quickly as you used to. Each person thinks they are the only person coming up and talking to you, so you can't brush those people off because that's their one experience at it. And the fact that you have had it happen a lot is your problem, not theirs. It can get difficult, through an airport or running to the store to pick up something.

Of course different stars react differently. Bea Arthur is very remote and very distant, and doesn't particularly appreciate it. She still would be very polite. Mary Tyler Moore was always very polite, but would always travel with somebody to get her through. I'm used to traveling alone, but it gets more and more difficult as the show gains in popularity. Sometimes, if I'm at the market, people will just walk down the aisle and put their hand on your arm and just squeeze it. Or you'll be walking down the street, and they'll just say, "Hey, Betty." It's funny, Allen's image was so different. We'd go someplace and they'd say "Hi, Betty. Hi, Mr. Ludden." It's just the different feeling that people have. Sometimes, they'll stand a short distance away from you and whisper thinking you can neither see nor hear.

What has made Golden Girls *a hit?*

The show tells people that you don't fall off the planet when you get to be 35 years old. Inside, you're thinking and looking out from the same perspective that you always did. If you were a dull young person, you're going to be a dull older person.

The Golden Girls *watch TV (Bea Arthur, Rue McClanahan, Betty White, and Estelle Getty, l–r).*

There always was the token funny old person on a TV show who would say outrageous things and do outrageous things—that was the humor of it—and the old person was brought in to play against type. We play against type some times but we don't stereotype.

You had your own show for 14 weeks. It was canceled. What happened?

The audience was expecting Sue Ann Nivens. They weren't expecting Joyce Whitman. When Lou Grant went on to the *Lou Grant* show, at first they were expecting to find the Lou Grant they had known on *Mary* and they found another Lou Grant completely. But he had a firm year's contract, so he stayed on the year. They canceled us at 14 weeks. CBS executives admitted that that they canceled the show too soon. Also, we were at 9:00 on Monday nights against football and by the time football went off, we were canceled.

The executives wanted an instant ensemble, but they did stereotype, cartoon casting. The ensemble worked so beautifully on *MTM*, they thought, "Well, we'll have another ensemble group." The pilot of *The Betty White Show* was the best pilot that had come out. It was the sure-fire hit of the season. The writers were Ed Weinberger, Stan Daniels and David Lloyd. I didn't know until after we did the pilot that they had already been signed to go over and do *Taxi*. I didn't find that out until after the fact, and I got the second team. The difference was horrendous.

Mary almost died the whole first year, but she had her year, and that year is so important. Then the audience got to know her during the summer reruns, and by the time they started back in the fall, the audience was aboard.

How much fan mail do you get?

Probably a couple thousand a week. My fan mail stays pretty high because I do so many things. I get all the animal mail, I get picture requests of course, I get a lot of widow mail from newly widowed ladies who ask, "How do you do it? Is it ever going to get better?" That kind of thing.

You can't possibly respond to all of that mail.

A widow letter I do. That's one lady who's got a problem, who's hurting, and she doesn't know that I get others like it.

I also have a secretary who sorts through the picture requests which are just automatically handled. Anything marked personal, she will open and sees to it that I see all those. I answer if it's something specific or from somebody very, very old who has something cute to say about *Golden Girls*. They always get at least a line, if nothing else. The animal mail is usually in more depth because a lot of them are technical questions.

A big surprise has been that people are so quick to sit down and write what they like. I can't get over the lack of negative mail. It still boggles my mind that people have time to do that.

If the mail dropped off a lot, you might not like that because it would be an indicator of . . .

Oh, you haven't heard me complain about the mail. No, not at all. Of course, that would be an indicator. Sometimes, it goes up to 5,000 a week, if there's something tremendous happening. When they canceled *The Betty White Show*, you wouldn't believe all the mail that came. Look what it did for *Cagney & Lacey*. It put them back on the air. That was strictly a mail campaign.

The amount of mail is another indication of the responsibility of working in television.

I think it's a tremendous responsibility. That's why I will never endorse any kind of a political cause, no matter how strongly I feel. I will work very strongly for my animals, but as far as telling somebody else how they should vote, or for whom they should vote, I've been wrong too many times. Nobody's going to say it's good to be cruel to animals. But to say this man is better than this man, who am I to say that? So I stay completely apolitical. A lot of people would do it only because I said, "You should do this." They wouldn't think it through. They'd go, "Well, if Betty does, if that's the way she feels about it, sure I'll do it."

You wouldn't believe the power. And you've got to be aware of it and respect it or you can abuse it.

Henry Winkler

HENRY WINKLER

Henry Winkler is best known for his 11-year portrayal of Arthur "Fonzie" Fonzarelli on *Happy Days*. His characterization is so much a part of Americana that The Fonz's jacket has been on display at the Smithsonian in Washington since 1980.

In the late 1970s and early 1980s, kids everywhere imitated The Fonz's signature gesture, popping two thumbs up and saying "Aaaay!" But, Winkler is cautious about his success and fame: "Success is not normal. We are not built to be that kind of successful. The mind and the ego are very delicate."

Happy Days began in 1974 and was expected to focus on the relationship of two characters, Richie and Potsie; instead, the show came to center on the relationship of Richie and Fonzie. Winkler brought unusual dimension to the character from the beginning, revealing both The Fonz's bravado *and* vulnerability.

Winkler first went to Emerson College and was later classically trained at Yale's Drama School, where he received his master's degree. There he learned how an actor approaches comedy versus drama: "You play comedy like a drama and drama like a comedy. You play a comedy as if it is a drama. You don't know that it's funny. You play it dead seriously. Comedy is very serious. If you act as if it's funny you blow the timing, you blow the elegance, you blow the comedy."

Winker has appeared in numerous theatrical features, most notably *The Lords of Flatbush* with Sylvester Stallone, and *Night Shift* with Michael Keaton. He now directs and produces and heads his own television production company with his wife, Ann Daniel. His most successful production to date has been *MacGyver*, which ran on ABC from 1985 to 1992. But like most anyone else in television, he also has his list of failures. In 1986 he executive produced *Mr. Sunshine*, an ill-fated series, but to his credit probably the only one in the history of the medium to feature a blind person as its lead character. Winkler executive produced and played the title role in another situation comedy, *Monty*, a program about a right-wing TV talk show host, based on Rush Limbaugh. *Ryan's Four*, a program about four interns, which Winkler coproduced with David Victor, who had created both *Dr. Kildare* and *Marcus Welby, M.D.*, appeared briefly in 1983. Most recently, Winkler has begun producing *The Hollywood Squares*.

We met at his offices at Paramount Studios in the late 1980s. He was sporting about three days' growth of beard. After the interview, he took me aside to advise me about a question I had about another topic. He wrapped his right arm firmly around my shoulder and spoke to me as if he had a crystal ball. As he explains in the interview, his attitude when providing advice, as himself or as The Fonz, is one of absolute confidence.

I started off as I did with most interviews by asking about his background. Winkler began reeling off the story of his life and his childhood.

☆ ☆ ☆

I was born to a middle class family in New York City. My parents had escaped Nazi Germany, and so I never had any grandparents.

The Fonz advises Richie Cunningham (Ron Howard).

I did very poorly in school because I have dyslexia and I'm in the bottom 3 percent in math. I thought I was stupid for a very long time. My parents were very strict and dyslexia was not even known at that time, so I was called lazy most of my life—not meeting my potential. But at 7 years old, the age of reason, I began to understand that I needed to act.

I also knew early on how to solve problems for my friends. I could tell them how they got into a problem, what they should do, and what would happen if they did what I told them. I have no idea how I knew this stuff, but I would click in and listen and say, "This is what it is," and boom, boom, boom.

The Fonz was a problem solver for people as well.

Absolutely. He totally springs from my rib. I had enormous input in the writing from day one.

What were your first roles?

My first role was a tube of toothpaste in nursery school. Then, Billy Budd in the 7th grade. I was flunking mostly everything and the only gratification I was getting was winning dance contests, talking to my friends, and doing the plays.

In college I had to take the same geometry course four times to finally graduate. I did not come out of this emotionally until I was 33. At

Winkler with Erin Moran

one time my self-image was probably at my ankle. Now it is at least at my sternum.

For years I carried the sense that someday, somebody is going to find out I really can't act, and that I am no good. Now that I am successful, I wonder if can do it again in another area? The feeling's still there. But, I will tell you that I'm having a much better time now being more in control, and not so put upon by the emotional pain.

After college you went to Yale for your master's degree.

That was a tremendous moment in my life. Being accepted to Yale. At Yale I worked very hard. From 1967 to 1971 I did 70 plays. And that's every kind of play. My second year at Yale I would be killed on stage, I would get up, take a bow with the rest of the cast, run down the street, change my costume, and then be the star of a cabaret.

Was The Lords of Flatbush *your first film?*

It was my first feature film. I made $2,000. After *Lords of Flatbush* and working in an improv group called "Off the Wall," I moved to California for "one month" with $1,000 in my pocket, just to see what it was like. I have not gone home yet.

The $1,000 went a long way. I slept on somebody's couch and I was able to talk myself into situations that allowed me to survive. Then I got on *The Mary Tyler Moore Show*. I had four lines. I sat at a little table all by myself when Mary had a dinner party and I was able to ad-lib 4 lines into 12.

How did you audition for the role of The Fonz?

I went into the audition and my hair was relatively long. There were stars that I had already seen on television coming out of the room so I thought my auditioning was ridiculous.

I told them I was very nervous, but from the moment I stood up to read the part I made one choice: that the person reading with me would sit down and that I would be the only one standing. An actor makes one choice. It's an attitude. The Fonz is cool. Nobody stands when The Fonz is talking. So I just made that up. That is part of my training, to always take an attitude.

Had you seen the script? Was it a cold reading?

It was cold. But because of my dyslexia, I could never read cold because I would miss and stammer on words and it would sound like Greek. But I have the ability to memorize the essence of a scene and make the words up as I go along. I have concluded that by necessity people with dyslexia become great problem solvers.

After the audition, I was asked to come back, and on my birthday, at the end of the month, a producer called me and asked if I would like to play The Fonz. I said, "If I can show the other side. When I take my jacket off at home, I've got to be a different human being." I wanted to show something other than the typical hood.

Couldn't they have said, "Who the hell does he think he is?" and you might have lost the part?

That's right. I don't know. I think about that all the time. I went for broke. I had the chutzpa. At the time I literally asked myself, "Where did you get the nerve to just say that?" I went with my instinct. When I speak to young people, I say, "Your instinct is more powerful than you will ever know and when your instinct comes clear, do not second guess yourself, no matter what."

Who was The Fonz?

The Fonz was a guy who was scared and who *also* had a school problem. He took care of others in friendship and he was a problem solver. And of course that is me. Every character that you ever play is close to yourself, is who you are. So he was loyal, but you did not mess with him.

Is The Fonz dead now? You don't play him anymore.

No, not for one minute. The Fonz will never be dead. Every time someone turns 3 he gets a new audience. Children start to relate to him at 3.

I did it for 11 years. It is the longest running straight series: 255 episodes. I'm very proud of him.

You have your own production company now.

It's called Winkler-Daniel. My partner is Ann Daniel. Ann Daniel was the senior vice president in charge of production for ABC for seven years, and is one of the most extraordinary women I know.

Let's talk for a moment about the business of television. Do the time pressures that actors are forced to work under result in a poorer product?

Yes and no. The time is short, but the time forces you to invent; ergo, a lot of great stuff comes out of that pressure. When you have the time you become a fat cat, you get awfully lazy. Television, theater, and movies are like mercury. Each adjusts to the area it's got.

I have had people tell me that directors in episodic television sometimes come to the set and have not read the script and as a result cannot really direct the actors.

Yes, that's true because they only got the script a few hours before. That is why you have got to know your stuff as an actor. You're taught in drama school that only one out of every 10 directors will actually direct you. You better know your craft. It's like the country tilts and everybody that looks good falls into Hollywood, do you know what I mean? This is the one thing I'm a snob about. There are 25,000 card-carrying actors. But there should be a test because most of them do not take the time to train themselves. There's so much to it. It takes an enormous amount of concentration and an enormous amount of trust to deal with rewrites.

Of course, I will never have acting partners the way I had on that show. First, Ronnie Howard was an acting partner that will probably never be duplicated in my professional life. Then, Scott Baio and Marion Ross, who are so unique I can't even begin to tell you. Erin Moran was wonderful. Oh, I had some incredible people to work with.

You've played drama and you've played comedy. Can you talk about the difference?

You play comedy like a drama and drama like a comedy. You play a comedy as if it is a drama. You don't know that it's funny. You play it dead seriously. Comedy is very serious. If you act as if it's funny you blow the timing, you blow the elegance, you blow the comedy.

Why does it work the other way? Why do you play drama like comedy?

Because nobody walks around like this all day. [*Winkler gets up and stomps around the room with a grim look on his face*]. You're living a life and you have a sense of humor and a particular part of your life is tragedy.

Dueling with Robin Williams as Mork.

Principal players, Happy Days

What concerns you the most about the way the business is run? What do you wish would change?

Oh . . . so much, really. I wish that things didn't cost so much to make. It's really getting out of hand. The industry has to reexamine the pay structure. What irritates me is that a lot of the corporations that now own the studios and networks are not filmmakers. They are corporate people. They are not bad people. But you don't make movies or television without loving the process.

You executive produced MacGyver *and I assume you're developing new projects. Are you often in on network pitch meetings?*

Oh, I pitch all the time. That's my job as a producer.

In pitch sessions, do you hear things from some network executives that indicate that they don't adequately understand drama?

Absolutely true, but I have been very lucky because I have been able to sell a lot of stuff. I have had people who have trusted me. And I have had people to work with like Ann, when she was at the network, who are brilliant about material.

But there are also people at the network who you sit with at a meeting and you think to yourself, "One of us should get out of the business." Because sometimes what that person is saying has no relevance to the process of making television.

What do you do in such instances?

What you do is you problem solve. You find out how to get around the problem. If you go to somebody higher up, what are they going to do? They're not going to say, "Oh yeah, bad person. I'm going to fire that person." You have to go back and face that person again. And sometimes you bring in your idea and all of a sudden your idea is being done by another company. The person said no to you and took your idea and gave it to someone else to do. Ideas are stolen sometimes.

You had opportunities to make enormous sums of money from cigarette and clothing advertisements. To my knowledge you never did those ads because every kid in the country looked up to The Fonz.

It's true. I was offered a *tremendous* amount of money. But it was very easy to turn down. At that time it was not right for me. I might very well do it now. Sir Laurence Olivier does it.

Is there a point at which the money doesn't matter?

The money always matters. I like money. I would like to have more money. I like money a lot, but you must put it in proportion and so far, and I'm knocking on wood, I have never done anything for money. I have done it because I wanted to do it. I have never fallen into the trap of living beyond my means so that I was forced into a position.

Given all of the residuals you must receive, it's hard to imagine how you could live beyond your means.

But it starts to creep in. By itself, my car started to turn itself into a Rolls Royce dealership. It would just turn off Sunset Boulevard into a Rolls Royce dealership and I had no control. It starts to overtake you. And you must exert great will power not to allow it to do so. Also, when you become a celebrity, you immediately become a public figure. People adore you. People expect you to become an authority on stuff you had no idea about 10 minutes ago and you start to replace all the homework you never did with cotton. So you're actually living on no structure whatsoever. You start to believe that you are more than you are. And when the reality hits that you are still the same guy, everything starts to shake and fall down.

Why does the public put you on a pedestal?

It's hard for people to take responsibility for their own actions. They look outside of themselves for the answer and they are hoping against all hope that *you* have it. If you don't have it, they discard you like Kleenex.

Furthermore, if you dare go for that pool of power that people imbue you with, they resent it. Power comes from other people thinking that you have power; ergo, you have power. If you believe you have power and go for the power, it becomes a mirage. Instead, you use what you need. You must find a steady stream—the yin and yang of power—which is very, very important.

Can you elaborate on what you mean by the yin and yang of power.

There has to be a steady stream of releasing. Because I'll tell you something, there is a lot of energy and I literally felt it objectively. I was the King of Bacchus in 1977 in one of the major parades down in New Orleans. There are doubloons with my picture on them that are thrown to the masses. Four million people are in the streets yelling up to you.

You know about the mirror exercise? About the energy that comes off you?

Tell me about it.

All right. Just put your hand up for a minute. Let's hope I can do it. Put your hand up a few inches from mine just like a mirror. Don't move. Feel anything between us?

Yes, I know what you're talking about. It occurs in tai chi and in the martial art of aikido. The word "chi" in tai chi or "ki" in aikido means energy.

Imagine 4 million people giving you ki. My psyche hurt. I literally was overloaded by that energy to the point where I was only a shell. I literally was sapped of all my energy.

I wonder how the Pope feels.

Trust me that he feels close to God. I mean it's big. The feeling is too big to hold in your body. The problem is if you think it's you, that you are more important than you are. That's why you have so many actors who go off the deep end. Because you're never prepared for success. *You are never prepared for success.* Success is not normal. We are not built to be that kind of successful. The mind and the ego are very delicate.

Speaking of success, I know The Fonz is in the Hollywood Wax Museum and his jacket is in the Smithsonian. Is your name also out on the Hollywood Walk of Fame?

Yes. I love that I have a star on Hollywood Boulevard. It's under the portico of the Pantages Theater.

Do you think it's healthy that we make so much of actors in this culture? That they become "stars."

If they were happy with themselves people would look to themselves. Europe has a 1,000-year-old tradition. Their actors are not deities. They are well respected members of society who do what they do. Here in America, if you make a mistake and your project doesn't make a lot of money, you have very few chances to continue to do what you dreamed of doing. In Europe, people will take small roles. They say, "Hey, I'll do this part. It's fun."

What does this say about American culture?

It says that the most important thing is money. The process of doing it, which is the most fun, is no longer what's important, that's what it says. It says that success is not that a human being has met a potential, it's that a human being has helped meet a big *monetary* potential.

If you hadn't gotten the call to play The Fonz what do you think would have happened to you?

I don't know. What if I had waited an extra day? I had been debating, "Do I go to Hollywood, do I not go to Hollywood? Should I go for a month? What do you think? I'll be scared out there. I don't know anybody." I think maybe I might have had a movie career instead.

Jason Alexander

JASON ALEXANDER

Say the name "George" to most anyone and they may well think of George Costanza; that's how deep an impression Jason Alexander's *Seinfeld* über schmuck made on tens of millions of viewers. But there's more to Jason Alexander's range and talent than what we see in George. Alexander is a seasoned musical comedy performer, who won a Tony for Best Actor in a Musical in 1989 for *Jerome Robbins' Broadway.* He prefers drama to comedy; has appeared in 23 films, including *The Mosquito Coast* and *Shallow Hal*; and played Harry Truman in the one-man play *Give 'Em Hell Harry.* Alexander also does the voice of Duckman in the cartoon series *Duckman.*

Little, rotund Jay Greenspan grew up in New Jersey, changed his name to Jason Alexander at 15, and left college early as his career began to take off. He is a serious student of acting, training for 14 years with his primary acting coach, Larry Moss.

We learn in the interview that "George" owes a lot to Jason Alexander's skill as an actor and to Larry David's neuroses. Alexander began playing George as if he was Woody Allen, both in his audition and in the first episodes, until he learned that George was based on Larry David.

We also learn how the *Seinfeld* ensemble invented as they rehearsed and often directed themselves. And if you are wondering about a career in acting, Jason Alexander suggests how you should approach that decision.

Alexander virtually reprised the George character in his own short-lived series, *Bob Patterson,* about a motivational speaker with low self-esteem. The program lasted only five episodes. More recently, he played A.C. Gilbert in *The Man who Saved Christmas,* a TV movie about the creator of the Erector set. The interview took place in 2000.

Probably at 5 was the first time that my family did the big journey down from New Jersey to Miami Beach. It's a three-day drive. I have a sister who's about 12 years older than I am. Her record collection was unusual for the time in that it wasn't filled with Beatles and Stones and The Doors and that kind of stuff. She had a theater album collection. So on the ride down to Florida, my mother would say, "Hey, let's sing some songs," and I started singing the scores of *Man of La Mancha* and *Fiddler on the Roof.*

In those days, I was a very, very heavy kid. So I got picked on a fair amount. And it dawned on me at a pretty early age that if I could make people laugh with me, they wouldn't laugh at me. But not thinking I had my own sense of humor, I just copied others. Bill Cosby, Mel Brooks, Woody Allen, Robert Klein, George Carlin, and Richard Pryor. Instead of just learning the material, I picked up on how to deliver a performance and did this with the Broadway musicals as well.

When George's perfect girlfriend dumps him because of religious differences, he's quick to embrace the Latvian Orthodox religion. From Seinfeld: The Conversion.

I saw your Broadway musical, one-man performance on PBS. You seem to love musicals and really put the songs over.

I definitely prefer the stage as a performing outlet.

In film and television there's a lot of "hurry up and wait"?

Absolutely. Particularly in *Seinfeld.* And we used to shoot shows that were way too long. So to get them down to size they would just nip and tuck and if I had a speech that was five lines long they might use lines two, three, and five.

With most situations comedies very few lines would be cut.

Oh, absolutely. They didn't come at it from a trained sitcom writers' point of view and that's why everything worked out so well. They came at it from a comic's point of view. Comics put all their material out there for the concert film and then you cut back the stuff that wasn't gangbusters.

When you mentioned mimicking different people, it occurs to me that having watched the early episodes of Seinfeld . . .

Woody Allen.

You anticipated my question. How conscious were you that you sounded very much like Woody Allen in the early episodes?

The way I came to *Seinfeld* was I got sent four pages for an audition and they said, "Put this on videotape." I was in New York and they were all out here in L.A. So, you know, with four pages, you're lookin' for a fast impression of what this could be. And I remember thinking, "Boy, this stuff really feels like a Woody Allen sketch." So I said, "Well, let's go with that." So I thickened my New York accent and ran out and grabbed a pair of glasses.

The reason the change began to happen was we got about five or six episodes in and there was something in some show and I said to Larry David, "Jesus, Larry, you know, this would never happen in real life and if it did nobody would react like this." And Larry said, "What are you talking about? This happened to me and this is *exactly* what happened!" And I went, "Oh, oh, oh, oh, oh." That's when it dawned on me that Larry was George! And so then, all I had to do was a blatant Larry David imitation [*laughing*]. You look at the second season and part of the third season of *Seinfeld*, I'm doing a killer Larry David.

Henry Winkler tells how he made a big decision when he auditioned for The Fonz. He didn't do what they wanted. He stood up and just took over the whole audition and became The Fonz. In your audition, someone might think that you were making the wrong move by sounding like Woody Allen. That you should try to sound different.

The only thing I thought about was that it was impossible, back in those days, to get a television series that's doing its work in L.A. from New York. It's almost a courtesy thing. They put some people on tape "just to see." It almost never works out. So I didn't invest in it. But I said, you know, as long as I'm going to do it, let me at least stand out on the tape. You *do* look for an opportunity to make big choices. You don't want to play it close to the vest. They're seeing it via tape. They're not gonna catch the energy or the nuance, so you go for big large gestures.

Winkler also says that in television you really have to direct yourself and that you have to be a seasoned actor to know how to direct yourself. Is that true in your experience?

Most television sitcom directors have nothing to say to you as an actor. On *Seinfeld*, I think part of why we became an ensemble so quickly is that the four of us directed each other. The director would be standing there watching it, but we would find our own business, we would find our own patterns and, you know, by the second season we got to know the camera placements well enough that we could almost do it in a way that we would know how the shots would look.

Can you give us an example of a moment or two from Seinfeld *where you or your fellow actors found or invented some business?*

One of my favorite scenes that Jerry and I ever did was a very long scene where George had been fired and he and Jerry were in the living room talking about what other careers he might follow. It's about a five or six page scene. We physically approached it like it was not going to be a *long* conversation, like it might be a *short* conversation. And we approached it fairly straightforward and as grown-ups. But as George started to think about the things as a kid that interested him, my physical choices became more childlike until eventually I was sitting on the floor of the living room, cross-legged with my legs under the coffee table and my chin kind of on the table and Jerry starts talking to me like I'm a baby. That was business that we found.

It wasn't in the script, nor from the director?

No. We found it. At first, when we put it on its feet we'd just kind of stand in place and talk to each other. And we always knew that to stay static too long was uninteresting. So we were always looking, particularly in that apartment set, for something organic to give anything some color, or some movement. But as I was doing the work on this scene, I could just kind of feel myself getting younger and younger, looking for childish choices.

In another episode, Jerry is dating a girl who was a dirty talker. We had a scene in the coffee shop where I was demanding that he tell me what she said. As written, he was supposed to whisper something and I was just supposed to have a funny reaction. I said to the prop guys, "Give me a plate that has French fries on it," and I got a full ketchup container, you know, a squeeze bottle of ketchup. So I listened before I was about to put the ketchup on the fries, so when I heard what Jerry said, I squeezed the ketchup container hard as if it was like something having an orgasm. That's a chosen piece of comedy business. Actually, they were all worried that we wouldn't get it on the air.

One does have the sense with Seinfeld *that there weren't a lot of egos involved. That the four of you worked extraordinarily well together.*

Oh, absolutely. There was an incident during the pilot between Jerry and myself where he came over to me on the second or third day of rehearsal and said, "You know, I hate to do this but, you know, I heard this line a certain way when we wrote it and would you be very upset if I gave you a line reading on this line?"

And I said, "Absolutely not. I have no problem with it, the caveat being, if I understand it, I'm happy to do it but if it's something that's strange or doesn't make sense to me, you wouldn't want me to do it because it would be weird."

Then I said, "As long as we're talking, you can always give me line readings because I assume you're going to make me funnier. However, in this scene that we're doing here, can I ask you what the hell you're playing? Because you've written a scene where you take one side and I take the other and then we switch two times, and if you don't play your side fully, I can't do anything with my side."

I sort of gave him an acting coach's speech about how to play the beat that he had written. And nobody had any problem with this. I was giving him a little acting coaching, he was giving me comedy coaching, everything was fine. And when Julia was added to the show after the pilot it was the same. Michael always had a clear vision of what he wanted to do. He was trying to flesh out something that was very, very thin, and we would encourage him to use what he had, which was that amazing physical comedy.

We each found the other three to be incredibly funny people. So we started to take joy in being amused by each other. And very quickly, instead of that thing where you go, "Jesus, the show's not gonna last, I'd better do something that makes *me* look good so that I'll get another job." Instead of that, we started going, "Hey, you know what would be good, *I* could do this line, but it's gonna be funnier on Julia. That's a funny attitude for her character." And she'd turn around and do the same thing. And Jerry would do the same thing or we'd say, "You know what? What would be funniest is if we just look at each other and let Michael come in and go ba, ba, boom." And so we started giving away material to each other or encouraging things out of each other. And that's the quickest way to build an ensemble.

Well, you did it. And I think the audience senses it.

It was an unusual ensemble. First of all, doing a show that featured four people was unusual. It's usually a single person's vehicle, or a couple, you know, a man and woman, or it's a large ensemble, like a *Cheers* kind of thing. So to have this very small ensemble was great. It was manageable and no one person had too much pressure.

And what made it even more extraordinary is—I always have to say this very carefully because it gives the wrong impression—we were *not* the most social company outside of the show itself. The four of us had very different lives; we did not go and hang out.

The hanging out was on the set.

Exactly. It all became about the process of working with each other. That was what was so extraordinary.

But let's take you back to your youth again. I've read a story about your preparation for your Bar Mitzvah, and also how you changed your name at a pretty young age. You really were on a track earlier than many actors.

My first track was actually magic. I was pretty convinced I wanted to be a magician. Theater was something that I experienced as an audience member

Flashing back with Jerry from Seinfeld: The Library.

and never thought about doing. And as I came to understand how difficult magic was, because I wanted to be a close up magician, it became pretty clear to me that it was going to take more discipline than I had.

We changed towns when I was 12 years old, we moved from Maplewood to Livingston, New Jersey. And by sheer accident the first kids that I kind of fell in with were these theater kids. And they pulled me into a production of *Sound of Music.* I played one of the Von Trapp kids. I just loved the atmosphere of the rehearsals. I loved the kind of people that I was suddenly amongst. Most of my friends before had been these kind of hyperintelligent kids, with no real social life. And that wasn't me either. And suddenly I was with people I understood. And then I got on stage and got a laugh.

Do you remember the precise line or moment that got the laugh?

Yep. I played Frederic, the older of the Von Trapp boys. They all come down and they're presented to Maria and the whistle blows and you step forward and you say your thing and I stepped forward and I said, "I'm Fredric, I'm 14," and then I look at the family and I go, "I'm a boy." And there's only two boys and you step back in. The audience just roared.

I was suddenly immersed because there were kids in this group that were three and four years older than I that had been doing theater for a while and that were going to New York and seeing shows. So, it became a very serious focus pretty much from that point on, and what cemented it for me was the same year, it was 1972, *Pippin* opened on Broadway. And it was a synthesis of everything I loved. It was magic, it was rock music of the day, and it was theater. And I looked at Ben Vereen and I said, "That is what I want to do."

So, can you tell the Bar Mitzvah story, assuming it's true?

[*Laughing*] Ah, it is true. I knew that I had to sing. I had seen *Pippin* and had started taking voice and other lessons. And my mother said, "Boy, you're really taking this Bar Mitzvah very seriously. You must be into it." I was into it but she didn't understand why. She thought I had suddenly found this religious fervor, as opposed to the fact that I really said, "This is a gig!" I mean my name is on the marquee, I'm in the starring role. So, it was a real performance.

And then you changed your name when you were 15? Is that right?

I did. I was performing with a children's theater group that was asked to do some of their original material as a potential television pilot and we had to join AFTRA. So, suddenly I was confronted with the possibility of having a different name. And seriously, if this had happened six years later, I might have kept my name. The problem with my name is that I was still a kid that was getting picked on. Greenspan was a very easy name to destroy on the playground. So I said, I gotta get some distance between this Greenspan thing.

Yeah, and who wants to run the Federal Reserve anyway?

Exactly. [*laughing*] It was a snap decision. My name is Jay Scott Greenspan. So I was going to use Jason Scott. But there was already a Jason Scott in AFTRA. And I said, "Well, jeez, my father probably feels awful about me even thinking about this. And his first name is Alexander." So I went, "How about Jason Alexander?"

Your production company is called AngelArk. What's the origin of that name?

Ah, I have a son Gabriel and a son Noah. Noah's Ark.

Yeah, but why those names?

Why Gabriel and Noah? Ah, Gabriel . . . we couldn't think of a damn thing that would sound good with Greenspan and we happened on Gabriel.

So your kids are using Greenspan.

I still use Greenspan. I didn't change it legally. Alexander is just a performing name.

I thought that as often as not, when actors change their name, that they make the full change.

You may be right.

When you're signing contracts you're signing Greenspan?

No, when I sign a contract I sign Alexander. I went to Social Security and I said I need to add a name, a legal a.k.a. to my Social Security number. I never wanted to legally change it. And in fact it's become a great thing because for the 12 percent now of the population that doesn't know that Jay Greenspan and Jason Alexander are the same guy, if I use Greenspan, it doesn't necessarily herald my arrival.

You can stay in a hotel without all those groupies.

Even if I had changed it, I'm not sure that I would have given it to my kids because one of the things that my wife and I are very aware of is trying to keep the kids separate from this phenomenon so that they experience their own lives and their own self worth. They're gonna have enough problems figuring all this crap out anyway. So they're Greenspan.

Did anyone in your family discourage you from your theatrical ambitions? I mean some people might have told you that you're fooling yourself, that no one's going to make a living this way.

My parents were extraordinary. First of all they came and saw every performance of everything I ever did as a kid. Secondly, they had to physically get me to the places that I couldn't go to. They took me to singing class, they took me to dance class, they took me to the auditions.

They never second-guessed that you could do it?

Sometimes they did and sometimes they didn't. What they knew was that this was really important to me. And it was not their job to decide whether or not I would be a success or failure. Life and time would do that to me. As a parent, all you can do is make sure that your child understands reality, and support their dream. You know, it's not even up to a parent to say, yes I think you're talented or no, I don't think you're talented. Because even that is a tainted point of view. I think the best thing a parent can say is, "I believe in you." My parents did beg me to go to college. "Please have a background in something else," they said, "in case this doesn't work for you."

And you did that for two years at Boston University, right?

I actually did it for three. The problem was, I was there as an acting student. I went to college for them.

But you were also already beginning to make money as an actor and so you left school. You've had six Emmy nominations according to one Internet site. For some reason, it didn't say that you had won an Emmy.

I've never won. I've had six nominations for *Seinfeld*. I've actually had more, 'cause I was nominated for some other things. I think I've had eight nominations altogether, but I've never won any of them.

Michael Richards, Jason Alexander, and Jerry Seinfeld (l–r)

Do you have any particular feelings about that?

Ah, mostly not. There was one year, which was actually the second year that I was nominated that I thought, "You know, as I look around I could sort of see that I should probably have that." And I didn't get it. After that point, I frankly don't know how anybody was beating Michael Richards. Michael won it three times. I don't know why he didn't win it every time.

The problem is that when they look at the Emmy nominations, the committee that decides, they're not even looking at whole episodes, they're looking at selected scenes from the episode that you submit. You're basically seeing four pretty solid actors doing some pretty funny jokes. And you see Michael. I would think he should stand out.

You were also nominated for a Director's Guild award for the first Seinfeld *episode that you directed.*

Right. I was nominated, didn't win.

Which episode was that?

"The Good Samaritan." The outstanding feature was a Kramer storyline that stood out. He was having seizures at the sound of Mary Hart's voice on *Entertainment Tonight*.

You've done some other directing. Do you have many aspirations along that line?

Oh, yes. Actually there's a film I just directed called *Just Looking.*

When I was looking at your roles in film, I counted maybe five films that I would consider dramas, not comedies at all. It's a general notion that it's harder to play comedy than drama.

True.

Do you take any particular pleasure in playing a dramatic role or a different kind of pleasure?

I prefer them, actually. I had an acting teacher in college who I think really had a good sense of me and he said, "You know, what's going to be the bane of your existence is that because of how you look, you're gonna be asked to play Falstaff, but your heart and soul is a Hamlet." I prefer the dramatic roles because they're closer to my heart. I never used to think of myself as particularly funny. Again, I was *channeling* funny people. I wasn't creating comedy myself until pretty late in my career.

Well, there is a warmth to George, as neurotic and nuts as he is. There's really a very human side to the character.

The pitfall of George is that everything he does is incredibly obnoxious and unlikable. So it's the things that you're choosing to play *between* those moments that have to bring him back to humanity and *believe* me I used to choose those moments because I used to think the character was reprehensible.

I've known a number of women who just hate George.

I'd say an equal number of people find him really annoying as who say he's the best character on the show.

I do think he's more central.

Well, he and Elaine, I think, were the most complex of the characters. And we got a lot of play. I mean Jerry didn't want to do that much and Michael was mostly a silent player.

The one character I've played where I was almost attacked on the street was in *Pretty Woman.* That was my first national introduction as a persona. I barely even noticed when it was released because we all thought it wasn't going to do well, that it would just disappear. And I was doing a Broadway show at the time and I remember walking around in New York and having women start to give me the dirtiest looks. Just scowls. And finally this one woman came right up to me and said, "I just hate you! I just hate you!" And I said, "I'm sorry, I don't think I know you." And she said, "Oh, how could you have done that to that girl? That lovely girl." And I went, "Oh my God, did you just see *Pretty Woman?*"

In looking for those human moments with George, was it that you wanted the character to be liked or did you want him more fleshed out?

All the decisions were attempts to squeak another laugh out. But the result was that it was showing a part of him that was more humane and gentler. Like when Jerry and George go into NBC and George is talking to NBC and saying, "*This* is the show. We're *not* changing it. *This* is the show." And acting like the asshole that he was. And then turning to Jerry, George says, "What do you think? Did I come on too strong?"

That was another laugh. It was hopefully a laugh that he was doing this asshole thing, and a laugh that it was all an act of bravura. But it also showed the ambiguity that this character had of, you know, I'm never enough. Nothing about me is good enough. Even my conviction is not good enough. So, it was just an insight into the idea that all of George's mishegoss came out of this incredible insecurity and lack of self-esteem. And I think that's why a lot of people have said to me over the years, "You know, I either know somebody who's just like George, or my friends tell me I'm just like George." To which I always say, "Well, you either need therapy or new friends."

Having interviewed Larry David and knowing that that kind of insecurity comes directly out of his experience and he's not completely beyond it yet, I would think . . .

Oh, no he's not! [*laughing*].

Is there some kind of special feeling or understanding you have for Larry David?

Oh yeah. Oh, absolutely. I sing Larry's praises. I know *Seinfeld* was initially Jerry's gig, and that part of Jerry's brilliance was the team he put together. And the choice of Larry David as his cocreator was inspiration. But I also have to tell you, between you and me and the lamppost, I think Larry had more to do with the voice of that show and what was unique about that show, than anybody else. And he was largely unsung for it.

I always thought that it was a painful thing for Larry to really be the genesis and the voice behind this incredibly successful phenomenon, and nobody knew it. People would think that the four of us were making up the show. And we weren't.

But certainly within the industry people had to know that Larry David was behind a lot of it.

I think Jerry got a lot of the credit. And God knows, Jerry was always there. Jerry works very hard and Jerry's a brilliant comic. But from what I know of these two men, and even seeing how the show changed, in my mind, once Larry left for the last two seasons, I firmly believe that Larry was the voice and the eyes and the heart . . . I think I'm probably the only person connected with the show that stands up and says that, and because of that, I think Larry and I feel a bond. In order to play George, I had to understand Larry.

Let's move on to a technical question. People who haven't acted often think that learning lines is very difficult. I know that it's an acquired skill and not really that difficult for most actors. Can you comment?

As I learned more and more about the technique and craft of acting, the memorization of lines only got easier because what most people are thinking about when they say, "Oh my God, how could you possibly learn that" is, if I gave you three pages of a text and I said, "Learn it," you have nothing invested in it so it's pure memorization. A lot of young actors who are winging it come to a script with pretty much the same approach of "I just gotta learn it."

I always say to people, learning lines is nothin'. *Doing* something with them is the problem. When the words mean something, when they have a reason to come out of your mouth, come out exactly as written, then you learn them more readily.

Let me ask you the standard question that you must get frequently from young aspiring actors: Should I be an actor, should I move to Hollywood?

[*Laughing*] Yeah, I answer this question about a thousand times a year.

The answer comes down to a couple things. The first answer I give is, if there's anything else you can do, and be relatively happy, not ecstatically happy, relatively happy, my suggestion is to do that. Because in some ways, the people that are pursuing this as a career have got to come at it from the point of view that they don't really have any other choice.

Why did you have to do it?

It seemed to me that it was the only place where something I innately had an ability for and interest in, and that gave me a sense of identity, all met. You know, I was not a particularly good athlete. I was a good student, I wasn't a great student. This I had a natural affinity for. On top of that, it was something that I enjoyed.

What you also have to check out is, do I want to be an actor or do I want to be a star? For everybody that wants to be a *star*, I go, you got problems, you need therapy, you don't need a career.

What I say to actors all the time is, you can't get my career, I can't get my career—it is an accident. In each and every case it's an accident.

Brad Pitt does not breathe a different kind of air than anybody else. When he began he was just an above-average, nice lookin' kid. Right picture, right time, caught the right imagination, and it began a roll of events. And had *Thelma & Louise* gone absolutely in the toilet and unseen, you might not know the name Brad Pitt today. So, you know, if I had done another pilot other than *Seinfeld* that year, I would still have been working. I was in the business already 12 years when I did the pilot for *Seinfeld*. I was making my living as an actor, I was working on

Broadway. I had won a Tony Award, which was my life's dream. You know, I was a success. But nobody knew who the hell I was.

And you were OK with that, I presume?

Absolutely! [*Laughing*]. The only time it was frustrating for me was when casting directors would say: name actors only. That was frustrating. Because I was locked out of a club without having a chance to try.

This is another thing I tell actors. I say, "Look, being an actor has a power to it. There is a certain power to standing on the stage and manipulating people's reality and emotions. That's what you're doing. You're creating false realities and you're manipulating their emotions with material. And it feels very powerful. And, of course, if you do it well enough, and you become a star, people treat you in a way that also makes you feel very powerful. But here's what you gotta remember. You have no power. The power that you're feeling is something that the viewer is loaning to you. It is not that *you* are powerful. You are participating in something that they *find* powerful and so they imbue that experience on to you."

In some ways, you're lucky that you had a 12-year career before your fame.

Sure. Absolutely. I've seen young actors bop into something that becomes a phenomenon and screw up their lives. Julia Roberts almost did it, at age 21. She became the world's biggest sex symbol. I think Julia was a virgin when that happened. How do you deal with that? So you have to keep that separation.

And if you're gonna be an actor—I always use this example—I say, "Look, there is no musician that picks up an instrument and kinda wings it. They have to learn to read music or they have to learn music theory. They certainly have to learn the technicalities of their instrument. There is no artist that just picks up paint brushes without learning technique, color mixing, perspective, they have to learn drawing, and everything they do on the canvas is a chosen thing, there are no half-assed attempts at anything. Actors are the only people that are sometimes given the name artist, that can get up and kinda bullshit their way through things and sorta, kinda, maybe do stuff and get away with it. And, it's reprehensible."

There are phenomenally successfully actors, and they have their place and I think they're fabulous, who really do one thing, and they can do it with an awful amount of skill and truth. I mean, great actors. Jack Lemmon, Tom Hanks, Jerry Lewis. They're persona actors. Tom Hanks, Jack Lemmon, they're *always* Tom Hanks and Jack Lemmon.

They're 85 percent themselves.

Right. But they have *enormous* skill as comedians. They have *enormous* sensitivity. And, they bring a great deal of truth to their work. Same thing can be said of Jimmy Stewart and Bogart, and, you know, all the greats. Then, every now and then, you will find an actress like Meryl Streep or you will find an actor like Olivier. These are people who can play anything, Shakespeare, Russian theater, children's theater, TV commercials, films . . .

And the last thing they want to do is present a singular persona. You are a character actor, or would you disagree with that?

No, absolutely not. In fact I, if I was a leading man, and I was still me, I would be a character actor because what I've done is take enormous pains to make sure that every character I play is resonantly different from anyone else. They should all be unique, individual human beings.

How do you do that?

I break down a script and know the story being told and get inside the mind of the characters. And then I start to create a physical character and a new physical life. I love to observe humanity. I have notebooks filled with observations about how people move through space, what they look like, how they speak.

In acting, it's taught, and correctly so, that there are four questions that always have to be asked and answered. I've been in plays where I don't know the answers to these questions after six weeks of rehearsal. But I find them in performance.

So what are the four questions?

They're not going to be anything you haven't thought of! Who am I talking to? What do I want them to do? How am I going to get it? What is in my way?

It's certainly very assumptive about human nature, at least in storytelling. That everybody wants something.

This is stuff that I'm putting in the book that I'm writing, which is about the technique of acting. The more specific you are in answering all these questions, the more honed and etched and crafted is your work.

What training have you had that was the most significant?

There was a man named Larry Moss who I found in 1982 and who I studied with for 14 years, in New York and then in L.A. Every actress that's won the best actress award at the Academy Awards for a number of years has thanked him.

How did you and Larry Moss get together?

I was doing a workshop in New York. There were two actors in it that I thought were very good and they turned out to both be students of his. He came to the workshop. I was someone, you'd give me a part, and I tried to apply all this shit I learned at school and you know, maybe it worked, maybe it didn't. He came up to me after the show. "My name is

Larry Moss. I wanted to meet you because you're very good, but I think I could make you a lot better". And I said, "Oh, really? How long would that take you?" Because I had studied with dozens of people by then and I frankly thought they were all full of shit. And he said, "Well, if you work pretty hard, I think I could change your career in a year." And I worked very hard and he changed it in 10 months.

What happened in those 10 months?

We began with the performance of songs. I would start to sing and Larry would go, "Hold it! Who are you singing to?" And I'd say, "What?" And he'd say, "*Who* are you singing to?" I'd say, "The audience." He went, "No, you're not." So we began from square one. And, he said, "You cannot sing, you cannot begin to express something unless you know who you're expressing it to." And so we began there. Then I'd open my mouth to sing and he'd go, "Wait a minute, what do you want them to do?" I said, "*What*?!"

He asked, "By the end of the song, what do you want them to do?" We took several weeks to figure that out, and I'd start to sing the song, knowing what I wanted them to do, and I'd get three lines in and he'd go, "What are they doing now?" And I'd go, "*What*?!" He said, "Well, you're conjuring someone specific, right? You're looking out over the audience, you're singing to a specific someone in your imagination, you know what you want them to do, so what are they doing right after you said that line you just said?" And I went, "Aha!" And he would just take me through this process, this choice, by choice, by choice, by choice process over and over. One piece of material, the next piece of material, the next one until I could do it without him.

There's a great story that Olivier has where he was doing, I think it was *Richard III*, live in the theater, and Ralph Richardson was in the cast. And Olivier had a night that was transcendental. It was the performance of his life in this role. But he was a miserable son of a bitch the whole night, in the wings and backstage, he just was miserable. And when it got to curtain calls, he barely nodded and ran off the stage and ran to his dressing room and slammed the door. And Ralph Richardson said, "This is bullshit." He went back to Olivier's room and he opened the door and he said, "Now what is wrong with you? You just gave the most magnificent performance of your career tonight, why are you acting like a jackass?!" And Olivier said, "I know it was a magnificent performance but I don't know why!"

And the secret of this, of a method like answering those four questions, is you *know why*. Because you're in charge of it. It's not chance.

This gets back to why people need to be serious about the art and craft of acting. Because if you're going to be any good at it, and odds are most people are not gonna make it, ideally you are at least interested in the artistry of it.

Absolutely. And on top of everything else you have to learn to handle the business side of it, which is a pain in the ass.

Jerry Seinfeld walked into that ensemble with the least amount of acting experi-ence, by far. He was a stand-up comic. He's not a fine actor at all. And that's OK because he was playing himself and he was playing a comic. But regarding the matter about finding a way to play something, I imagine he had a good learning curve?

Oh, yeah. Jerry is a good audience and a good natural riffer, you know, so, Jerry was very good at improv from a comedic point of view. So if he sees somebody going in a direction, he knows how to follow. He may not know specifically what he's doing but he can follow. He's going off of a comedic instinct as opposed to something chosen. But his instincts are very good. He doesn't have the instinct for finding the most interest-ing choice, but he certainly has an instinct for finding a funny choice.

How do you respond if I say that your look is that of an everyman? How aware of that are you?

Yeah, I always say that my intellect and my interest are beyond the ordi-nary. But my life experience, for the most part, has been pretty much of the ordinary. And, you know, my look, for better or worse—I think for better—is very, very flexible. I have no strong feature. I have a certain warmth to my eyes. People say that my eyes smile. My voice is neither high nor low. Towards the end of *Seinfeld* I certainly got heavier than not. But most of the time, now, I'm not fat, I'm not thin. It's something in the middle. I'm not tall, I'm not short.

There's no particular ethnicity about me. I don't have a strong nose, I don't have a strong chin. You know, it's none of that stuff. So what I have, is the ability to make myself present whatever I want to present. That's a great advantage.

Earlier you said the business is a pain in the ass. Does it squeeze the fun out of it?

Yes. Yes. In a world where they're going after Bill Gates, no one seems to have a problem with four corporations buying up every media outlet in the world. AOL/Time Warner.

You're saying that the business has become more of a big business.

It's called vertical integration. But the entertainment divisions of these corporations are incredibly small, and now they're part of a corporate strategy, so they must be profitable. Which means, from a corporate point of view, you put a guy in charge of your studio who knows how to turn a profit, who knows nothing about the art or craft of doing any-thing. But that's the guy you're now serving. So, my business becomes serving guys who know nothing about what we do.

But even forgetting the business side, how about this—the audi-ences have gotten worse. In the live theater now, we have to make an-nouncements: "Turn the cell phones and the beepers off. Don't take out wrapped candy. Please don't put your personal items up on stage."

You'll get half the audience that leaves before the curtain call because they don't want to be stuck in the crowd. And the other half, no matter what piece of shit they've just seen, gives it a standing ovation.

The level of crap audiences will accept is a phenomenon. And so what happens is you get writers, directors, and artists of all kinds who think that they've achieved something at the middle of their ability. And then the business encourages that. Also, the Internet is killing us. Interactivity is the buzzword of the day.

Personally, I wouldn't worry too much about interactivity. People will always be drawn to a good story. Audiences don't really want to be involved in the storytelling itself. Whether it's Sophocles, Spielberg, or Larry David, audiences want to be in the hands of a good storyteller. There will always be audiences wanting to experience good stories, told well.

I hope so.

I'm a believer in certain enduring truths about what is good. There are reasons that Sophocles and Shakespeare's plays were great and still hold up. Crap doesn't hold up.

I hope you're right.

Aida Turturro

AIDA TURTURRO

Aida Turturro plays one of the most intriguing and troubled characters in the history of television—Janice Soprano on *The Sopranos*. The demanding role calls on her to convey an array of intense emotional states, often all in a matter of moments. Her character starts one memorable episode in love and engaged to old flame Richie Aprile. That night, while having dinner at home, Richie hits her. A moment later, enraged and with next to no premeditation, Janice finds a gun and kills him. In a later episode she suspects that home health care worker Svetlana Kirilenko has stolen her mother's LP record collection. To apply pressure, Janice steals Svetlana's prosthetic leg and holds it ransom for the records. "Princess" in *Father Knows Best* she is not.

Turturro has appeared on Broadway, in over 40 movies, as well as in television series such as *Law and Order* and *The Practice*. Her film work includes "best friend" turns in *Angie* and *Jersey Girl*, roles in Woody Allen's *Celebrity* and *Manhattan Murder Mystery*, as well as work with her cousin John Turturro in *Illuminata*, *Mac*, and *The 24-Hour Woman*.

Aida Turturro discovered her acting talent in junior high school. In college, she majored in theater and then studied with acting coach Robert X. Modica. She auditioned for her *Soprano's* role like any one else, although James Gandolfini (Tony Soprano) *had* recommended her for the role. They had become friends performing in the 1992 Broadway revival of *A Streetcar Named Desire*. Like the other actors in this section, Turturro sheds light on the demands of television acting and on how an actor prepares.

I was a shy kid. I was in a drama class in junior high school with this great improv teacher. I was so shy that I sat in the back of the class for two years, praying that she wouldn't call on me. When I finally went up, I did a Vitameatavegamin improv, a Lucille Ball kind of thing. Not to sound corny, but it was like an out-of-body experience. I was really good and everybody was like, "Wow!" And I remember thinking, somehow I'm going to be an actress.

Going along with the shyness, I've read that you don't like publicity, that you don't read reviews, that you don't always see the films you're in.

I don't need to see what people say. I like to do the work, and I like to know I did a good job and that the people who saw the show liked it. That's what I want to know. It's nice when you walk down the street and people say, "Wow, I love your work." There's nothing like being in a show and people applauding you. We all want compliments. It's great to get approval.

But it's true, I don't like watching myself. I *can* watch myself on *The Sopranos* because I feel like I'm watching Janice. She is so much someone else to me that I can watch it.

Turturro with Dominic Chianese (Uncle Junior)

Some of the other characters you've played are more like you.

> Yes. Janice isn't me. Her neediness and her manipulativeness are not me.
> For example, I have a lot of friends. I'm a good friend. Friends are one of
> the most important things in life.

*You mentioned people coming up to you on the street. I'm curious what they
say. After all, one can nearly see the cogs turning in Janice's head when she's
going to manipulate a situation, and she is very manipulative. Jason Alexander
talks about a particular role he played and having people coming up to him and
being mad at him on the street as if he were the character.*

> A lot of people *do* that. With James Gandolfini, some people really think
> he's some mobster. But I get a high percentage of people, 90 percent or
> more, separating me from the character. It does annoy me when they
> *call* me Janice. They might make a joke, like "Stay away from Bobby."

Why do you think the public readily separates you from the character you play?

> I don't really know. Maybe because she's changed a lot, maybe because
> she has so many facets that they don't really know how to typecast her.

How has the character changed?

> Janice hasn't changed in *who* she is. Her *outside* has changed. She
> changes by what she wants to do, day-to-day. She was into what was
> convenient for her, hippieland, the spiritual world, the mafia girlfriend
> and the loving, easy girlfriend. She does what she needs to do. She's a
> chameleon for herself and what she needs.

I wonder if the public also separates you from the character because of how extreme the character is, the things she does? She stole Svetlana's leg. She killed Richie Aprile. The public wouldn't believe that you had actually done those things.

There *are* people who can do those things. That's a realistic murder. It didn't happen because she's a mean person. It came from a different place. She killed her boyfriend for so many reasons that came from inside. It's why women kill their husbands. Instinctually, emotionally, people might sympathize with her because even though she's so bitchy and manipulative and mean, it *all* comes from neediness. A lot of people relate to that. So many people come up to me and say, "Oh, my God, my friend, my aunt, my sister is just like that, you remind me so much . . ."

And I'm like, "Really? You know someone like that?" It's scary, but it's true that there are parts of her that are very common to many people. And so she stole the leg. Someone else might do something a little mean and you just don't find out about it because it was a relative. The murder was strong, but it *does* happen.

In the episode where Janice arranges for everyone to speak at Livia's wake, from your point of view, do you think Janice knew in advance that she would dish some dirt on her mother, figuratively speaking? It seems that she intended to have a nice ceremonial moment, but then couldn't restrain herself.

No, Janice doesn't plan everything. She doesn't *think* she's a manipulative person. She didn't plan it connivingly. Some things just come out unconsciously. How much came out, what came out . . . she didn't plan to get emotional about her mother. She's coming from her mother being Livia and coming from a very dysfunctional, maybe slightly psychotic background. She felt very neglected in childhood and this is how she functions. She runs away from things, she has trouble with her boyfriends. This is a troubled woman.

You've done a good number of other dramatic TV shows and over 40 movies. How does shooting The Sopranos *compare to the work on non-premium TV and movies?*

Television is a very hard medium for an actor because you don't have the time to do as much as you would like to do. You don't get as many takes. If you do a movie, you have the script for a while, you study it, you have maybe one scene one day, maybe two scenes another day. In TV you might have four scenes in a day. It varies. With *The Sopranos*, we're doing an hour show with no interruptions and filming it in nine days. By contrast, you do a movie in a month-and-a-half. Could you have been better in a particular scene? Of course you could. Give me five more takes.

Having done Janice for a while, there are some scenes that aren't brain surgery. But there are times when, if I could have just had a little

With Nancy Marchand (Livia Soprano)

more time in this scene, I could have gotten a little more fine tuning. And I'm *not* an actress who needs a milieu. I'm not a perfectionist, like a diva, or it has to be *this* side or *that* side of my face. I'm really into the work. Like the scene after I shot Richie, I looked over the dead body—we had already been shooting for 16 hours—and oh my God, I got one take and a master and that was it.

How would you compare shooting a Law and Order *to* The Sopranos?

You come in when you're a one-day player and you get more nervous, but they aren't hard scenes. *Sopranos* is complex sometimes. There are a lot of levels on *The Sopranos*. I had a scene with Nancy Marchand early on, and I was all shy about just starting work and I didn't want to be the one not knowing what the heck was going on in the scene. But thank God we *both* were confused. We both needed time to figure it out. You're working on a scene sometimes and you see it first on one level, and then there's another level, and you want to have that all in you. And you don't always have it. Other times it's a simple scene. I've got Janice in and out, it's not brain surgery, no problem.

I would have thought that the actual experience of shooting The Sopranos *would be somewhere between like shooting a movie and shooting a standard, one-hour dramatic television show, but I hear you saying that the time frame and pressures are a lot more like television than film.*

What we try to get out there is like a film.

I certainly feel that way on the receiving end.

But how you do it, the time to do it, you simply don't have the time. It's rushed.

How much rehearsal time is there?

We don't have rehearsal like you get on a movie. Between going over it once, and blocking it once, unless in some scenes it's not happening, there's no rehearsal really. We run it through once, and then you're trying to get the blocking technically and then you gotta go.

In television you have to largely direct yourself.

Oh yeah. It changes as seasons go on. You watch any show in the beginning, it's rougher. Everyone's finding their character, everyone's getting their rhythm. But as a family of actors grows, and the directors are there for a while, and the crew's together—don't forget it's a team on all levels—the crew starts to know everybody, the actors start to know each other, and things start to mesh. When you're on a show two years, you can do more and everyone's working together and you can pick up the shooting pace.

Let's say you have a lot of dialogue with Tony, James Gandolfini's character. You've got ten lines between the two of you, back and forth quickly. Will you have run those lines with each other at least once or twice before it's shot?

We're all pretty easy going people. I'll say, James, you got five, you wanna go over this? Other times you're getting makeup done so you run lines then.

As with most television shows, the directors change on The Sopranos. *How would you describe, from an actor's point of view, what the director is doing? And insofar as the director is changing, how much are they doing with the actors?*

It varies with the director and it varies with the actor. In television, it's not as much as in a film because you don't have the time and you have two takes. You can't be like, let's try it this way. If you've got it, you're happy. You're working between making the actors happy, getting the scenes good, and also coming in on time.

So how many times might you have worked it through with the director?

You'll have one rehearsal. You have to walk it through. You're figuring out your blocking and you're kind of reading the scene and maybe you'll

With James Gandolfini (Tony Soprano)

go through it again. But not like a major acting thing. It's a combination of blocking the scene and reading the scene and if you have questions, you ask.

If it's the beginning of the day, and you're not behind in the shooting, maybe you can do a few takes. If it's the end of the day you have no choice. Everything varies. But the time constraints are always there.

We're lucky to have some really great directors on *The Sopranos*. Some scenes are really hard and I can go to my director and say, "I'm a little confused about this. Can I meet with you before we shoot?" Or you call the writers: "I'm unsure what the intention is here, where are we going?" You could call David Chase. Our show is very open to questions and ideas.

Do the writers ever let you know what's going to happen to your character in a later episode so you can choose to play a scene differently?

Sometimes, directorially, you think you're going to make a choice but since you don't know what is ahead in the story—like maybe there are choices for the character that you don't know they are writing—you might have to play the scene in a different way. Janice might need to go *this* way.

Are there occasions on The Sopranos *where other actors are directing you, and you they?*

Sure. I'll ask Edie Falco, is that alright? I think people who respect each other if they're having a hard time, they'll ask the other actor.

You had worked with James Gandolfini before, on Broadway, in A Streetcar Named Desire. *I understand that Gandolfini played a role in bringing you to the attention of the producer, David Chase.*

Before I was on the show, James called me up and said, "You know, I'm doing this pilot, we're filming it. They might have a sister and you would be so great. I mentioned you to them."

Time went on and I saw the show the first season and I loved it and then I heard that they were going to have auditions for a new character. But they were saying, she's gotta be older. They thought I was too young for it.

I thought, if I'm not right for it, I'm not right for it. It got closer to their actually casting it and James said, you know they're starting the auditions, you gotta get in on this. So Peggy, my manager, said you're going to go in for the audition.

James said there was nothing he could do. "I'd love for you to do this, but I have no power." And I said, of course not. Like whatever. So, I went in and they loved me.

How many scenes did they have you do in the audition?

I read about four scenes. First I read with the casting person. They liked me. And I didn't go back for maybe two, three weeks. Then they had callbacks and I did ask James to read it with me to get familiar. So, you know, he was happy to do it. He loves me and thinks I'm great. I think he's great. We go way back. We were both fans of each other when we first started working and very supportive. And we have chemistry when we work together. Sometimes people just have a good working relationship and it's magic.

I went to the callbacks and some of the other actresses who were there I really respected. Luckily someone I really respected wasn't really right for the part.

So you saw them in the hall while waiting to be called in to do your scene?

Right. So one person is like my favorite actress and I was like, "Awhh, oh my God," but she wasn't completely right for the part. Not that many actors wow me but I'm like *in love* with her.

So it was a combination of yes, I'm a good actress; two, it's your part. Once in a while, it is *the* part for you. Not that you're a better actress than somebody else, but the combination of your own energies, and the right style.

Aida Turturro and James Gandolfini

Things were in alignment.

It's alignment. It's a combination of my acting and the feeling of the sister, and that was it. I got it. But James had nothing to do with it.

Actually, at the end of the season, where I killed Richie, he came up to me and said "You made me really proud of you," and that was nice to hear, not that I felt pressure to make anyone proud, I don't look at it like that, but it was nice to know he was happy because he recommended me.

Janice has her share of sexual scenes on The Sopranos *and some are unusual scenes.*

Thank God I haven't had to be naked 'cause no way will I do that. I had to do sexual, but I didn't have to be naked.

But there are those things that the men are demanding Janice to do. Are these difficult things for you to . . . .

Are you kidding? They're *so* difficult. You ask any actor. I can't imagine there's any actor, maybe 1 percent or 5 percent think it's easy. To be intimate or sexual in front of people and open that up? You're vulnerable enough when you're with someone and you're alone in your house.

But for some it's easier because they develop what Ronald Reagan called "Leading Lady Syndrome." He was always falling in love with his leading lady, so it wasn't as hard to do the romantic scenes.

But you're still doing it in front of people. Even if it's your wife. You're opening up that intimate sexual side in front of a camera.

You've had scenes, unlike any on TV, where your lover is holding a gun to your head while you're being intimate. And another time you're in bed and behind Ralphie and God knows what's going on. From the point of view of the mass audience, these are on the edge of kinky or more than kinky. Does that make it more difficult to play?

It was difficult. The gun scene was very difficult. All of it was difficult. You get nervous beforehand. Once you're actually doing it, you're not so nervous, you're just doing it. You're concentrating on it and you're not saying, "Oh my God I'm doing a sex scene." You're just trying to meet your objective. But beforehand, you're like, "How am I going to look?" You just feel weird. Everyone hates it.

Going back in time, what sorts of things did you do to support yourself before you could make your living as an actor?

I think it's very important as an actor to not play the starving actor role. I don't believe in being a poor person. I don't believe in depriving myself from life because I'm not making money acting.

I organized homes and cleaned houses for 16 years. I like to do it, I was proud of my job. I'm an amazing organizer. I still like to organize houses and I still do it for friends as gifts, but now I just come up with the ideas more.

I always think it's important that whatever you're doing, whether you're waitressing, or whatever it may be to make money, you should do it *well*. You should be proud of the work you do everyday. I think that's a big problem in our country.

Many people are alienated from their work.

They don't respect their work. They don't do their job well. It's like a fad today. Oh, I want to be an actor, I want to be a writer. For what? You can do other things. People think you do one movie and you're a millionaire and you can pay the bills. No you can't.

It takes time in this business, so I never sat there going "Oh, now I'm on Broadway" or "I'm in this movie so I'm done with other jobs." When I had a lot of money, I stopped.

Work, and do what you need to do so you make money, so you can take a cab, or buy yourself a nice pair of shoes or take yourself out to dinner. If you have to work a little bit more, do it. So many people work just enough to pay the rent. "Oh, I'm a starving actor." What is that about?

Well, of course there are some would-be actors and actresses who would say that cleaning houses was beneath them, or that they wouldn't be able to make enough money.

Well, that's their problem. I'm completely proud of anything that I do to support myself.

I believe in working hard whatever it may be. I don't think there's a thing between what you work hard at and what you don't work hard at.

There's nothing beneath you to "do" a job well. I have friends and whether they clean houses or they're millionaires, I don't think there's any distinction except for who the person is.

You and your cousin John both went to SUNY New Paltz. Is it a good school for theater?

Yeah, it was great when I went. It was well rounded. I liked going there because you don't just act. I did costumes, I did stagecraft. I did lighting design and loved my lighting classes. I was a master electrician. I learned a lot. I worked on shows. It wasn't just actor, actor, actor. It was a really wonderful place to be.

Have you had private coaching?

I studied with one person after I got out of college. I studied with Robert X. Modica, who John studied with and I think my cousin Nicholas. He's still teaching at Carnegie Hall. He's been around for a while. The Meisner technique. Studied with him for two years and loved working with him.

In your time with Modica, what was the thing that you learned most about being an actress?

It's the basis of my acting: working off the other person, and trying to be in the moment and honest. And not trying to act in your head or your thoughts.

Could you unpack that a little more? A lot of actors think their lines are the most important ones. They don't recognize that being in the moment and having the other line be responded to authentically is what needs to be done.

Yes. It's the whole scene even if you're not saying anything. Your reaction is important. And listening. You can have a scene and have nothing to say and just watching someone, and *that's* the scene. You're living the scene from moment to moment.

It's got to be fresh every time.

From start to end, whether you have all the lines or you have no lines. That's acting!

Janice is upset.

The Meisner technique is under the umbrella of method acting. Do you make a distinction?

Yes, but you mush it altogether. I learn it and I throw it out. I kind of just do my own thing. I think you should learn your techniques and I think you should throw them in the garbage after you're done. I don't mean throw them in the garbage, I mean like you can't act with techniques. You should learn them, work on them, and then you hopefully suck it all up in and then you go. You just do it.

I guess I've been blessed with it not being so hard for me. I can't speak for other people. Maybe I shouldn't say throw your techniques out because maybe some people need that help a little bit more. I learned a lot through method and Meisner.

I kind of think you study a little bit, you do it, and then you create your own form. Like the difference between Olivier and Dustin Hoffman [Olivier was known to be a "technical" actor whereas Hoffman is a "method" actor]. Different styles, but they're both great actors.

To take it full circle, when you were called up, years ago in school, and did that Lucille Ball bit, it sounds to me that you didn't even know what you were going to do exactly and it just happened.

Yes.

You were channeling a Lucy character, you were in touch with something and you had the gift.

I have to say I probably have a little gift. Not that I'm unbelievable, I never think I'm unbelievable. I think I'm a decent actress, I think I'm good. I'm lucky. Some days it's hard work, but I'm lucky that it comes a little easier to me. Not that it's always easy. Some days I go to work and I'm like, *how* am I going to do this scene?

I'm doing this script with my cousin John for example. Amazing part and I'm excited about it because it's hard. But *how* will I do it? I know I'll be able to do it. But it's scary at first because you don't know *how* you will do it. And that's the exciting thing. You know it will come but it's always a little scary because *how* does it come? It's a very organic thing. Now that's me. Some people do not work that way. Some people might sit down, they might study, they might write things, they might be technical, they might dissect the scene, dissect their objective, they might sit down with papers and pens.

A lot of HBO acting appears quite organic to me, especially The Sopranos *and* Six Feet Under.

You have really nice actors on HBO. I'm in love with *Six Feet Under*. There's a lot of leeway to be honest, a lot of leeway for real great situations and characters and there's a lot of great acting. And they cast things well. The actors are down-to-earth, good actors. Sometimes you see actors and they're fine, but you see the wheels turning, so to speak. Like last night I watched *Twelve Angry Men*, the old one.

One of my favorite films.

I'm sitting there and I'm going, *this* is a film! Today, how many times do you see a film that makes you feel that way? It's fine, it's simple, it's real, it's beautiful!

That's why I like Kazan's work a great deal.

Oh, God. It gives me a chill. I mean *Streetcar?* You don't feel like you're watching actors.

Can you comment on the roles that you and James Gandolfini played in Streetcar?

We were Eunice and Steve Hubble [*laughs*]. We were not the leads.

And that's how you met?

Yeah, we met on *Streetcar*. He played my husband and I thought, oh, this guy's going to be trouble [*laughs*]. But we had a *great* time, even with our little parts. We would go backstage and to our little upstairs apartment over Stanley and Stella's and we'd create things. What sounds should we make tonight?

How long did you run as those characters?

It was a six month thing, so we rehearsed for about a month and ran for about five months with Jessica Lang, Alec Baldwin, and Amy Madigan. It was great to be on Broadway. You can't say it wasn't.

Can you contrast working in film and theater?

I've been doing film a long time and I couldn't say that my favorite was theater, but I do *miss* it. It's just how things have happened. When I've wanted to do theater it's not around. At times when I could, I couldn't afford it.

It's quite a commitment.

Yes, theater is. I hope to do more. With theater you're out there and it's an immediate gratification. You're living the scene and the audience is there and it's *live*. It's so scary, and the adrenalin. There's a thrill of *living* it.

Many actors also like the theater because your scenes are in real time. You're not seven hours in your dressing room waiting for a scene to be lit, and then the scene being shot isn't even in the same order as it will appear in the movie.

Right. Theater is your perfect acting scenario. You've rehearsed a part and had four to five weeks to learn the part and to create. It's so much better.

It's been a long time since I've done theater. I'd love to have more of a combination of theater and film. Speaking of theater, you know, my cousin John's an amazing guy. He's not just my cousin, he's a friend. And he's a very good guy and an intelligent man. I worked with him on the film, *Illuminata. It* was like a show. We had rehearsal time and did exercises together as a troupe of actors which was so wonderful. I felt like I was doing a play inside a movie.

Like Shakespeare in Love.

Right. Exactly.

You mentioned Illuminata *just now. Earlier you said that in* The Sopranos *you didn't have to do any nude scenes, but you do show yourself in* Illuminata.

My first, and so far, only nudity. It was very hard to do. I did it because it was in the script. I was *so* nervous but you know, we all had to do it and my cousin's wife had a little nudity. It wasn't about nudity, it was an erotic farce. But it was very hard for me to do. And then my God, there's my *cousin* directing me. We were both so uncomfortable. But like with *The Sopranos,* when you have a chance to do *good* work as an actress, you get excited whereas sometimes you do a movie because you have to pay the rent.

I was going to say that people would kill to get on The Sopranos. *Let me rephrase that. I'm sure people would do most anything to get a role on* The Sopranos.

Paul Petersen

Yeah. Listen I *respect* my job. I'm appreciative of it. I've been so lucky, not only to be on a hit show—I don't feel lucky 'cause I'm on a hit show—I feel lucky because I'm on a show that *I* respect. I love the episodes, the writing, and the people are like a family. When this all ends we'll probably all have to have a Sopranos AA meeting.

You could form a recovery support group with Dr. Melfi. But seriously, all in all, it sounds like life's pretty good.

Yes, but it's been hard this last year. I lost my Dad, and my Mom two years ago. But I'm trying hard. You hang in there.

PAUL PETERSEN

A talented child performer at the age of 9, Paul Petersen became a Mouseketeer on the *Mickey Mouse Club* (and was fired just a few weeks later). He went on to become a household name in the role of Jeff Stone on *The Donna Reed Show* from 1958 to 1966, and recorded Top-40 hits along the way. After the *Reed* show ended, he began 25 years of serious drug and alcohol abuse, emerging in the 1990s as the nation's premier advocate working to protect the rights and welfare of child celebrities.

Petersen was a well-trained little performer when he began working for Walt Disney, but as will be seen, he didn't start off with the right attitude toward authority. His experience with the *Mickey Mouse Club* foreshadowed a future he could not know at 9, but one he was warned of by former child stars Mickey Rooney and Jackie Cooper.

Petersen relates one tragic tale of childhood fame after another. Our best and worst fantasies of life in the fast lane of Hollywood are made real. We see into the emptiness of celebrity.

Following the suicide of Rusty Hamer, his friend and former child star of Danny Thomas' *Make Room for Daddy*, Petersen formed the advocacy group A Minor Consideration. Now with over 500 members, the group of former child celebrities is dedicated to the protection of children in the performing arts and athletics, and has helped pass new laws in California, Kansas, Texas, and British Columbia. Petersen is now working toward federal legislation, and as the United Nations Delegate to the World Safety Organization, he is taking his message worldwide.

Petersen is the author of *Walt, Mickey, and Me*, a book about racing cars, as well as eight titles in the Smuggler series, a set of action/adventure books for children. The hero of the Smuggler series is Eric Saveman, a young James Bond type navigating the drug culture. Petersen lives with his wife in South Central Los Angeles where he works with impoverished youth.

☆　☆　☆

My mom was born with a disfiguring birth defect. The rest of her appearance was pretty striking and she could sing and dance. The moment

God gifted her with these children who had all their fingers and toes and knew how to carry a tune, she set on having us in the entertainment business and moved from small-town Iowa to L.A.

I was born in Southern California. My parents and grandparents worked at Lockheed. Then we were driven back to Iowa because of the postwar depression. Come 1951, Lockheed was hiring again and so the whole family came back out here. By that time I was already taking singing and dancing lessons.

I have an older sister, Pam, and my baby sister, Patty. Pam quickly lost her taste for the business when I struck gold. She was 14 and her brother was already on a TV series—how could she do better?

Your mother wanted to live through her kids, theatrically?

No question about it. I was taking singing lessons, dancing lessons, drumming lessons, and piano lessons. When I got my job on the *Mickey Mouse Club* it was validation in her belief in my skills because I did win a competitive audition. Out of 5,000 other kids, they only hired 16 Mouseketeers and I was one of those.

Did you enjoy all the lessons?

I hated the practice. When you're taking four different kinds of lessons a week, even if you only do 30 minutes a day for each element, you have two hours of practice each day. For a kid who'd rather be outside playing with his chums throwing a baseball, that's a big chunk of time.

Was your success bittersweet for your mother?

In the end, even she said, "I enjoyed your successes more than you did and I suffered more when you failed." She was totally invested in this ambition. You can imagine with what I do now, with A Minor Consideration, how painful it is for my mother.

What she didn't see, but she does see now, is that there are lots of facets to success. It just amazes her now to see people compliment me as a *man*, not as a performer, not as a celebrity, but for the work I do as a *man*. And she had never, in small-town Iowa, recognized that that kind of success is the most substantial. It surprises her that achievement really can be validated, it doesn't have to erupt overnight, it can be the product of a life's work.

I've heard you use the word "abuse" about your childhood. Is that at all metaphoric?

No, that's literal. There were straps and coat hangers and slaps. It was a wildly alcoholic family from my grandfather to my mom and my dad. It was a turbulent household. The kid who gets himself fired at 9 years old was a handful to raise. I admit that to anybody. I have always been a confrontational and aggressive person.

Age 9, during his weeks as a Mouseketeer.

Were the straps and hangers and slaps related to poor performance or practice?

If you don't give your 100 percent effort and your mom is sitting right there with a strap in her hand, you get punished.

Would this ever be in the presence of another adult who was teaching you?

Not in front of the teachers. The teachers were themselves abusive. It's so easy to understand. The coaches and teachers are living through you, *too*. Their very success depends upon *you* becoming a success. My teacher, Sally Sargeant, for singing and dancing, got tons of clients because she could say one of her pupils was Paul Petersen.

What did you do before you landed your job as a Mouseketeer?

The expression I use is "showing early foot." It's a horse racing expression—the sprinter that jumps to the lead and hangs on. Before I ever went to the Mouseketeers, I was getting standing ovations all around Southern California. I would go perform in places and just rock people. I enjoyed performances because, after all, that's what you do it for. And I loved that applause and I liked to stun people.

You've always had a noticeable dimple. Would the people advising you talk to you about how to show that off, how to smile more?

Oh, absolutely. We are trained early on that our entire body is an instrument and that's from fingertips to eyebrows. I can remember Sally Sargeant saying, "Lift those eyebrows!" in dancing class.

You also become very skillful at manipulation. Kids are good at it anyway, they truly are—it's a survival mechanism. But when you become professional at it, then you're talking about something *deadly*. You become *great* at lying, and those deceptions, you *think* are all *outward* directed. What you don't realize, until you're older, is that those deceptions are also *internalized*.

So you learn to fool yourself as well.

Yes, then as an adolescent, and I feel this rather keenly, you begin to have a distaste and cynicism towards other people who are your victims. As surely as if you were a pickpocket. But in the fooling of them, you can mask all sorts of large and growing character flaws.

If you're masking them intentionally, one might think that you might be more aware of them in yourself than someone else would be.

Not necessarily. Remember, the purpose of all of this manipulation is to *please*, it's *not* to feel better about yourself, it's not for growing self awareness. And when this process came to an end I felt, "How come everybody else has got a smile on their face, and I've got this crushing headache?" That's what Ricky Nelson's song, "Garden Party" is all about [*singing*]: "You can't please everyone, so you've got to please yourself."

One of the times when this might have played itself out is the moment you left the stage. There's the Paul Petersen out on the stage, and then there's you back in the dressing room.

Of course, and that's why I stopped doing live performances. You know, as a teenage idol, I was out on the road with the *Dick Clark Caravan of Stars*. And there were some big acts out there. There were The Drifters, The Supremes, Gene Pitney, Tom Jones, The Temptations. And the fact was, because I was on a *television* show, all the big screams and the closing act came to rest on *me*. And I hated it. I hated the stupidity of the audience who didn't recognize that the real talents were The Drifters and Gene Pitney. But I had a hit record *and* a television show.

I found myself really disliking the mob psychology exhibited by people when they get in large groups. I don't like the smell, I don't like how easily they can be twisted and bent with what amounts to stage tricks. At first I traded on that because I felt this competitive need to show these real singers that I had a place with them on the road.

And then I didn't like myself very much for doing that because who I really respected was the guitar player with The Drifters. And I really did respect Gene Pitney, and I really did think that Diana Ross was extraordinarily talented. And I began to say to myself, "What the hell am *I* doing here?" I began to dislike myself for using my talents for what I thought, and I still believe, is purposeless. It doesn't enhance the human condition.

How unusual are you in this?

Only in that I have found the words to encapsulate these feelings. And that's why people come to me, because they often have these unspoken, unspeakable sensations.

I sat down once with Tony Dow from *Leave it to Beaver*. This happened 25 years ago, and mind you, we were both in our late 20s. We recognized that the trouble with our early success was that it had driven out the spice and the ambition of being a young man trying to make a mark. We had *already* made a mark, and found that it was lacking.

You're stripping away a very significant myth of American culture. So many people envy stars and they don't realize that perhaps they're envying the wrong people.

That is exactly the case. To meet a Mother Teresa was really an epic event because *there* was a person who eschews celebrity and takes all of their worth from their actions, and they're *real*. To have people come up to me asking for autographs, and some truly great person is standing right beside me . . . here's where I come down on that: there's something wrong with *them*, not *me*.

But you also blame the industry as much or more than the public.

Well I do, because the industry sets its sights so low. What happened to trying to enrich the environment? What happened to eye-opening drama that reveals the human condition?

You seem to believe that popular culture inculcates stupidity and shallow, vapid values.

Absolutely it does. And unfortunately, the outward trappings of success solidify that point of view. There are a lot of marginal people in the entertainment industry making huge amounts of money. I mean these people are not talented, they cannot hold their own in a wide setting. Meeting them is a disappointment. They have no animating sense of principles on which they operate. Conversely, let me say that meeting Paddy Chayefsky [Paddy Chayefsky wrote the teleplays for *Marty* and other early TV classics and the movie *Network*] was like an atomic bomb going off because he was brilliant. Watching Spencer Tracy and Katharine Hepburn work on *Guess Who's Coming to Dinner* was an amazing experience.

You were on the set?

I was free to go on any set at Columbia pictures.

And you made a point of watching them?

You bet I did because Cary Grant, with whom I worked in 1957, told me I *had* to do that. He said, "Go seek out the brilliant people"—that was his advice. I don't think I was born to be mediocre, and frankly, being a bubble-gum star on a modest television show, whatever its success, is being mediocre.

Let's go back to your audition for the Mickey Mouse Club.

The winnowing process was brutal. The day I was there, there were about 1,500 kids on a big sound stage. You'd start to perform, and if you weren't good enough, it was, "Thank you. Next!" Pretty soon it was down to 700, and then it was down to 200, and then it was down to 50, and out of that 50 they pulled out five kids and I was one of them.

How pumped were you that you saw yourself getting winnowed into that final group?

I thought that the lessons and practice had been worthwhile. That's really what I thought. I am a competitive person. I do not like to lose—especially in something I *know* I'm good at. If it came down to singing and dancing and impressing a panel of judges, I could do that.

When I was 9 years old on the *Mickey Mouse Club*, I was the *size* of a 5 year old. I had this baby face. I had this gap-toothed smile. And so I looked like a 5 year old, but with all these skills.

You had twice as many years of experience pumped into a little kid's body.

That's why virtually all kid actors are small. The list is endless: Roddy McDowell, Davey Jones, Rusty Hamer, Lee Aaker, Robert Blake, Gary Coleman, Mickey Rooney.

Besides packing a lot of talent and expertise and savvy into a smaller body, the small kid's got more shelf life, too.

Well that's *exactly* the case. I have a friend whose parents denied him the medical treatments he needed to overcome his dwarfism because he was a hot commodity as an actor.

There have been rumors over the years that some child actors are actually given drugs to thwart their growth.

That's absolutely true. Judy Garland was not given just B12 shots in 1939, '40, and '41; she was given illegal drugs which started a lifelong struggle with addiction. They were to keep her small and slender and to maintain her girlish figure. Now mind you this is a girlish figure in *Hollywood*. That means boyish hips and a huge chest, and that was certainly Judy.

It's not just Hollywood with its share of quack doctors. Elvis Presley had 16 doctors giving him prescriptions. Ask the East German women's Olympic team, which is currently suing the government, for the decades-long drug abuse that they suffered at the hands of physicians to help stop menstrual cycles, to reduce their stature.

You claim that stage parents tend to be working class.

All blue collar. White collar families don't put their kids into this business because they have the *wit* to understand that there will be terrible consequences.

There are exceptions to this.

Not really. The equation is simple: time and money. Consider the investment you have to make. And if you make that investment on your child's behalf, when you are yourself a professional, you're losing money! I can tell show-business parents every day: if you would invest this energy and this treasure into your own adult career, your family would be better off. Professionals, on the other hand, understand that careers last 30 or 40 years. They appreciate that athletic careers come to an end, often brutally, because of injury.

What is held up as successful in our culture is *so* wrong-headed that people who are true heroes, day-to-day heroes, are not celebrated and they should be. Nurses, doctors, policemen, the guy who picks your garbage up every Monday without fail, the postman, the people who do all of that, volunteer at the church and who are lining up to be foster parents. Those are heroes.

How did you get fired from the Mickey Mouse Club?

I did not understand that kid actors are not supposed to be children. They are supposed to be little professionals and I was not a polished professional at 9 years old. Sorry! I was a 9-year-old boy.

During the weeks that I was there, I got into a couple of fistfights, I had been absent from the set more than once because in 1955 they were building Disneyland. The little cars from Tomorrowland were on the lot and easily stolen. And on a sound stage there are ladders that go up into the darkness, 40 or 50 feet. How cool!

Because I was so small, they called me "Mouse," and I hated that. I hated that frigging hat. All of us hated the hat.

You felt like you looked like a dork?

Well, didn't you?

Well, as a Mouseketeer that was your job.

Kids don't know from jobs. What they know is that you look ludicrous wearing a hat with two big mouse ears on it. In any case, this nickname Mouse was just too much for me.

Anyway, one man, his name was Lee Travers, he was the head of casting for Disney during this era, a big fat man. He continued to call me Mouse. One Friday afternoon, he came up behind me, put his hand on my shoulder, and said, "How you doing Mouse?" I whirled around and punched him in the stomach and said, "Don't call me that, fatso!" Standing behind Lee Travers was Walt Disney.

I got home that afternoon at 3:45. The phone rang at 4:15. My mom answers the call, listens briefly, and makes me take the phone to hear that I had been discharged. I looked up at my mom and asked what discharged meant, because I didn't know. She said, "You've been fired."

Was I suddenly devastated? This is my exact thought process, and believe me, I remember this vividly, I was only two months short of my 10th birthday. I thought, "Oh my God, I have to give back the new bicycle I just bought."

And your mother?

On the important things, the love and support were there. My mother understood, that this boy, whose behavior had been called "abominable" by Mrs. Karnes, my third grade teacher, *was*, in fact a handful. Also, she understood that what I needed then was to focus on getting work. The solution to losing one job is to get another.

So you didn't catch hell for being fired?

Now, do I know kids for whom that did happen? You bet. And I've seen it in the flesh. I've seen it right after auditions, where a kid didn't do well. I've seen them beaten in parking lots. I've seen them screamed at and hair pulled. Any professional kid actor has seen it.

Within three months I was in a famous "Mr. Manners" commercial and in a Ford Theater drama. Within a year, I was starring in *Playhouse 90.*

And you couldn't have done these things if you had remained a Mouseketeer.

You've got it. I got to grow and develop, particularly with the acting skills, because I wasn't locked into the stupid chorus. I had the satisfaction of going on to bigger career achievements.

This whole business of living is a giant adventure of exploration and discovery and there are some hard knocks. What celebrities are asked to do is to adopt an image and then hang on to it. For children it's particularly cruel because children need to grow and develop and they do so in unexpected and wonderful ways. If you limit them by saying, "You're only going to be a shortstop, or a quarterback, or a gymnast, or a singer," you are taking away their options. I hated that more than anything. That all people saw in me was the all-American boy who was able to amuse them.

This crucible, if you survive it, does in fact, allow you to be hardened and toughened. It does help form you. Children who erupt into sudden prominence, if they survive, later in life, are often quite extraordinary.

When we spoke before, you talked about the sexual allure that also attends the success of young stars.

Richard Shickel, the film critic, wrote about this in a devastating fashion. When you look at Shirley Temple movies, what you are seeing is a nubile, young, rounded, prepubescent female sitting on a man's lap and making the world's troubles go away. She was always dressed provocatively and yet played the little girl, always the heroine.

I think I see that, but I'm troubled that I see it. I think that I shouldn't be seeing that. She's just supposed to be a sweet little girl.

It's right there, and that's an essential ingredient. That's what Nabokov was able to explain to people in *Lolita*.

Are young female stars especially likely to be sexually abused at the studio or elsewhere?

There are two elements to this. First, it's a hugely protected environment, so you are watched closely—after all, you *are* an *investment*. But, especially for young females, they are objects of men's lust. The teasing starts very early for an adolescent female in Hollywood. The crew is composed of men in their 20s who are pretty lusty individuals who are sitting there focused on a developing female.

Wouldn't a crew member be afraid that he'd get fired if caught fraternizing with a fourteen year old girl?

Nearly all early infatuations with Hollywood starlets is with a member of the crew. A production assistant, a grip, a cameraman.

Not another star?

Seldom, because other actors are already seen by actors as not quite all there. They're too focused.

Is it different for a male star who's going through adolescence? The grips and others were probably not hitting on you, but other things were happening?

What's happening is that you are losing control of your vocal chords, you have pimples, you feel gawky, you're uncomfortable with your body. It's all that adolescent stuff that guys go through. There are also women at a studio and a lot of them are just like their male counterparts—pretty randy and sexually active.

And status seeking?

That too. It's kind of fun for an older woman to nail a young celebrity.

Did that happen frequently?

As frequently as I could get it, you bet.

Usually with women older than you?

Well almost always, until I got into my stride at 16 or 17.

So when you're 14 or 15 you were having sex with women in their 20s and older?

And older. Even at the studio, when everyone was on their lunch break, the joke was: Paul was going to "funch."

In your dressing room?

In my dressing room, in my car, at the nearby Hollywood Professional School, at apartments close to the studio. Of course. My God, I was 16 you know—life is an erection. It was always a pleasure. My grandfather had it right, sex only comes three ways: good, better, and best. It was never a chore.

You were having sex with women who were old enough to be your mother.

You don't understand the nature of celebrity. At age 14, I'm picking up my own paycheck every Thursday. I'm doing all of my finances myself. I'm making beaucoup bucks, and I'm a celebrity. In the culture we live in, not only today, but back in 1959, those elements are seen as making you quite eligible. For these women, there was a feeling of validation for their own sexuality and a sense of triumph.

I was no longer naive at 14. At the same time I was taking advantage of any female that came my way that was halfway attractive and I was myself being subjected to sexual objectification, and I hated it. I was a teen idol. I wasn't just a kid on a television show. This is your face on the cover of magazines, spreads in all the publications around the world. I had hit records.

Remind me of the titles of the records.

Lollipops and Roses, She Can't Find Her Keys, My Dad.

There were girls screaming at your appearances?

Well of course. That whole thing that Bing Crosby, Frank Sinatra, and Pat Boone did. I was doing the Fabian, Frankie Avalon thing. Young girls, for the most part, would see me as some sort of sexual trophy. What I'm trying to explain to you is that at the same time I had the opportunity to take advantage of women coming into their sexuality, I was being subjected to that kind of humiliating objectification, where on sight, someone saw you as a trophy.

On The Donna Reed Show *with Shelly Fabares, Carl Betz, and Donna Reed.
The show ran from 1958–1966. Betz is seen here engaged in a world record
arm stretch, not an unusual skill for a 1950s father.*

*Did you have anything like a "normal" relationship with a teenage girl during
this time?*

No way.

When did you have your first normal relationship?

Frankly, I started to string what I would call a normal relationship together with five or six females at a time. I had a core of girls who I really
liked as people. Hayley Mills, Donna Loren, Regina Groves, Cheryl
Holdridge. These were girls who I took on the publicity dates because
they knew how to behave. They were wonderfully attractive, and I liked
them. They became my girlfriends. Intimacy is not even an issue I discuss when it comes to these people. They were the ones who were en-
meshed in the same struggle I was.

Let's move from sex to money.

I was 13, and I got an IRS notice that I was being audited. My father was
not financially astute and when I walked into the IRS office he had my
records in a shoe box. The IRS guy looked at my father and said, "Don't
you think with your son's income you ought to be paying attention
to this?"

He humiliated your father in front of you.

Well of course, but dad deserved that humiliation. My father *liked* it when I was introduced as his son. He didn't like it when he was introduced as my father. So he had to keep his distance from me. There's no stopping a superchief and I was on a fast track.

You bought a house when you were a teenager?

I bought my mother a house when I was 15. I bought my first house when I was 17. I had a house in Beverly Hills.

And you had a couple of cars at 16 or 17?

My first car was a '61 Pontiac Ventura 348. I was into drag racing. I had nice cars, you bet. At 17 I traded out of the drag racing cars and bought a Cobra.

When did drugs start becoming a part of your life?

I was living such a high anyway that drinking didn't enter my life until *The Donna Reed Show* came to an end, at age 20. I had six months of enforced idleness when there was no work and the culture had changed so radically around me, I began to try to hook up with my generation. This was 1966. The Beatles are the rage, long hair, sex, drugs, and rock and roll have arrived.

And you could avail yourself of all of them.

You've got it exactly. And people were happy to help me down this road.

You had not abused anything much until the Reed *show was over?*

There was no need. I had been drunk, but I didn't think about smoking dope or popping a pill, or even getting drunk in public, because I had a public image to live up to. But more importantly, I was already pretty high. Things were going pretty good. I was also focused on a relationship with the woman who would become my first wife, Brenda Benet.

Was she also an actress?

Brenda Benet was already a working actress. She would leave me to marry Bill Bixby.

She left you for the Incredible Hulk?

You've got it. Only he was then on *My Favorite Martian.* But again, a public breakup.

What's that like, to have the press feeding on you when you're already hurting?

Brenda and I talked about this before she committed suicide. It was a shame that I didn't know what was going to happen in my life, the predictable consequences of my early fame, because she was really a grand gal.

My shrinking professional opportunities created a lot of tension in a marriage that, frankly, ought to have lasted. I was crazy in love with her, and she with me.

So you took it hard.

Oh, absolutely. By the time our marriage had come to an end in the spring of 1969, I had, in the span of three months, lost a three-and-a-half acre house in Encino to a mudslide; both cars were repossessed; I had missed the unbelievable opportunity to play in *Johnny Got His Gun*—I wanted that part so bad I begged Dalton Trumbo to let me have it; my dog died; and Brenda left me. It was a tough spring.

Did your drug abuse accelerate?

Oh, absolutely. By that time I was a complete mess.

What were you using then?

Everything except the needle. I'm honest about this. The acid was there, the cocaine there, and the marijuana was there. And, of course, under all of this was the alcohol. I wouldn't wish this upon anyone.

How aware of it were you? Were you in denial?

I have never been able to *not* think, or to not feel. For better or worse I am built this way. I am empathetic to other people and I am aware of my surroundings. Even in the midst of a drug-induced haze, or an alcohol haze, I still feel things. But it was painful. Of course, I wrote about it, I talked about it. Even in the midst of all of this, I was writing and selling scripts for *Marcus Welby*. After all, that's what I was being raised and trained to do.

Donna Reed and Carl Betz were teaching me on rehearsal mornings how jokes worked, how you string together moments to have people understand emotionally the points you're trying to make. That's what made the absence of work so particularly painful. I had been raised and trained to be a professional thespian and there was no work.

Mickey Rooney had warned you of this.

He came into my life in 1969 at the house that had been destroyed in the flood.

Did he know you had a drinking problem then?

No, that wasn't it. The problem I had was trying to make an adult life out of the wreckage of early fame.

Which he knew a lot about.

You bet. He had done it himself; he was in the process still, in 1969. It was pretty amazing to open up your front door, and there stands Mickey Rooney. He sat me down in my living room and said, "Now listen, Paul, this industry is *not* going to let you work for *25 years.* You've got to get out of town, and get your education, and then if they're going to let you work, *maybe* it'll happen."

Did you take him seriously?

Well, I'm looking at this guy who was himself out of work sitting there in an orange Nehru shirt, with a big peace symbol hanging off his chest.

You could be thinking, "Well, that happened to him because he's a schmuck. It's not going to happen to me."

That's what happens to all kid actors in this process. You think you're unique. It's only an old goat like me who looks back at 150 years of entertainment history in America starting in 1850 that recognizes that this is a process.

It sounds like Rooney was really well motivated here. He was being a good guy.

Oh, he was! He was trying to help, and he remains constant in that purpose to this day. The person who really drove this point home to me, finally, was Jackie Cooper while I was writing *Walt, Mickey, and Me.* The research for that really disturbed me because so many of the Mouseketeers were living lives of quiet desperation. They hadn't profited emotionally, or financially, or professionally. I looked at them and said to myself, "Wait a minute. In 1955 they were the best and the brightest. What the hell happened?"

When I explained to him the trouble I was having getting a handle on all of the Mouseketeers, he said, "Paul, you have to look at this as a process. You can predict future events by looking at the nature of the child's fame, the composition of their family, and the type of education they are receiving." He used his own life as an example, sharing with me the last negotiation he had with Louis B. Mayer when he was 19. Louis Mayer knew what was going to happen to Jackie Cooper.

What was the nature of that negotiation?

Jackie Cooper at that time was making $1,900 a week [1941]. That's big-time money. Louis Mayer said to him, "Look kid, you're getting hair on your legs now. I'll put you under what we call our starter contract so you can learn to be an adult actor." He made him the offer, but the offer was for $200 a week, and Cooper and his mother turned it down.

Louis Mayer was looking out for Cooper.

Of course he was. He was saying to Cooper that if he wanted to have a career, he had to learn to be an adult actor.

You mentioned your first wife's suicide, but as I understand it, it was Rusty Hamer's suicide and other suicides that were formative in the creation of A Minor Consideration.

Without question, because that's where the rubber meets the road. It's hard to ignore someone taking their life. You can justify or rationalize people doing bad things to themselves, but when a person ends up putting a bullet through their skull, something's amiss.

There were three former child actors, all of whom were friends of yours, and all committed suicide within a year, weren't there? One who hanged himself on a school fence?

That was Trent Lehman of *Please Don't Eat the Daisies.* He hanged himself on the schoolyard fence of the grade school he was pulled from to be an actor. Tim Hovi hung himself in his garage, with the garage door set on the automatic cycle so that it opened and closed like a theater curtain, up and down. He did it just in time for his kids' arrival home from school. The one that hit hardest, for me, was Rusty Hamer whom I had known from the beginning. He spent 12 years on *The Danny Thomas Show.* We were from the same era, we were the same age, we both owned Cobras, we had the same kind of celebrity.

I had talked to his brother a couple of weeks before. Rusty had left Los Angeles, started on his trek to destruction and ended finally in Louisiana. I had stayed in contact with him. But I never intervened. I never showed up on his doorstep when he was fat and addicted to drugs and prone to violence. He ended up in a dilapidated trailer in one of the poorest parishes in Louisiana, working as a short order cook for his brother. Even his brother couldn't keep him employed because he'd pull out his .45 and blow holes through things, getting loaded all the time. What was painful to me was that I *knew* this. I had talked to John at Christmas, just a month before Rusty's suicide, and it would have taken nothing to hop on a plane.

How did you hear about it?

I was in bed with my wife at 7:00 A.M. The CBS morning news came on saying, "Former child actor Rusty Hamer, who starred for 12 years on *The Danny Thomas Show*, committed suicide this morning in De Bitter, Louisiana." I sat bolt upright in bed and—I try not to minimize this, but I don't want to overstate it either—I heard a voice, I felt an honest-to-God presence on my shoulder and the voice said, "This is your task." I turned directly to my wife and I said, "That will never happen again. There will never be another kid actor taking his life without me being there."

Inside my brain, there was a voice not only telling me what my task was but how to go about it. I was being told by *my* God that he had a job for me. That morning, the first phone call I made was to Jay North who had played Dennis the Menace and was in the same boat as Rusty Hamer and probably much more dangerous to the civilian population. He had a list of people who he was going to kidnap and kill. He had asked for my support to help get him a motor home. He did this in front of me and Jimmy Hawkins who'd been on *Annie Oakley.*

He wanted to get a motor home to do what?

Because there's no death penalty in California he had to kidnap the people and take them to Nevada to kill them so he could get the chair.

He wanted to die, but he wanted to finish some business first?

That's correct. Jay North, who was also fat, and also prone to violence, and also deeply disturbed, was my first phone call. And when I told him about Rusty, he got really quiet, and I said, "Jay, you have to let me help," and he agreed.

From Jay, I made five other phone calls to the kid actors currently in trouble at that time, January 1990. All of the previous 13 years that I'd spent out on the stump trying to explain to people—badly, because I was drunk—about how much pain there was in this profession, suddenly, with this mission of mine to help other people, I began to help myself.

How soon after you heard about Rusty Hamer were you on the phone with Jay North? Within the hour?

Five minutes. That morning, the core elements of A Minor Consideration's mission became clear and the momentum hasn't stopped.

Within six months, we had 12 committed people who were going out on the talk show circuit to tell the truth finally about their drug addiction, fame, the estrangement from contemporaries, the obliteration of any sense of family life, and what it felt like. We were using all of our performance skills to make people *feel* this. Within that first six months, we had five people in treatment.

But within a year, with a lot of early successes rolling in, I had my friend Lee Aaker, who played Corporeal Rusty on *Rin Tin Tin*, at my house. Lee had been sober for 13 years. I was still struggling with my drinking. Lee and I together lost Christmas of 1990. He fell off the wagon, I fell off the wagon, and the two of us went through a three-week blackout, woke up on January 3rd, and looked at each other and went to the doctor. I haven't had a drink since that day, and neither has Lee.

You now have about 450 members?

485.

When we last spoke, you told me, "We haven't lost anyone else, except for River Phoenix." Can you explain that?

Fourteen months before River Phoenix died, a young reporter called me in the middle of the night. The reporter had been at a night club on Sunset Boulevard, and was scared to death, because he had just seen River Phoenix and five other pretty prominent young actors shooting up heroin in the bathroom at this nightclub. It was 1:30 in the morning. This was the first time I was told that there were major drug problems in River's life.

I've kept my connections to the drug community because they come and tell me things, and it didn't take very long to know that this was the case. I arranged an intervention because the promise I made that morning, to not let this happen again, still animates me every day, I won't let it happen. We confronted River in his home.

"We" being . . . ?

We being Dr. Stan Zeigler, who was instrumental in providing virtually the entire psychological and scientific base for this group. He's a Yale-trained psychologist. Greg Lougainis was his most prominent patient at the time. Along with Jay North, we confronted River. The guy's reaction was unbelievable. Standing in the doorway he said, "What are you talking about drugs? I don't even eat meat, I'm a vegetarian. I don't do heroin." He closed the door in our face and he was dead in 13 months.

One wonders if some of the people who'd gone that day had been more of his era, things might've been different?

Sometimes the most effective advocates are not names. I am an intimidating presence to people in their 20s. Whereas a younger member of our group finds a way. In River's case, there was no time to do that.

If you got a call about a guy like River Phoenix again, the people who went over to see him would be different?

Not only that, the setting would be dramatically different. The setting would now be in a work environment. There are tools to use that for a performer are truly intimidating.

Do you mean at the studio or on location?

In a studio, in front of people, and saying, "Your job is at risk."

You can't slander, libel, or malign them in front of other people?

When I tell you that I intervene, I am telling you that I walk on sound stages where there are problems and it becomes very quiet.

They know what you're about to do?

You bet. If there is a drug addicted star performer of a series who happens to work with children and I show up, I'm there because somebody called me and there's a reason.

A guy could lose his job, and he could come back and say, "You ruined my career."

Except that I've got the goods. The people, for example, around Robert Downey Jr., *wish* that I had been there. The people around Christian Slater *wish* that they hadn't kept me at arms length, and I think in the end that River Phoenix's family would have to acknowledge that they wish they had called me.

How careful are you in knowing that you aren't working off a report that could be felonious?

On the serious stuff I am careful, you bet. As I said, I keep my connections to the drug world. I know who the dealers are. I would have to have multiple sources.

Let me understand—you'll go on a set in front of how many people?

However many are there. It doesn't matter to me.

And what will you say? Would you do it to a 16-year-old actor?

I have done it.

If a kid is quite young, you come on the set, and what do you do?

Well generally I will come into the schoolroom environment first and say, "Here's what's at risk. First, your work permit is on the line here, because you can't pass a drug test."

Do they give them?

That's the nice thing about being 16. You're so stupid you don't know that the guy talking to you is handing you a load of shit. But I do have the tools. There are "conduct unbecoming" clauses in the constitution and by-laws of the Screen Actor's Guild.

So you could make a case that this guy could be stripped of his work permit.

Absolutely. I am a court-appointed advocate for children.

Do you threaten it, or have you actually done it?

I haven't had to do it. The threat of exposure is generally enough. I have gone to the parents' homes and knocked on the door. Generally, if they're around my age, they know me already and I have the reputation that I will show up anywhere. If I see parents buying a new Mercedes or airplanes, or suddenly living in a $1.5 million home when neither one of them have a job, somebody's going to hear from me. If it isn't me, it's going to be one of the 16 or so real activists in this group who will show up. I am so confrontational on this issue that it puts people off, politically speaking. I don't play Screen Actor's Guild politics very well. The guild is pretty much an assemblage of very liberal, nonreligious people who are driven by their agendas. I have an agenda too, but I come to them as a very conservative, Christian fellow, and it's off-putting.

When you had your epiphany, right after you learned of Rusty Hamer's death, were you already a practicing Christian?

Of course. You can't struggle with alcoholism as long as I have and not recognize that there is a higher authority. Spirituality is such an essential ingredient to recovery, and I had been struggling with this demon for so long that the only glimmers of hope I had ever had came from a spiritual base.

How common is it that parents exploit their actor children? Some maybe don't even realize that they are, and others know exactly what they're doing?

Yes, that's true. In fact, the rare exceptions are people like Jodie Foster's mom, Ron Howard's parents, Fred Savage's mother and father. Those are rarities.

And they've bent over backwards to be sure that they're not doing anything wrong?

Vance and Jean Howard, when they came to our initial focus group at the Screen Actor's Guild, stated the case quite bluntly. This should be taken as a primer for *all* stage parents, or sports parents for that matter. Number one: You do not *ever* change your lifestyle *no matter what* your child's success. You live within your own means and you never move. If you're going to get a kid engaged in the turbulent world of big-time sports or the performing arts, it's important that they have neighborhood chums, a home school, and that they *know where they live.*

Can you comment on Macaulay Culkin?

Well there is the perfect case in point. The moment *Home Alone* became such a big hit, Kit Culkin, who was himself a minor player as an actor, became the manager. He got the money Macaulay deserved—and he did deserve the big pay day for *Home Alone 2*—but Kit was unable to grasp the importance of the very things I just mentioned: staying anchored and not altering the family's lifestyle.

After the purchase of five luxury condominiums in one building, the mother and father got into a nasty custody dispute and divorce which cost Macaulay *a lot* of money. Macaulay, who hadn't worked in years, married his 17-year-old sweetheart and is, in the eyes of the law, an adult man. Kit Culkin was not invited to the wedding.

You gave me a statistic once that, proportionately, drug and alcohol abuse is three times as high for kid actors.

Three times the national average means that three out of every four kids who go through this process that we're talking about will have substance abuse problems.

Is the figure also multiplied like that for people in the industry generally?

No. That is the lovely fiction—that people think this business is so different from other businesses. I've been in a lot of businesses, and frankly, I find very little difference in the publishing business, the entertainment business, or the transportation business.

Let's back track one more time. How did it come about that you went to Yale? This was right after Mickey Rooney and Jackie Cooper talked with you.

When I got to Connecticut, the year was 1970. It was on the strength of a screenplay that had been purchased by a Connecticut company called Ampersand, which was headquartered in New Haven. My best friend, the man who rescued me, David Oliphant, owned a company called Academic Industries. When I moved there, I was staying at the New Haven Motor Inn. I moved there with two suitcases.

Had you already been accepted to Yale?

Hell, no. I was there to work with him. Someone suggested to me that since I already had three years of college credits at UCLA, and was short only a few credits of getting a degree, I might finish up at Yale.

What subject?

English and History. I took advantage of an admissions policy that Yale University had instituted like many premier universities did, their Community Outreach Program. The program allowed me to come and audit these classes. I was already holding a contract for three books with Simon & Schuster, looking at people who would've killed to be published.

I had an early string of books. The first book was on high-performance driving that was a contractual obligation that I took over from Carroll Shelby, who was the creator of the Cobra. Herb Alexander, who was the senior publisher at Simon & Schuster—I knew his son, we had raced cars together many years before—gave me a chance to write this book for him. When I delivered it, camera ready, Herb gave me a three book contract to write a series of books called The Smugglers, which was an action-adventure series.

How would he know you could write that?

I think because he had read my screenplay *A Thing Called Honor*, and because he knew me personally.

What happened to you at Yale?

For the first time I recognized that I could play at that level. I no longer felt that I was handicapped by my early fame. I didn't feel that I had been cheated educationally. Looking around at some very bright people, I felt that I had their skills and then some. And I feel that way today.

Because I was on *The Donna Reed Show*, I *had* avoided finding my place in the pecking order. Kid actors as they age are forever looking over their shoulders wondering if they're worth it. If they really had deserved that opportunity.

Why do you live in South Central?

I live in South Central because this is where the work is.

Wouldn't some say that the work is in Beverly Hills or Hollywood?

No, the work is with children. I know I talk incessantly about high-profile kids in sports and entertainment, but our culture is being damaged from the bottom up. When I take these kids to summer camp at YMCA camp they do not have the basic tools of civilized behavior. They do not know how to say please, thank you, excuse me, and I'm sorry. And believe me, since I am generally three times the age of the other counselors, I *am* a presence. I make sure that at least those core values are passed onto these kids—at least to behave. Since I am a rather loud person, the message gets through.

What is your neighborhood like?

I live around 146th and Western, which is at the southern end of South Central. I live in a truly diverse and wonderful community. I've got the Ramirez family to my left, the Johnson family to my right. The kids know me here. I volunteer at the YMCA.

You told me the other day that it grounds you to be coming back to such a place, versus up in the hills.

It does, because these kids' concerns are not at all what the privileged kids I generally am dealing with are concerned about. These kids are struggling to learn to read.

It's so important to me to do the work, and this is the street where my wife was born 40- some years ago. Because we made a commitment to A Minor Consideration, all of our resources are poured into that. And frankly, it makes us, not bulletproof, but darned near so from the retaliation of a very powerful industry.

Given the way we've talked, someone might think that you had a bad experience on The Donna Reed Show. *Can you capsulize how much you enjoyed being on* The Donna Reed Show?

I did. I had a private tutor for eight years—a woman, Dr. Lillian Barkley with *three* doctorates. But more importantly, Carl Betz, who played my dad, had gone to Carnegie Tech. He loved the arts, he loved fine writing, he loved fine food and wine.

Carl pushed me *always* to look for finer things and better things and to educate myself. You can't imagine what fun it was on my 14th birthday to get from Carl the complete works of Shakespeare. Over lunch on the set, he would, through memory, and me by reading, go through Shakespeare for the first time. We would read Shakespeare over a plate of spaghetti and he'd have a couple of beers. That's how cool it was. Donna Reed never once worried about my acting ability or whether I knew my lines. She cared about me as a person. She wanted me to sharpen my wits and to get my education and to learn this craft.

Was it difficult for you or your parents that you had these two surrogate parents who were so accomplished?

It was only difficult for my parents. It wasn't difficult for me at all because I had it good and I knew it.

But it was tough on them.

Of course it was. And for my siblings. And for four of Donna Reed's children who I consider my brothers and sisters. For many years, they were resentful of the time that Shelley Fabares and I took from *them* because *we* had their mother all day. In any case, all of these forces were consciously considered by Donna Reed and Carl Betz.

I know you've had new laws passed that protect child entertainers in California, Texas, and a handful of other states. And I know you've taken A Minor Consideration's message to Canada. I suspect your message has begun to go further still. Are you the main voice leading this cause in the world?

I'm the only one. I am now the United Nations Delegate for the World Safety Organization. I have similar initiatives in Canada, Mexico, and Ecuador with more coming in the Southern Hemisphere.

Federal legislation sponsored by Tom Harkin and Sam Brownback should hit the Senate floor in the spring of 2004. As soon as the federal legislation is announced, we go to the National Administrative Office that runs GATT and NAFTA and ask that these commonsense rules for children be "imposed" on the entire continent. If America installs child labor laws for entertainment on a national level the rest of the countries (primarily Canada and Mexico) must comply.

From there I hope to introduce our "solution" to the United Nations General Assembly. I believe we can have a global rule in place, at least for kids in entertainment, and if we're really lucky we can apply our standards to the rest of industry. It's so simple. A safe workplace. The children own the money they earn. Employer-supplied education if kids work on a school day. Mandatory savings for the kids until they reach adulthood. Imagine if we can play a part in leaving this legacy behind.

Give me a good summation line.

I suppose the summation of all of this, since it's so difficult to really share your life fully with people, is my favorite Nabokov quote which is this: "I know more than I can express in words, but what little I can express could not have been expressed had I not known more."

The Agents

During television's early years, talent agencies sometimes directly produced television programs. Years later, with the demise of the studio system, talent agencies once again became critical packagers of talent and now wield considerable power in a town where power and agentry are synonymous.

Agents are constantly on the phone, putting deals together and keeping them from falling apart. They manage talent (writers, directors, and actors) and see to it that talent agrees to work with other talent.

Agents typically start their careers in an agency's mailroom, often at William Morris, America's oldest agency. Though I first interviewed Jeremy Zimmer, Bill Haber, Jay Bernstein, and Ray Solley when they were working elsewhere, by coincidence, *all* of them had worked at William Morris at one time or another, and two started out in the William Morris mailroom. Zimmer explains why the mailroom is a smart place to put a fledgling agent:

> The only true commodity that an agent and his agency sells is information. You're a purveyor of talent. The talent needs you for your information about the activities of the marketplace. By starting in the nerve center of the mailroom you learn the importance of the commodity of information.

In the interview, Zimmer is often brash and outspoken. Bill Haber, diplomatic and cautious, couldn't be more different. Haber cofounded Creative Artists Agency (CAA) in 1975 and headed CAA's television department when we spoke.

Around the time Haber was starting CAA, Jeremy Zimmer was a young man, on his way to becoming a parking lot mogul before an altercation in the lot left him with a knife in his chest. He stopped parking cars but couldn't get another job until his grandfather, Dore Schary, once the head of MGM, set him up to work in William Morris' mailroom. Zimmer would later join the industry's largest agency, International Creative Management (ICM), and then cofound United Talent Agency (UTA).

Jeremy Zimmer

Jay Bernstein started out seriously starstruck in Oklahoma. He would tell his parents he was at athletic practice and take the bus downtown to watch movies instead. He began in Hollywood working three jobs: the mailroom at William Morris, parking cars, and the night shift at a ball bearing plant. By the late 1970s he had become the most prolific publicist in Hollywood, successfully promoting numerous actresses and deliberately modeling their public images on movie actresses from the 1940s and 50s. (Farrah Fawcett was his Betty Grable.) Bernstein is a very serious student of stardom and has his personal trainer read a star biography each week so that while he works out they can discuss career trajectories.

Bernstein was also one of the originators of the "team" concept in personal management, which puts an actor or actress together with an agent, a personal manager, a business manager, a public relations agent, and an entertainment attorney. Bernstein has headed many such teams, had lots of clients, and been fired 600 times. Asked why he is fired so often, he explains that it is an occupational hazard for a publicist: once you get stars where they want to be, "the air becomes rarified, they become deified, and that's when you get nullified." No wonder Bernstein finds the industry so brutally competitive. "I don't know what the rest of the world is like but I know that here in Hollywood people have a tendency to think that the greatest sound to hear is that of your fellow man crumbling."

When Ray Solley and I did our second interview, he was an agent at William Morris, but a very different kind of agent, putting television production and syndication deals together. Solley grew up in Kentucky in a religious household, went to college, and then moved to Chicago, where he helped produce *Soundstage* and *Sneak Previews* for PBS. Solley now runs his own consulting company and he knows a lot about the mechanics of the business. His is the single best interview in the book if you're interested in the business side of the industry and how it's changing. A lot about the business can also be gleaned from the interviews with Arla Sorkin Manson, Bruce Sallan, and Lee Rich, among others.

JEREMY ZIMMER

Jeremy Zimmer is a film and television agent in Hollywood, representing writers and producers. First at the William Morris Agency, long an agent at International Creative Management—the largest talent agency in the world—Zimmer eventually left to help found United Talent Agency (UTA) in the early 1990s. Since starting UTA, Zimmer has been associated with Gary David Goldberg and the creation of *Spin City*; Dick Wolf and *Law and Order*; Tom Fontana, who produces *Homicide* and *Oz*; and David Chase the creator of *The Sopranos*.

Zimmer takes and makes hundreds of phone calls each day in a business where the phone has been likened to a bayonet. Throughout most of our first meeting at ICM in the late 1980s, he fondled and twirled his telephone cord. (We talked again in the late 1990s.) I began to think of him as attached to his phone cord as if it were an umbilical, the cord through which he receives the life's blood of his profession: information. As he says, "The ability to wield the information and influence equals power, and power is your ability to deliver talent or not to deliver talent. It's like the old west with telephones and pens instead of horses and guns."

The interview begins with his rise from parking cars and being stabbed to how he became an agent, starting out in the mailroom—the launching ground for all young agents. We focus more on the life of an agent than on the films and TV programs he has been associated with, but in so doing, we learn a lot about the business. Zimmer is unusually colorful and outspoken and he has quite a sense of humor.

☆ ☆ ☆

What in your background led you to become an agent?

When I was 6, I used to let people see my sister naked and charge them a quarter. Actually, my grandfather was Dore Schary, who was the head of MGM for many years and a writer and a producer. My father was a TV producer but stopped when I was 8 and became a stockbroker. My mom was a novelist.

I knew some celebrities, but it never made me want to do show business. I didn't know what I wanted to do. I didn't have any clue at all. I was a terrible high school student and I was terrible in college.

I went to Boston University and dropped out after a year and a half. I started parking cars for the Boston Red Sox just to make a living, developed some ideas about how to increase the space, the amount of cars you can put in a lot, and impressed some people by doing that.

I figured out a way to double the price you could get away with on reserved spaces. I had insights into how to get people to do what you wanted and pay what you wanted them to pay. I sort of figured those things out early and gained insights in how to impress someone with your ingenuity and your ability. I was 18 years old and I was making $75,000 to 100,000 a year in cash.

Then, when I was 19, I got into some trouble. There was an attempted robbery in the parking lot and I was stabbed in the chest. I was in intensive care for a while. Then I moved down to Connecticut and was recuperating at my mom's house. Once I got stabbed I was out of the parking lots and never went back. I didn't know what to do. I tried to get a job in a Xerox store and I couldn't do that. I tried to get a job as a shipping clerk in the Franklin Mint—figured I'd work my way up at the Franklin Mint. I couldn't get a job there. After about four months of striking out getting my own jobs I was scared to death and I was thinking about going back to college.

One day my grandfather just kind of descended upon me and said, "You're going to have an interview at the William Morris agency in New York. You are going to wear a tie and a jacket and you are going to say, 'Yes sir' to whatever they ask you to do. And you are not gonna be a wise guy. And that'll be that."

I showed up at William Morris and met with a fellow who was on the phone the entire time. I next met with the chairman of the board. He was a lovely man, over 70 years old. He couldn't really hear what I was saying. It was one of those interviews where I just said, "Yes sir" and I got the job.

I immediately went out and bought seven new Ralph Lauren suits. But I was hired as an agent trainee which means I was in the mailroom. So I showed up my first day in my beautiful Ralph Lauren suit and spent the next two weeks in the subways delivering packages. You know, Bobby Vinton's teeth and things like that.

Bobby Vinton's teeth?

We had to go pick something up and bring it back to the office to be pouched out to Vegas. We picked up this package, and I said, "What's in here?" I opened it up and it was Bobby Vinton's teeth.

Is the mailroom the normal entry position for most new agents?

Yes, at William Morris, Creative Artists, and at ICM. I was in for a very short time. Then I was promoted and made a secretary to two young agents. I answered about a million phone calls a day.

So one learns the business by handling the mail and telephone traffic for a number of months and getting the sense of who people are and who's talking to whom.

Yes. The only true commodity that an agent and his agency sells is information. You're a purveyor of talent. The talent needs you for your information about the activities of the marketplace. By starting in the nerve center of the mailroom you learn the importance of the commodity of information.

It's truly an osmotic process learning to be an agent. You learn to talk like an agent, think like an agent, and react like an agent. But you can learn all those things and still not be a good agent unless you have an instinct for it. You have to know what works and what doesn't work. Knowing that a square peg doesn't fit into a round hole. You don't put an actor or writer in the wrong project.

But obviously some people have better judgment than others.

Maybe. Why?

Don't some people have a better sense than others of what makes for a good television program or film?

Anybody who believes they have a better sense of what makes a good product is screwed. You've got to operate from your instincts but you can't believe your instincts are better than anybody else's. Otherwise, you're gonna miss out on terrific things. You can't think that what the other guy is going after is no good. You gotta believe that what he is going after may be good, too, and you've got to go after it as well.

You're saying that no one really knows what's going to be a hit.

Absolutely correct. Because if somebody knew what was going to be a hit, then that person would run a studio that produced and distributed nothing but hits. And there is no company that has done that in film or in television. If I knew what would always sell, I'd be making a couple million dollars a year telling people. I sure wouldn't give it away for free and let you go and run a studio somewhere with my secret.

You can get the best actors in the world and the best scripts, but you don't know if you're going to have a hit. Bill Cosby had a number of unsuccessful TV series before he had a hit and Mary Tyler Moore's last two series failed.

What does this fact of high uncertainty mean for the agent?

It gives the agent power. It means that I can represent an idea or a script or a new person and that person just may be the next sensation. If an executive sitting there in his office is uncertain, he's gotta listen to me. All of a sudden there is a lot of power in my belief. If I come up and say, "This guy's got it," he's gotta listen.

But people are saying that constantly in Hollywood aren't they, always hyping their projects?

Right. It's all about who's hyping it. It's all about reputation and frequency of delivery.

What are your main priorities as an agent?

My first priority is the people I work with in my agency. But, when you boil it all down, what I try to do at the end of the day is try to put people together with people, writers with producers, producers with actors. Merge like minds.

How does a new writer get to you?

Through referrals, people I know tell me about a good writer, through a witty and intelligent query letter, through luck, through me hearing about them.

What do you say to the claim made by some writers that many Hollywood agents and producers cannot competently judge written dramatic material.

I'd say that's what writers said about agents and producers in the 1920s and 1930s. That's probably what Homer said about the ancient Greek guy who ran the Greek theater 4 million years ago when he said, "Listen, Homer, babe, I don't think this works." I mean, so what? That's part of the whole downtrodden writers' syndrome.

Some writers say agents are reading scripts on boats, on planes, and in cars and that you don't give the kind of attention to the material that it deserves. As a result, sometimes things are missed or not understood.

I've missed a lot of things. A lot of material has come to me that I have passed on that has been successful. Or where I passed on writers who have become incredibly well-known and highly paid.

Am I right that saying no to something that succeeds later elsewhere is a much less egregious error than saying yes to something that fails?

The good part about being an agent is you don't get to say yes. You get to say yes to things you want to sell, but you don't always sell them. That's not a failure necessarily. But I don't finance movies or television series, so my failures are on a lesser scale.

To the person who is putting money on the line, it has to be safer to say no than to say yes.

Yes, but if you're in a job where you have to say yes, there's a reason why you have to say yes. These companies aren't structured and financed to *not* make movies and television shows. It's like you never know if a line of chairs will sell, or if a line of shirts will sell. But if you're a clothing manufacturer you can't not make them. You've got to. Otherwise you have nothing to sell. Just like me—I never know whether a client will make it or not. That doesn't mean that I don't sign them.

When you're thinking about whether a project will work, do you think about the audience?

Yeah, you think about the audience, but once again if you base your thoughts on what the audience will like, you're screwed. Because you never know. Still, at every step of the way, you're thinking about how something will come together in a way that will attract an audience. So, yes, the audience is at the end of the chain. The only reason you're in business is because of the audience. But if you sit there and only make products that you think an audience will want to see, you will fail.

Is research on what people want to see made available to you on a regular basis?

Yeah, but we don't utilize research much. The production houses and studios use it to create marketing and advertising plans and to help decide how much money to spend or where to spend the money. But marketing studies have limited value. For every movie or television show that has tested huge and did well, there's something that tested huge and didn't do business.

Can you comment on critics and academics who say that the television and movie industries have become too commercial?

If you look at most of the critics who cover the entertainment industry, all they want to do is be *in* the entertainment industry. The guy from the

Washington Post now wants to be a producer. The guy from the *LA Times* is now working over at A&M Films. These guys come out here and write some little fluff pieces about some big executive and they get jobs. If somebody said to you, "Hey pal, do you want to come out here, you know a lot about television? Do you want to come out here and make $150,000 a year and drive a Porsche?" You'd say, "Where do I sign up?"

Money and power and glitz and glamor and perks talk. Most of the people who write about the entertainment business make $40,000 a year and think they're smarter than whoever they're talking to and they think they can do it three times as well. Then they come out here and they are just as big a pain as I am.

I was interviewed on PBS's *Nova* program and talked about the business and got 400 letters from people all over the country who have written things, who want to be in the business, who have a cousin living in Pacoima who is a struggling actor, and could I meet with him. It's like the old saying, "Everyone has two businesses; their own business and show business." Everyone is interested in show business. People are fascinated with the business and how much money's involved. Everyone thinks they can do it. Everybody has fantasies and they think that's what it's all about.

At ICM how is an agent paid and performance measured? Are you salaried?

Yes, plus you get a bonus based on performance. Performance is measured by a combination of the revenues of your clients and the overall contribution you have made to the company; that is, your ability to sell other people's clients, your ability to assist in the putting together of projects, and your ability to garner and transmit information on the activities of the marketplace.

Are there partners at ICM?

No. We're a publicly held company. We're traded over the counter. We are a subsidiary of the Justice and Talent Group.

Roughly, what does an agent earn in salary and how much might a bonus range?

The bonus can range, from what I've been told, from 2 percent of your salary to 100 percent. The mean salary is around $100,000. But there are a lot of people making $30,000 and there are a lot of people making $300,000. I'm *not* making that much more than when I was a parking lot man.

When someone works in production and owns part of a hit movie or television series, they stand to make enormous amounts of money. I would think that an agent might want to move into production.

And they often do. I've been offered opportunities. And it's something I may desire to do at some point. But the upside of being an agent is tremendous job security. You have a guaranteed salary every year. All your overhead is taken care of and you have got very good perks, a complete expense account.

Studio jobs are a lot scarier for a lot of people. But if you have a basic talent and an ability to play the game in this business, you will succeed almost endlessly. If you don't burn too many bridges, bust too many people's balls, and make too many stupid, glaring mistakes you'll only succeed up.

Once again, it's the square peg and a round hole. Every transaction has a critical apogee, a point at which it happens or it doesn't. If you're not smart enough to recognize the critical apogee and you go on beyond it and you torture a process and you make things happen that shouldn't have happened or you make things that should have happened not happen . . . if you keep doing that, you obviously don't have the touch and you won't last. It's just touch.

You're always walking through a mine field. There are a lot of mistakes to be made, there're a lot of opportunities to screw people. Because you're in the business of information and influence.

A producer has a project, but a studio or production company isn't sure they want to commit to it. I'm in a passing conversation with the studio head who asks what I think of it. If I don't like something the producer did to us or if the producer screwed one of our clients or something like that, I might say, "Let me tell you the truth—I think it'll turn out to be a bomb," or you could say, "It's not very good, we've seen it before. You know that producer really can't deliver." Or "There're a lot of no-talents working with that guy."

People run a great risk in crossing a powerful agent. It also sounds as if you feel that you can't take insults lying down.

It's true. It's individualistic as well as corporate. If somebody screws over a client of the agency, you as an agency have to respond to that. You have to say, "This won't happen to clients of our agency." That sends out a signal to the buyers and also sends out a signal to the clients that you are protected by virtue of the power of your agency. Because that's what agencies represent. Large agencies represent information and information is power. The ability to wield the information and influence equals power and power is your ability to deliver talent or not to deliver talent. It's like the old west with telephones and pens instead of horses and guns.

What kinds of things do you do to gain clients or to hold on to existing clients? Is it necessary that you go to parties?

Yeah, I go to parties. Part of what you do is try to steal clients from other agents. Other people represent them and you try to let them know that you offer a better quality of service. Wait one second while I take this phone call.

When you're on the phone you talk cryptically and use very short phrases.

You have, like, 150 to 200 phone calls a day. You gotta shorten them up.

By talking that way you communicate to the other person that you have other calls?

Right, no nonsense, let's get down to it. Hi, what's up, OK, good, yeah, 'bye.

It's my understanding that some of your clients, an actor or a writer, might go to a party and have five ICM agents surrounding him. What are you doing when you're doing that?

You're showing him that's he's represented by a company, not a person.

Do you like that part of being an agent?

Yes. Because when I'm in trouble with the client it's good to know there're four other people who are going to help me pick up the slack.

Let's move on to the topic of television and movies' impact on society.

I think that television and film are responsible for 99 percent of the creation of role models in our society. I think if you look at the typical development of a typical family, it's patterned on *The Flintstones* or *Ozzie and Harriet.* The husband's a hardworking guy who's assumed to be a schmuck.

The entire women's movement and subsequent sexual revolution and the battleground we lived through in the 1970s and early 1980s was a result in our change in hero worship from John Wayne to Woody Allen—the sexual uncertainty that men all of a sudden had.

Do you think the attention span of the American public is growing shorter?

What did you say? I wasn't listening.

Is the attention span of the American public growing shorter?

Probably, yeah.

Everyone I've talked to in Hollywood and in publishing believes that it is and many believe that as a result, they must produce products that are adapted to a shorter span.

Look, the delivery system for information has changed. Is it better or is it worse? I don't know. You can now get information more quickly, in a more shortly defined and more encapsulated version. Does that make it worse or better? I don't know. Our attention span is shorter, but are we less informed?

What if, as a result of entertainment values dominating mass communication, the level of political discourse in the society has declined?

Look, some guy gets elected because he's better than everybody else. I believe that leadership responds to the environment. I believe that if the sheep are asleep, it doesn't matter how loud the bell rings, they ain't goin' anywhere.

Then the question becomes, are they naturally asleep or have they fallen asleep because they have been grazing for too long on too much easy-to-eat grass?

They are asleep because they have been grazing on grass that is satisfying to them. The sun shone on them all day and they are in a pasture which they love. And that's why they're asleep. When it starts to rain or hail, or the grass turns brown and ugly, or there is a leopard among them, they will wake up.

You understand what I'm saying? It's like Jeff Greenfield is sitting there saying in one of his commentaries, "You're all asleep," and the people watching agree with him but they're watching him say these things about the power of television and how horrible it is on a 36-inch, rear-projection screen.

You're right. They're a little numb, but they're happy. People in America are, for the most part, happy. I've been in other countries. It doesn't look that great to me. I love it here.

I really feel I'm blessed. I think we can all worry that television is ruining the masses, or that smog is ruining the masses, but I kind of look to myself. On an individual basis it's up to every man to heal thyself. The theorists who sit there and worry about the masses should wake up.

Would you like to say anything about the negative image of the Hollywood agent?

The negative image of the agent is fostered by people who have struggled for recognition and either found it or not found it but have come through it the hard way, or by people who have been represented badly by agents, or by people who resent paying a buck to somebody to gain entry into the world of the marketplace. That you have to pay somebody leaves a negative taste in some people's mouths.

The negative image is of a nonprofessional agent. I'm completely professional. I carry around in my mind 50 deals amounting to $5 million worth of business. Deals that I know inside and out. Most people within the industry don't feel that way, other than the writers who hate agents and who hate producers and who hate . . .

I know I've sounded very cynical. What I do want to say is that I think that most of the people that I work with during the day care about and love television and movies. And yeah, we also have to make movies and television shows that are stupid but make money. Because those products support the system. People don't understand that we make a range of products. They think that we're all named Morty. We all have pink earrings and drive Cadillacs and have casting couches to take advantage of starlets. That's really not the way it is. I could make five times more money in the real estate business or any other business using the amount of wit, instinct, and energy I put into this business. It's not about money and it's not about power. It's really about being involved everyday in a business that I really love.

It's been over 10 years since we last talked. When did you start UTA?

Around 1991–1992.

There were a number of founders, yes?

There were eight of us, of whom four remain.

How does UTA differ, in its clientele, in its thrust, than, say, ICM or CAA?

UTA has benefited from an open philosophy and an ability to identify young talent, invest time and energy in that talent, stick with that talent as their careers burgeon, and then reap the economic rewards of that development. We have been less inclined to poach and more inclined to develop.

How different is it being in charge?

When I was at ICM I was involved in senior management, ran departments, but I always looked at the guys right above me and said to myself, "If only they would, . . . ," really believing that somehow they were holding me back. *Now* I find myself in the position where there's really no one for me to look up to. Now I see all the guys looking at me thinking, "If only I would . . . " *Now* I realize that it's not at all about the people who you work for. It's really that the responsibility for your opportunities lie largely within yourself. That is what you come to realize, and I think that's part of adulthood—that there is no "If only." I no longer live my life with that idea: "If only certain things would occur."

What are you doing in television these days?

I represent Gary David Goldberg—I helped him put together *Spin City*—and I work with people who've created a lot of shows for Nickelodeon.

What has been the effect of cable on the industry?

It's been good for the audience. There's a broader spectrum of places for people to find the kind of show they're interested in, which has also allowed people to do edgier, more intense, critically interesting programming. We're representing David Chase, who created *The Sopranos*, and Dick Wolf who does *Law and Order*, and Tom Fontana who does *Oz* and *Homicide*.

In the old days a network would want to do a 40 or a 50 share. These days no one even thinks about doing that. David Goldberg was doing *Family Ties* and that show would do a 45 share, which means that half of everyone in America who was watching TV was watching *that* show. It was huge. These days a giant hit is doing a 20, a 22.

Which is still an amazing bunch of people.

Right, it's a huge amount of people, but the expectation of the network is no longer to do the huge numbers they once did.

And the industry has gotten tougher. The large corporations that came into the industry pumped a huge amount of money into it and executives and stars were able to start making huge, vast sums of money which made the tone of it much more intense. It's no longer a bunch of guys doing well and hoping to someday have a house in Vegas or a house in Palm Springs. We're now talking Jags, three or four residences, lots and lots of money, and with corporate America breathing down people's necks, the tone changed.

And when you are really able to stick around for a while in one of these big companies, we're talking $30, 40, 50, 100 million, and I think people started getting a lot more serious, people became greedier and bloodier and more intense. And it wasn't just fun anymore. Plus, the real estate and mergers and acquisitions market businesses went into the toilet in the late 1980s and all those "best and brightest" turned their eyes toward Hollywood and they came out here, so it was no longer sort of a gentlemen's extended family business. It was the guys who've been competing their whole lives to get into the best colleges and go to the best business schools who were coming out here. And so a combination of events contributed to make the business much more competitive and much more cutthroat.

Are business relations more coarse as a result?

Actually in a weird way, less coarse in the sense of that old grotesque stereotype of the agent who was very coarse and sort of, hey baby this, and oh baby that. More civil, yet deadly.

Not long ago, studio executives only stayed in the same position for a few years. They thought they weren't moving quickly enough if they didn't change jobs every two to three years. Now I'm hearing that people want to stay much longer.

Right. What you'll find is that studio executives stick around because the stock advantages are so good.

If the market goes sour, will that change?

That'll change for a while, but the reality has become the long-term play of becoming a part of a big corporation and hanging on for your stock, people playing the corporate game much more intensely because they want to move up the stock ladder.

By virtue of people staying longer, more stability could be brought to the industry. In the past, an executive would leave the network or a studio and a lot of deals would then fall apart.

Well, it does bring more stability to some degree, but you also find that a lot of people are sticking around for a long time. They don't stay around

Bill Haber

by taking hard positions or completing projects—they stay around by riding the political wave in the most adept manner. It's all about figuring out which wave is going to break fast and how to get on it.

BILL HABER

Bill Haber cofounded Creative Artists Agency in 1975 with Michael Ovitz and three other agents. Heading CAA's television department, Haber helped create the industry's most impressive client list of actors, writers, directors, and producers. For many years, Haber was one of the most powerful agents in the industry.

CAA is housed in one of the most stunning buildings in Hollywood, a beautiful, modern creation by I. M. Pei. But few Hollywood offices match Haber's for a different ambience: dark, hardwood walls covered with original, nineteenth-century paintings. I didn't expect to find a television talent agent in such a space.

Haber is a cautious and diplomatic man, an agent's agent: calm, poised, not one to stand out beyond the talent he represents. But we see in the interview the lengths to which agents, and agencies, will go in competition for, and protection of, their clients.

Haber left CAA in 1995 to head-up Save the Children, where he supervised 4,000 employees in 41 countries. But he kept his hand in entertainment. While at Save the Children, he brought *The Scarlet Pimpernel* to Broadway and produced CBS's *Jack and the Beanstalk* miniseries and NBC's four-hour production of *The Uprising*. In 2001, USA Cable announced that Haber had been named president and CEO of TRIO, a division of USA Networks, a cable program service emphasizing the popular arts.

I've heard two different schools of thought on whether the cream rises to the top in the television industry or whether there is a lot of undiscovered talent out there that's having a hell of a time breaking in.

They're both true. The cream does rise to the top in the television business but television in not about *good*. Television is about a lowest common denominator. However, so is democracy. Not just our business. What happens is the whole population comes down and TV now lowers itself to the lowest common denominator. But the cream also rises. A certain person has been given a gift as a comedy writer and that gift allows most everything he or she touches to work—it's not a coincidence. Whether you do or don't like David Lynch's work—he's a client of ours—he is given a gift.

There's been a long-standing controversy in Hollywood about what percentage of product the networks should be able to own versus the studios. What's your view?

Agents are not principals, and not being a principal, we have no opinion on this whatsoever.

You must have some view.

My personal feeling is not relevant to any of this discussion. As an agent-executive of this company, all of our clients have different opinions, and as their employee, I honor whatever their opinions are. As a principal of CAA, an agency representing principals, we have no opinion whatsoever.

An agent must be a good diplomat and that's what you're doing with me now, understandably.

I may have personal feelings about it, but that has nothing to do with this discussion. You're interviewing me as a principal of an agency—not a principal. In the entertainment industry, I'm not a principal. There's a difference. I have very strong feelings about this, I have for decades. We are not employers, we are employees.

Can we go back a little bit to the history of the founding of CAA, why you left William Morris, and why some of the others left?

Five of us thought there was a different response to changing times and five of us also believed that there was a hole in the industry at that time for another agency. I had some very good friendships at William Morris and they're a fine company and will probably outlast all of us. They've been in existence over 100 years.

As I look around your office, you have a great number of exquisite paintings which appear to be mostly nineteenth-century, and which I presume are originals, and a lot of other fine artwork. I see nothing that speaks to popular culture. You were talking about the lowest common denominator earlier. Can you comment on what the industry produces and what good or bad it does for the society at large? What I'm getting at is, I see someone who has surrounded himself with high art and obviously has an appreciation for that. You may love Top Gun as well.

Two of the paintings are nineteenth-century French, the one behind my desk is nineteenth-century Italian even though it looks French, and the one by the door is a very well known nineteenth-century Boston painter named William Churchill; it's the only American piece up there. I happen to like old, beautiful things. It's my own personal preference. You see the building I'm in is as modern as you can get.

I think that television is able to accomplish a great deal for large numbers of people and you need both. There's nothing wrong with the Roseanne Barr show and there's nothing wrong that the highest grossing picture one year is *Home Alone*, which doesn't require that you're a nuclear physicist to understand. There are people who want to go see *Hamlet* and *Cyrano* and who will enjoy *Hamlet* and *Cyrano*, and then people who want to go see *Home Alone* will enjoy *Home Alone* and that's exactly what happens with the television industry.

We are moving from broadcasting to narrowcasting. It used to be that in the broadcasting business you would see *Peter the Great*, and it maybe wouldn't be viewed by that many people; but still 30 million people would see it even in failure and so that did something for the population. I would be personally involved with two or three projects a year that wouldn't make me any money but which I believe would change the opinions of this country, and you would watch it on one of the broadcasting networks. Now we've moved into narrowcasting and as an individual you make your selection from 50 places.

It certainly opens up lots of opportunities to make product.

And a lot of people will have trouble making the very large amounts of money you've typically read about.

In the 1950s, on Wednesday nights, stores closed and people stayed home to watch Lucy. *They talked about it the next day. There was some shared common experience, there was a "culturally integrating" function that television could play. That's changed.*

I think they'll still have shared cultural experiences. Everybody was surprised that the country had a cultural experience from PBS's *The Civil War*.

But it still only reached 15 million people, and that was after months of reruns. By network standards, that's a failure.

That's still a lot of people. The time where you're disappointed because it wasn't 60 million people is over. The only time you'll have that is on the Super Bowl or a presidential speech, or a news event. You will never, ever see that again in this country.

Does the industry regulate itself as well as it ought to? Doesn't it frequently fall victim to excess?

I think that men of substance who are buying into television and broadcasting companies at the moment are very conscious of how they may operate, and men who are not of substance are not. And I think it's probably the same in any business. There are presidents of networks who will put a show on the air knowing that it will not get an audience but believe that if 15 million people will watch it, it was worth doing; they will take the risk for that one particular time because it's something they owe this country as a broadcaster. There are men in very important jobs who are doing that, and there are men of little substance in very important jobs who only care about the economics of it.

I've heard it said that an agency's client, typically an actor, might go to a party in Hollywood and he may be surrounded by CAA or ICM agents. There may be five agents who will attend the party with him. Why is that done?

Well, maybe 10 people wanted to go to a party, maybe the food's good, maybe the music's good, maybe the house is nice.

Doesn't an agency sometimes want to make a display that says, "This client is ours," or, "He or she is well protected by us"? There's also a sense that sometimes agents will want to retaliate in kind if they feel they've been hurt losing a client to another agency and they have to let the industry know that if the client gets stolen, that you're not just going to take it lying down. It's almost a war time mentality. . . . Does that ring true for you at all?

I guess the two phrases that come to mind are, first, that I read somewhere there's safety in numbers and second, you have read long ago that you do upon others as others do upon you.

Isn't it to do unto others as you wish they would do unto you?

I understand that. It changes over the years.

How does CAA go about attracting a client from another agency?

We have a policy that we do not initiate conversations with other smaller agencies' clients that come to this company. We usually call the agent of that company and say, confidentially, "Somebody's leaving you and has asked to meet with us." Our business is not so needy that we need to hurt a small company that needs the income from that client. But we interchange clients with other large agencies all the time. It's the nature of the business. They take our clients, we take their clients, clients shift, clients go around. It's a no-holds-barred game and it's the agency business in the large companies.

It is true that an agency might make a physical display at a social engagement by almost surrounding their client.

We often go out in large numbers together. We like each other and there's comfort in numbers—that's human nature. But we also often will show a client our regard for him by having a large number of people there.

If we're taping a pilot someplace, we may have 10 agents show up because that is our way of showing that that pilot is important to us and that the producers producing it are important to us.

Might the director, see it as a form of intimidation?

I've never heard of an instance of it. If I send 10 agents to a show we don't represent and most everybody involved in the show is represented by another agency, the other agency would not be happy with that and would be uncomfortable that I've done that—and we do it often.

You do that often?

Yes.

What are you trying to do there?

We're trying to show people—the prospective employers of ours—that we would like to have them as clients, and that this is how we treat our clients, and if they come with us we'll treat them that way.

I think of a shoot as not being that open an environment. I mean, one needs to have a pass to get on the lot.

We're talking about a television pilot in this particular case. If we were on a film location and we were trying to steal Sydney Pollack off of *Havana*, we would send one agent because that's not disruptive and makes a connection. But when you have a pilot going, you've got an audience with 500 people sitting there.

We also do it with a show that's already on the air and a series. We have agents who just go and cover shows that we do not represent—two or three of them on a Friday night.

But is it more likely that this happens at the pilot stage because there might be some way in which the deal hasn't been totally consummated?

No. You just do it at the pilot stage because the stakes on pilots are so high. Everybody shows up at those. The agency business is not as complicated or mysterious as you or anybody else thinks it is. We are salespeople.

Are there one or two things that the public thinks about the way the television industry operates that are just out of sync with reality?

I would think so. I think that they think that the entertainment industry is basically dishonest, that it has a substance abuse problem, that we have no loyalties, and that we are self-interested and self-driven. None of that is the truth. None of it. There are extraordinary loyalties to each other, in most areas of our business; words are given and kept. I have personally never been anyplace in 25 years where there has been serious substance abuse.

Television has always been, in our industry, more of a business. Motion pictures is a business, but it's more ego driven. It's always been that way, it'll always be that way—because of the amount of product you have to deliver. But it's a business that has extremely decent people, who are very socially interested, who have wonderful backgrounds, who are very loyal to each other, who have very good intentions, and I would be very pleased if my children ended up in the industry.

There's no question that it is an incredibly competitive business. People have told me that they sometimes secretly relish another person's failure.

It is true that this is an industry where those in it relish each others' failures. It's very easy to understand the psychology behind it. When

Jay Bernstein with Farrah Fawcett

another fails, it strengthens you and the fact that you're aware of the failure means that you're a part of the system, which makes you more important. If someone else fails it means you haven't, and when you fail you're no worse than anyone else, so I can understand the psychology of it. It's also an industry that really relishes the failure of a big film—and it's a terrible mistake because the failure of a very expensive movie damages the industry.

How so?

Because it makes it that much harder for a major filmmaker to make the next movie for tens of millions of dollars and it hurts everybody.

Could the industry do something to change its public image?

To begin with, they're too busy to worry about it, and secondly, it's always been an industry that generates enormously large amounts of money and that will always be subject to jealousies. It'll never change.

JAY BERNSTEIN

Jay Bernstein is the most successful manager and publicist in the history of television, having engineered the stardom of Farrah Fawcett, Suzanne Somers, and hundreds of other stars. In the 1970s, Bernstein was rarely seen in public without a female star on one arm and an ornate walking stick in the opposite hand. Said to be the last flamboyant man in Hollywood, Bernstein's cane collection now exceeds 300 and he claims to have been fired by over 600 stars.

Bernstein moved from publicity into television production and has succeeded twice with *Mike Hammer* and *Houston Knights*. Our first conversation took place at Bernstein's house, once the home of Carole Lombard and Clark Gable. We met in a parlor overlooking Hollywood. A maid served canapés. On tabletops and in wicker baskets are dozens of articles about Bernstein. His offices are downstairs. On every wall are news clippings about himself, photos with stars, and magazine covers displaying the smiling faces of Farrah Fawcett and Suzanne Somers. Against one wall is a door with his name, taken from the mobile home that he inhabited while directing an episode of *Mike Hammer*.

Bernstein insisted that I tour the house. We skipped the garage with Alan Ladd's wife's Rolls Royce, but he did show me elephant tusks from the last elephant legally shot in Kenya and his bathroom with "the largest indoor Jacuzzi on the west coast." After the tour, he seemed compelled to explain himself, even before I asked my first question.

Let me get one thing clarified. A lot of people think "ego" is a negative word. I don't find ego negative. Ego is like gasoline, and I can't run on unleaded with what I've had to do. So if I say, "Hey, look at this story on me, and look at this on me," it's only to save time and to give somebody a better picture of what's going on. Because if you don't have a strong ego, you're not gonna last very long in this town anyway, because the minute you start asking people, "What do you think?," or "What do you think I oughta do?," or any of those kinds of questions, you're already screwed because most of the people in this town aren't really on your side.

I don't know what the rest of the world is like, but I know that here in Hollywood people have a tendency to think that the greatest sound to hear is that of your fellow man crumbling. I don't subscribe to that theory, but if one year I had died, it would have meant to some people that the time slots at 8:00 on Wednesday with *Mike Hammer* and 10:00 on Wednesday with *Houston Knights* would be open for somebody else to put their series on. I think that's the very sad part of this town.

I'm not originally from Los Angeles. I'm from Oklahoma City. I was an overweight kid, wasn't good in sports, and instead of being laughed at on the playing field it was easier just to tell my parents that I was at practice. Instead, I would get on the bus, go downtown, and see Alan Ladd, Tyrone Power, Robert Taylor, Clark Gable, or Gary Cooper and I would live through those role models.

Are you saying that your childhood wasn't particularly happy?

I had a great childhood—I just wasn't athletic. But I grew up in a time where we had role models. Mine happened to be actors, but there were others available. There was Harry Truman, Eisenhower, MacArthur, Patton, and Bradley. This was politics before Watergate; the military before Korea and Vietnam; and sports before drugs, big money, and commercials. You had DiMaggio and Joe Louis and those people. I had the movie stars and I was someone who just loved the movies. I knew that I wanted to be in show business but I knew that it wasn't gonna work to be an actor because all the actors were so good looking. The ones I just mentioned were leads. The female lead was always put between the first male lead and the second male lead—guys like Gig Young or Tony Randall. I would have been the third male, so I decided that if I could only be third in my chosen profession, I better choose another profession.

I came out here and got a B.A. at Pomona College in Claremont, California. That was as close as my family would let me get to L.A. My mother and father are still married and that's where a lot of my traditional values come from. They're celebrating their 53rd wedding anniversary in August.

I came out here to meet Alan Ladd and to get into show business. What I didn't know was that they weren't expecting me. I finally got a job in the mailroom at William Morris. They had a six-month waiting list for a $40-a-week job. I couldn't afford to live on $40 a week, so I got another job in beautiful downtown Burbank in a factory making ball bearings on an assembly line from 8:00 at night 'till 2:00 in the morning. On the weekends I parked cars at Lowry's, the famous restaurant on Restaurant Row. After three months I wrecked a car at William Morris and they fired me. They said it was my fault and made them party to a big lawsuit.

A kid in the mailroom's father was Sheldon Leonard [producer of *The Danny Thomas Show, The Andy Griffith Show, The Dick Van Dyke Show,* and *I Spy*]. The night I got fired I went to their home. I hadn't cried since maybe I was 11 years old, but I cried because I wanted them to know how unhappy I was, and I also thought that maybe Sheldon Leonard might be able to help me.

You mean, you faked crying?

No, I actually cried. I've felt like crying lots of times since I was 11 years old, but it was not until I was about 22 that I allowed myself to give in to that. The tears streamed down my cheeks and the next day he called me and I had a job at Rogers and Cowan, the big public relations firm, for $55 a week. I kept the job in the ball-bearing factory in Burbank and the job parking cars.

Why did you want so much to be involved in show business?

Show business was bigger than life, and living in Oklahoma, life looked very boring to me. Everything in Hollywood seemed bigger, better, and more exciting.

In the beginning I was starstruck. I loved it when Gregory Peck called me and asked me if I would come to his home to help his son who was running for political office. I was thrilled when Henry Fonda called me and asked if I would do something for Peter Fonda.

Can you still get those thrills now?

No. It's changed. I know those people. I came in at the last days of the old studio system, when the studios made people stars. They gave them five movies a year, taught them how to dance, how to sing, how to dress, did their press. What I did for a period of time, in my own way, was to replace the studio system. Because nobody built stars.

When I started, the only people who had people managing their careers were nightclub artists. In those days, a manager would go into a town with Sammy Davis, Jr. and make sure that the sound equipment was working, that the lights were working, that he got paid by the promotor. That's what a manager did. Only one or two managers ever had an actor as a client.

I'm a pioneer. I started the personal management business for actors. Now there are probably 100 personal managers. But I started it. I was the first manager to handle more than one client. I was the first manager that turned it into a business. At one time I had over 25 clients. Nobody had ever done that before.

With Suzanne Somers

With Olivia Newton-John

Just like those billboards on Sunset Boulevard, with all the movies advertised. I started those. Those billboards used to be for suntan lotion and liquor. I did everything. I handled companies in all their entertainment-related situations. AT&T, U.S. Steel, Procter & Gamble, General Foods, General Mills, Ralston Purina, Dr Pepper, Kodak. Anything they did on television I would publicize to America.

But when I got tired after 16 years of doing all this, I took three unknown ladies and said, "One of the three is going to make it." I hoped that would get me out of the PR business. They were Farrah Fawcett, Suzanne Somers, and Kristy McNichol. So I made three out of three.

I linked up with Farrah before *Charlie's Angels*. She had already done the pilot, but she was only supposed to be the third lead. The lead in the show was Kate Jackson. She had these two assistants, Jacqueline Smith and Farrah Fawcett. Kate Jackson made twice as much money as Farrah Fawcett. And Farrah had third billing, just like Suzanne Somers had third billing in *Three's Company*.

What did you do to make Farrah Fawcett as big as she was?

What you need with everybody's a point of view. Because I'd seen so many movies, Farrah Fawcett to me was Betty Grable. She had the most famous pin-up picture during World War II. She wore a white bathing suit and looked over her shoulder. The reason she was shot from the back was because she showed up pregnant for that photo session.

So I said, "Since Farrah's my Betty Grable, I'll do my own pin-up poster." That's where that poster came from in the red bathing suit. The poster was bigger than *Charlie's Angels*. Most young guys of that era had their first sexual experience with Farrah. She just wasn't present for it.

If they were older, they wanted a wife just like Farrah. Women wanted to be like Farrah Fawcett. She was the real *10*. And also my version of Grace Kelly and Betty Grable. She made millions of dollars from Farrah Fawcett shampoo, the posters, the lunch boxes, and everything else that she did. Stars were hotter for longer than they are now. Farrah was hot from 1976. She was the leading role model for at least another decade.

Suzanne Somers to me was Marilyn Monroe and Judy Holliday. Kristy McNichol was the little girl next door, Margaret O'Brien or Shirley Temple. So I used the older stars as role models for these stars to create that point of view.

Sometimes the model can be more than one person. When I managed Mary Hart, who's on *Entertainment Tonight*, she was a 32-year-old Doris Day, the girl next door. A 32-year-old Debbie Reynolds with all that perkiness, and a 32-year-old Shirley MacLaine, the daredevil.

I insured her legs for $2,000,000, and that stunt netted her at least $10,000,000.

How does a star's team work?

Let me explain what everybody does. If you're Switzerland and you're going to invade Russia, you better have a good army, navy, air force, and marine corps or you're gonna lose. So it's called the "team." I was one of the originators of the team concept.

An agent is a person who gets an actor jobs. You're paid 10 percent. The personal manager is someone who says, "Don't take that job."

There's also a business manager that should be taking care of your money so that you're not gonna end up broke. The public relations person is someone who lets people know what you're doing. Maybe it's a two-hour movie for television. Their job is to do the best they can to make sure that the public watches it, or at least knows that you did it, how well you did it, and what the reviews were. Then we have the entertainment attorney, who is important because there's an awful amount of small print in Hollywood.

You've said that you've been fired by 600 clients and the press talked about Farrah "dumping" you. Why do you get dumped? If you're doing a great job, why don't they hold on to you?

Once you get them where they want to be, the air becomes rarified, they become deified, and that's when you get nullified. I was making over a half million dollars a year from Farrah Fawcett in commission and I was making half a million dollars a year from Suzanne Somers. That's a million dollars. These people might figure after a while that they don't need you anymore. I mean, you don't call home to your Mom and Dad every day to say thank you. It's very painful sometimes, but I've learned to deal with the pain.

I'm someone who's been in the business for over three decades. I've been a puppet, a pauper, a pirate, a poet, a pawn, and a king, and I can remember the time that I was each one of those things.

Insofar as you modeled Suzanne Somers and Farrah Fawcett after older stars, I wonder if you've modeled yourself after anyone?

I thought I'd like to be remembered like Colonel Parker, Elvis' manager, or P. T. Barnum. P. T. Barnum said something that I never liked, "There's a sucker born every minute." So I said no, it's not that group either. But when you have lived as long as I have in this business, then you have to have some kind of role model for yourself and my role model at the moment—I've been studying him for the last three months—is General Douglas MacArthur. He was a very interesting, powerful, controversial man. A man that some people hated, a man that some people loved, a man that everyone had to respect.

I'm a traditionalist. I believe in what MacArthur believed. Honor, duty, and country at a time when people believe primarily in power, money, and position.

People are more and more into themselves because after the 1940s and 50s, we had the 60s. The 60s were a very strange time in this country. The 70s became a reaction to the 60s and I'm studying the 40s and 50s right now to see what it would be like today politically and philosophically if we hadn't had the 60s and the 70s.

I tried to say in my first *Mike Hammer* movie with Stacy Keach that we should get back to a time when our neighbors aren't strangers and folks take care of each other. People in television will say there is no reason to make a drama if you can't sell it into syndication and they try to find a way to do things more cheaply. I think that is wrong.

Are decisions in television more financially motivated now than, say, 10 years ago?

Absolutely, because the people who run the studios are nice people, but they are businessmen, they're accountants, they're agents. You don't have the same creative forces. You don't have the studio heads who were creative men *and* businessmen.

You're talking about doing something that's for the benefit of the society but at the same time you're a man who has lived off the incomes of other people. Money certainly makes an impression on you. You live in an enormous house. You're as much a part of Hollywood, or more so, than almost anyone in Hollywood.

I would say that's true. Except, remember Stacy Keach who was the star of *Mike Hammer*? He was a traditional American hero. The minute they were going to nail him for possession of cocaine, they were going to start trashing Dirty Harry, they were going to start denigrating an American James Bond. They were going to say they're just a bunch of actors, they're just a bunch of phonies. What I did is take 17 months out of my life and I went across the U.S. and on radio and television and said that in this country I believe people should only pay once for a debt, or a mistake. We believe in giving people a second chance. I said, "I'll never work again in show business, unless you put *Mike Hammer* back on the air."

I did it because there was nothing left to believe in. Farrah Fawcett was my reaction against green hair and spiked bracelets. Linda Evans was helping women not to commit suicide between 30 and 40. Farrah Fawcett by accident was the first 30-year-old star. What I worked on, based on Joyce Brothers' suggestion, was to make women perfect at 40.

So my point about money is that I had two mortgages on this house and I was heavily in debt, because I didn't work for 17 months. But I have been financially well off and I've been broke twice in the last decade and I'll probably be broke again. I nearly lost my house, but I didn't care because what I wanted to do was to prove that the American people could be proud of themselves by bringing back someone and giving them a second chance. Stacy's a nice man who made a stupid mistake. All heroes don't all have to all fall by the wayside just because one person who was a hero made a mistake.

I went out on a limb for what I believed in and I won't just make a television show to make a TV show. People say, "Why don't you have five series on the air?" Because I haven't found five things that I believe in.

What was it about Mike Hammer *that made it worth making?*

He's a man who shows urban traditionalism. I think in one show only, out of 52 hours, did he ever take a dime to help anybody. He took $20 and it cost him that on cab fare in the next scene. I want to show people helping each other for no reason except for a sense of honor and duty and country and some kind of pride in what they believe in.

There was a blind woman who was beat up on a bus and walked 15 blocks on a major street in L.A. and no one helped her. If Mike Hammer had been there, he'd have helped her. If Mrs. Fletcher on *Murder, She Wrote* had been riding her bicycle, she'd have stopped.

I understand that you were watching Entertainment Tonight *and found out that your house had burnt down?*

December 7, 1984, Stacy Keach went to London for the drug thing that happened in April of '84. He went back to pay a large fine, and instead they kept him for six months. I went into shock. I didn't go into real shock, but I was pretty shocked. I went to Palm Springs and on December 12th, on *Good Morning America*, they said, "We interrupt this program to tell you that Jay Bernstein's house has burnt down." Then that night on *Entertainment Tonight* Mary Hart stepped away from the Teleprompter and said, "If Jay Bernstein's watching, and if anyone knows where he is, I would like him to know that I feel, like a lot of us do, that as bad as it seems right now, he can pick himself up and handle all of this." They showed a picture of Stacy going into prison and they showed a picture of my house.

The kitchen and the garage were damaged. I had Alan Ladd's wife's Rolls Royce. The Ladds had become friends of mine. David Ladd gave the car to me. And I had a 450 SL Mercedes-Benz that burned. I had it for 11 years and it was in mint condition. The whole house experienced smoke damage.

So my business was gone and the star of my series was in jail. I had eight more episodes to do. And I had no house to come to and close the blinds and escape.

But Mary Hart said, "I know he can do it," and so I sent her a long-stemmed crystal rose. Finally, I thought the time would be right to help her. Because she'd really helped me more than anyone as far as letting me pick myself up like that Sinatra song: "You pick yourself up and start all over again."

I have been broke twice because I'm not interested in just accumulating money. If I had done that I would have been a rich person. I'm not. But I do a lot of things. I work 18 hours a day, 6 days a week. I hire myself as a producer, and then as a producer, I hire myself as a writer. I've written five scripts. I hired myself as an actor and I acted in a two-hour movie. And I hired myself lately as a director. I directed the last episode of the *Mike Hammer* series. I think that Warren Beatty and Woody Allen and I were the only three people who were in seven guilds at that time.

What is it that drives you?

Every year it will change. Now, I think there is some relevancy to what I'm trying to do with traditionalism. Like I must have thought

Producer Bernstein with his cast on the TV movie The Wild Wild West, *from left, Robert Conrad, Emma Samms, Bernstein, and Ross Martin.*

there was some relevance to Farrah Fawcett being representative of apple pie, Chevrolet, and baseball, and I suppose I felt there was great relevance with the idea of being perfect at 40, instead of at 30, with Linda Evans.

I think we have to separate two things. I'm not necessarily what I would consider a good person. I think in many cases I'm probably an asshole. Sometimes you've gotta be a tough guy. I'm not saying dishonest; you've just gotta do things in order to have the opportunity to give people the messages that you want to give them.

What I'm trying to do is reach millions of people with the microphone I have [*Bernstein holds up a miniature toy microphone to make his point*] and give them something to hang on to that they never even heard about. For example, remember the three guys: one played a fife, one played a drum, and one had a bandage on his head and one on his leg. What was that called?

I don't recall.

You are the 54th person I've asked. I've only had six correct answers. The Spirit of '76. They were minutemen. The point is that people don't care about those things. George Washington is a man on the dollar bill that you see standing in a boat holding that staff or whatever it was. To me, General MacArthur became the George Washington of my generation. So if I can help in some small way and give people something to hold on to, by having an audience of 20 to 40 million people a week, then I think I have to do this until I'm not around here to do it.

It's just that if I didn't do this, if I didn't work to make women perfect at 40, who was going to do it?

Changing ground—what makes a star a star?

A star is someone that people care about. For example, is Elizabeth Taylor married? Is Tom Cruise married? Those people are stars that we care about as people and people want to know about them. Is John Travolta married? You have an idea, but if I asked if Robert Loggia, or Roy Scheider, or Nicol Williamson was married, you wouldn't know. That's the difference between a star and a fine actor. There are many fine actors, but only a few stars.

I am a student of this business. Even when I take an hour Monday, Wednesday, and Friday to exercise, the deal that I have with my exercise person is that I pay him, whether I show up or not, as long as he reads me a book about the business a week. And, while he exercises me, all we talk about is what's in the book. My new exercise trainer has been with me for the biographies of James Cagney, Steve McQueen, Burt Lancaster, and Frank Sinatra. Now, what's gonna happen next is he's gonna read the Sinatra book by his daughter and then he's gonna read the Kitty Kelly book. Then we're gonna discuss the difference. So, while I'm exercising that's all we talk about. I asked him to compare James Cagney and Steve McQueen as far as their careers, how they thought of their directors, how they felt about studios.

You call yourself a traditionalist, and one traditional institution is the family, and yet you didn't have one until now.

I didn't have a wife and children because my family was this town. I probably *am* Hollywood. Because when I wake up in the morning, I hear a clapboard and it's "Take one." And when I go to sleep at night I guess the last thing I hear at night is, "It's a wrap." I don't know the difference between the real and the unreal. I have been here too long to know.

With the rise of cable, how has the introduction of so many additional channels for product affected the industry?

The more outlets you have, the more shows you have. The more shows you have, the more actors you have. The more actors you have, the more choice the audience has and the less chance of anyone ever becoming a star. Ten years ago we could still build a star.

Is the industry even more competitively focused today versus ten years ago?

When there is so much product, people are going to have to go to a lot of extremes to sell a whole lot of things. And the competition has made it so bad that everybody has forgotten the rules and they're just going for the bottom line. It's not good for anybody except those people who are going for money.

How much has the industry changed?

I've always loved glamor. I only came here because of the glamor. That was a magnet to me. I don't know if I still would have been here if I had known it was going to become so mundane and not really good for the people. I came for heroes and heroines and I'm not thrilled when I see an ad with David and Goliath and Goliath's eating a sandwich from some particular company and David hits him with a stone and kills him, so some 7-year-old kid can go to school and say to the big kid, "give me your sandwich," and if he says no, the kid hits him in the head.

I don't know of anyone who was shooting people in schools years ago. It's a different world now. How does a kid find someone to be like? The mean, the average, that they now see, the mean now is negative.

There's no way to stop it because television is only catering to the sponsors who are catering to the people. There's nothing about what's *good* for the people except how to make money. We've changed gods.

Ray Solley

RAY SOLLEY

Ray Solley has held many different positions in the television industry over the past 25 years, and with many different companies. When we first talked in 1987, he was at CBS. When we spoke again 10 years later, he was an agent at the William Morris Agency in charge of packaging of series and specials for basic and pay cable.

Solley received a master's degree in telecommunications from Indiana University and held his first job in public television at WTTW in Chicago where he worked on *Soundstage* and as a producer of the original *Sneak Previews*. From PBS he moved to Los Angeles as a talent coordinator on *The Tonight Show Starring Johnny Carson*. His story of the energy he put into his Hollywood job search and how he got started with Carson will prove instructive to anyone wanting to get a start in the industry.

His experience as director of programming for Paramount TV involved overseeing *Entertainment Tonight* and *Solid Gold*. At Samuel Goldwyn his job was to create programming and develop ideas for their first run syndication department. At Goldwyn, he helped develop *American Gladiators*. At CBS his job as an executive-in-charge-of-production involved finding, developing, and polishing ideas that would meet the needs of CBS' four largest stations. At William Morris, he sold dozens of programs, including *South Park*, to Comedy Central.

Solley increasingly works in syndication and cable and runs his own consulting company, The Solley Group, which provides strategic business advice to television production companies nationwide. Having done so many things, having been both a buyer and a seller in television, gives Ray Solley a keen perspective on the industry. Solley's an especially likable and self-effacing fellow, someone who can work well with the enormous array of intense players one finds in Hollywood.

What are some of the problems with how work gets done in the television industry?

One of the biggest problems in television is time. You never really have a chance to sit and talk, and more importantly, you never have a chance to sit and analyze something. Things are happening so fast; there are so many deadlines. Another problem is that people sit around quoting William Goldman's line "Nobody knows anything," so therefore anything can happen, anything can be a hit. Brandon Tartikoff said, "all hits are flukes." Actually, "all hits are flukes" is a much more reasonable theory to have than "nobody knows anything." If nobody knows anything, then you just look at the marketplace, and you say, "*Wheel of Fortune* works, so why don't we get a Vanna White look-alike and try to rip off the wheel." You end up with everything being imitated because your operating philosophy is what is working now.

Ray Solley, producer of PBS' Sneak Previews *celebrating with Gene Siskel (l) and Roger Ebert. WTTW-TV, Chicago, 1981. Everyone in 1981 wore glasses in the shape of television sets.*

Solley with his clients, the kids from South Park.

You've got to come up with something that seems like you're doing your job, that you are delivering something new, that you are aware of the marketplace, and you can change quickly with it, and that you can report to your bosses and stockholders that in "x" number of months, when the new season or the second season or the third season or the fourth season starts up, you've got answers in front of the audience.

You're saying that bad decisions get made because of time pressures.

Everything is always done under deadline. There is no such thing as a leisurely pace in television. Even in public television there was never a leisurely pace.

And the problem is not the number of creative people, or the brain power that you can apply. The problem is that there are so many people up top, that almost every corporation and company you get involved with is top heavy. The decisions have to go through too many people above. I don't care how high a concept it is, from the time it has gone through three management layers, back to the writers for rewrite, back to the producer, filtered through directors, associates and everybody else out in the field, and then it goes through the postproduction phase, dozens of people have altered that product. If it comes out anything like the original idea, you are massively lucky.

Another reason TV is the way it is here in Los Angeles is because it is bottom heavy with freelancers. Every time you do a project in this town, you have got to get a freelance person, who has no real allegiance to you. But you have got to get 10 people to do one thing. If you go on a film shoot, you will see tons of people, van after van after van.

When I was at WTTW in Chicago, a small group of production people had total control, complete vision over each show. I could always go to bed after taping a *Sneak Previews*, and know that I had done everything I possibly could to make it as good as I could.

How do you fix commercial TV?

You don't. I have been in tons of situations where you look at the clock, and say, "This is as good as it is going to get." You say, "Well, close enough." There was a writer in the paper the other day who had a great line, he said, "Why do you think we call it commercial broadcasting? Because it is broadcasting commercials." Unless you realize that the reason television exists is to deliver an audience to an advertiser you will constantly be frustrated.

So how frustrated are you?

I love mass broadcasting, mass communication. It is frustrating in that you want everybody to believe and follow your viewpoint. Don't let me forget passion. That is a word I keep coming back to. It's a matter of struggling to get to a point where you have power to help mandate those ideas that you like, because that is the only way that you can really transform and have an effect on the business that you love. For example, *Sneak Previews* changed the face of movie reviewing on television. It *is* the form. One show can do it. The goal is to try and come up with another show that will be breakthrough, that will form the new formats, that will rewrite the old rules.

What are some of the old rules?

People come into my office and they pitch ideas. Always, one of the first questions is, "What is it that you want?" They want to find out, among their arsenal of ideas, which one has a better chance of getting a "yes." Since none of us like rejection, why bring up an idea that the guy hates?

The other question that they will ask is, "What time period are you looking to fill?" Early on at CBS, I said I refuse to answer that question, because I firmly believe that a show idea that has a producer behind it that has passion, that will be the show that will be different and break through. If somebody believes that this thing has to be on the air, then eventually it will find its way on the air.

How important are personal contacts?

The business and the industry operate on who you know, and more importantly, bringing those people along with you from job to job. A certain kind of loyalty revolves around who you've worked with before. If somebody delivers for you once, they'll deliver for you again, so you keep bringing them along with you. It's like the last episode of *The Mary Tyler Moore Show*, where they are all huddled together with their arms around each other, and they have to get a Kleenex and they all move as a unit, they sort of shuffle across the room together. That is exactly how the production community operates, because if you are under pressure and you have to deliver something good and your reputation is on the line, you do not want to be trying out new ideas, you do not want to be trying out new people. You have got to deliver dependable results. That is not so much a criticism of the business as just simply an admission of it. This is the way that it works.

What would you rather be doing; buying or selling?

I really like buying. I like buying because I like to know everything that is going on. Also, selling is much more emotionally draining. You are selling an idea that you absolutely love, or that you see a financial upside to, and every time somebody says no, that just nicks the dream.

Buying isn't all fun. It is the hardest thing in the world, for me and for most people, to tell somebody that they don't like an idea or don't like their pilot, or they don't want to have a meeting with that person. Giving rejection to somebody, I don't care who you are, or how long you have been doing it, is the next worse thing to firing somebody. We would like to say "yes" all of the time. However, it is the nature of management, of bureaucracy, to come up with three reasons why something won't work.

Why three?

It is just my rule of thumb. Once you as a producer or as a seller can work through those three objections, then maybe the idea could sell. It seems to me that my job is to bring up all of the internal reasons, internal to the company, why this idea won't work. I have to bring up the objections that my general managers would have if they were in the room. Now the other side of when you say "no" is because the idea is simply something that doesn't spark you, doesn't involve your imagination, seems like a rip-off, or has been pitched to you six times before last week, or you know that you couldn't in your wildest dreams get one or two key people in the organization to get behind it. The final reason is you don't trust the producer's ability to pull it off.

You have to pitch sometimes. How do you prepare?

You don't take a complicated idea and try to walk somebody through every detail. What you do is you try and pull together all of the major elements you have, you send tapes, you send paper. I don't go in and just pitch a two-sentence idea; I never do that. I will prepare tapes, I will send treatments. I'll leave behind whatever printed material I have.

What is the strongest thing you would say?

Here is an idea I really love. It meets several needs at once.

What is the most ambivalent thing you would say?

Here is an intriguing idea, what do *you* think?

If you are getting pitched almost every day, what percentage stop right there?

Five out of six. The job of screening things out is based on the assumption that some people will never know how bad it gets. What you have got to constantly do is remind people that they are not seeing the majority of stuff, because the majority of the stuff is not suitable for their needs.

At staff meetings and division-wide meetings at CBS we have to point out that here are three or four ideas that we are pursuing, and let's sort of highlight the three or four most outrageous ideas we have heard in the last six months so you guys understand what we are up against. We are screening things so that you are not bothered in your incredibly hectic day with an idea that has no relevance.

Let's talk about what you do.

I find and develop and polish ideas that meet needs of CBS' largest four stations, in non-primetime periods. I deal with non-primetime, first run syndication. I am able to look at an idea and have a reaction as to whether it will work for us or for somebody else. There really are no rules, there are no objective yardsticks to apply to things. You can present a show to six different people and get six different reactions. If it's really bad you'll get 18 reasons why it's bad. If it's really good, you will all agree that it's good, maybe for different reasons, but you will all agree that it's good. The objectiveness of television is unified in good programs. We can all agree that *Moonlighting* is great. We can all agree that *All in the Family* was great. We'll never agree on why *Super Train* was bad.

Are writers sometimes being told "no" for what seem to be ridiculous reasons because the buyer doesn't want to tell them the truth?

The truth could be that the idea is so fundamentally flawed that it would take an hour to go through all the legitimate, honest reasons, and the buyer is saying, "Why should I spend the time and the energy to help somebody whose idea, even if he brings it back to me and it's perfect, I'm still not going to buy?" There is a theory nowadays in television that says since people are changing the dial so quickly, zapping it so fast, you better grab their attention in 30 seconds or less and keep it, and always be changing. And if the TV is on while people are fixing food or getting the kids home from school or off to school or whatever, you've got to grab them. The viewer's got to be able to go in, catch what's on, and come out and go in and catch it again.

There are syndicators and there are sellers whose main goal is to get something into national syndication. They don't care what the content is. You get the feeling that a lot of sellers would just as soon be selling a test pattern as long as it got cleared and they could get their commercials onto the show. It's a vehicle for a commercial.

And I find that the conservative, southern, moral part of me finds that attitude offensive because viewers watch TV for the story, for the experience, and they zap through the commercials. That doesn't mean you have to get rid of the commercials—that is a foundation of the business—but it does mean that I as a programmer have to serve several masters: the stations, the syndicators, the advertisers, the viewer. But there are a lot of people who believe you simply put on something to get an audience to a commercial. The responsibility that people like me have is to understand that every time someone brings an idea in, you are now holding their dream and their psyche in your hands. I've been on the other side of the table. Every time you crush their idea, or you betray it, or you manipulate it to a negative end, you are toying with somebody else's life—their hopes and dreams—and I think that's morally wrong.

Is there a downside to being moral in this industry?

Not in the long run, but in the short term, in an effort to be fair, you can easily lose your leverage. Leverage is based on manipulation, and information, and if for some reason you are evenhanded and fair, you begin to lose the ability to cut out and draw turf lines because you're trying to please everybody.

What's the screen credit for you?

Executive-in-Charge or Executive-in-Charge-of-Production.

We have developed a lot of one-time-only specials that are spinning out into ongoing projects. We did an animated children's special for Christmas. It went toward a commitment our stations have for children's programming. We will end up with a package of three great animated shows for kids that we will run in access, between 7:00 and 8:00 Eastern time. We will have brought to the marketplace and brought to the stations a new show that meets a new need.

And you are happy with this show?

Absolutely. It started out strong. It was an idea that worked from the beginning. The stations loved it. It was much better looking than it had any right to be, for the money we put into it. It ranked number one for its time period in L.A. All the elements came together, and you say, "Let's go to bat again."

I've been on the periphery of some shows that one or two of our stations have bought, that I find less attractive. Like *The Newlywed Game*. But I was stunned at how much I liked the new version of the game. I had to oversee the production of that a little bit.

There is a kind of exploitive nature to the show.

No doubt about it. But we get a ton of syndicators coming into us. They will pitch an idea and we will say, "This is awful. We are CBS, we will never put this on the air." Their response is, "But wait a minute, it will get ratings, it will make you number one in the time period." Our response, I hope, will continually be, "Right. We could put on pornography at 7:00 and be number one. We don't do that because we have an obligation to ourselves. The federal government says we have an obligation to our viewers. We also have an obligation to what our corporation stands for." CBS has an image to uphold because there is a certain channel and station and network identity.

What does CBS stand for?

Probably for conservative, family values.

What do you say to the charge that TV aims for the lowest common denominator?

When I was at PBS, the director of broadcasting for WTTW early on said that the one reason commercial TV is the way it is, is that producers and programmers think that the audience has no intelligence for information. It's not true. They have a great deal of intelligence, but very little information. If you clearly tell people what you are telling them, if you tell them what you are showing them, they can figure it out. Everybody in Los Angeles will tell you they don't program down to the audience. That they don't go "lowest common denominator." That they don't want to dumb it down. The reality is that they do it through research and they do it through numbers.

Given your background, why did you pick television instead of radio?

It was easier to tell a story with pictures. Basically, my whole background was in speech, drama, and theater.

How far back does that go?

At least high school or junior school. I was doing dramas in church. Acting in them. I was performing and singing with groups. Performing arts have always been an important part of my family. My mother ran arts and craft courses for a park district in Louisville, Kentucky. My father was in a performing group and directed lots of drama in his career as a Christian educator. My sister is a classically trained singer.

Then you went to college?

In college my career took two moves. One was a major in speech and drama. The second path started more casually. My roommate was in charge of student government and one night said to me, "Why don't you start a radio station for us"?

What school was this?

Kentucky Wesleyan College. Eight hundred students, real small. I went with it and I was having a ball. I created and ran the radio station on campus and I built it up using my own record collection. Then I went to grad school at Indiana University in telecommunication. I wanted to move from radio to TV. I wouldn't give up those two years at Indiana for anything. I learned more about the larger issues of television, the ethical and business issues, than I did on how to focus a camera or how to edit. The things that come into play more and more often are a sense of history about the medium, about FCC decisions, about ethics. When I make or read about a decision in television now, I'm able to put it in context with many others that have gone before.

One night, I went to a party and learned that there was a production internship in Chicago. WTTW had been traditionally one of the four or five flagships of PBS. They were producing *Soundstage* and *Bookbeat* and other things. It's Chicago. They are the third largest market in the country; an obvious move up for me.

WTTW had 500 applicants from all around the country. Every year they pick one or two. They narrowed it down. I flew in for the interview. They were concerned that I was overqualified. Here I am, I have a master's degree in radio, TV, and telecommunications. I *wanted* to be an intern for chickenfeed. It was like 7,000 a year. I said I would be willing to learn for a year. The other person they hired didn't even know what the word "dub" meant in TV.

The first year I was fortunate to be assigned to Thea Flaum. We started doing experimental TV shows. One of her first assignments was to do a special on comedy in Chicago. We had David Steinberg and

Shelley Berman. I began to get a feel for big time TV. The next thing you know we are assigned to make a show with Roger Ebert and Gene Siskel.

What was your screen credit on Sneak Previews?

It started out as a production assistant. Then moved to associate producer, then I coproduced one of the episodes that won an Emmy. I produced it for a year and a half with Siskel and Ebert, and for nearly two years with Jeffrey Lyons and Neal Gabler after that. I was with WTTW for a little under seven years.

What made you marketable to Hollywood?

Two things. One was working and producing and developing a national breakthrough show. There is no doubt about it. *Sneak Previews* got me in the door. What made me saleable after I got in the door was an ability to do "quality entertainment TV."

Why did you leave WTTW?

Jeffrey Lyons was appointed the cohost of *Sneak Previews* against the recommendations of Thea and me. We recommended Rex Reed. We believed Rex Reed and Neal Gabler would have been a better pair. Or at least provide more of a dichotomy of viewpoints that would have provided some sparks. When that happened I realized that I had done everything at WTTW that I could possibly do. I looked around Chicago. I couldn't find anything that I wanted to do. I didn't want to do news.

I then went into the station virtually every weekend for months and took out the *Hollywood Reporter Blue Book*, which is a yearly publication that lists names, addresses, and personnel at positions. I wrote about 65 letters asking for interviews.

One person who I talked with when I was in L.A. on business said, "If you are going to make a move out here, treat it like an assault. Go after it and really market yourself. And do it in a time frame that makes sense." I sent out the letters and then came out here for the Academy Awards on a two-week vacation. I took 10 days following the awards and did 25 interviews. One referral sent me to NBC. I interviewed with Peter Lassally, the producer of *The Tonight Show*. He seemed impressed. They were looking for a new talent coordinator. When I went back to Chicago, he wanted me to send him a packet of information and do two things. First, he wanted me to come up with a bunch of questions for three or four different celebrities.

He gave you specific celebrities?

Yes. Brooke Shields, Roy Scheider, Shelley Winters. I was to come up with questions that they might not have ever been asked. Peter also asked me to come up with a packet of guests that they called civilians. I went and I scoured the *Star*, *True Grit*, *The National Enquirer* and the local papers all around the country to try and see who would make a good interview with Johnny. I sent Peter a packet with not only clippings from newspapers, but contacts, phone numbers, questions, and potential answers based on a preinterview that I did with the actual people I found as part of my research.

It seems as though you thought, "I have a chance of a lifetime, and I'm going all out."

Totally. Not only did I do that, but when they decided to hire me they said that they were going to use one of the civilians I'd found. It was actually two little girls who told jokes for a penny. I knew that kids work well with Carson. One of the biggest thrills of my career was sitting on a girlfriend's couch in Chicago, watching my first booking on *The Tonight Show* 2,000 miles away, before I was even on staff.

How long were you at the Carson show?

About six months.

Why did you leave so soon?

When they hired me they were a little threatened by Alan Thicke.

They thought he was going to be younger and hipper than Carson and steal audience share, and you were younger?

Yes. And also that I would bring in a breath of fresh air from Chicago. You have to remember that Los Angeles is as parochial as Washington, D.C., or New York. I had booked a lot of things for *Soundstage*. And from *Sneak Previews* I knew the movies. When you bring in someone who is young, who is unaffected by Hollywood, who has a track record at PBS and in another city, you hope that maybe you will get an infusion of new material.

Can you say anything about Thicke and that whole business?

Well, the joke at Carson Productions was Johnny's joke: "What's the difference between the *Titanic* and the Alan Thicke Show? On the *Titanic* there was entertainment."

Why did you leave?

I left because they felt that I was not delivering to them all that they hoped I would deliver. For whatever reason I was not living up to their expectations and they did not live up to mine.

Then you went to Paramount. What was your job there and your title?

Director of Programming for Paramount TV. It turned out to be overseeing *Entertainment Tonight* and *Solid Gold*.

What is meant by overseeing?

Being on the set every single day. Overseeing the production process. I was involved in all the staff meetings, was involved in some decisionmaking.

My boss was making a lot of the decisions, and I would be the onsite supervisor.

How long did that last?

About a year and a half. What I had to get over when I got here was that people in Los Angeles don't stay in one job for years and years like I had been accustomed to in Chicago. To move as quickly as I did for the variety of reasons why I moved was not a negative thing.

Do you imagine you'd ever go back to PBS?

Yes. I would go back if I was in charge of the whole shebang. If someone said to me, "You have the PBS network, how do you want to program it?"—yeah, I'd jump at that.

How has TV changed in recent years?

I have seen a couple of commercials, especially for teenage clothing, that if you zap through them in 10 seconds, if it's a 30-second commercial, you get the same message as at normal speed. The logo appears over and over. With the VCR people speed through ads.

And people now have cameras in their homes, and people have their own little network at home. TV has been demystified. You no longer sit around and say, "Oh my God, television must be telling me the truth because they are all-knowing." You can't go to Rockford, Illinois, anymore and go in with a camera crew and say, "We are here to do TV," and have them bow and scrape. They will be cordial, they will be polite, but they are not going to be in total awe of you. They've seen a crew before, they have a camera in the house, they know that what you're doing is not magic.

What do you think is the future of the networks?

CBS is going to be in trouble and it could well be that one of the networks will go out of business in a couple of years. Before that happens, whoever is in third place going out, on their way out of business, they are going to try any crazy idea any producer has. The changing TV economy can't support three big networks. Network TV depends on a certain amount of coverage and a certain amount of revenue and viewership to support this huge monster that we have.

How do you learn how to develop and produce TV?

There is no school where you learn how to produce something. There is no course you take. There is no rule book. It's a matter of finding a good mentor and learning as you go.

It's been 10 years since we last talked about the business. What's your title at William Morris and what do you do?

Packaging Agent in Charge of Basic and Pay Cable. That means I'm responsible for taking our clients' projects and adding certain elements, like a director or a writer, or other proprietary pieces, optioning a book, whatever it might be. Then turning that into a package that's salable to a cable network á la Lifetime, Comedy Central, MTV, A&E, HBO or Showtime.

So you maximize the sales potential of a project?

Yes. It's easier to sell something if all the "creative auspices" are recognized and wanted by the buyers. We had a project come to us from an alternative comedy company here in town. I hooked them up and packaged them with a production company that is very well thought of at MTV. The idea probably could have sold by itself, but the buyer eventually would have said, "Well, who's going to produce it, who's going to direct it, how do I know you can deliver this idea?" The same thing with a couple of projects on Comedy Central. The idea is to do some of the initial development and legwork on these projects, so you take them to a buyer and it's that much further along, and they have that much more incentive to buy the program.

How is an agent compensated?

We're all on salary, and though there are great rewards and bonuses if you do well over the year, we are not tied to a particular property or client. We are able to work for all of the clients at the agency based on our area of expertise.

It would probably be a mistake if you were working on a direct commission basis. Your judgment needs to be geared toward the long-term interest of your agency.

You always want to sell and you always want to get it sold. But you can't sell something to somebody who doesn't want it, number one. And number two, if they decided they want it, you need to be able to have passion in the project, or the producers, or the idea, or the creative auspices. You need to *believe* in it. If you promise something and the client doesn't deliver and you try to skew it just to get the sale, it will be a long time before that buyer will trust you again.

When do things hit a wall so that you can't make a deal?

They hit a wall in either one or two places. Either in the initial pitch, because the buyer hears something and they throw up an immediate knee jerk reaction that says, "No!" They react negatively and then you can't move them off of it because they stick with their first reaction. Or it hits the wall in the deal. Everybody loved it in the room, you loved it when you start trying to make the deal, and then someone concludes that the numbers are not appropriate for the level of client that you're selling.

Last time we talked, you were at CBS. Why did you leave?

I left CBS because they were going through a massive restructure. I survived the Turner potential buyout. I survived the Tisch purchase until they decided to downsize.

I was hired by the Samuel Goldwyn television company to create programming and develop ideas for their first run syndication department. I developed and helped sell their daily exercise program called *Body By Jake*. Made 100 episodes of that, and then further developed and launched and sold *American Gladiators*.

Didn't you name a couple of them?

I named several of them: Nitro, Malibu.

What state of mind were you in when you named them?

It was a production team that did it, not me completely. But it took two years of development to work out the details of the characters, the games, and the rules of the show.

Some people reading this book might ask, "It took you two years to develop American Gladiators?*" Why does it take two years to develop such a show?*

Partially it has to do with other irons the company has in the fire, and it also has to do with the marketplace. Is there anything else similar or competing out there, are there openings at the stations, are there clearances, are there places where you can actually sell this thing? And there are half a dozen ways you could do that program. Everything from a backyard kind of *Battle of the Network Stars*, to huge David Copperfield stunts. And do the gladiators become prototypes? Are they real? Are they good? Are they bad? Are they athletes or are they not?

Can you describe how a herd mentality develops in the syndication market? Many readers don't see the ads in the trades that read "30 percent minimum share in all urban markets among women 18 to 49. Buy Rikki Lake for your fringe slot."

As soon as *The Rosie O'Donnell Show* was on the air its impact was felt quickly at every agency in town—including ours. We had phone calls from syndicators and buyers saying, "Do you have another Rosie?" Meaning, "Do you have a star that people sort of know the name of. Do you have a thin Rosie, a young Rosie, a black Rosie, a male Rosie?"

Coming out next year will be about four court shows because now with the success and the rebirth of *The People's Court* and *Judge Judy* there are other people trying to get in on that.

And a few years ago virtually everybody had a talk show. There must have been a dozen different talk shows out there. So the herd mentality is when the syndication industry goes in one direction with a genre. It used to be game shows, then it became court shows, and then it became talk shows. Until you oversaturate the marketplace, then you back off. Cable is different because the herd mentality doesn't exist there. Why? Because there are so many different cable networks. Each has their own brand, each has their own niche.

What happened after Samuel Goldwyn?

I realized after two years of working there on a variety of shows that I really needed to stop and smell some roses. I'd been on the fast track in L.A. for a long, long time, my own personal fast track, and I wanted to be my own boss. So I started a consulting and production company that helped new people with good ideas find appropriate buyers and develop projects. I did everything from booking stars for interviews and helping William Morris develop a talk show, to doing some distance education video projects with Yale, Duke, and Notre Dame. So I really got my fingers in a variety of different pies and talked to a lot of independent producers, buyers, and cable operators and syndicators that I would not have done if I'd stayed in one place at one desk.

What was your thinking then, and how did you launch your company?

When I decided that I wanted to go out on my own I rented a dining room in a restaurant and invited about 10 or 12 top producers that I had worked with, or known of, through the various jobs at CBS and Paramount and Goldwyn, and laid out to them that I would like to be their consultant. These are one- or two-man operations. They're all so busy doing what they're doing, making money with the shows they had on the air or were producing, that they weren't looking 6 to 10 to 12 months out and developing something for next season.

They couldn't afford me as a staff person, but maybe they could afford me as a consultant. I'd help them when they really needed extra assistance looking at a project, writing up a treatment, selling it, pitching it, setting the meetings, doing the follow-up, analyzing it. I began to work from project to project, and was able to make a very good living for seven years being an independent consultant.

And the move to William Morris?

I had known Mark Itkin, the senior VP for cable and syndication, for 10 to 12 years. I first met him when he was what they call a "baby agent" and he was selling me people and projects when I was at Paramount. Over a lunch he said, "Have you ever thought about being an agent?" He expected me to bring all my contacts in the world of syndication and cable into their office and not have to work my way up through the mailroom, which is how the traditional route goes. I came in at a relatively high and appropriate level and jumped right into the mix and made the kind of deals, contacts and contracts that we needed to be a presence in a marketplace of cable that is expanding exponentially every single quarter.

The networks used to be precluded from owning their product, their own negatives. How has that changed the industry?

It's changed it enormously. The days of licensing a program to a network and owning it and creating your own library and having a huge asset base to create a company, then make a fortune selling your library of shows overseas, has dwindled. TV networks are producing in-house, through CBS Productions or NBC Productions, for example. And cable networks want to produce and own the shows they air themselves because they want maximum control of the revenue stream by selling it to foreign outlets, or online, or to CD-Rom, or to create another asset out of that same piece of tape.

The rulemakers have also caused the enormous growth of mega-companies. We're seeing everything being vertically integrated. In other words, you have the big companies, like Viacom at the top. They can take a piece of product and run it vertically through their entire pipeline.

Do you see things as having loosened or tightened up? And the studios, they've been hurt, yes?

Yeah, because they're near the top of the food chain, and they really did create and control a lot of the product. It's loosened things up in that shopping product to top buyers is slightly easier because you clearly see who the megaplayers are. But fewer big players means tougher deals with fewer options elsewhere.

We're seeing a huge consolidation now, with big companies buying other big companies. At some point, the American public and the government and the industry, all at the same time or within a year or two of each other, will realize, "Wait a second, we've created this huge, multi-headed monster, and everything's looking the same, we're spreading the talent too thin." There are not enough good producer-writer types and creators to go around, and prices are going up. What we've got to do is see if it can be either deregulated or broken down a little, and if it can, then we can begin to decentralize. Somewhere, in the next 10 years, there'll be some happy medium.

The pendulum has swung from the early day of first run syndication when you went to a convention and you saw 30, 40, 50 different companies of basically equal stature and equal clout, to now, where it's about 6 or 8 different companies of huge clout, and everybody else is like little boutiques that don't really control anything.

Some people fear that with fewer companies running more of the world's media there'll be greater homogenization. At the same time when there's a huge multinational corporation, is there sometimes more wiggle room, more freedom in each of the subsidiaries, than some critics would think?

There is freedom and wiggle room within some of those divisions. But the wiggle room isn't in producing something that is odd and unusual and stand-alone and idiosyncratic, because the reason you have the big conglomerates is so you can share the assets. If you bring in something that is a weird stand-alone project and can't be used anywhere else by anybody else in the company, *that* doesn't serve the company well. You need to have product you can flow in all different elements and departments of the company.

How do you see the multichannel cable world developing?

There are about 308 channels on the air or in some stage of active development so that you'd want to track them. In other words, they plan to be real. On paper, they have the necessary financing to be real. About 40 to 45 of the current [2002] national cable channels are measured by Nielsen.

I'd been doubtful for some time that 500 channels would happen.

The 500-channel universe was a phrase coined by John Malone of TCI. It is not going to become a reality in terms of new, original, broadbased cable programs and channels. It may become a reality with highly targeted niche channels, and with digital compression and other technological advances. But a large number of those channels will be used for pay per view, for interactive TV, for on-demand, or near-demand programming. It'll be used for multiplexes so that there will be multiple feeds and choices of a network's programming, like HBO 1, HBO 2, HBO 3, and so on.

The same movies starting at two-hour intervals.

Yeah. It's all about shelf space. So if you're Discovery, you want to have three or four places for your product and have it digitized so that anybody can get your product pretty much anytime. But you need the channel structure, the capacity for that. You may see some niche things, but now we're finding that unless a cable operator like TCI or Comcast actually funds the development of the channel it's not going to get launched. Somebody dreamt up the idea of "The New Age Channel." It didn't go anywhere. It's such a niche, you're better off writing a book, you're better off starting a magazine.

Why couldn't there be leverage on that?

You either have to have advertising support, or you'd have to have a cable operator devote a very expensive and potentially profitable cable channel slot to it. When you go to digital you may see a lot of these things crop up, but they will not have the overall social impact of Lifetime, ESPN, or A&E. So I think you'll still have this large number of people watching television as a communal operation. It will be around national events. It will also be around affinity groups.

I sold *South Park* to Comedy Central. I made the deal that sold the show. We had a bidding war between MTV and Comedy Central. But the point here is that they're getting a 3 rating on their Halloween special, but that is way more percentage points than they normally get. However, it's developed a cult following. A lot of people college age, and slightly younger, are watching it and talking about it, and there are Web sites devoted to it. It's in a different class.

Tell me about your Distance Education experience.

What I loved about Distance Education is that we were using all the elements of TV entertainment: director, graphics, music, opening titles, closing credits, lighting, special effects, multiple cameras, all the tricks of the trade. The studio looked like we were producing a talk show, without an audience. Lots of wood, lots of flowers, lots of leather couches. And lots of books. We turned a huge studio into an enormous study and the walls were full of books—real books that were bought at auction—that looked "antiquey."

You knew when you were dealing with a professor versus a television person. TV people would come in and look around the set and go, "Oh, wow, you built this, it's real, you spent some good money on it, and it doesn't fall down." The professor would come in, go over to the bookshelf, and then cock his head to the right to better read the titles of the books. The professor would start pulling books down off the set to read them!

Some faculty say that Distance Education can be every bit as interactive as a classroom.

Our feeling was that distance education needs to be upgraded because just one professor speaking over a one-way camera to a bunch of students in satellite classes is not at all what it is about. What it's about is getting the information out, showing you something maybe you couldn't see normally, and then using the online component to create group discussions.

We have some students who really like it and say, "I'm getting more contact with faculty on the Internet." And many professors feel they get to know certain students better online.

Students will say, "I don't want to raise my hand in the back of this room, but I *will* send him a question when it pops into my brain at one in the morning. I will think about how I *want* to say it. Then, when I get the response back, I will think about how I want to respond to that."

What direction did you need to give the professors?

There are techniques to communicating to a large group of people through a camera: don't shout to the last row of your lecture hall, make it more intimate and talk to me, five feet away from you.

I loved doing it. I loved creating something that was familiar yet totally different. I, as a viewer and user, was in exactly the right demographic. I was looking, and still look, for places where I can go to learn about topics and disciplines that I didn't have the chance to study earlier in my life.

A Different Kind of Executive

Though there are only three executives in this final section, there are eight in the book. Network and studio executives move around a lot, do different things in their careers, and often spend time as producers. Thus, you'll find most of them in other sections, often in The Pioneers chapter.

A big part of being an executive is learning to say "no." An executive may well reject 99 out of the 100 pitches he hears. Production companies, studios, and networks are in the business of making television shows, so they must also say "yes." But since saying yes means committing millions of dollars to a project, they pick their shows and series cautiously. You *can* get fired for saying "yes" and spending the company's money on a program that fails, but it's *unlikely* that you will get fired if you say "no" to a series that ends up being a hit for another network or production company. At least you didn't spend the company's money. Put another way, it is understood that even the most capable executives will pass on material that in retrospect they should have approved.

Once a program is in production, from the point of view of producers and writers, the best executive is a hands-off executive, an executive who lets the show be created unencumbered. If a problem comes up that the executive can help with, producers and writers will want her to get it solved, but otherwise many writers and producers would prefer to hear as little as possible from network executives. Some executives do give advice that producers and writers welcome and find very useful, but most producers and writers tell more stories of how they experience interference from executives in the form of phone calls or "notes." Many complain that unknowledgeable and inexperienced executives provide much unwelcome and erroneous advice.

For models of what many creative people like in a network or studio executive, I recommend the interview with Grant Tinker who, while president of NBC, was probably the most admired man in television because he afforded his producers and writers great freedom and protected them from

Frank Dawson

interference. The interview with HBO CEO Chris Albrecht also focuses on the need to provide freedom and latitude to artistic talent.

David Levy was a very different sort of network executive, one who very much wanted to influence the content of programs once they were in production. But his real conflicts were with the network itself. Levy worked as a vice president at NBC until he ran into his own conscience, ultimately forced to leave the network as he tried to halt what he believed was a decline in its moral standards.

Lee Rich has been a producer and an executive, but because he started in advertising in the industry's early days I put him in Chapter 3 along with Tinker and Levy. Another executive, Bruce Sallan ran ABC's movie division but has spent more of his years as an executive in independent production. Ray Solley has spent time both as a network and studio executive and worked as agent. Because he is most involved in putting deals together you will find him with the other agents.

The three executives who *are* featured in this section aren't at all typical. Frank Dawson worked in development and supervised series television while he was at CBS, later worked at Universal, and now is in independent production. Dawson's story is particularly moving and important, I think, because it sheds light on how racism plays itself out in the industry. Gerry Laybourne's story is no less interesting. She built and headed Nickelodeon over a period of 16 years, then spent a short time at Disney before launching her newest venture, Oxygen. Lastly we have Chris Albrecht, the CEO of HBO. Albrecht helped make possible a great deal of the very successful, original work at HBO where he's played a significant role in the creation and development of *The Sopranos, Six Feet Under, Sex and the City, Curb Your Enthusiasm*, and *Band of Brothers*.

FRANK DAWSON

Frank Dawson's story is both inspiring and frustrating. As a child, his talent helped move him out of a difficult urban environment. When, as an adult, he hit a glass ceiling at Universal Studios, Dawson had risen further than any African American executive in the U.S. television industry. In reading his account we know that his is just one story among thousands of people held back by racism.

Dawson was often one of the first, if not the first black, in any number of positions: from the time he left New York City to a private boarding school, then to Cornell, then the Newhouse School at Syracuse University, and then to CBS. At CBS he was an associate programming executive on *Magnum, P.I., The Incredible Hulk, Simon & Simon, The Dukes of Hazzard, The Jeffersons, Private Benjamin*, and *Alice*. He also started the Los Angeles chapter of the CBS Black Employees Association. Then he moved to Universal Studios as director of comedy development, where he worked on *Charles in Charge, Miami Vice*, and *Square Pegs*.

His frustrations in producing *He's the Mayor* tell us a lot about television production practices. We learn that black writers and executives are channeled away from drama to comedy. A vicious cycle is set in play: because most of their screen and production credits are in comedy, they are typecast as only being able to produce in that area. At a deeper level, it seems that blacks are confined to comedy because many in Hollywood believe that there are not large enough American audiences prepared to watch blacks in dramatic roles as fully realized people with the same aspirations and human qualities as anyone else.

Dawson left Universal in 1993 and formed his own independent production company, NuHouse Media Group, to develop and produce television series, movies for television, and cable television features. Dawson is also a professor of communications at Santa Monica College. He lectures extensively as an advocate for media education in schools.

The first thing that really made an impression on me as far as images and media were concerned was when I was in the 6th grade and won a photography contest. The Henry Street Settlement was an organization on the lower east side of New York that provided afterschool activities and kept kids off the streets, and was one of the things that kind of saved my life. It's been in existence for over 100 years, originally founded as an institution to help immigrants adapt to the new world.

I became fascinated with taking pictures. My mother got me this little box camera. I lived two blocks from the East River, and right across from the Brooklyn Navy Yard and a fireboat company. I took a picture of a fireboat, and the picture won first prize. The feeling that I got from winning that award! The prize was a developing tank. I got into this photography class at the Henry Street Settlement and began developing my own pictures.

Why do you think your photo won?

I was always an observer. I would always look at things when I was riding the subway as a kid, or walking down the street. I would always compose in my mind, pictures of people, images of people and then think about who those people were based on this little picture I'd made up in my mind of them.

You'd tell stories to yourself.

Exactly.

Why do you think you were doing that?

I don't know. I was being raised by my mother; my father was not around very often, wasn't involved in my life. Maybe it was a way for me to kind of escape from some things.

How well did you know your father?

He would come around. In fact, he lived with us 'till I was 5.

Can you remember when you were 7 or 8 kind of longing or missing him?

Sure. Sure. Every time he came and visited was difficult.

Bittersweet.

Yeah. It was nice having him there, but then he was gone, you know.

The next thing for me was a little later on. I'm a kid who got out of the projects of New York City through the efforts of my mother, my church, and the Henry Street Settlement.

I used to read everything I could get my hands on because my older sister read everything. She'd finish something, pass it down to me, and I'd just read it. But I wasn't a good student in school because I didn't pay attention. I didn't care—misbehaving and that kind of thing. But because I read everything I always did well on standardized exams. And so through the efforts of my church I got a chance to take an exam for a private school and did really well on it, and I became the second black student to go to a private boarding school in Westchester County. Peekskill, New York, 50 miles north of New York City.

I was 15 years old and going through a very difficult time in not having my father at home, getting in little bits of trouble in a neighborhood where most of the kids my age got in a lot of trouble. It was a critical time in my life and I got this opportunity to go away to boarding school.

You didn't have any doubts that this was the right thing for you to do?

My best friend was the first black student to go there and I went to visit him on a parents weekend. I was an average athlete because I came from a family where my mother didn't let me stay out all night and play basketball. A lot of other kids in the neighborhood played it 24 hours a day.

And you're not the tallest guy in the world.

So that was my attraction. I could go to school there and I could really be a basketball star, which I couldn't in my neighborhood.

Were you really good athletically when you got there?

I graduated with the director's trophy as the most outstanding athlete in the school. I was captain of the basketball, football and baseball teams.

How were your academics?

Graduated third in my class out of 26. I had never had any kind of academic orientation at all. The school changed my life. Here I went into this completely different cultural environment, with all of these rich white guys who had a preconception of who I was as one of only two black kids. And, obviously, at boarding school you live together with these guys.

Here were all of these guys who thought that black kids were dumb, but great athletes. Here I am fitting the stereotype as an athlete, but I had to show I had something on the cap also. I was put into an environment where every night there was study hall. You couldn't leave campus. There was nothing else to do—you might as well study.

In those years, was there anything else that relates to what you do now?

Yeah. In boarding school, my way of communicating back home was to write letters to my mother about my experiences. And my mother loved my letters. Every time I would go home for a vacation she would just talk about my letters and what a wonderful writer I was and how visual it all was, and she could just see everything I talked about in my letters. I wrote so visually. It identified for me that I could do a kind of descriptive writing that was very visual.

Over your years there, did you win over the other 24 members of your class?

Some never, but from most I got a grudging respect. I did make some close friendships, but my best friend that I came from the neighborhood with is the only one I'm in contact with today. And sometimes I kind of think back on the experience and it's almost like it didn't really happen.

What did your mother do?

My mother was a school aide in the local public school.

Of all the things she might have done, she gravitated to an academic environment. Where did that come from with her?

West Indian background, family values. My mother's family is originally from the West Indies and that's really part of the culture. The importance of education is really strong. A West Indian kind of value.

So how did your family come to the states?

My mother's father is from a small island and came over during the Spanish-American War.

Black people got to the West Indies through the slave trade.

Exactly. But slavery ended earlier on those islands.

Is that one of the reasons that people in the West Indies had their act together?

Exactly. Because they were used to running their own affairs and running their own country.

That's quite a lesson.

It is. There's a whole different orientation.

I presume you went to college right after boarding school.

I went to Cornell University. Majored in sociology. Graduated in 1972. My freshman year at Cornell, I was involved in a building takeover that ended up on the cover of *Time* and *Life* and *Newsweek* magazines. The last event prior to the building takeover was the burning of a six-foot cross on a black woman's residence. We all came together over that. We were forced to arm ourselves with guns after taking over the student union. There was escalating frustration over the university's policies. I was in the first class of minority students recruited from the inner city to go to Cornell. We were different than what they were used to.

How many were you?

Fifty of us went in and took over the building.

Was Harry Edwards there then?

He was at the university teaching at that time, in 1968.

How many black faculty did you have at Cornell in those days?

Well that was one of the things. One of the demands was an increase in black faculty, and a reexamination of the entire curriculum that was completely Eurocentric at the time.

Our activity led to the development of the African Studies and Research Center at Cornell, which today still remains as one of the foremost programs in the country. That came out of us taking over that building. We didn't go in the building with guns, nor with that kind of intention, but while we were in we were attacked by a white athletic fraternity in the name of taking the building back for parents' weekend.

Housed in the student union building was the student radio station. And one of the assignments I had during the building takeover was to check the Teletype machines, because the UPI and AP Teletype machines were in there.

It was the first time I'd ever been in a radio station in my life and I'm sitting there looking at the AP and UPI Teletypes and I'd see dateline: Ithaca, New York. And it's a report on what we're involved in.

Distorted?

Completely. I'm sitting there. I know what's happening. I'm in this and yet this is what's being reported? I called my mother in New York to let her know that I was all right and my mother's going crazy.

Were there TV crews around too?

Oh yeah. TV crews. Everything. This was major. I saw the power of the media in that my mother believed this report that she heard on CBS from Walter Cronkite over her son. Here I was, in the building, telling my mother, and for her, no, that wasn't what was happening. The press listed demands that we had allegedly made that were completely outrageous and made no sense whatsoever.

She was also disturbed that you were doing something wrong?

Oh definitely. I'm the first in the family to get an opportunity to go away to college and what are you doing with it?

After the political stuff, I got on the air as a DJ with my own radio show and produced a radio documentary on Attica in 1971. The inmates from inside the prison, along with William Kunstler, called us.

Then we did a show where people would scour newspapers and periodicals to find out things of interest to Third World people because it was not being included in any other news report.

What was the name of that show?

Sounds of Blackness. Then I went to Syracuse and branched into television. I was selected by a professor to direct everything that came out of the graduate lab. He said I had a knack for it and I stayed calm under pressure and stuff like that.

After Syracuse, I went back home to New York City, tried to get a job in television. I wanted to be in production, but production really wasn't happening in New York at that time from an entertainment point of view. It was all news and it was advertising. So I didn't get a job, but I got an offer from Cornell to work on a program called *Nightsounds* that ran for 12 years in Ithaca. I did it for two years.

So how did you come to L.A.?

My sister lived in Los Angeles, she and her boyfriend both worked at CBS. Not high-level kind of people.

That makes it a lot easier to move out when you know somebody there and in the business.

Right. I went out and visited for three weeks. Went on some job interviews, didn't get a job, but I came back and told my wife, "We're going to move. We get out there and I'll get a job. It'll be cool." Packed up, big garage sale, sold everything, moved across the country by car.

How quickly did you land something?

Two months. I was interviewed at CBS and they told me I was *overqualified* for an entry-level position, yet they promoted from within so they couldn't give me a job I was qualified for.

That's a catch-22.

My sister-in-law's boyfriend knew of an opening in the film department as a vault attendant, which is like the first rung in the film editor's union. It's just like it sounds: in the basement of CBS, all the shows at the time were still delivered on these big 35 mm reels and my job was to catalogue those reels as they came in from the production companies, and make sure they came in on time.

This is pretty easy? But you got your foot in and you got a union card.

Exactly. I did this for less than a year. I had an opportunity to move up to the next rung and become a projectionist, which was more money, and I needed the money at the time. But the difficulty I had with that job was that the projectionists ran all the dailies for all the executives upstairs. And I knew if I became a projectionist and they *knew* me as a projectionist I would never be a programming executive 'cause they'd always see me as the projectionist. So I passed on that job even though it was more money.

And the whole time you're keeping your eye out for other stuff?

Yeah, I'm going out and interviewing for stuff. I'm lobbying. The best thing about the job was that it was in the advertising department so we worked with the writers who wrote all the advertising and promotional spots.

    I watched what they did. I had written over 100 radio commercials when I worked in radio so I knew the format. CBS decided to create five staff positions. After they hired the fourth person I went and camped out at the vice president's office and said, "You got one job left. That's my job." I turned in all of these scripts and I said, "I can do this work." It was a difficult transition to look at somebody who's in the film editor's union, which is blue collar, and this other job was a writer's job that got you into the Writer's Guild. They didn't have anybody black who had ever had that job before as a writer-producer at CBS.

He gave in eventually.

He said, "Look, if this doesn't work out you know you're not going to be able to go back to that other job," and I was like, "Cool." He was a guy who wanted to do the right thing, but had to be nudged to do the right thing. My wife was pregnant. He knew I needed the work, and I was willing to take the risk.

So you're writing promotional copy?

The White Shadow was one of the first regular series that I was assigned to. My job was to work with the producers on the show to look at the episodes when they were delivered and decide what the best way to sell that episode was for on-air promotion. I'd write a script, sit in a room with an editor, select the shots, and *bang*.

    CBS had this executive intern program, but they had never hired anybody from inside the company. They hired the sons and daughter and nieces and nephews of executives in the business straight out of UCLA and USC, so the CBS employees association put on a lot of pressure that they let somebody from *inside* have a chance. So they decided, OK, for the next group they would allow *one* internal candidate. They did this big thing in New York and Los Angeles having people apply and go through this series of interviews and out of about 300 people that applied, I got the internship.

    So many people told me it's not going to happen. The guys that I worked with in the film vault, they used to see me sitting down writing stuff and they'd say, "What are you wasting your time for man? You know you're going to be a film editor."

How many people were in the intern program?

Three a year. People in the company kind of knew of me. I had started the Los Angeles chapter of the CBS Black Employees Association. In talking with other black employees at CBS I found that they had more education than the people that they worked for, yet they were relegated to all these lower-levels jobs but all they were doing was griping about it.

Because of the Cornell experience, this is who I was and that's what I did. I had the ability to do it and in a way that the company had to deal with it. Because I did it in a very organized fashion.

I had them look at the statistics that we had put out in terms of the educational levels of the black employees who were stagnated in all of these positions and not moved up. But my whole approach was what we could do to make this better, to benefit both the company and the employees. It wasn't an antagonistic kind of thing, so they had to deal with it. They began to mention the CBS Black Employees Association in their brochure as a thing that was good about CBS.

The internship was great. It was like going back to school again. For one year I got a chance to move around through every department that programming dealt with at the network. I was sent back to New York for three months to live in a hotel, on an expense account, lunches at The Russian Tea Room, encouraged to see as much theater as I could digest for three months, and I'm like, "This is the New York that they sing about. I love New York!"

I was from New York, but I had never seen New York like this. I moved around to every department and the people that ran those departments knew I was there from "corporate." I was somebody who could come back at some point and maybe be their boss, so people had to kind of like be cool with me, but they were also very open and shared information. And because I had started in the bowels of the company I was learning this company from the ground floor up. Knew everything about CBS.

Each time you would go into these all-white environments, how tough was that for you?

It was difficult but it was something that I think I was very good at because of the experiences that I had had at the boarding school and at Cornell.

You'd been trained in a sense to live in the white world.

Right. But I had a more popular view of TV than these guys who had grown up in a completely different way. A lot of their approach to television was real ivory tower. They weren't out there among the people. I'd take a two-week vacation and I'm back at home in the projects in New York.

You could bring something to the table that no one else could.

Exactly. And I had a really good connection with the creative people. A lot of times creative people don't respect suits, the executives. But I was a different guy. It was easier for them to recognize that about me, that I developed that kind of rapport and there was appreciation for me in that regard. But at the same time I think there was this lingering kind of thing, a real limitation on how far I could go. Because I was this black guy.

How would that come out?

It was just from a movement standpoint. I'm here at CBS. The two people who came in as interns with me both had no experience in the company, both came directly out of college. They come out of the program as managers, and I'm made an associate program executive.

So I see that they're moving ahead, and I'm still sitting there going, "What about me?" And they say, "Be patient, Frank, your time will come." It became very frustrating to me. And there was a perception that I did not have this universal view because I did these other things, because I was someone who was obviously an advocate for other social issues and things happening for blacks in the company. For them, I could not *also* be this mainstream programming guy who could program a network with everybody's mainstream interests in mind.

You didn't want to be vice president of movies? You wanted to program the whole network?

I was interested in taking those incremental steps, but those incremental steps were being denied to me. I hit the glass ceiling at CBS and stagnated.

Briefly, what does an associate programming executive do and how long did you do it?

Two years. Programming executives at the network are broken into two areas, into development, which is where you work with creative people developing new series to go on the air, and current programming where you supervise the production of shows that are on the air. You work with producers of production companies of shows that are already on their air, supervising scripts, giving them comments, you're kind of the liaison person between the network and the studios. I was in that area.

In such a position you begin to be a known quantity in the business.

Exactly. I had been over to Universal because a couple of my shows, *Magnum, P.I.* and *Incredible Hulk* were produced there. I had to be over there for the dailies to see what film had been shot, and that kind of thing. The first year I was put in drama. *Magnum, P.I., Simon & Simon,* and *The Dukes of Hazard.* Escapist stuff generally. That was the popular stuff.

And the comedies?

> *The Jeffersons, Private Benjamin,* and *Alice.* I went from drama to comedy after the first year. After a year in drama you know, "okay, here I am, it's time for me to get my own shows." But the guy I was working for who was head of drama would not give me my own shows. He said, "No, you don't have enough experience. It takes 20 years of experience to be able to do this." "But I've already done this job at least as well as all the other people." He was a real old-school conservative guy. So I sit down with Harvey Shepherd, who's running the network at the time and say, "Harvey, you know it's time for me to get my own shows," and he goes, "Look, Tony's a very conservative guy. It's a very difficult area, you know—it's personality. It's probably not going to happen with him. If you want to move ahead I suggest you move into comedy." Black people, they always want them in comedy. I want to be serious.

There have always been more black executives in comedy than in drama?

> Certainly. And writers.

Is that because there are more black performers also in comedy? Is there some notion that blacks can entertain, but only do comedic stuff? Ironically, I'd argue that it's generally much harder to produce really good comedy than drama.

> Which is what I learned when I went into comedy.

It's very hard to make someone laugh every 30 seconds.

> That's right, it's much more difficult. So finally I realized, he's right.
>
> The guy who's running the comedy area was a really giving kind of guy, Peter Stern. And I learned a lot under him. I moved into comedy, and after two months I was given my own shows. The first show that I was given was *Private Benjamin;* the second one was *Alice.* And then *Flo,* which spun out of *Alice.*

Are there other reasons that historically there have been more blacks given the opportunity to produce and manage comedy than drama?

> Because I think comedy is less threatening. You could take this all the way back to minstrel shows. People feel more comfortable about other ethnic groups if they're funny. So that's the kind of plantation that we were relegated to. And blacks are given opportunities only in comedy and then don't explore more dramatic things that allow us to be humanized and more fully developed.

Comedy makes people like cartoon characters. If you fill the person out, now that's threatening to many mentalities. This is a full-blown person, with thoughts and experiences, and subjectivity. How did you then get to Universal?

> Another black executive working at CBS at the time, Roy Campanella, Jr., was a good friend of mine. They had contacted him first, but he wanted

to be a director. He wasn't interested in another executive job so he told them about me. We were the only ones in the industry at the time.

The whole industry?

The three big networks at the time, ABC, CBS, and NBC.

You took a big bump in pay when you went to Universal?

About $15,000, which was a lot at that time. I think when I came out of the executive intern program, I was making 20 and maybe I went to Universal at 45, so it was a big bump for me.

At Universal, what were you in charge of?

I was director of comedy development, developing new comedy television series for sale to the network.

So now you're out to lunch a lot, and breakfast, and dinner and taking pitches all day long and everybody you run into has an idea for a sitcom and you're saying "no" a lot more than "yes."

That's the job.

What shows did you develop that got on the air?

The first one was *Charles in Charge*. There are tons of others that came and went. *Domestic Life* with Martin Mull. *He's the Mayor* was the first project that I really wanted to do, that had African American characters. It was a show that was originally developed before *The Cosby Show*. A writer came in and pitched me a show for Bill Cosby, called *City Hall*, where Bill Cosby was the mayor. The guy worked for Norman Lear and I knew him as good idea guy, but he was a terrible pitch person and he didn't inspire confidence in the room. So I told my boss about it and he said, "Okay, fine, bring the guy in." After the meeting, my boss says to me, "I love both of those ideas but this guy I can't take into a network room to sell." He says, "I'll pay this guy some good money, we'll buy the idea outright. You find somebody else to write it and we'll move forward with it."

You could have a writer who is quirky and odd in a pitch meeting, maybe he doesn't dare to pitch it, but he could be on the show and write it.

Yeah, it was odd.

Was the writer black?

He wasn't just black. From an appearance standpoint he probably fit more of the stereotypical mold of what my boss felt was a guy that was not intelligent, was not articulate, a good guy but he just was kind of appalled by this guy.

But the guy could write.

He wouldn't have been my first choice to write the script either.

But it was his concept?

It was his concept. So it ends up that he got some good money for optioning the idea, he gets a royalty if the show goes forward and he gets a royalty on every episode of the show that gets produced.

By now Bill Cosby's got *The Cosby Show*, so he wasn't available. It got changed around: what about a guy who's the first black mayor of the city, but he's also 24 years old? So it's not only about a black mayor, but it's about a young mayor. We went into ABC and sold the idea. We hired a black writer to write the script, another black writer, who had come through Norman Lear. Most of the black writers at that time in comedy had come through Norman Lear.

Like The Jeffersons. *How many writers on that show were black?*

Maybe eight in total, and maybe half of them were black.

Was most of the original concept of He's the Mayor *preserved?*

Most of it was changed. So the writer comes in and writes a number of drafts of the script. I think we did like 13 drafts of that script before we found the guy at ABC to step up to the plate on it. He did maybe two drafts of the script and the studio lost faith in him, said, "This guy can't do it." They didn't like the script, they didn't like the tone of it, they didn't like the characters.

What did you think?

I thought it was fine. It was different. It was a different look, but they couldn't see it.

Totally beyond race, aren't there some executives who, if they can't see how something is very much like other things that are on the air, that they're going to get freaked out by novel material?

That happens very often. Even probably more so today. When I first came into the industry a majority of executives would make decisions based on their own gut kind of feeling about something. An idea came in and they'd say, "Yeah, I like that idea. Let's go for it." Today, these guys sit down and they look at the research first. What do the numbers look like? They like it if there's something else that's been on like it that they can relate it to. Oh, it's another *Friends*. Today, most of the things that get on that are good are the result of the person producing or creating the idea being such a powerful producer that nobody can fuck with them. They let them do it the way they're going to do it. Nobody tells Bochco how he's going to do his show. Nobody tells David Kelley how he's going to do his show.

Steven Spielberg did Amazing Stories *for TV, with a solid two-year deal regardless of the ratings. No one's ever had a deal like that before or since.*

But at least there's a singularity of vision. He gets to do what he sees in his head.

Going back to He's the Mayor, *did they tweak it too much and wash out the guts of the thing?*

The network bought the thing because the executive producer is guaranteeing the script. So the network and the studio say, "Okay, from now on the drafts of the scripts are going to be written by him, not by the black guy that you hired to write the script." So this guy begins to write drafts of the script. We hated it and the studio hated it.

So the thing is really in trouble now.

Right. So we go though 13 drafts and this thing just isn't right. And then the 14th draft of the script comes in and we go, "Hey, this is pretty good."

Someone else wrote it for him.

Now we've got a script that's workable. The network says okay, let's go into production. Here's the money, the license fee, *bang.* Got to cast it.

At the time, as far as black actors were concerned, at that age, there weren't any major stars to kind of plug into this. We originally developed the show for Arsenio Hall because ABC had a deal where they went around the country and signed 12 comics from around the country to this overall holding kind of deal to develop shows for and that's one of the reasons ABC bought this project. We were developing it as a vehicle for Arsenio Hall. But before we finished the script, Arsenio's deal ran out, and ABC lost confidence in him and they didn't re-sign. So now we've got to take three guys into the network for them to say who's got the role.

They get to pick the one they want.

Yeah, which is why you try not to take in anybody you really don't like. So we took in a guy from Broadway who was mostly a dancer. Melvin Van Peebles, who's a big star and a big director now, and Kevin Hooks. We all liked Kevin because Kevin was really credible as a mayor. You could believe that this guy could be a mayor of a city.

How much did you tip your hand that you liked Kevin Hooks best or would that be the worst move of all?

We didn't at all. We just figured if they made the wrong choice we'd fight about it afterwards. And if it's their idea they're really happy. So they chose the right guy, we got Kevin Hooks, but at first he didn't want to do it because he was really getting into his directing career and had stopped acting. But his father, Robert, convinced him to do it.

Robert Hooks founded the Negro Ensemble Company in New York. His father thought it was a good opportunity for him to star in a network television show. Kevin did it and we were happy. I convinced the studio to hire a black director, Oz Scott, the New York director who'd done *For Colored Girls Who've Considered Suicide When the Rainbow Is Enuf.* He'd directed Richard Pryor in a feature film. I got them to hire four black writers as part of the staff on the show. I knew competent, qualified, good people and I think the studio always thought I would recommend people because they were black and not because they were good. My thing was, "They're black *and* they're good."

Besides Norman Lear's shows, had there ever been many black personnel on a network program?

To my knowledge, no. I was very proud of it and it ran 13 episodes. Initially, we had a good shot. When ABC announced their schedule we were coming on Tuesday nights at 8:30 P.M., right after Tony Danza's show *Who's the Boss?*, which was a very successful spot—the "hammock" position—right after and we already had the promotional campaign, you know, *Who's the Boss?* and then *He's the Mayor,* and we were going to copromote Tony Danza and Kevin Hooks, two young guys. We had it all together.

And the demographics.

Exactly. Perfect audience flow. But the network didn't see it that way because they made a deal to pick up a show from Alan Thicke, *Growing Pains.* And when NBC cancels *Diff'rent Strokes* ABC decides, "We're going to pick it up. We think there is life in Gary Coleman. And because *Diff'rent Strokes* is a black show, it needs to be with another black show. So we're going to pull *He's the Mayor* from that Tuesday 8:30 P.M. time period and give it to *Growing Pains* and we're going to put on *He's the Mayor* Friday nights at 9:30 P.M. following *Diff'rent Strokes.*" The life has already gone out of that show, and the second half hour is against the number one show in television on CBS, *Dallas.*

They're probably thinking that the black audience for Dallas *isn't very big so they're going to get the black demographic that whole hour. They've already started to marginalize the show.*

That's where we were defeated.

And you felt the show could have a very broad demographic.

Yes, you know and we had Pat Corley, and David Graff who came out from *Police Academy* as the mayor's adversary. It was not an all-black show.

How disappointed were you when they changed the position and went to Friday?

Completely. I knew it was going to fail. I knew it was impossible for the show to be successful then. I was angry and frustrated. I'm going to prove something to network television: that we've got a show with black characters in it that is going to be of interest to a mainstream audience. I knew from audience flow and everything else that at 8:30 P.M. behind *Who's the Boss?* we had a winner. I mean *Growing Pains* went into that time slot and ran for *eight years.* We had a winner there. We had a real opportunity to open the door.

This is one of the ways hegemony works. Through all kinds of preexisting expectations, notions, and prejudices, the assumptions and tenets of racism reproduce themselves and play themselves out.

Even though you say you knew it was going to fail, you're still watching ratings, you haven't turned your back on it, right?

We're trying to do everything. We're trying to get as much promotion as we can out of the network, so people will find the show.

Are you thinking, too, that if this gets any kind of traction that we're going to maybe get them to move it?

We're trying to get them to move it, but they lost confidence.

So how do you find out when you're not renewed? Is it a phone call?

Well, they order 13 episodes, so you're looking to get the back nine.

"The back nine." A term from golf.

Yeah. "The back nine," although that term has disappeared because it's rare now to even get an order of 13 unless you're somebody with established talent who's real powerful. Six episodes is a normal kind of order for a new show now. Like when I worked on *Square Pegs.*

Great show.

That's when I was an associate program executive at CBS. We ran full season, but never with a full order. All the executives would say the show was over, it's canceled. But Anne Beatts would go into Harvey Shepherd's office and they'd battle and she'd come out with two episodes.

Anne Beatts. I respected her so much in that she never gave in to what the networks wanted to do to her show. She did that show the way she wanted, you know, she fought the hell out of them and got through an entire season on that show.

So how long were you at Universal? How many years?

Total of six. But only as an executive for four. And then I hit the glass ceiling there.

Your title when you first came in was director of comedy development and then you went over to the dramatic side.

After my first year as director of comedy development, my boss and I were having a little friction. He felt that he wanted a guy who was more

Geraldine Laybourne

open to doing things the way he wanted to do them without having a lot of opinions. I saw a different way to do things and I would kind of question things. I had just come off a successful season. I got a network television show on the air at a studio like Universal that is not known for comedy. And we had been battling to get into the comedy business because it is more profitable. So, I got a show on the air, yet the president of the studio calls me and says, "We're going to move you into current programming." I'm like, "What?! I want to be in development, I want to *create* new shows," and he says, "Well, we've already hired somebody to take your place." He had hired an agent to come in and be his director of comedy development. So they were giving me this position in current programming and I was just floored.

I asked for and received a new position that allowed me to work as both a development and current programming executive. I served as director of programming and supervised production of *Miami Vice* and *The Insiders*, while also developing new comedy series for the next couple years. Then, after I was passed over for the position of Vice-President of Comedy Development I left and formed my own production company, Nuhouse.

GERRY LAYBOURNE

Gerry Laybourne is one of the most celebrated executives in television. She turned Nickelodeon into the most highly rated 24-hour cable programming service, reaching a larger audience of children than ABC, CBS, NBC, and Fox combined. Through careful research and a clear philosophy about children and children's television, Gerry Laybourne created the Nickelodeon brand. She then expanded the brand by launching and distributing Nickelodeon to other countries, developing theme parks, and creating Nickelodeon film, toy, and publishing divisions. She also oversaw the development of Nick at Night.

Nickelodeon has won most every award for which it is eligible. Laybourne has won numerous awards also, including the Annenberg Public Policy Center's Award for Distinguished Lifetime Contribution to Children and Television. *Time* magazine named her one of the 25 most influential people in America. In 1995 she was inducted into the Broadcasting & Cable Hall of Fame.

Laybourne spent 16 years at Nickelodeon, becoming president in 1986. In 1992 she became vice chairperson of Nickelodeon's corporate parent, MTV Networks. Then, in the late 1990s, she spent two challenging years with Disney/ABC, where she oversaw current cable programming, before taking on her most challenging position yet as the founding CEO of Oxygen, which launched in February 2000.

With the success of branding a network for children behind her, there was a great deal of excitement when Ms. Laybourne announced in 1998 that she was going to start a new cable network for women with partners like Oprah Winfrey and Marcy Carsey and Tom Werner, the creators of *The Cosby Show, Roseanne* and *Third Rock From the Sun*. With this combination of players, she quickly raised somewhere between $300 and $450 million in start-up capital. Oxygen began life by simultaneously launching on the Internet, but ran into difficulties early on marrying the two media. As a result, it has undergone at least one programming makeover.

We learn in the interview how Laybourne came up in the industry, how she remade Nickelodeon, and how she is now working to turn Oxygen into a success. After receiving her bachelor's in art history from Vassar, she received a master's in elementary education from the University of Pennsylvania. Early in her career she spent time as a teacher and researcher and has long been an advocate of media education. The interview took place in 2001.

☆ ☆ ☆

How does my childhood relate to my work as an adult?

I believe we get made in our childhood, so the first thing I would say that's relevant is that when I was three years old a TV was delivered to our house. Somebody actually came and plugged it in. My mother said, "Hello, television," and the guy turned the television on and somebody on the television said, "Hello out there in television land."

At three, I was convinced that TV could see me. So I would dress up and when my favorite show, *Hopalong Cassidy*, was on, I would sit, and put a nice little table with a cloth in front of it and wear my best dress.

My mother claims that I begged her to spin me around and send me into television land. My mother was a creative person—she had been a radio producer and soap opera actress—and she kinda tortured us because she would wait until we got to almost the end of a story and then she would turn it off and make us write the ending.

She wasn't really trying to torture us, but she would never let TV interfere with our dinner. So, if dinner was ready, we had to leave it at whatever point and then we'd have to tell her what the story was and what we thought was the ending. I think that was a great kind of an exercise.

And then the other influence was my dad. I was sandwiched in between an older sister and a younger sister. And they were both quite spectacular in their own right. And I think my dad looked at me and said, "You know what? You're going to be my business daughter."

He really cultivated me as a businessperson. I became the family treasurer and he took me to his office on Saturdays, and to business meetings, and he would describe companies to me and I—as a little 8-year-old—had strong opinions about what he should or shouldn't invest in. So I think that that gave me a confidence about business that I surely don't deserve to have because I never went to business school.

My mother was also a social activist. She raised money for school bond issues and was very integral to electing politicians. She was a community leader and she raised her kids to believe that they had to go out and do something that would make a difference. So it was a good counterbalance to dad, who was a stockbroker. We were raised with the expectation that we would both do good and do well.

You were raised in Plainfield, New Jersey. Did growing up in New Jersey have a particular impact?

I think it had a huge impact. My mother was from North Dakota and so I was the only kid raised in New Jersey who summered in North Dakota. Because she was in New Jersey and because she had such a love of drama and the arts, we were ferried in to New York from New Brunswick on the New Brunswick bus. We would go in every Saturday afternoon and go to a play on Broadway. And so we had an uncommon exposure to really great theater.

Is there anything about the so-called "attitude" of New Jersey that made a difference?

I think so. It's more like being a second child. So I have a double dose. I'm a second child from New Jersey. You have to try harder.

Actually, I was really comforted if the people I was hiring were from New Jersey. These strong women: Sandy Cavanaugh, who was one of the first people at Nickelodeon, was raised in Watchung, New Jersey. It was just comforting. It's like, man, if you can make it through New Jersey . . .

Well, they say if you can make it in New York you can make it anywhere, but you think New Jersey may be tougher?

I think it is. You have a chip on your shoulder. You kind of stutter when you say where you're from.

But I would just want to tell you something about your work and what it meant to me when you spoke at MTV that day because I felt so strongly that my job was to add something to kids' lives. It wasn't enough to do no harm, which I think is what most broadcasters before we started doing Nickelodeon would think, "Well . . . this won't hurt a kid."

My goal was, "How will it *help* a kid?" And this came out in my first question that I would ask any producer, "What does this do for kids?" And when you talked to us at MTV, you talked about the fact that people who were depressed tended to watch more TV than people who were not depressed and that they got more depressed the more they watched. I didn't know whether I interpreted you right or not.

Close enough.

It influenced me tremendously. Because I also see Oxygen as an antidote to the kind of cliché of what women will watch. That women want to watch these "victim of the week" movies that make them feel worse about themselves. And so, the very root of both Nickelodeon and Oxygen comes out of optimism and curiosity and how can we introduce people to new things and how do we actually make them feel better about themselves.

Well, we did a phenomenal number of focus groups. I would go to the focus groups with my executives to hear from kids. We heard that they felt that we were on their side. And they felt like they had a friend in TV. And they knew that they could count on us to never sell them short.

Or talk down to them.

Or talk down to them. And, so we did that. But we also had longitudinal studies. One of the questions we asked early on was, "Do you think Nickelodeon understands you?" And 93 percent of kids thought we understood them, which I thought was pretty amazing.

Tell me about the early years at Nickelodeon.

Those were great years. We had no money. We had a horrible boss who had antediluvian ideas about management. He was an old-fashioned broadcaster and he thought that the only way you could reach kids was with a very officious sounding male announcer, a bombastic male voice. And, God, that just didn't make any sense to me at all, because that was the voice that you would instantly tune out. And so we had four years of the luxury of learning with absolutely nothing at stake.

So not having a lot of money at risk helped?

Right. We had no money. We had no audience and we had no programming. It was a scramble. And my poor kids had to stay at home every weekend with me and lie in bed and watch Czechoslovakian cartoons. "Please Mom, no more TV," they'd plead.

You were looking at world cinema?

We were trying to find anything we could find to put on the air because we had no money. Nickelodeon was gonna exist because cable operators wanted to have something that was clearly positive to offer the community. So a lot of the early days we were just running old PBS or Canadian shows, or compilation series from around the world. And we built our subscribership. By that point we had a notebook full of things that we wanted to do.

When one guy left and they fired a couple of other people they looked at me and said, "We don't know what to do with you. But we know we shouldn't fire you." I thought to myself, "They really want me to run it!" Really all I did was take the entire staff, which was about 20, away to a room at 75 Rock and I said, "OK. We all know what's wrong with Nickelodeon. If you want to, let's make this something great."

What was one of the first things that you did that got you on the right track?

I had been fascinated by what MTV was doing. They were younger than we were but they came out of the box with a bang. They listened to their audience and they spoke back to their audience in their vocabulary, in their medium, in their style. And what I felt Nickelodeon needed was to do just that. That it needed to become a home base. I didn't believe it needed to worry about its programs so much as it needed to worry about what it was going to stand for. So the "us" versus "them" became our rallying cry, which was us (Nickelodeon and kids) against them (unfair authority figures). It wasn't against adults. It was against unfairness.

We borrowed things from the Revolutionary War. We had declarations of independence, and kids' rights, and mission statements. It really had to do with galvanizing around an idea. "What can we do for kids?" And we did some pretty interesting things. For instance, one of the first exercises my new management group did was take commercials that were being shown on Nickelodeon and show them to focus groups. We got kids to talk about how they liked being talked about. It was so obvious to us that, man, never use an *adjective* with a kid! Never tell a kid it's funny. Never tell a kid it's cool.

Let them see that it's funny.

Be it! Never say it. Be it. Let them discover you.

You believed early on that kids see through phony pitches.

Oh! All you had to do was sit there! And also, it's lazy. In the promotional world, if people use a good word, they think they've achieved something.

It's presumptuous to tell the person what it is. If it's really that good they ought to be able to see it for themselves.

That's right. Fortunately, we had some real geniuses. Just unbelievable people who didn't come with preconceived notions about how anything had to be.

What kinds of things have they gone off to do?

The original programming/production team of Debby Beece and Geoffrey Darby are working with me here at Oxygen. Thank God. Scott Webb is also consulting with us. Scott is the first creative director we hired and he had optic neuropathy, making him legally blind. And what's interesting about that is, if you think about the Nickelodeon orange logo and how powerful it is, part of the reason it is so bold and clear is because he saw the vision so internally.

When I met him, I decided in one minute that he was the personification of what we wanted Nickelodeon to be. He was so clearly the embodiment of being slightly naughty but also deeply decent, and playful. Extremely playful.

Some stayed at Nickelodeon, like Herb Scannell and Cyma Zarghami, and others left to start new enterprises, like Betty Cohen with the Cartoon Network, Anne Sweeney with FX—who's now president of Disney Cable Networks—and Rich Cronin with the Game Show Network.

Let's go back years earlier. How did you initially make the leap into television?

I was starting out to be an architect. I met my husband, who was setting up film programs for AFI and Title I programs in inner cities. And he was teaching kids about the media and he was one of the first media literacy educators. He worked for John Culkin. I was fascinated. And so I went to graduate school and worked with him. But it was always in media education, so it was always around making things with kids and seeing how they saw the media. So, I'm not really your standard classroom teacher. I taught for a very short period of time and then I went into the not-for-profit sector working with the Center for Understanding Media doing projects with kids, showing avant-garde, independent films to kids to try to see what they would tolerate.

With Maureen Gaffney, we created a splinter group called The Media Center for Kids. And we did lots of programs in the schools and libraries where we made stuff and watched kids watch stuff. And so it was quasi-research, quasi-creative. We decided to create a company to market the work of independent filmmakers to television.

What were some of the other key steps between that time and first starting at Nickelodeon?

Eli Noyes, an independent filmmaker, introduced my husband and me to Thomas Watson, the CEO of IBM, who provided funding to Early Bird Specials, a company we created to market the work of independent filmmakers to television. And we pitched ideas to all the networks and to this little, tiny, new network that was just starting, called Nickelodeon. This was in 1979. They hired us to do two pilots. And then they hired me to join the staff.

Let's jump to a wholly different place, to a more recent and different kind of transition—to when you left Nickelodeon and to the relatively short time you were at ABC and with Disney, and before you started Oxygen. You were commuting to the west coast then. I'm wondering if you ran into some of the kinds of management practices like the ones that you'd experienced early on at Nickelodeon. Or did you have a great time but Oxygen just seemed like the next thing to do?

Bob Iger, Michael Ovitz, and Michael Eisner had courted me as they were putting together Disney and ABC. But there was tension putting the two cultures together because the Disney folks were unbelievably bright and aggressive and the ABC folks were very proud, rigorous and solid and had many beliefs that they held dear. It was clearly not the time to be building new assets—integration was the primary focus. I left Nickelodeon to build new things and that just didn't materialize.

I imagine that there were one or two things that you did do that you were pleased with?

I was able to put in a great management team at the Disney Channel and to get it on a path to move from pay to basic. When I arrived there it was in 14 million homes, and when I left it was in 42 million homes.

I supported creator-driven animation with *Recess* and *Pepper Ann* for ABC's Saturday morning programming and a rich original agenda for Lifetime.

But I was unable to get the new ideas—the educational channel, ABZ—or ABC 24-Hour News off the ground.

What is your aim now with Oxygen?

To create something meaningful for a constituency I care a lot about: women.

The reason that I wanted to do Oxygen independently was because I believed in the possibility of combining the two media and having them work together in a really concerted way. I didn't see that happening at the big media companies. They would take their Internet properties and put them in separate companies that they would then take public and monetize the value of the crazy Internet world. To me that was so wrong. I'm a trademark builder. I'm a lifestyle brand builder.

And you want the "creative" to lead the way?

Right. And the only way that you could get TV and Internet to work together is if they had the same goals, in the same company with the same compensation and the same everything. And so that's what we're struggling to do here. That was the reason for doing it. And the other reason for picking women as the audience was that women were underserved by cable. It would've been easier for me to do this with kids because I spent my whole life with kids. And kids are the ones who are on the forefront of accepting the computer. But we would have had trouble getting carriage for another kids service. We've done very well with Oxygen's distribution. We've got commitments in 44 million homes at this point.

I imagine you feel as if you are still struggling because you're trying to create something that really hasn't been done before. An industry trade recently referred to you as the "queen of convergence." I don't know if you like those kinds of titles, but you are trying to bring about a difficult convergence thing here.

We're the first to admit that our interest in convergence was probably premature. Trouble is, when technology advances at Internet speed, you can either be early or you can be dead. We've opted for the former. We're still doing it, but we've had to downsize our interactive business because there's no business model. And so a year ago, we had 200 people working on the online side and today we have about 70.

Is it partly that it's much harder to find a way to make a revenue stream out of online activities than with traditional media?

Yes. That's absolutely true. Fortunately, AOL/Time Warner is one of our investors, and so we're working closely with them because they're the media company that's really in the forefront of all of this.

How involved are Marcy Carsey, Tom Werner, and Caryn Mandabach [who created The Cosby Show]*?*

They are very involved as investors, as producers and as suppliers of product. We have *Roseanne* and *Cybil. Cybil*'s on the network now. *Roseanne* we get in a year. And they are involved every week with a programming call with lots of advice and counseling and they are developing shows for us.

What's Oprah Winfrey's role?

Oprah also is an investor, producer and supplier. Oprah continues to produce shows for us. And her Web site is part of our family of Web sites. She learned about the Internet and the computer by doing the show; Oprah goes online for Oxygen. Now she e-mails in notes and comments!

How quickly did the name "Oxygen" come to you? Was it meant to mean it's like a breath of fresh air?

It came from feeling that creative people were being pressured to deliver impossible results and that consumers were being pressured to buy constantly. I felt like the world was suffocating in its demands on creative people and consumers. I woke up one morning with the idea that what the world needs is some breathing room! Oxygen! That's what we need.

Gerry Laybourne at work in her new digs at Oxygen.

Earlier, you said that you're very attuned to your environment. This was when you were picking up on difficulties with the ABC/Disney merger. I've read that your office at Oxygen is right out in the middle of the company, just as it was at Nickelodeon. You're not hiding away someplace.

Our daily TV show is shot right outside my door. And two opposite entrances to it are part of a longer corridor. The architecture of offices always, for all of my spaces, has been important. But here we took over the old Nabisco Baking Company and so we have an extraordinary loft space. We took metal tire stands that normally hold tires at automotive shops and created desks. And we put them on a spine together with desks on roller blades that move up and down. So, my desk is on the spine. But there's a plexiglass wall that enables me to close doors so that I can have private conversations. But visually, I'm on the "zipper," as we call it.

Could you put into words what you mean about being in tune with the environment, and about your management style and philosophy?

Lots of people talk about the glass ceiling for women. And I think it's one of the most hurtful expressions because it provides a really concrete image for women to worry about. For me, what's really dangerous is the glass floor, or the 12 glass windows that an executive gets—where the CEO gets protected from their consumers and their staff, where they're sealed away and have layers of management that keep them from getting the straight scoop from anybody. I did not like it when I was at Nickelodeon and got my 12-windowed office and was in a corner. And nobody felt like they could come in. I didn't like it. I felt left out. So when we redid the offices, I built a desk in a shared space. People could walk through and I had a conference room where I could go for private conversations.

Spaces. They're little fiefdoms. People complain about our office space. It's too noisy. We have bands playing here some days. There're problems with all spaces.

How important is research?

It's completely possible to use research for good and research for bad. All I can say is, I want to make a difference. So, for me, the research that we did with kids told me that they felt pressured in growing up. They felt they were being hurried out of a childhood. They wanted a place where they could just be kids where they could have humor that was appropriate to them.

And there was nothing goody-two-shoes about Nickelodeon. But there was a goody-two-shoes foundation of Nickelodeon, which was very much on the side of the kid. On the side of how do we make them feel better, how do we make them feel not alone, and how do we make them laugh at some of the crazy things that happen in their lives so they're not jaded by it?

A lot of it has to do with the intention. There are certainly more people who are in the TV business for the intention of making money than there are people who are in the TV business for making a difference.

Don't get me wrong. One of my prime goals with Nickelodeon was creating a business that would be secure and that nobody could take away from kids. We weren't creating something that nobody was gonna watch. But we were trying to get at the roots of kids' problems so that we could help them. And we hit gold. Because they *did* want a place where they could be kids.

You've obviously made a good living and I imagine that you could say, "Hey, I'm just gonna quit this. I'm just gonna go off on a desert island or I'm gonna get into something entirely different." But I don't hear that at all from you. I get this feeling that you practically leap out of bed in the morning. What continues to animate and motivate you?

Young people. I feel like I've been with the same group of people my whole life. You know, first they were *my* kids, then they were my audience at Nickelodeon, and now they're my employees. I love this group. I love watching their brains work. Most of these people grew up on Nickelodeon. Basically, I guess I've just stuck with this one group!

So, do you feel they keep you young?

I think it keeps me sharp. My mother, who died last year at 84, had the youngest brain of anybody I ever knew. Her newest friend was 24 years old. I don't have any choice with her as a role model. She just never liked old thinking. She never liked old thinking from young people or old people, and I think I'm just blessed with her as a role model.

Has there been some time or some moment when you thought, "I'm gonna hang this up for a couple years"?

No. Nobody really understood my leaving Nickelodeon. I loved it so much. I loved the people and I loved the company. But I felt like I was getting stale. I'd hear in the hallways, "Well, Gerry wouldn't like this" and "Gerry wouldn't like that." Horrifying.

You'd become one of those people.

I don't want to be there. And so I knew that I was going into dangerous territory by going to Disney and ABC. Because I had lived a spoiled existence. I had been able to be an entrepreneur. Ran my own thing. The company was there for me. And never asked a question. There were budget limitations but my judgment was never questioned. So I knew I could run my division without interference. And I knew I was spoiled. But I wanted to test myself. I wanted to test how much had I really learned? What do I really know? And I discussed it with my kids. We had a family breakfast.

This was in November '95. And also, the contract negotiation with Viacom had taken a turn that was very much about me retiring at the end of five years. But clearly I was not ready to retire. I was 48 years old. And my kids did not want me to retire. Their response was, "Mom, when you're ready to tell 'em, just call us and we'll be there and we'll pack your desk." And you know you have more to offer. I did it really for selfish reasons, in a lot of ways. I felt like I wanted to test myself. And it's been quite a test.

Even though Oxygen isn't spoiling you, in the way that you might have felt toward the end of Nickelodeon, you're back to a similar shop it seems to me.

I'm back to a similar shop, although it's much harder. I thought I worked hard at Nickelodeon. It is much harder to have your own company. I *thought* I was an entrepreneur at Nickelodeon. I was not an entrepreneur. I had none of the burdens of an entrepreneur. I had all the benefits of feeling like one without the burdens.

You didn't really know that then.

I didn't know that and, you know, we never know that. If you knew how hard it was gonna be, would you do anything? It took me four years to have a second child. Thank God I did.

Chris Albrecht

CHRIS ALBRECHT

One fitting way to end a book about creativity in television is with the person some have called the most original mind in television, Chris Albrecht. In his position as chairman and chief executive officer of HBO, Chris Albrecht is responsible for the overall management of the world's largest premium television company: HBO operates networks in the United States, Europe, Asia, and Latin America.

Albrecht became CEO in 2002, following seven years as president of HBO Original Programming. He continues to direct day-to-day operations of both West and East Coast original programming for the network and for Cinemax.

In 2001, the network received 94 Emmy nominations, and won 16. At the awards ceremony, as they stood at the podium with Emmys in hand, 20 different winners personally thanked Albrecht. After all, Albrecht has been involved in the development of *The Sopranos, Sex and the City, Six Feet Under,* and *Curb Your Enthusiasm.* He gave the green light to the $120 million production of *Band of Brothers.* The cultural significance of these programs is hard to overstate. *New York Times* film critic Stephen Holden, for example, has called *The Sopranos* "the greatest work of American popular culture of the last quarter century."

Albrecht has been with HBO for 18 years, starting in 1985 as senior vice-president for original programming on the West Coast, then serving from 1990 to 1995 as president of HBO Independent Productions where he developed and produced comedy series such as *Martin* and *Everybody Loves Raymond* for CBS.

Before joining HBO, Albrecht was an agent at International Creative Management (ICM) where he signed talent like Jim Carrey, Keenan Ivory Wayans, Billy Crystal, and Whoopi Goldberg. From 1975 to 1980, Albrecht co-owned the Improvisation nightclub in New York City. He started there as a standup comic.

In the interview, we see how Albrecht thinks about creativity, its sources, and what an executive needs to do to unleash others' creativity.

How far back can you go in your life to something that you used to do that is very similar to what you do now at HBO?

> Playing with my toy soldiers. Setting up strategies, laying out the troops to come up with an imaginative game plan that was not only going to be fun, but might even prove to be intelligent in terms of making sure the good guys won. I did it every day. I still have a toy soldier collection.
>
> It's all about setting up a strategy. It's all about trying to keep your imagination open. I think games like that help keep your imagination

open so you're always trying to be open to inspiration while at the same time consciously working through the options.

How far back does your interest in comedy and the management of talent go? Is there a life theme there do you think?

All through school I was interested in plays. In fifth grade I played Curly in *Oklahoma*. We also did the *King and I* that year, which gives you an idea of how much school work we got done.

But the first definite building block to what I do today came in college when I became a dramatic literature major and when I read all the great plays from the Greeks on upward. That gave me, not only a sense of dramatic structure, but a sense of character development, certainly a sense of quality, a sense of the fact that stories are allegories that are told and retold throughout the history of our species. That good stories seem to take hold in each time period, but find a new language to be told in.

You're keenly interested in Jungian psychology, and in a deep understanding of the human experience. Why do you think you gravitated to dramatic arts? Why not English or psychology?

The pretty girls were in the drama department.

An interesting answer.

And a true one. An honest one (*laughs*). I was walking around Hofstra. I was a polysci major, I was a philosophy major, and every time I turned around and saw somebody that I thought I was interested in, a friend would tell me, oh yeah, they're in the drama department.

So your interest in drama does spring from the primal.

It's a good combination to incorporate both spheres of our being, right?

I guess the other part of that answer is that when I went to the Improv, early on, as a comic, and later as the guy who ran the club, I would see the creative process in motion every day. I saw the time it took, and the immediate relationship between the performer—who was also the writer, the producer, and the editor—and the audience, and how the comedians worked in crafting their act, collaborating with other peers in the bar, or outside on the street, going over stuff and talking with one another. I really had a sense that while there was a magic to what they did, there was also a *lot* of dedicated work.

What happened with your own comedy and acting career?

It was never a passion of my mine. I wasn't a big fan of staying out late at night and waiting to go on in a club for free. Although I was a comedian, I was also a bartender or waiter. When Bud Friedman asked me if I wanted to manage the club for him while he and his wife went to Europe for three weeks, I said yes because I needed the money. But I adapted to

Robert Iler, James Gandolfini, and Edie Falco—The Sopranos.

it really easily. I utilized some of the same skills, putting one foot in front of the other, while keeping my imagination open for inspiration.

I imagine that your experience of working closely with comedians at the Improv was very formative for you. That it is directly relevant to what you're doing at HBO, especially in helping you encourage others' creativity and to know, also, when you can "greenlight" a production as you did after seeing the pilot of The Sopranos.

I think if there's a direct line in my career, it has been trying to experience my own artistic talent in the entertainment industry, and then giving other people the opportunity to experience their talent. Then, as an agent at ICM, I started to manage and handle the the careers of those people while also learning the business side. Like we were talking before, you have to experience both sides of your being.

When I got to HBO, both aspects, understanding the business side and the creative process, let me put it all into play, where I had a real impact in inaugurating the larger and more intensive creative process—being involved early on in script development for example. I was able to combine the experience I had in understanding talent, and what was important to them, and the very practical knowledge that I gained from being an agent in a large industry and sitting in on all those staff meetings. It wasn't instantaneous, and I certainly had great people around me: Michael Fuchs, Rich Potter and later, Jeff Bewkes, helped me learn the ropes, and we came up with a style that ended up working for us.

It's said that you know how to stay out of the way. To know when, and how, to pick the places where you're going to give a producer some input. I imagine it takes discipline.

I think it takes experience also. When I first came here I didn't necessarily stay out of the way. Sometimes I'd get more involved, out of a choice of mine, or in trying to support an executive who worked for me who was intent on managing a process a little more closely than I might have instinctively. I used to have arguments with people about certain things until I realized that in 90 percent of those cases, there wasn't a right or a wrong just a difference of opinion and that ultimately what I really wanted to do was rely on the total vision of the person.

A successful creative endeavor really is like a house of cards. There's a reason why the people make the choices they do, and if you start to change one you can't anticipate the impact on the others.

You said in another interview about your Jungian analysis that "the idea that we're all connected in the collective unconscious is an extremely important part of what makes entertainment successful. You can't translate that literally, but you can be aware of the ideas behind it: that the psyche has a structure, that the unconscious is a very powerful force, that we're all on a journey, striving for individuation and wholeness. If you understand that, you have a better grip on what's relevant, resonant, and rich about human experience" (LeBarre, 2002). The house of cards analogy and this quote make clear that you try to practice holism, you want the artist to be permitted to experience and communicate a gestalt in their work. Everything is interrelated.

I think it is, especially in the creative process, and especially since I'm relying on the magic and hard work that comes out of someone else's efforts, not my own. And also from a very practical point of view.

There was a guy named Jack Rollins. Jack was one of the old school guys who managed Woody Allen and won the Academy Award for *Annie Hall.* Jack also handled Mike Nichols and Elaine May, Tony Bennett, and Robert Klein. Jack said to me, a long time ago, as he was spitting pieces of cigar out of his mouth, "Listen to the gut of the performer. What's right for them, what they think is right for them, because nine out of ten times it will be right." It's a very clear directive.

You know how you hear things and they go in one ear and out the other? That thing went in one ear and got stuck in my head for the last 20 years.

HBO is widely thought to be an especially good place to work. The organizational culture and climate are unusual in the industry. There's also an extraordinary longevity at the company with many people having been at HBO for 10, 15, and more years. Being a fan of the programs you make, and their organic quality, and seeing your appreciation of how everything is optimally interrelated, I have to think that the programs HBO produces, and the creativity that is permitted, are outgrowths of, and feed back on to, HBO's organizational culture. You've been at HBO for a good chunk of time, going on 18 years. How much did you inherit and how much did you help make happen?

I think we all inherited a lot from Michael Fuchs who had the total belief that HBO was this incredibly unique place, that it was better than other places, that it was bold and risk-taking and daringly differently. He ingrained that in us, although many of us would look around and think that we weren't really fulfilling that vision. There was a certain Vaseline on the lens that Michael was using for himself.[1] He'd see through that lens and make it a little bit prettier picture than it really was. Then, when Jeff Bewkes took over, he had the skill as a manager to open up what had been percolating under Michael.

HBO *isn't* just a place. It's an idea. Those of us who have been here for a long time came to realize that the idea isn't just something on paper. You really had to understand what it really meant, what it really meant to you, and what the opportunities that came from it were.

So you'd be living and practicing the idea.

Yes. I think the great thing about HBO is that there is a shorthand between people who work here, and not just in the programming department. You go from programming to marketing to scheduling, to on air promotion, the media relations people, to the affiliate people out in the field down even to the finance guys that go out and make the deals: everybody, in the key roles especially, and to a great extent in several layers below them, understands this intuitively now because *they've* been going through the process. So when you have that kind of a shared vision and immersion in people, then there's a consistency to everything you do that really starts to add up to something.

To a whole that's greater than the sum of the parts. Can you give an example? How something got done, early on in your experience, that exemplified to you a different approach and attitude to decision making at HBO? How it was a different kind of company?

We were trying to develop shows here on the West Coast. This was years ago. Michael Fuchs was down in Florida with Garry Shandling. They talked about an idea for a series that was set backstage at a late night talk show. Michael always thought that was a good idea. For anyone else, that idea would have gotten developed and watered down into a pilot. But he literally gave Garry a commitment for the *Larry Sanders Show*. We were all asking, should we make a pilot, should we do this, should we do that? And Michael said, "Nah, nah give him his head, he knows what he's doing." And it turned out to be true. So I realized that this wasn't about being locked into a process, it was about being open to the opportunities.

---

[1] Vaseline on a camera lens is often used to impart a fuzzier and more romantic focus.

In television, it has to be extraordinarily empowering to a writer, producer, or performer who's used to how things are done elsewhere, to be given that kind of trust and latitude, to know that he or she has the opportunity to make a bunch of shows, that he needn't be looking over his shoulder every minute worrying what the network or studio is thinking. And that he doesn't have to force—and potentially ruin—an innovative concept into a particular model, a pilot, that wouldn't do it justice but might impress the network brass.

Last question. HBO would seem to be revolutionizing what's possible in the medium. There's a notion that network television will change down the line. What do you think is going to happen?

I think that there will be a slow erosion of the network business model. Not that it will collapse, but at some point its own weight will necessitate a great change, and the first person on the broadcast side to figure out how to reinvent one of those networks will be a true pioneer. At the same time, I think you'll see more vertical integration, and people in big companies aligning their own downstream windows to make the ever increasing investment in programming affordable.

Unless something comes up over the horizon that I don't know about, it's going to be a slow process of change that I think will eventually result in a sea change. There's no one sweeping thing on the horizon that's going to come in as some deus ex machina and save all of us, or provide the way out of the wilderness.

References

Arhneim, R. (1957). *Film as art.* Berkeley: University of California Press.

Associated Press. (2002, June 7). TV creators ask for Fed merger study.

Bloom, A. (1988). *The closing of the American mind.* New York: Touchstone.

Bourdieu, P. (1984). *Distinction: A social critique of the judgement of taste.* Cambridge, MA: Harvard University Press.

Boyd, J. (1968). *Above the law.* New York: The New American Library.

Bruner, J. (1994). The "remembered" self. In U. Neisser & R. Fivush (Eds.), *The remembering self: Construction and accuracy in the self-narrative* (pp. 41–54). New York: Cambridge University Press.

Cantor, M. C. (1971). *The Hollywood TV producer: His work and his audience.* New York: Basic Books.

Capra, F. (1971). *The name above the title.* New York: Macmillan.

Cawelti, J. G. (1976). *Adventure, mystery, and romance: Formula stories as art and popular culture.* Chicago: University of Chicago Press.

Conway, M. A., Rubin, D. C., Spinnler, H., & Wagenaar, W. (Eds.) (1992). *Theoretical perspectives on autobiographical memory.* Dordrecht, Netherlands: Kluwer.

Corporation for Public Broadcasting. (1978). *A qualitative study: The effect of television on peoples' lives.* Washington, DC: Author.

Csikszentmihalyi, M. (1975). *Beyond boredom and anxiety: The experience of play in work and games.* San Francisco: Jossey-Boss.

Csikszentmihalyi, M., & Beattie, O. V. (1979). Life themes: A theoretical and empirical exploration of their origins and effects. *Journal of Humanistic Psychology, 19,* 45–63.

Daniel, D. K. (1996). Lou Grant: The making of TV's top newspaper drama. Syracuse, New York: Syracuse University Press.

Desser, D. (2000). The martial arts film in the 1990s. In W.W. Dixon (Ed.), *Film genre 2000: New critical essays* (pp. 77–109). Albany: State University of New York Press.

Epstein, J. (2002). *Snobbery: The American version.* New York: Houghton Mifflin.

Ettema, J. S., & Whitney, D. C. (Eds.) (1982). *Individuals in mass media organizations: Creativity and constraint.* Beverly Hills: Sage.

Feldman, D. H. (1999). The development of creativity. In R. J. Sternberg (Ed.), *Handbook of creativity* (pp. 169–186). New York: Cambridge University Press.

Gans, H. (1974). *Popular culture and high culture: An analysis and evaluation of taste.* New York: Basic Books.

Gardner, H. (1983/1993). *Frames of mind.* New York: Basic.

Getzels, J. W., & Csikszentmihalyi, M. (1976). *The creative vision: A longitudinal study of problem finding in art.* New York: Wiley.

Gitlin, T. (1983). *Inside prime time.* New York: Pantheon.

Hall, S. (1973). Encoding and decoding in the television discourse. Birmingham: Centre for Contemporary Cultural Studies, Stencilled Paper No. 7 (revised as Hall, 1980).

Hall, S. (1980). Encoding/decoding. In S. Hall, D. Hobson, A. Lowe, & P. Willis (Eds.), *Culture, media, language* (pp. 128–138). London: Hutchinson.

Hart, M. (1959). *Act one: An autobiography.* New York: Random House.

James, C. (2002, May 18). For fall, TV looks back, and back. *New York Times*, p. B7.

Kubey, R. (1991, March 6). The case for media education. *Education Week*, Vol. X, 24, 27.

Kubey, R. (1992). A critique of *No sense of place* and the homogenization theory of Joshua Meyrowitz. *Communication Theory, 2*, 259–271.

Kubey, R. (Ed.) (1997/2001). *Media literacy in the information age: Current perspectives.* New Brunswick, NJ: Transaction Publishers.

Kubey, R. (1998). Obstacles to the development of media education in the United States. *Journal of Communication, 48*, 58–69.

Kubey, R. (2000). Television and the Internet: Pitfalls in forecasting the future. *Knowledge, Technology and Policy, 13*, 63–85.

Kubey, R. (2002, Winter). The future of television: On missing human nature in forecasting, Part II. *The Journal of the Caucus for Television Producers, Writers and Directors, 17*, 7–9.

Kubey, R., & Csikszentmihalyi, M. (1990). *Television and the quality of life: How viewing shapes everyday experience.* Mahwah, NJ: Lawrence Erlbaum Associates.

LeBarre, P. (2002, September). "Hitman." www.fastcompany.com/online/62/hitman.html.

Levy, D. (1992). How sex and violence came to network television. *POV.* Producers Guild of America, pp. 10–13.

Lowenthal, L. (1957). Historical perspectives of popular culture. In B. Rosenberg & D. M. White (Eds.), *Mass culture: The popular arts in America* (pp. 46–58). Glencoe, IL: Free Press.

MacDonald, D. (1957). A theory of mass culture. In B. Rosenberg & D. M. White (Eds.), *Mass culture: The popular arts in America* (pp. 59–73). Glencoe, IL: Free Press.

Marc, D., & Thompson, R. J. (1992). *Prime time, prime movers.* Syracuse, NY: Syracuse University Press.

McBride, J. (1992). *Frank Capra: The catastrophe of success.* New York: Simon & Schuster.

Munsterberg, H. (1916). *The photoplay: A psychological study.* New York: D. Appleton.

Newcomb, H., & Alley, R. S. (1983). *The producer's medium: Conversations with the creators of American TV.* New York: Oxford University Press.

Newcomb, H., & Hirsch, P. (1983, Summer). Television as a cultural forum: Implications for research. *Quarterly Review of Film Studies, 8,* 3, 45–56.

Piirto, J. (1992). *Understanding those who create.* Dayton: Ohio University Press.

Powdermaker, H. (1950). *Hollywood the dream factory: An anthropologist looks at the movie-makers.* Boston: Little, Brown and Company.

Prelutsky, B. (2000, January/February). The sensitive guys. *Emmy.* (For Prelutsky's interview with Zwick and Herskovitz, go to http://www.angelfire.com/tv/onceagain/archives/febart.html.)

Ravage, J. (1978). *Television: The director's viewpoint.* Boulder, CO: Westwood Press.

Rose, B. G. (1986). *Television and the performing arts: A handbook and reference guide to American cultural programming.* Westport, CT: Greenwood Press.

Rosten, L. C. (1941). *Hollywood: The movie colony.* New York: Harcourt, Brace and Company.

Sarris, A. (1962/1979). Notes on the auteur theory in 1962. In G. Mast & M. Cohen's (Eds.), *Film theory and criticism: Introductory readings* (2nd edition) (pp. 650–665). New York: Oxford University Press.

Sarris, A. (1968). *The American cinema: Directors and directions, 1929–1968.* New York: Dutton.

Schatz, T. (1988). *The genius of the system: Hollywood filmmaking in the studio era.* New York: Pantheon.

Shils, E. (1959). Panel discussion. In N. Jacobs (Ed.), *Culture for the Millions? Mass Media in Modern Society* (pp. 155–200). Boston: Beacon Press.

Sultanik, A. (1986). *Film: A modern art.* New York: Cornwall Books.

Thompson, R. J., & Burns, G. (Eds.) (1990). *Making television: Authorship and the production process.* New York: Praeger.

Thomson, D. (2002, May 26). A mogul of the best and worst kind. *New York Times,* p. 11.

Truffaut, F. (1954, January). La politique des auteurs. *Cahiers du Cinéma.*

Walters, J., & Gardner, H. (1986). The talented student: A validation of the creativity-intelligence distinction. In R. Sternberg & J. Davidson (Eds.), *Conceptions of giftedness* (pp. 306–331). New York: Cambridge University Press.

Wolfenstein, M., & Leites, N. (1950). *Movies: A psychological study.* Glencoe, IL: The Free Press.

Photo Credits

Index

References to figures (photos) are indicated by *f*. Footnotes are indicated by *n*.